On Rope

North American Vertical Rope Techniques
For Caving • Search and Rescue • Mountaineering

On Rope

North American Vertical Rope Techniques
For Caving • Search and Rescue • Mountaineering

By Allen Padgett and Bruce Smith
Illustrations by Pandra Williams

Vertical Section
National Speleological Society

Design and Production by NSS Special Publications Committee
David McClurg, Chairman

On Rope

Published by the National Speleological Society
Cave Avenue
Huntsville, Alabama 35810
205/852-1300

Library of Congress Catalog Card Number 87-60477
ISBN 0-9615093-2-5

Printed in the U.S.A.

ON ROPE LIABILITY DISCLAIMER

WARNING. Serious injury or death could result from the use of techniques and equipment described in this book. It is the reader's responsibility to seek qualified instruction on the use and precautions of vertical rope work. Experience tends to be one of the best teachers, however a mistake or misinterpretation of this material could have irreversible consequences. Every person practicing vertical rope work should use good judgement and a lot of common sense. This book is sold with no liability to the authors, editors, critiquers, publisher, or the Vertical Section of the National Speleological Society, expressed or implied, in the case of injury or death to the purchaser or reader.

Table of Contents

PHOTOGRAPHS

Acknowledgements

Throughout its two and a half years of preparation, *On Rope* has been reviewed and critiqued by dozens of people. Their efforts have brought field-proven reliability to the contents of *On Rope*. It is the input from the reviewers that has allowed the authors to push aside the myths and write and illustrate what really happens. The process has been cumbersome, but effective. After the initial research and writing, each chapter was mailed to a number of reliable sources, many of whom were officers in the Vertical Section of the NSS, who critiqued the chapters for content, accuracy and reliability. After retrieving the input, the authors sorted out the information, often during marathon get-togethers. The consolidation became the best-of-the-best, so to speak. This in turn was presented again to other key critiquers. Adjustments seemed never-ending. Because so many gave so freely to this project, *On Rope* the first North American SRT book, is now a reality.

Pandra Williams, the illustrator brought life to the ideas and information with her talent and skill. Stella Twilley provided her expertise with her mechanical illustrations of the post chapter projects as well as appreciated last-minute proofreading. Sally Wheeler, Pam Long and Jean Cassidy, the editorial helpers, played key roles in the successful completion of *On Rope*. The photographer, Mark Wolinsky, has added interest and quality between the covers. The critiquers, who spent many long hours pondering opinions, facts, and consequences were:

Gary Storrick	D.C. Province
Darrel Tomer	John Weinel
Steve Hudson	Dan Twilley
Bill Bussey	Shari Lydy
David McClurg	Mike Fischesser
Larry Caldwell	John Markwell
Bill Cuddington	Dick Newell
Richard Schreiber	Kyle Isenhart
Bob Wells	Forrest Gardiner
Ed Strausser	

Other individuals who cooperated or played important roles in the book's research and development were Jeanne Pridmore, Vickie Nixon, Tim Setnicka, Rane Curl, Linda Starr, Marion O. Smith, Joe Domnanovich, David McClurg, and John Scheltens.

A special thanks is extended to the Chattanooga Police and S.W.A.T. team, including individual thanks to Sgt. Bill McCray, Mike Williams and Mike Robbs. Joe and Jean King of Mountain Ventures in Scottdale, Georgia played a key role in helping Pandra through the voluminous diagrams that were necessary. There are others who also played a part in helping with information research. We also wish to thank them.

The authors and illustrator want to extend a special public thank-you to their spouses, Karen, Marilyn and Mike, who endured the grossly underestimated amount of time necessary to compile *On Rope*.

The NSS Special Publications committee would also like to thank several volunteers who helped produce the camera ready materials for the printer: Larry Pardue, Janet McClurg, Linda Starr, Kathy Grossman, Barbara Schaefer, and David Belski.

Profiles of the Principals

ALLEN PADGETT (NSS 10371F). Padgett first began caving with a high school biology class in 1963. He was introduced to organized caving in 1967, where he learned a great deal from the early TAG (Tennessee, Alabama, Georgia) cavers. With the TAG group he participated in many explorations and discoveries in the Southeast. An early concern for safety and an involvement with a near tragic vertical accident prompted a desire to learn, teach and share knowledge. Padgett was Safety and Techniques chairman of the National Speleological Society from 1979 to 1983 and has been an active member of the Vertical Section of the NSS since its beginnings.

Also active in search and rescue, Padgett is a member of the Mountain Search and Rescue Team of the Georgia Department of Natural Resources. In cave rescue, Padgett along with his wife Karen, are members of a local rescue team. Padgett puts aside a little time each year to act as an instructor at the annual NSS National Cave Rescue Commission workshop. As a Game & Fish ranger since 1971, vertical rope applications have often been a part of his work.

Padgett's varied background in the areas of vertical work, combined with his drive for safety, go together to provide the beginnings for others to safely enjoy the *On Rope* experience.

BRUCE SMITH (NSS 12458F). Smith began caving in 1961 at the age of 13 with an Illinois Explorer Post. In 1968, he began vertical caving with half- inch manila rope, two Hieblers, and a book of directions. Through contacts in the vertical world, information was acquired and Smith became a vertically knowledgeable person.

Experience and a lot of research helped gain him the recognition of being the first editor of *Nylon Highway*, the publication of the NSS Vertical Section. He has been active with the Vertical Section since its beginnings.

Smith considers himself a generalist, able to review and analyze all different techniques and designs of vertical work. To further his generalist aims, Smith makes it a practice to try out new devices and techniques as they are developed. His goals focus on the publishing of reliable, usable vertical information and the enjoyment of all aspects of vertical work.

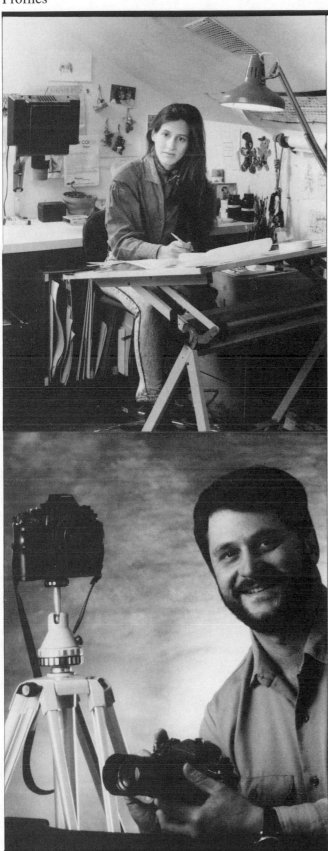

Prejudice is avoided and logical thought can be expected. "After all," he says, "I started with a manila rope and two Hieblers that never came off the rope accidentally."

Though originally a West Virginia caver, Smith relocated to Chicago to teach at Hamburger University. Currently, Smith and his wife, Marilyn, own and operate a McDonald's Restaurant in Chattanooga, Tennessee. Smith practices his vertical work in the TAG area (Tennesee, Alabama, Georgia) or in his old favorite, Hellhole Cave, West Virginia.

PANDRA WILLIAMS (NSS 27513). Williams received her BFA from the Atlanta College of Art in Georgia. She is currently freelancing as an illustrator in Atlanta, and raising two girls with her husband Michael. The whole family enjoys caving, camping and the great outdoors. She is a member of the Nature Conservancy and a new member of the NSS.

Photo by Michael Williams

MARK WOLINSKY (NSS 11438). Wolinsky was born and grew up in the Tennessee mountains and the Cumberland Plateau. He started caving in 1967. His interest in vertical work began in the early '70s. He has twice been president of his local grotto. He is presently a member of the NSS, American Cave Conservation Association, Sierra Club, Nature Conservancy, Georgia Forestry Association, Society of American Foresters, American Forestry Association, Tennessee Cave Survey and several cave organizations.

Wolinsky is a self taught, outdoor stock photographer. He specializes in underground photography such as mines or caves, cliff photography and scenic photography. His work has appeared in such publications as *Atlanta Weekly Magazine*, *World Book Encyclopedia*, *Chattanooga Life & Leisure Magazine*, *NSS News* and the *Speleonews*.

Wolinsky is a registered forester in the state of Georgia and shares his time between his hobbies, forestry and photography.

1 About On Rope

1 About On Rope

A new book on ropework has been needed for some time. Since the technology explosion began in the 1960s, many changes in equipment and technique have occurred. For example, manila rope has been replaced by nylon. Then braided nylon replaced laid nylon ropes. Now several different braided ropes are available. In addition to the myriad possibilities in materials, many clever climbers began to have ingenious ideas that led to sweeping changes in equipment and thus in techniques.

On Rope contains descriptions of all the practical equipment and techniques of ropework commonly used in North America. This book explains what is available, what it does and doesn't do, where to get it, and how to use it properly and safely.

Who needs *On Rope*? Anyone who needs to know about the equipment and skills necessary to go up and down a fixed rope needs to study this book carefully. Included are cave explorers, mountaineers, fire and rescue teams, S.W.A.T. personnel, tree surgeons and forest rangers. *On Rope* will help these people, from beginners to old-timers, approach the topic correctly. The sequence of chapters and many illustrations lend the book to natural use as a classroom text or as a reference book to be consulted again and again.

Abundance of Gear. There is a vast abundance of rope-oriented equipment for sale and a lack of information on its proper use. In addition, the woods are full of semi-trained, word-of-mouth trained and I-think-it-works-this-way "experts." People looking for information on ropework are often without resources. There is really no set standard as to the competence that an instructor may claim to have. Instructors are often judged by the drops or caves they have done. "Experienced" old-timers are often not up to date as to current trends, methods, and systems; and too cocky or embarrassed to ask. These old-timers are encouraged to update themselves and remain current. *On Rope*, along with quality instruction and hands-on practice, will produce competent vertical people.

North Americans. The basic North American is an individual working alone or as part of a team working toward common objectives. In Europe, vertical types look alike and climb very much alike. In North America, if two climbers have an identical rig, it happened by mistake. The wonderful thing about this individuality is that it encourages innovation, experimentation and discovery. North Americans, primarily cavers, began to define the technology in the 1940s and developed in the 1950s the three-knot system presently in use. The 1960s brought advances in technology combined with greatly increasing numbers of people taking to the out-of-doors. Then during the 1970s and 1980s the type of gear and its availability expanded exponentially.

The number of rope users in-

Fig. 1-1. On Rope's own special couple, Dilbert Lunker and Murphy Law.

SIDEBARS

Sidebars are used to include information that does not fit with the flow of the text, but which is useful nonetheless. Often sidebars deal with lesser points or widespread, but faulty information or techniques. As in a magazine, they add information to the comprehension of the text. Most sidebars are short, but some are multi-page with illustrations. All are black type in a gray background. (Gray backgrounds without type are graphic elements not sidebars.)

creases dramatically each year. The fire/rescue market, realizing the importance of the technology, has emerged as America's largest user of rope and related equipment. With that growth comes the increased challenge to educate and train these people in the proper use of single ropes and their associated equipment.

On Rope. The design of *On Rope* needs a bit of explanation. Measurements are in feet and inches. Sexual discrimination has been lessened with the balanced use of feminine and masculine pronouns and the illustrations feature Dilbert Lunker and Murphy Law performing expertly the do's and don'ts of the vertical world (Fig.1-1). The superimposed dark circle with the dark slash through the middle is the obvious symbol for unacceptable, unsafe or dangerous (Fig.1-2) technique.

Each chapter concludes with a list of references used to prepare and document the information. These lists are not to be considered an exhaustive bibliography; but rather a generally available reference for further study of topics discussed in each chapter.

Workshops. Appearing at the end of several chapters are home-workshop projects. For the dedicated, these projects go step-by-step through the construction of some of the more important items that must be made by the user, because they are unavailable in stores or through catalogs. A complete list of materials, cutting, fitting and assembly instructions are included with each project.

Glossary. Technical terms are usually defined in the text then introduced. However, if the reader happens on an unfamiliar word, consult Chapter 14, the glossary.

This compilation not only defines words used in the text, but terms likely to be encountered in training classes or contacts with other rope users.

Except for two chapters, we wrote the *On Rope* text. We spent one year finalizing the original outline. Each chapter was reviewed repeatedly by a board of 12 critiquers, each of whom are experienced. Over the two and a half years of production, these people provided input, direction, suggestions and encouragement. Then, after all of the input, we were the final jury. It is very likely that we have missed something along the way, due to the complexity of this topic. Subjects such as mountaineering and rescue were left to the specialists. With regard to SRT (Single Rope Techniques), there will always exist differing opinions. We tried very hard to remain objective. We're sure the future will reveal that some of the practices detailed in *On Rope* can be improved by some technique or piece of equipment yet to be developed. We have been and remain open to suggestions, criticism, new ideas, techniques and equipment. Contact us through the National Speleological Society office. The address is in Chapter 12.

On Rope is a practical approach to North American ropework skills. Whether you call it ropework, vertical work or SRT, the technology of all the different users of rope has one common goal, getting *On Rope*.

Quality Instruction Needed. Please realize that *On Rope* can provide the information, but it is up to the reader to seek quality instruction to prevent the blotter effect from occurring. The techniques and equipment shown in this book are safe if used correctly.

Fig. 1-2. A figure with a slash means unacceptable, unsafe, or dangerous.

2 Rope

2 Rope

From the early days of caveman Alley Oop, the search for a better rope has been ongoing. Naturally occurring ropes, such as vines, were the beginning of rope evolution (fig. 2-2). Through experimentation with the early technology of weaving, early man braided natural fibers to form primitive ropes. These ropes were made of hair or other natural fibers such as cotton, wool or plant fibers. Unfortunately, natural fibers are subject to deterioration and rotting. The natural degradation of natural fiber ropes forced modern man to look for a new solution to an old problem.

EVOLUTION

E. I. duPont deNemours and Co. introduced nylon in 1938. Patented by chemist W. H. Carothers, this fiber proved to have more uses than anyone could have imagined at the time. During World War 2, natural fibers were suddenly in short supply. Mountain troops and sailors needed strong weather-resistant rope and thus the war machinery at Dupont came out with nylon rope. Twisted into a laid construction, it was light for its strength. This 7/16 inch rope had a tensile strength of about 3000 pounds did not rot, and was easily inspected for wear. In the early days after the war, nylon rope was expensive and hard to get. As a result, the natural fiber ropes were carefully used for many more years.

Over the years nylon has proven to be the preferred rope fiber for many reasons. The molecular structure of nylon makes it possible to extrude very long continuous slender fibers that have exceptional strength and natural elasticity. These features can be seen in common monofilament fishing line. Ropes, however, are made of multifilament bundles of nylon, where the natural elasticity of the material is enhanced by the construction weave and twist (fig. 2-1). It can be bent sharply, has a high melting point and excellent abrasion resistance. The combination of these features make nylon the material of choice for the manufacture of quality rope.

Early nylon ropes did have their problems, however. After the war, markets were small and nylon ropes were primarily used on sailboats. The concerns of the marine trade became the design criteria for ropes. Out of this market came Goldline (fig. 2-3). Mountain climbers using this marine rope revealed the need for an improved version of Goldline that displayed better abrasion resistance. The rope, which became known as Mountain Lay Goldline, was twisted tighter and displayed better abrasion resistance. For many years it remained the standard to which all other ropes were compared. It withstood shock-loading well, but under normal working loads the rope was stretchy. Because of its twisted (laid) construction, a climber would spin like a top if suspended in free space (fig. 2-4). As the nylon fibers twist and entwine about each other in laid rope, they come to the outside surface approximately every two inches. When subjected to abrasion, the fibers break, and the rope slowly becomes a collection of two-inch fibers. Although the rope appears to be holding up well to abrasion, in reality it is seriously weakened. Other than abrasion, nylon has one other problem in that it decomposes photochemically (degrades) when exposed to ultraviolet radiation or sunlight. Years after the introduction of gold solution-dyed rope, it was revealed that gold-color yarns actually deteriorate faster under ultraviolet radiation. Rope manufacturers now recommend that ropes 1/2 inch or less in diameter not be made with gold yarn.

Samson Two-in-One

As rope use evolved, the search for a better rope continued. Frustrated with the

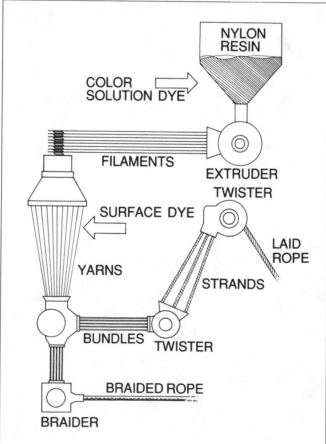

Fig. 2-1. The rope making process.

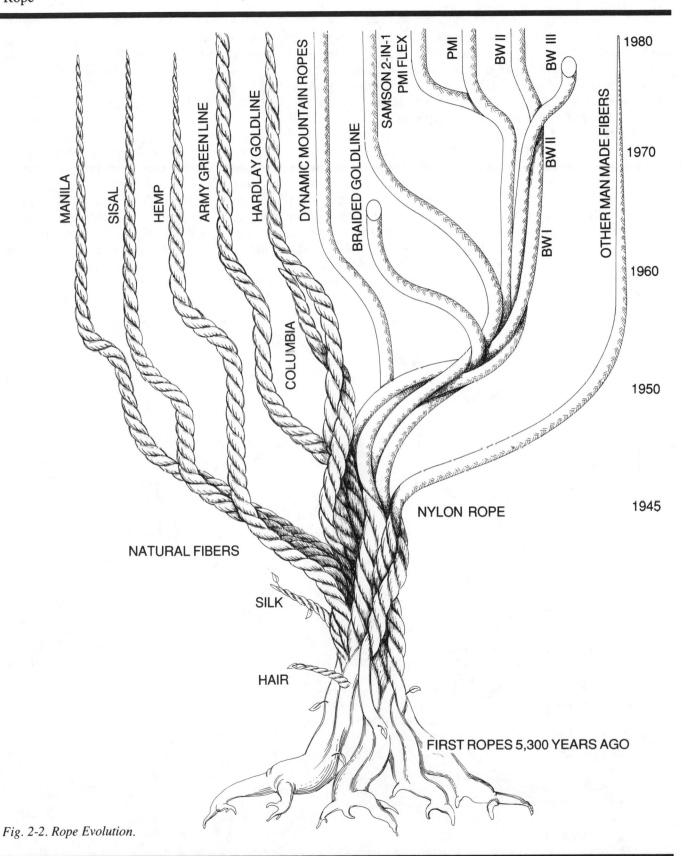

Fig. 2-2. Rope Evolution.

problems of laid rope, the marine market produced an alternative rope, a braided rope woven around a smaller braided rope core (fig. 2-5). It was named Samson Two-in-One because two yarn bundles cross over one yarn bundle in a braided pattern. This rope solved the spin problem because when loaded it did not unwind like laid ropes. Unfortunately, most of the other problems with rope remained. Stretch under a working load was better, but still Sampson was a very stretchy rope. Its softness of braid and lack of abrasion resistance was a problem. The braided sheath on braided core construction

means that the outer portion of the rope, which is subject to abrasive wear, is responsible for half of the strength of the rope. Any abrasion to that surface seriously weakens this type of rope.

Because of the braid-on-braid construction, a break in the sheath at any point would allow the outer braid to slip, exposing the unprotected inner braid. If a climber is always careful while rigging and using the rope, Sampson Two-in-one performs well, but climbers are not always conscientious about their equipment. Because circumstances have not always allowed for proper

rope protection, many ropes were damaged and the search for the elusive "better" rope continued.

Blue Water
In 1966, in the rural Georgia town of Whitesburg, there was a textile mill making nylon rope for the marine trade. This 7/16 inch rope with a trade name Blue Water, was a hard, tight-braided sheath woven over a collection of parallel inner-core fiber bundles (fig. 2-6). This stiff white rope was discovered by cavers, who began to use it extensively. The way Blue Water was constructed solved many problems. It was a static rope,

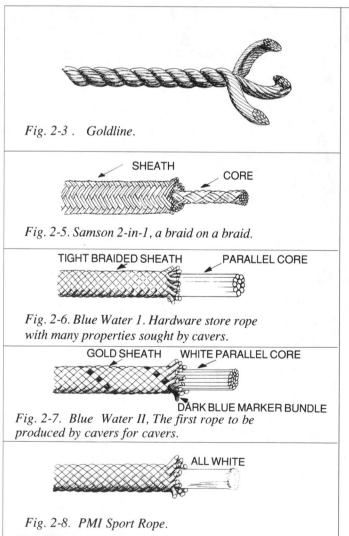

Fig. 2-3 . Goldline.

Fig. 2-5. Samson 2-in-1, a braid on a braid.

Fig. 2-6. Blue Water 1. Hardware store rope with many properties sought by cavers.

Fig. 2-7. Blue Water II, The first rope to be produced by cavers for cavers.

Fig. 2-8. PMI Sport Rope.

Fig 2-4. The problem with laid rope. Uncontrollable spin and stretch.

meaning that under a working load, it stretched very little. The tightly braided sheath protected the rope from abrasion and the parallel core supported 80% of the load. The plain 7/16 inch rope had a tested strength of over 5000 lbs. and survived the rigors of caving and climbing better than any previous rope. A market demand problem developed because of a lack of marine sales. The cavers' purchases did not contribute enough to justify the continued manufacture of Blue Water and the factory discontinued production.

Realizing the potential market, Dick Newell, a caver and textile engineer in Georgia, bought the trade name and purchased some used rope-making equipment to make rope in the basement of his house. On Sept. 1, 1969, Newell began producing Blue Water II. Blue Water II soon became the rope standard with its spiral blue stripe amidst gold fibers (fig. 2-7). It was the first rope to be produced by cavers for caving.

For the first time rope users had access to the rope design and manufacturing process. Newell and other members of the local caving club (The West Georgia Grotto of the National Speleological Society) were able to make prototype ropes, use and test them, and constantly refine the manufacturing process.

In 1971, the DuPont Company introduced its super blue 707 nylon. This beautiful light blue fiber was supposed to be more abrasion resistant. Using this fiber Newell introduced Blue Water III. Field use and actual rope testing did not bear out the promise of increased abrasion resistance. DuPont ceased production of the super blue fiber and Blue Water III passed on like the Edsel automobile. However, the rope market grew larger and production of Blue Water II left the basement and, again, was made in a fac-

Fig. 2-9a. Graphic representation of a nylon molecule.

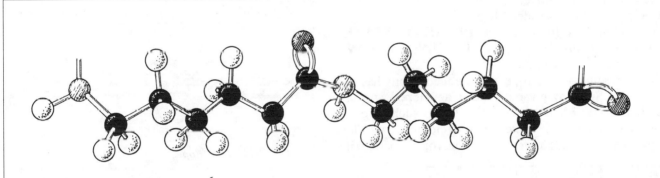

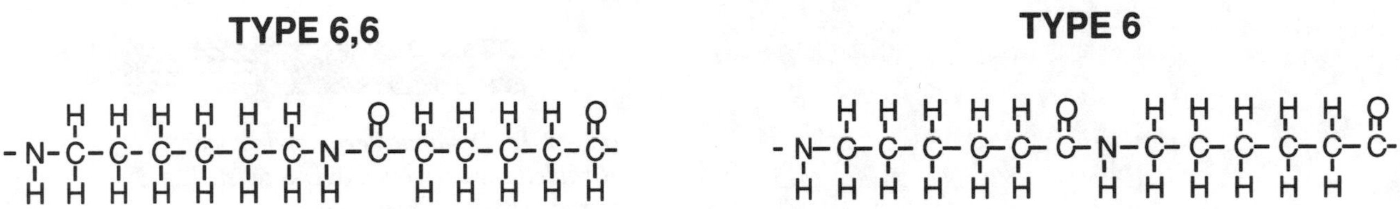

TYPE 6,6

TYPE 6

Fig. 2.9. Nylon is available in two types, 6 and 6,6.

tory devoted to rope.

Currently Blue Water manufactures many specialized rescue and fire service static ropes and has developed an American dynamic rope. They also continue to develop new ropes, rope-use devices and rescue equipment.

Pigeon Mountain Industries

In 1976, a group of cavers (many involved originally with Newell and Blue Water) decided that competition was good for the rope market and founded Pigeon Mountain Industries (PMI) in Lafayette, Georgia. With fresh ideas and enthusiasm, these experienced cavers designed a rope for the severe conditions present in cave rope use. PMI Sport rope (now called PMI Max-Wear) resulted. This firm white rope featured a 7/16 inch-

diameter braided sheath over a parallel core (fig. 2-8). With cavers descending into deeper, more complex, often wet vertical caves, the need for an abrasion-resistant rope was met. For rope users desiring a more flexible rope for slings or tight knots, PMI Flex (now called E-Z Bend) was developed. As the market for rope and rope accessories expanded, so did PMI. From its meager storefront beginnings, the factory now produces rope for many uses around the world.

PRESENT STATE OF EVOLUTION

Rope technology has now been developed and specialized to such an extent that deciding what to look for in a rope is perplexing.

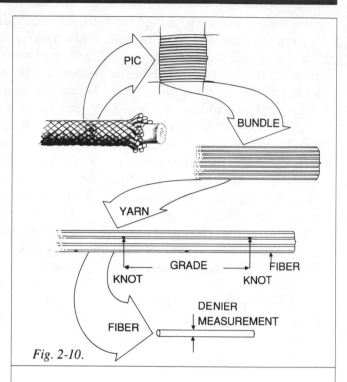

Fig. 2-10.

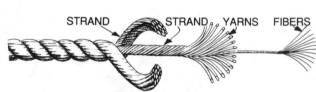

Fig. 2-11. Laid Ropes.

Fig. 2-12. Solid Braid.

Fig. 2-13. Dynamic kernmantle rope. Braided sheath woven over a twisted-strand shock-absorber core.

Fig. 2-14. Static kernmantle. A protective sheath woven tightly over a load-bearing parallel-fiber-bundle core.

No one rope will do it all. New ropes are continually being developed to meet the needs of specialized applications. These needs are met by changing materials and construction methods. Decisions as to what factors are important must be made. In a real sense, advantages and disadvantages must be traded off and compromises made to select the best rope.

Applications include: • Shock-absorbing ropes for the rock climber • Strong low-elongation ropes for rescue • Floating ropes for marine use and river rescue • Low-elongation, shock absorbing ropes for European style caving and tree surgeons • Soft responsive rappel ropes for S.W.A.T. teams • Colored ropes for multi-rope management challenges • Abrasion resistant, no-spin, low-elongation ropes for cave explorers.

FIBER TYPES

Natural fibers should not be considered for lifelines or other important uses. Quality control in a natural product is difficult since natural fibers tend to rot and degrade. These problems of degradation occur not only during use, but often occur in storage and are often not evident upon inspection. Manmade fibers are the focus of this discussion.

NYLON (Ni'-lon). Nylon comes in two basic types: type 6 and type 6,6. Though both have similar properties, type 6,6 has a higher melting point and a greater average toughness than nylon type 6 (fig. 2-9). DuPont 707 nylon is type 6,6. Perlon is a European trade name for a type 6 nylon. Where wet nylon may lose 10-15% of its strength, other fibers show no reduction when wet. However, other fibers tend to be considerably weaker than nylon. Nylon remains the superior rope fiber in that even wet, it maintains the ability to absorb a shock load where other fibers cannot. Ropes of nylon are very strong and have a high shock-load absorption capacity. Construction design can affect the abrasion resistance of ropes. By changing the number of times per inch the yarn bundles cross (pics per inch) and the tightness of these bundles, abrasion resistance can be enhanced. Another design factor is the actual diameter of the fibers extruded from nylon resin. The unbroken length of these fibers is reflected in the grade of nylon (the distance between knots joining fibers back together) (fig. 2-10).

POLYOLEFIN (Pol-lee-ole'-fin). Polypropylene and polyethylene are two useful polyolefin fibers that have a positive flotation property, which is useful in water sports and river rescue. Because of their exceptional acid resistance, polyolefin ropes are useful in industrial applications for lifelines near acid tanks. However, polyolefin's low melting point and low abrasion resistance makes such ropes a poor choice for most climbing activities.

POLYESTER (Pol-lee-est'-er). Dacron and Terylene are trade names for polyester fibers. Wetting has little effect on breaking strength. However, these fibers cannot handle shock loading or repeated loading as well as nylon. This is caused by the fact that the fibers have a low elongation at the breaking point. The main advantage that polyester fibers have is good resistance to most acids and alkalis.

KEVLAR (Kev'-lar). DuPont Kevlar is a high-temperature-resistant fiber that is extremely strong. It has a very low elongation at the breaking point and is highly susceptible to both internal and external abrasion. Kevlar lacks the capacity of longitudinal dynamic energy absorption and breaks easily if bent too tightly, such as in a knot. Having exceptional strength and latitudinal absorption ability makes Kevlar the fabric of choice for bulletproof vests. Internal abrasion of Kevlar affects heavily used articles. A vest worn daily must be replaced in 5 years. Little application exsists for this fiber as a climbing rope. However, it is used as a lightweight substitute for steel cable on climbing chocks by mountain climbers.

CONSTRUCTION

Rope construction methods, in conjunction with the fiber type, will determine a rope's properties. Twisting and weaving the various fibers uses mechanical properties plus the basic property of the fiber to produce a rope for a specific application.

Laid
These ropes consist of bundles of fibers, called strands, which are twisted or laid around one another. Usually, three of these strands are twisted into the finished rope (fig. 2-11). Larger laid ropes incorporate either seven strands or 21 strands. Most commerically available laid ropes used by cavers or climbers incorporate a Z twist (fig. 2-11), which is commonly called a righthand lay. The spiral construction of these ropes causes them to untwist under a load, which causes spinning, kinking and stretching. During use this stretch translates to a bounce. If the rope happens to be touching a ledge it will begin to abrade. The open-twist design allows for inspection of the rope, but the degree of fiber degradation cannot easily be detected visually.

Solid Braid
A solid braid rope is a large thick braid of fiber bundles that does not contain a core as found in many other rope types (fig. 2-12). When subjected to abrasion, the rope loses strength rapidly. Most solid braid ropes are unacceptable for use as a lifeline.

Dynamic Kernmantle
The term "kernmantle" describes a rope construction in which the kern, a high-strength inner core, is covered by the mantle, an outer braided sheath. The term "dynamic" de-scribes the load absorption ability of the rope or simply its ability to act as a shock absorber to catch a falling climber. Most ropes of this type are made by braiding a sheath over a twisted core strand bundle (fig. 2-13). These ropes commonly found in rock climbing have sacrificed other factors such as abrasion resistance to achieve their superior shock-absorbing ability. If severe falls are to be encountered, a dynamic rope is necessary to prevent injury to the climber.

Static Kernmantle
Static kernmantle ropes are constructed of a braided sheath woven over parallel continuous fibers of the inner core (fig. 2-14). These ropes stretch only 2% or so under working loads. A safe working load is commonly defined as 1/15th of the breaking strength of life-safety ropes. Because of the core type, the rope does not spin when loaded and has very little stretch. Typically, the core supports 70% of the rope's strength, allowing the sheath to suffer abrasion without affecting the strength of the rope significantly. Though not as good a shock absorber as dynamic ropes, static ropes have the ability to absorb shock-loading. However, they do it quicker and harsher than dynamic ropes. Static kernmantle ropes have high abrasion resistance and overall have many excellent caving/climbing/rescue qualities.

ROPE STRENGTH
Man-made fiber ropes have tremendous strength for their size, but it is important to choose one that is strong enough for safety's sake. A safe working load is commonly defined as 1/15th of the current breaking strength of the rope. If the rope's load is to be 400 lbs., it would be desirable to have a rope with a breaking strength far in excess of 400 lbs. Using the 15 to 1 formula, it will be necessary to use a rope that tests in excess of 6000 lbs. When a life is at stake, this somewhat conservative working load is recommended.

Rope strength or tensile strength is determined using a machine that pulls two cyclinders apart at a predetermined rate. The rope to be tested is wrapped around these two cylinders or drums (fig. 2-15). There are several factors that can influence the breaking strength of a given rope:

- The rate of pull.
- The temperature of the rope.
- The age of the rope.
- Whether the rope is wet or dry.
- The type of knot or the diameter of the anchor.
- Overall length of the sample.
- Source and history of sample.
- Integrity of the tester.

After the tests have been run, it 's important to interpret the test data. Are there enough samples to be significant? Is the breaking point stated at a **maximum** value (the best the rope can do)? The figure stated may be the **average** strength of several pulls or the **minimum** value (no sample failed less than this). Often a figure is stated and no explanation is given.

The purpose of laboratory testing is to set standards that will always be the same, allowing for fair consumer comparison of products. Results from laboratory tests and real-world applications, which cannot be accurately measured, are often far apart. A rope's strength when tied with a knot, looped through a carabiner, then bent over the edge and hanging in a waterfall is not the same as in a laboratory test. Hence, field-strength figures may not be even close to laboratory results.

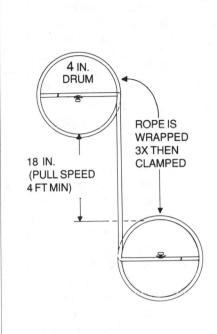

Fig. 2-15. Federal rope strength test, standard 191A, method 6016.

ABRASION RESISTANCE

North American-style ropework places a large demand on rope as compared to European styles. The European caving methods protect the rope at all costs. In North America, the rope is protected only if it has to be, if even then. There are numerous places at popular drops where rope wear has worn deep grooves into the rock! This means the rope must be ready for the demands placed on it by the North American style of SRT (Single Rope Techniques). A study of accident report histories bears out the fact that most nylon ropes hold up well.

The intricate subtleties of rope construction make a large difference in abrasion resistance. Whether the test is run dry or wet with flowing water can make a significant difference. (A caving rope test is shown in fig. 2-16.) No official standard exists for abrasion testing. Several conclusions can be drawn from the known methods:

• Kernmantle ropes are better able to protect themselves than laid ropes (Padgett 1983).
• Water flowing on the test surface can change results significantly (Eavis 1974).
• A grooved stone alters results significantly (Eavis 1974).

The use of a static rope lessens the bounce of the rope and results in a lower abrasion rate. While a tight outer sheath may help to keep grit particles out of the fiber bundles, proper care and cleaning can extend rope life and remains the most important factor. Ambient abrasion from being hauled about in the real world also affects rope life.

LOAD ABSORPTION

To what degree is load absorption necessary? General rope use places a varied amount of loading and un-

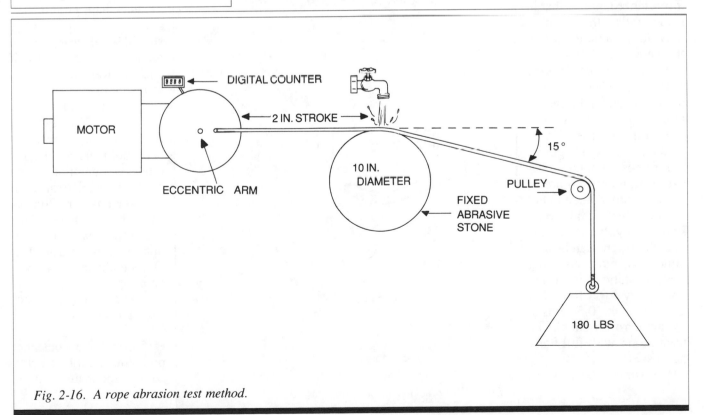

Fig. 2-16. A rope abrasion test method.

loading on the rope as the rope is rappelled and climbed. However, the natural elasticity and construction of nylon rope handles this load application well. Load absorption ability becomes an important feature when the system sustains a sudden shock load. This shock-loading occurs if an anchor fails and the back-up anchor is suddenly snapped into service.

Another type of shock-loading occurs if a climber falls onto the rope. The term used when measuring or describing falls involving shock-loading is fall factor (fig. 2-17). The fall factor is arrived at by dividing the length of the fall by the length of the rope in actual use. It is important to realize that in some falls, the climber may not be able to sustain the shocks and forces involved without injury. Much depends on the harness worn and if the anchor point can sustain the load. Because of the North American style of rigging, the forces generated because of anchor failure or shock-loading result in fall factors less than one. Forces involved in less than factor one can be sustained by most climbing rigs and static ropes. If the possibility for a force fall greater than 0.5 exists, dynamic ropes should be used along with full body harnesses.

If using a static line to

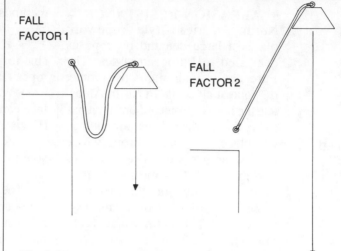

Fig. 2-17. Fall factor rating. Fall factor equals fall distance divided by rope length.

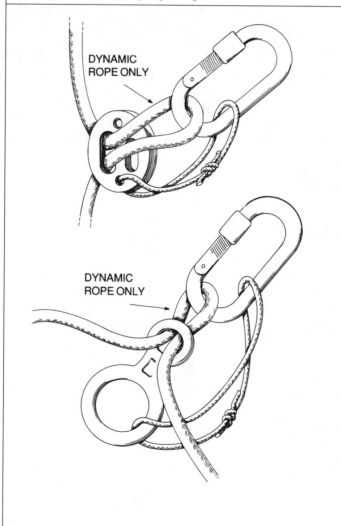

Fig. 2-18. Mechanical belay devices.

belay a climber on less than factor one falls, a mechanical belayer (Sticht plate, Figure 8, etc. fig. 2-18), could stop a fall too quickly. Traditional body belays could be employed, but they are often difficult to get out of and often the belayer receives rope burns. Body belays backed up with mechanical belays may be the answer. A Münter hitch could provide the security of a mechanical belay and the absorption of a body belay. See Chapter 9 for a complete discussion on belaying. Static ropes are very useful for protected aid climbing because of their low stretch and ability to absorb the fall forces present. If lead climbing is to be done (fall factors greater than one) a dynamic rope is a must. Care should be taken at possible abrasion or cut sites if anchors were to fail or a fall were to occur.

OTHER FACTORS
As with any consumer decision, there are always other considerations to be made. Rope price can be an important factor. Competition in the marketplace has kept the prices for quality rope reasonable. One should beware of bargain rope.

Other things to consider are:

• If there is a consumer problem, can it be resolved with the manufacturer?

• Is there documentation that assures product quality control?
• How does it "feel"? Is it knotable? Are the colors desirable?
• Above all, is it the right rope for the job to be done?

ROPE CARE

After all the investigation and the final acquisition of the right rope, it is important to care for it properly. The term "lifeline" is very apt and describes the rope's function well. If rope were always thought of as a lifeline it might receive better care.

Cutting Rope

There are several things that should be done to a new rope. First prepare the rope ends so they won't unravel. Prior to cutting, wrap the rope with a piece of tape, cut it with a sharp blade, and finally melt the ends to fuse the fibers together (fig. 2-19).

Washing Rope

A new rope is naturally slippery, which keeps the rope soft and supple and the fibers adjust favorably depending on use. Washing a new rope tends to remove the natural slipperiness, causing it to become dry and brittle. This, in turn, shortens the life of a rope. So as not to prematurely dry out a new rope, it **should not** be washed, rinsed or soaked before initial use. After the fibers have set themselves in use, it's advantageous to soak the rope to shrink it slightly. This tightens the sheath so dirt will not penetrate. Shrinkage is usually less than 10%. Many manufacturers allow for this shrinkage when measuring new ropes for shipment.

An excellent way to wash a dirty rope is to take it to a laundromat with a big round **front opening** commercial washer. Typically, these have a large round sight glass in the front door. Make sure it is glass instead of soft plastic as it is possible to damage the rope with abrasion from a plastic lens. To load the rope into the machine, it is best to loosely bundle the rope into a large mesh bag, then stuff it all into the machine. The next best way is to just stuff a loose bundle of rope into the machine making sure all the rope is in the drum and not caught in the space between the drum and the door.

CAUTION: Washers, especially top loading ones with a central rotating agitator should be avoided. The rope tends to become very tightly snarled about the agitator and severe abrasion can result, not to mention the possible washer damage.

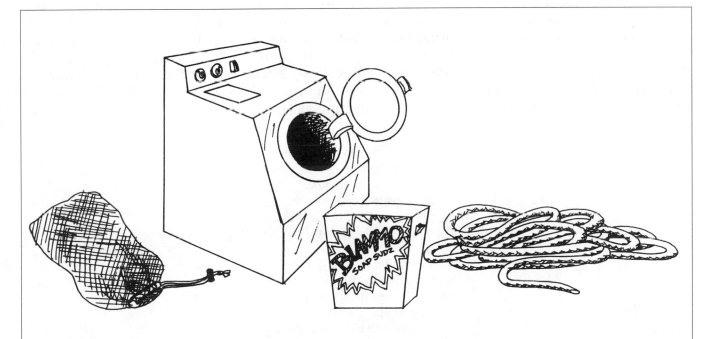

A front-loading washing machine is excellent for washing dirty ropes. Avoid top loading washers, especially those with central rotating agitators.

For a new rope, after first use, use cool water and a very small amount of mild soap (like Ivory Flakes, not a detergent). On an older dirty rope, to remove grit and grime, use a good quality laundry detergent instead of soap. The idea is to suspend the dirt particles and clean the rope. Most commercial detergents are safe on nylon, but some include additives that could be harmful to rope. It's important to carefully read the label to be sure it's safe for synthetics.

CAUTION: Never use Chlorine Bleach on a rope.

Nylon can stand immersion in 180°F water indefinitely with no degradation. However, shrinkage of the weave will occur. To prevent shrinkage, set the water to cool or warm for a very dirty rope. The hot water in most laundromats is about 140° F.

All indications point to the fact that fabric softeners are not a good idea. Fabric softeners have from time to time been recommended as a way of softening well used stiff ropes. Instead, recent tests on aging rope indicate fabric softeners substantially weaken rope. It is proposed that this weakening is due to the bonding of free hydrogen molecules from the softener to the nylon polymer, actually changing the molecular structure of the rope's nylon.

After washing the rope, air dry it away from direct sunlight to prevent ultraviolet degradation. Never use a clothes dryer as they can quickly exceed safe temperatures.

Marking a Rope
Every rope should be marked as to the length and owner. There are several ways to mark a rope:
• With commercially available rope labels, owner, length and age can be written, then sealed with the attached plastic tape (fig. 2-20).
• Colored marking pens (like Marks-A-Lot) can be used to add colored bands to identify the owner and length of the rope. The owner code can be a three-color sequence. The method as shown in fig. 2-21 uses bands of varying width to indicate the length of the rope.

CAUTION. Phenol-based markers can degrade a nylon rope.

• Clear shrink tubing with an inserted label makes an excellent homemade marker.
• Whipping the ends with colored thread sets each rope apart.
• It is possible to surface-dye rope. A rope dyed different colors also allows a climber to pace himself during a climb. A 300 foot white PMI could be soaked in blue dye for the first hundred feet and red dye on the last 100 feet. Read the label on the dye before you begin.

Using The Rope
As a practical matter, rope must be gathered, coiled or bundled for ease of use and ease of transit. The best way, in most cases, is to place the rope in a protective bag (fig. 2-22). This will keep it clean and allow for transportation ease to and from the place of use. Others may opt for a

---

ROPE DYEING
As a manmade fiber, nylon's quality control can be assured. Pure nylon is naturally white, but has the ability to absorb color dyes. There are two basic ways to dye nylon:
• Solution dyeing is the adding of color to the nylon resin, which can result in a less strong finished product.
• Surface dyeing is the adding of color to the yarns after the nylon fibers have been formed. This does not weaken the yarns at all, although the color bond is not as good as with solution dying.

backpacker's coil (fig. 2-23). For long ropes, up to 600 feet, a rope pack may be the answer (fig. 2-24). Inside the pack is a metal frame to wind the rope on so the rope occupies a minimum of space. Even larger ropes may be carried in army duffle bags. Forsaking a bag, the next best way to transport rope is to wrap it into a cavers/mountain coil (fig. 2-25). Another method of transport is to chain the rope. This works well on very flexible ropes (fig. 2-26a) and very well with webbing (fig. 2-26b).

Nylon is an extremely inert material. This means very few things will react with it and cause damage. Basically, only strong acids, alkalis, oxidizing and reducing agents are known to be dangerous to nylon.

NYLON HAZARDS

- Sulfuric acid (battery acid)
- Other strong acids
- Chlorine
- Hydrogen peroxide
- Bleaching compounds
- Phenols, cresols and xylenol

While in storage or transit, a rope's worst enemy is acid. Keep lifelines separated from the vehicle or headlamp batteries (fig. 2-27). Place the rope in a rope bag and keep them apart, so they won't accidentally come in contact. For example, always put the rope in the trunk and lamp batteries on the floor of the back seat. In trucks, vehicle batteries are not always under the hood, so be cautious. At home, store ropes and electric lamp chargers in separate rooms. Don't pile ropes on concrete floors, as acid is often used in concrete work and lasts for years. Chemical damage to ropes can occur and not be visually detected. It can be an unseen killer.

It is always advisable to protect any rope from unknown chemicals in the interest of safety. For reasons mentioned earlier with regard to fabric softeners, substances and compounds such as gasoline, oil, antifreeze, and other hydrocarbons containing free hydrogen may weaken a rope as much as half of its original strength after prolonged contact.

Keeping the rope clean and free of these substances will greatly extend the working life of a rope.

DON'T Step On The Rope. Grinding in grit particles under the soles of one's boots can cause the rope to suffer internal abrasion and find itself being cut from the inside out. As the rope is used, think of ambient rope abrasion. This is the damage to rope fibers from being hauled about, dragged through the mud, and pulled over rocks. Dragging a rope down a crawlway or up a climb abrades the rope surface just like an unprotected rub point on a drop. The only difference is that the damage is not usually localized. Ambient abrasion also adds grit and grime to the interior of the rope. Rappelling on a dirty rope will cause more grit to be worked inside the fibers, causing further weakening. A dirty or partially wet rope can provide an uneven friction surface upon which to rappel, causing an unnecessary hazard.

On any drop, pad the rope where necessary (See Chapter 4). However, to protect against severe abrasion in

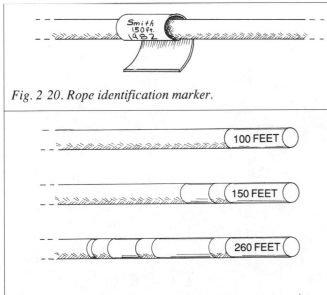

Fig. 2 20. Rope identification marker.

Fig. 2-21. Indicating rope length by band width.

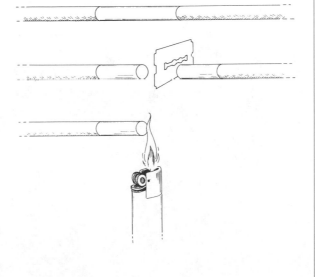

Fig. 2-19. Rope-end preparation methods.

Fig. 2-22. Rope
bags protect a
rope from ambient
abrasion.

Fig. 2-24. The
rope pack uses
an internal frame.

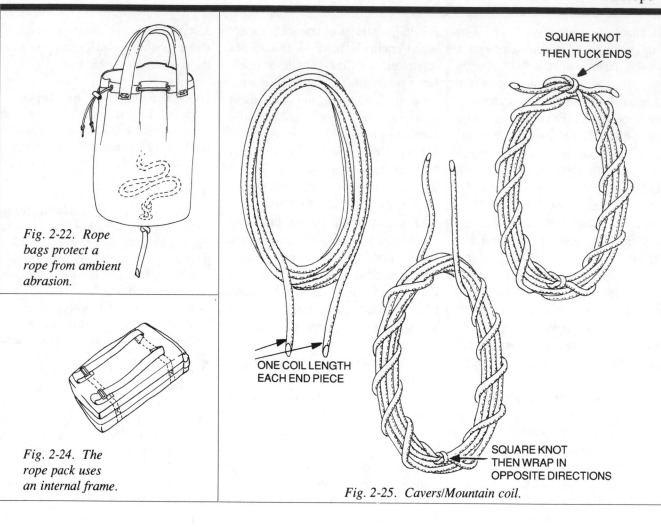

SQUARE KNOT
THEN TUCK ENDS

ONE COIL LENGTH
EACH END PIECE

SQUARE KNOT
THEN WRAP IN
OPPOSITE DIRECTIONS

Fig. 2-25. Cavers/Mountain coil.

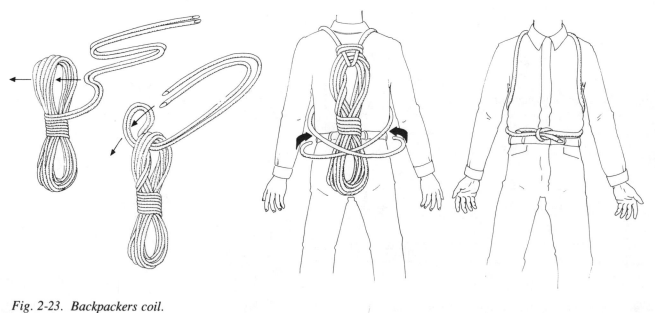

Fig. 2-23. Backpackers coil.

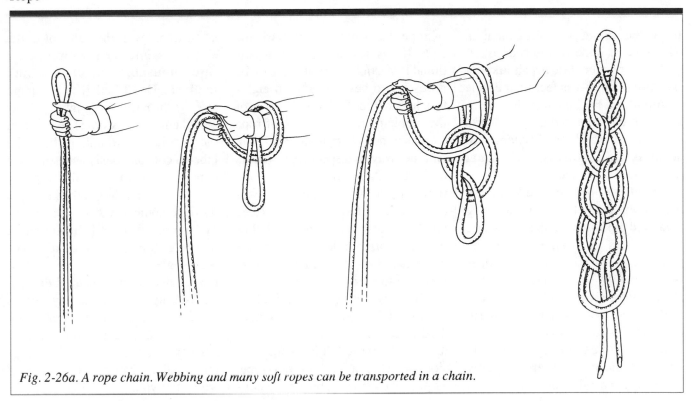

Fig. 2-26a. A rope chain. Webbing and many soft ropes can be transported in a chain.

those impossible places, the rope can be retied a short distance up or down to change the wear points. This won't stop abrasion, but it will avoid the concentration of extensive abrasion at any one place. Each time a rope is used, alternate the end that is tied off. This helps provide for even wear on the entire rope, thus maximizing its potential life.

Rope Inspection

After a hard trip, the rope is usually muddy and gritty or at best just covered with aluminum residue from rappels. Before reuse or inspection, it needs to be washed. A clean rope and well cared for equipment are the signs of an experienced, competent climber. Dirty "crudded up" rope or gear is no status symbol.

One quick way to get the surface mud and dirt from a rope is to pull it through a rope washer (fig. 2-28). Another idea is to use two stiff nylon-bristle scrub brushes while blasting the whole rig with a water hose (fig. 2-29). These methods will remove a great deal of the surface dirt and grime. Don't stop here. Allow the launderette and soap to finish the job. After washing, the rope should be

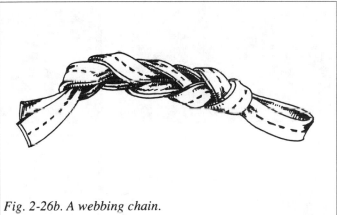

Fig. 2-26b. A webbing chain.

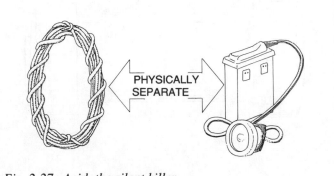

PHYSICALLY SEPARATE

Fig. 2-27. Acid, the silent killer.

inspected along its entire length. This can be done as the rope is re-coiled or bagged. Gloves should not be worn to do this as feeling the rope is important. Feel the rope for fuzziness and changes in diameter due to damage. Also feel for any changes in stiffness (fig. 2-30), as these occur at any point of damage.

Study the rope carefully as you are feeling it to check for excessive wear and puffs—core fibers that tend to be clean and white protruding from the sheath (fig. 2-31). A booger is a severely worn place possibly showing core strands (fig. 2-32). If a puff, booger or any marked change in diameter or texture exists, it is definitely time to cut the rope. It should be cut at the problem area, usually resulting in two shorter usable pieces of rope. Remember to re-mark the ends. If it is desirable to test a questionable section of rope, it will be necessary to have at least an eight-foot length, four feet on either side of the problem area. The piece of rope can then be taken to a local lab. Another way to inspect rope wear is to look at the surface fibers of the rope with a 10X magnifying glass (fig. 2-33). Examine the fiber bundles (pics). If, in these bundles over a majority of the rope, there are more than 50% of the fibers broken, it is time to retire the rope.

If a rope has taken a hard fall or been used for some other non-standard use, such as a tow rope for a car, it should be retired. It is a hard decision to retire a faithful old rope. Ropes are expensive, but surely non-comparable with the value of a life. When it is time to retire a rope, cut it into unusable pieces. Think **lifeline!** Don't sell it at a garage sale or throw it away intact. If for sentimental or historical reasons an old rope is kept around, it should be labeled conspicuously as retired and kept separate from all other ropes.

This section has looked at rope, its development and its properties. The proper care and protection of rope as a lifeline is a critical aspect of high-angle ropework. Often, all that is available for a vertical pitch with no back-up or redundant system in place is a single rope. This single rope deserves the respect and the care from the climber who uses it properly. If all these things are in place, it won't fail you.

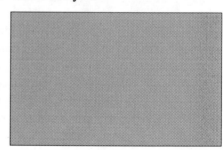

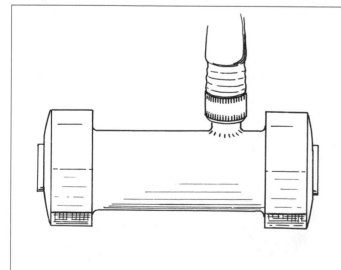

Fig. 2-28. Pull through rope washer.

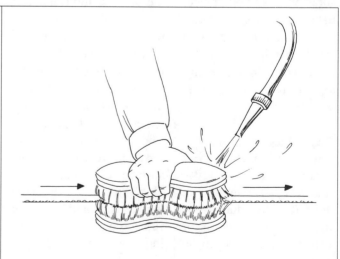

Fig. 2-29. Washing surface dirt.

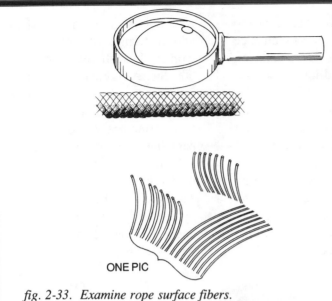

ONE PIC

fig. 2-33. Examine rope surface fibers.

WEBBING

Webbing, (sometimes called **tape**), is essentially flat rope. Its most common usage is for slings and harnesses. The sizes that are most often used are 1 inch webbing, 1 25/32 inch parachute webbing and 2 inch seat belt webbing. Webbing is made in two forms: flat and tubular. Both appear flat, but upon examination from the end, tubular webbing is, in fact, hollow (fig. 2-a). Tubular webbing is usually stronger and more flexible than flat webbing.

Tubular webbing is constructed in two very different ways: • Spiral structure, (shuttle loom construction), which is very strong, and • Chain structure, (needle loom construction), which is weaker.

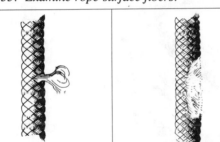

Fig. 2-31. A puff is strong indication of internal damage.

Fig. 2-32. A booger is a warning sign.

Fig. 2-a. Webbing: flat and tubular.

Some types can come unraveled like a knitted sweater when one thread is cut. Both chain and spiral look somewhat alike. Careful examination is required to tell the difference. To check, roll the webbing 90° between your fingers and examine the crease now on the top or bottom (fig. 2-b). The chain structure has a seam which joins the webbing together. The preferred spiral structure has no disconformity along the edge and has continuous ribs (fig. 2-c). Chain-structure webbing commonly occurs in flashy multicolor webbing. Examine all webbing carefully prior to purchase.

Webbing withstands abrasion well, but is not indestructible. It is not a kernmantle construction, so the outside surface is the load-bearing surface. Examine the webbing fibers in the weave and retire if 30% of the fibers are worn (fig. 2-27) at any place along the

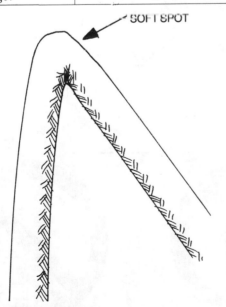

SOFT SPOT

Fig. 2-30. A change in stiffness can be an indicator of internal rope damage.

webbing.

Webbing is commonly tied or sewn to make loops or harnesses. The water knot (see fig. 3-20) is best for tying webbing into slings. However, sewing is the stongest, neatest and most secure way of joining webbing together. Prior to sewing, seal the ends with a hot wire or flame. The best method of sewing (fig. 2-d) is a series of parallel longitudinal runs. The sewing area length should be three times the width of the webbing. There should be at least nine passes made when using a sewing machine. Nylon thread should be used and, if sewn on a machine, make abso-

lutely sure that the thread on top and in the bobbin are nylon. See Chapter 10 for more details on stitch patterns and the proper use of a sewing awl.

Quality 1 inch inch tubular webbing has a strength of about 4000 lbs. When rigging with 1 inch webbing, attempt to make the webbing as strong as the rope by doubling the webbing. Knots and bends affect strength, so a safe working load should be less than 350 lbs. The most common 2 inch

webbing is of the flat variety with a strength of 5500 lbs. Its working load should not exceed 500 lbs. Any buckles or hardware used with webbing should be of parachute quality and able to withstand heavy loads. Most parachute buckles are made for 1 25/32 inch webbing. Webbing is used in a life support capacity and should not be compromised by the use of plastic or cheap buckles. When using a buckle with webbing, the loose end should be backed up, either by threading the loose end back through the buckle or by tying it down with an overhand knot.

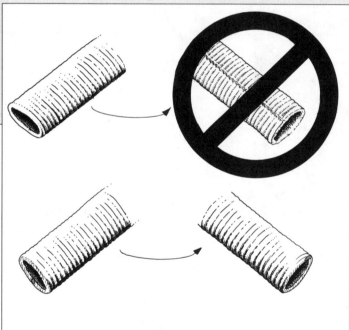

Fig. 2-b. The edge seam will often tell the quality of the webbing.

Fig. 2-c. Webbing rib comparison. Spiral is best for strength.

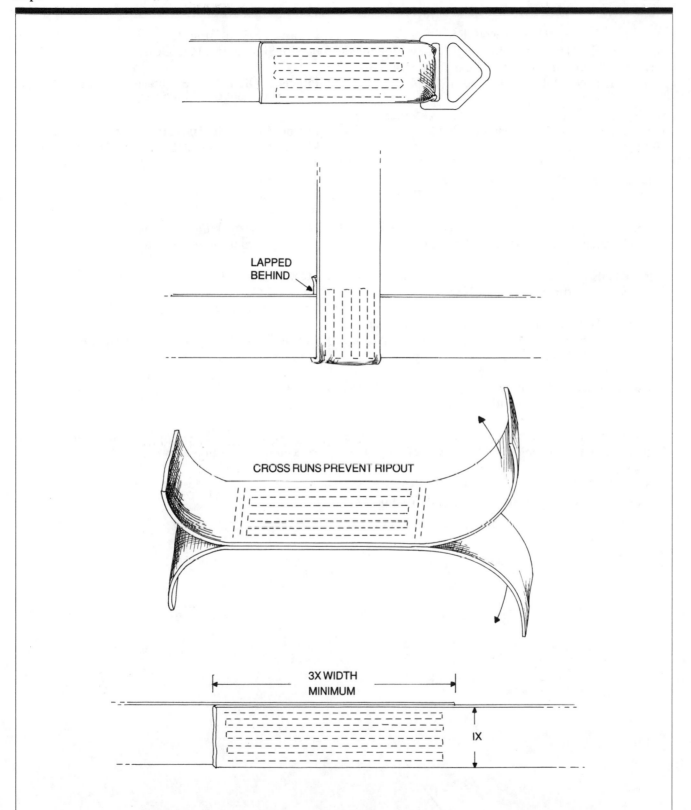

LAPPED
BEHIND

CROSS RUNS PREVENT RIPOUT

3X WIDTH
MINIMUM

1X

Fig. 2-d. When sewing webbing, the seam should be three times the webbing width with at least nine passes of the sewing machine using nylon thread on both top and bottom thread bobbins.

REFERENCES

Eavis, A. J. "The Rope In Single Rope Technique Caving." *Transactions British Cave Research Association*, Vol. 1, No. 4, Dec. 1974, pp. 181-198.

Eavis, A. J. "The Weak Link." *Union International de Speologie Equipment Commission*, Bulletin No. 1, Nov. 1980, pp. 15-17.

Georgia Emergency Manual Agency. *Rescue Specialist Manual..* Atlanta, Georgia.: GEMA, 1983.

Isenhart, Kyle. "Abrasion testing of Ropes and Slings". Paper presented at 1977 NSS Convention.

Isenhart, Kyle. "Care and feeding of Rope." *Nylon Highway 1*, Vertical Section of NSS, (1973), pp. 3-6.

Isenhart, Kyle. "The Selection, Use, and Care Of Ropes For Vertical Caving." *Caving Basics*, Huntsville, Alabama: Natl. Speleological Soc. 1987, pp. 69-72.

Judson, David, ed. *Caving Practice and Equipment*, London: David & Chales Ltd., 1984, pp. 59-66.

Montgomery, Neil. *Single Rope Techniques*. Sydney: Sydney Speleological Society, 1977, pp. 1-9.

Newell, Dick. "Development of Caving Rope." *Nylon Highway 5*. Vertical Section of NSS (1976), pp. 5-8.

Para-Gear Equipment Co. *Product Catalog., Number 50*, Skokie, IL.: Para Gear, 1985.

Padgett, Allen. "Rope Abrasion Testing." *NSS News Vol. 41, No. 9,* 1983, pp. 234-7.

Pigeon Mountain Industries, Inc. Guide to Buying Rescue Rope, Pamphlet, Lafayette, Georgia: PMI, 1982.

Smith, Bruce. "Aging Rope." *Nylon Highway 25,* Vertical Section of NSS (1988), pp. 1-6.

Setnicka, Tim. *Wilderness Search and Rescue.*, Boston: Applachian Mountain Club, 1980.

Steele, Bill. "On the Ups and Downs of Vertical Caving," *Caving Basics,* Huntsville, Alabama.: Natl. Speleological Soc., 1987, pp. 62-67.

Thrun, Robert. *Prusiking*, Huntsville, Alabama.: Natl. Speleological Soc., 1971.

Tryckare, Tre. *The Lore Of Ships.* Sweden: 1963, pp. 140-141.

Van Nostrand's, *Scientific Encyclopedia, 5th edition*, Princeton, NJ.: Van Nostrand, 1973, p.1029.

3 Knots

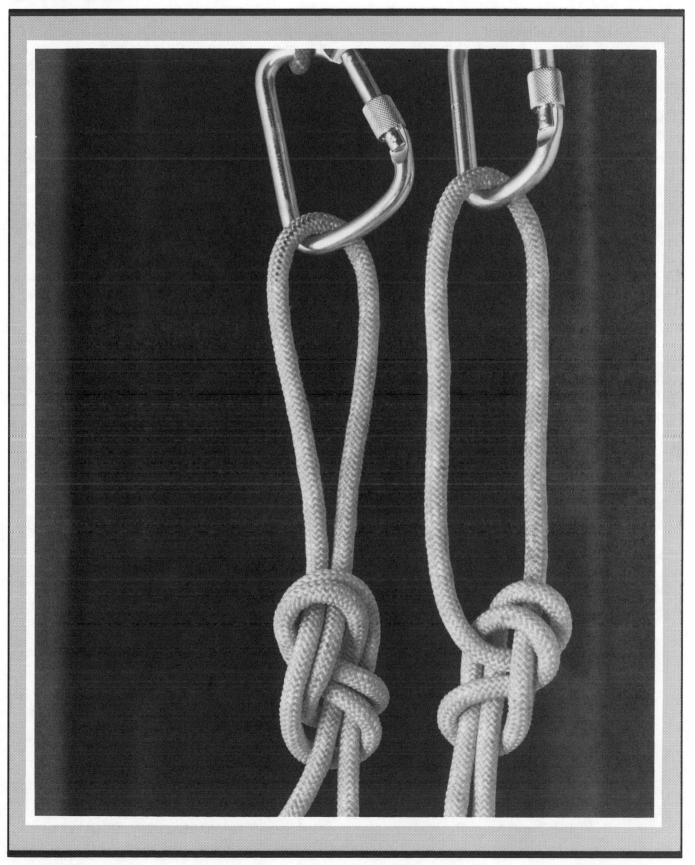

3 Knots

Vertical ropework demands a skilled rigger. The rigger ties off the ropes and pads, and weighs the advantages and disadvantages of one tie-off point over others. Securing rope is a critical skill that should be mastered by all vertical cavers and climbers. After the rope has been attached to its anchor by the rigger, it should be closely examined by each member of the party before use. After all, it is a critical link upon which lives will depend.

A skillful rigger does not need a vast repertoire of knots. In fact, some say knowing a bowline and a figure eight knot and all their variations can accomplish all ropework needs. Knowing a few knots and knowing them well is far better than being familiar with dozens of knots about which one feels only vaguely comfortable. The purpose here is to discuss the practical, usable knots and their variations that have proven repeatedly useful when operating at high angles. In Chapter 4 these knots will be put to practical use when we discuss the subject of rigging. Climbing with knots and the Ascender Knot will be discussed in Chapter 6. The Prusik Knot is covered here.

Knots are essential to a successful rigging and are the focus of this discussion. Knots should be as simple to untie as they are to tie. They should not be able to work themselves loose and should be simple, allowing for easy inspection. Knot size is a factor that sometimes becomes an important criterion in selection. A compact knot may be necessary if it has to travel through a pulley or if it becomes necessary to climb or rappel over it. Understand, also, that a rope's fibers undergo stress whenever they sustain bending or twisting. As a general rule, a rope oriented in a straight line will maintain the greatest original strength. The opposite is also true; the sharper the angle at which a rope is bent, the weaker it becomes at that point. In fact, summarizing test results of rope strengths from the dozens of published charts, one can conclude that a rope's efficiency is reduced to approximately 50 percent of its original working strength at a tight knot.

Knot Efficiency.
Knot Efficiency or the remaining relative strength of a rope after a knot has been placed in it, is a debated topic and varies with the

Fig. 3-1a. Undressed. An undressed knot may reduce strength by as much as 50%.

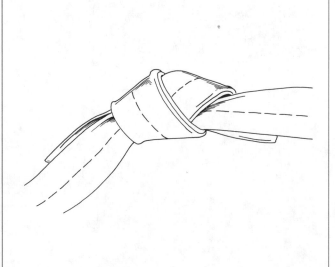

Fig. 3-lb. Dressed. Does not reduce strength as an undressed knot does.

rope type, diameter and source of your data. A knot should be selected because of what it can accomplish. Consider all the options at your command, taking into consideration the approximate 50 percent strength loss. Somtimes knot efficiency may be sacrificed for the priority of "compactness." These factors are the rigger's decision.

Finishing.
Finishing a knot involves two activities:

• **Dressing a knot**

• **Setting a knot.**

Dressing.
Dressing a knot involves the orientation of all the knot parts so that they are all properly aligned, straightened or bundled, and so that the rope parts of the knot look like the picture books. Neglecting this activity may result in an additional 50 percent reduction in knot strength (fig #3-1).

Setting.
Setting a knot involves tightening all parts of the knot so that all of the rope parts touch, grab and cause friction upon other parts of the knot so as to render it operational. A loosely tied knot can easily deform under strain and change in character. For instance, an effectively set bowline, requires tension in three directions at the same time (especially with limp or soft rope (fig. 3-2). Even the decorative double carrick bend takes on a completely different appearance after the knot has been set (fig. 3-3).

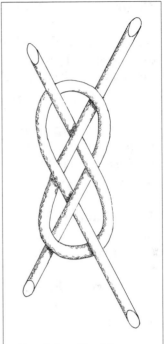

Fig. 3-3a. Double Carrick bend is tied in this manner.

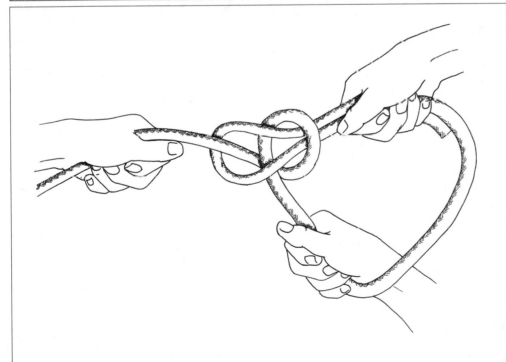

Fig. 3-2. Setting a knot renders it operational. Setting involves tightening all parts.

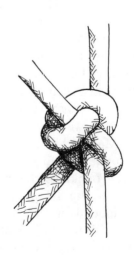

Fig. 3-3b. Double Carrick bend after setting.

Common Knot Tying Terms

Bight. A doubled section of rope usually taken from the center of the rope that doesn't cross itself—compare with loop below (fig 3-4).

The Standing Part of the Rope. Includes all the rope that is not fastened at the rigging point (fig. 3-5).

The Running End (or End). Refers to the end that is not rigged or the free end (fig. 3-5).

The Working End. The end that is used to rig with or tie off to something (fig. 3.5).

Loop. A turn of the rope that crosses itself (fig.3-6).

Knot Names.

The names of knots can be an extremely confusing issue. Clifford Ashley, one of the foremost experts on knots and their names wrote a book in 1944 about the subject. He has often been referred to as the last word in knots, yet, 40 years later many knot names have changed.

For example, a common Prusik knot was known to Ashley as the Magnus hitch. When a publication attempts to write a definitive piece on knots, their names and how to tie them, the confusion compounds itself. *On Rope* does not wish to add to that confusion, but rather to present the most common names that are recognized by several sources as well as field experts. With no offense to Ashley, some knots names do not agree with the last word in knots.

Categories of Knots.

A majority of rigging/sling knot sources classify knots into three major categories.

- **End-line riggings**
- **Mid-line riggings**
- **End-to-end tie-offs**

The first two types lend themselves to main riggings, while the end-to-end tie-offs have predominate sling application.

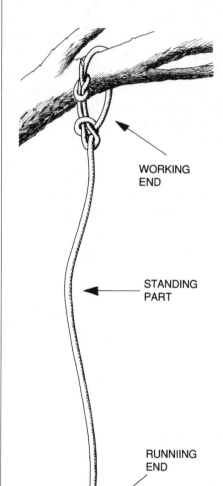

WORKING END

STANDING PART

RUNNIING END

Fig. 3-5. Rigged rope parts.

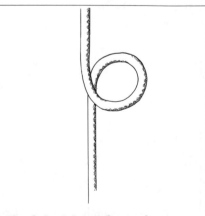

Fig. 3-4. A bight of rope—a loop that doesn't cross over itself.

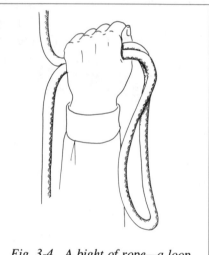

Fig. 3-6. A loop of rope that crosses over itself.

End-Line Knots

Bowline.

The bowline is a multi-purpose knot that is as easily tied as untied (fig. 3.6). If tied wrong, the knot will fall apart into some unknown tangle. Its loop size is easily adjusted. It has a high efficiency rating but has been known to work loose during repeated loadings, especially with softer ropes.   It's best to back up this knot with an overhand knot (fig. 3-7). The end of the rope should be oriented on the inside of the major loop, never on the outside (fig. 3-8). On the outside of the loop the end is vulnerable to snagging. Snagging may cause inverting of the knot, resulting in a slip knot. Actual test with 7/16 inch rope in 1985 indicated there was no knot strength difference between the two ways of tying, inside or outside.

Experienced climbers advise that each participant be able to tie this knot quickly, with one hand, around the waist with eyes closed. One never knows when he will be precariously stranded on some ledge, holding on with one hand while trying to fasten a rescue rope around his waist with his other hand. This is one knot that has to be dressed and set. If left loose it can distort and turn into a slip knot.

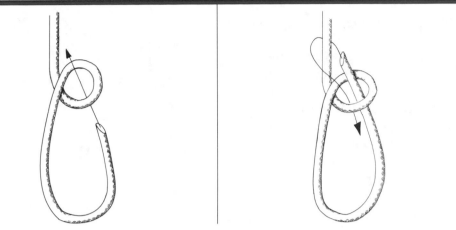

Fig. 3-7. Tying the bowline. It is considered one of the preferred knots and a "must know" for rigging.

Fig. 3-7b.

Fig. 3-7c.

Fig. 3-7d. It's best to backup a bowline with an overhand knot.

Fig. 3-8 Bowline strength is not reduced if tied backward, though it is more vulnerable to snagging and inverting into a slip knot.

Mountaineering Bowline

The Mountaineering Bowline (fig. 3-9) is a variation of the bowline. It has other common names such as **Double-Knotted Bowline** or **High-Strength Bowline**. Ashley calls it a **Double Turn or Round-Turn Bowline**. Setnicka, editor of *Wilderness Search and Rescue*, claims it has a five percent strength advantage over the regular bowline.

From all indications, it is becoming the preferred rigging knot in North America. Like the bowline, it is easy to tie and even easier to untie even after heavy and repeated loading. Dressing and setting, followed by an overhand knot, are minimum requirements when finishing this knot.

Setnicka depicts another bowline tie-off, which he claims he learned from his Yosemite Mountaineering School, that involves tucking the end back through the eye (fig 3-10). This seems to be very practical, maintains the compactness of the knot, the cleanness of the loop and can be used with many bowline variations. This backup variation yields an uncluttered loop center allowing for multiple hookups.

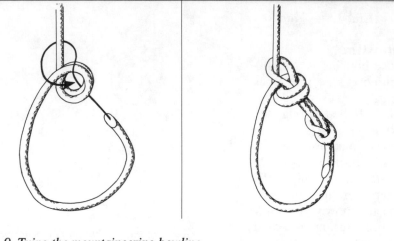

Fig. 3-9. Tying the mountaineering bowline.

Fig. 3-10a. Starting the Yosemite tie-off with a bowline.

Fig. 3-10b. Yosemite tie-off on a bowline.

Fig. 3-10c.. Yosemite tie-off on a mountaineering bowline.

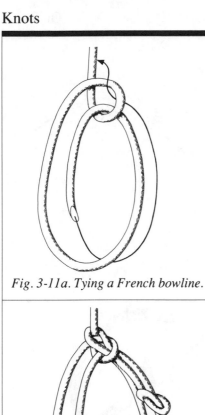

Fig. 3-11a. Tying a French bowline.

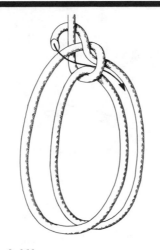

Fig. 3-11b.

Fig. 3-11c.

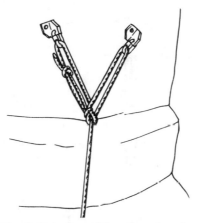

Fig. 3-11d. French bowline rigged as a self-equalizing anchor (SEA).

Fig. 3-12a. Tying a figure eight.

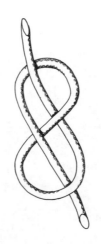

Fig. 3-12b.

French Bowline

This knot is occasionally called a **Self-Equalizing Bowline** (Fig. 3-11) and is another variation of the bowline. Its use, as the name implies, is for the attachment of two anchors where equal tension is desired and the direction of pull may change.

If one of the anchors fails, the knot has enough internal friction to slowly readjust to the one anchor without a sudden jolt to the climber or the remaining anchor. However, this knot has been known to cut itself if the loops are allowed to adjust under a load. Again, dressing, setting and backups are important.

Figure Eight

The Figure Eight Knot (Fig. 3-12) has so many purposes and variations that some say it is the climber's secret weapon. As an end-line knot it is a recommended knot for tying off the running end so the climber doesn't rappel off the rope as discussed in Chapters 4 and 5.

Figure Eight on a Bight

By forming a bight with the running end of the rope, an easy, reliable loop can be formed for hauling or lifting gear. The Figure Eight on a Bight (Fig. 3-13) has terrific applications to carabiner clip-ins, trolley line hook-ups and primary riggings from the middle of the line and reanchors. It is the preferred end-line safety knot over the Figure Eight knot because it supplies a loop at the end of the rope that could assist a climber during an attempt to changeover from a rappel to a prusik system. (This procedure is covered in Chapter 7).

It is possible to tie this knot incorrectly, resulting in about a 10 percent strength loss (Montgomery) (Fig 3-14).

The Figure Eight knot can be used as a primary end-line rigging around an anchor, such as a tree (Fig. 3-15). First tie a simple Figure Eight knot, loop the end around the anchor and rethread the end back into the knot following it backwards. Don't forget to dress and set this knot.

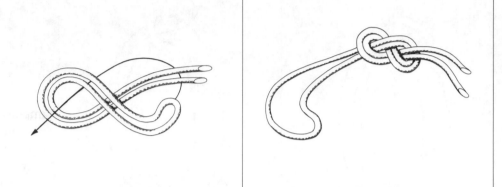

Fig. 3-13a. Tying a figure eight on a bight. One of the preferred knots and considered a "must know" knot for rigging.

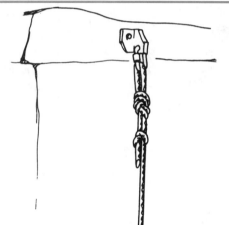

Fig. 3-13b. Figure eight rigged to a bolt and hanger with a carabiner.

Fig. 3-14. Tying a figure eight on a bight with the standing line taking the short radii of the first bend weakens the knot.

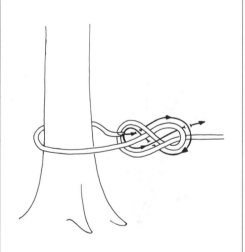

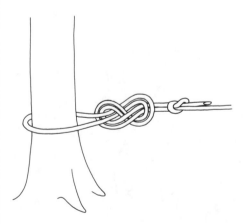

Fig. 3-15. Practical use of the figure eight bend.

Mid-Line Knots

Often, there is a need to tie a knot in the middle of a rope for a carabiner clip point, a gear transfer line (zip line) for that time when only 100 feet of rope is needed for the drop and all you brought was a 600 foot rope. It would be senseless to lower several hundred feet of rope into a muddy pit when much less is needed. Mid-line knots have numerous applications and should be a ready part of a climber's knot repertoire.

One of the better mid-line knots is the **Figure Eight on a Bight**. See the previous section for discussion of this knot. This knot is sometimes referred to as the **Middleman's Knot**.

Bowline on a Bight

The Bowline on a Bight (Fig. 3-16) is another variation of a bowline. It has a high knot strength, a redundant coil, and remains impossible to untie while still around an anchor. However, the coils do not easily adjust as with the French bowline, but it remains one of the recommended knots to use when rigging self-equalizing anchors. Dressing and setting, as always, are important.

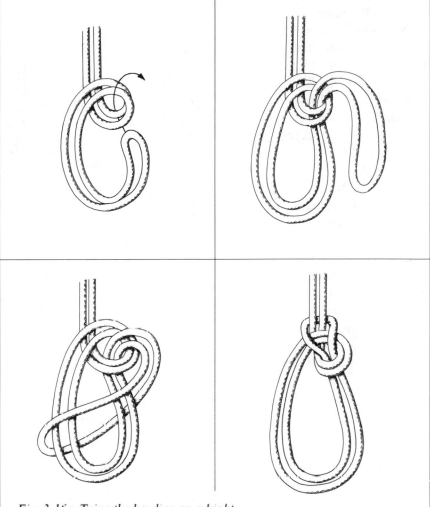

Fig. 3-16a. Tying the bowline on a bight.

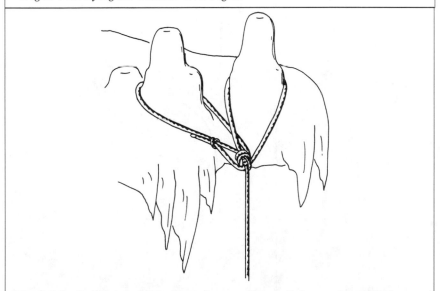

Fig. 3-16b. Bowline on bight, rigged as a self-equalizing anchor (SEA).

Double Bowline

The Double Bowline is another variation of the Bowline. It is sometimes called a **Three Loop Bowline** or **Triple Bowline** and becomes very handy when securing the mid-line to a large object.

Simply bight the rope, wrap it around the object/anchor and tie a regular bowline with both ropes (fig. 3-17). For years this knot has been used as a harness to lift injured victims or for attaching a litter to the multiple loops, etc. Harnesses and litter bridles for the most part have replaced this application.

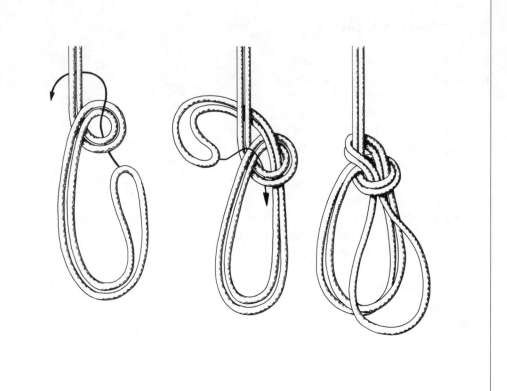

Fig. 3-17a, b, c. Tying a double bowline.

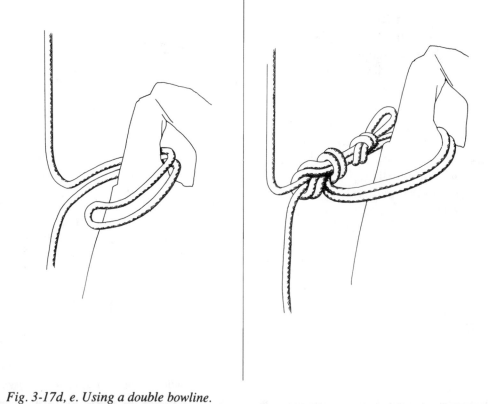

Fig. 3-17d, e. Using a double bowline.

Butterfly

The Butterfly (fig. 3-18) is a compact, somewhat complicated, mid-line rigging. It is probably the best mid-line rigging knot there is. Once mastered, the number of situations in which this knot is appropriate and useful are many. Its important feature is that it provides for multi-directional pull. Also, because of its symmetry it is very easy to inspect. It is important to dress and set this knot, and it seems to work best with softer ropes.

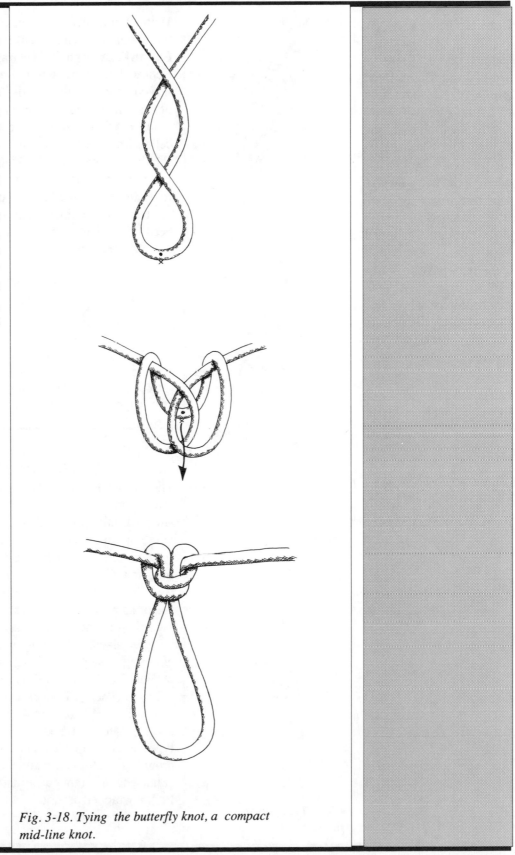

Fig. 3-18. Tying the butterfly knot, a compact mid-line knot.

End to End Tie-Offs

Figure Eight Bend
The Figure Eight Bend (fig. 3-19) is also referred to as the **Flemish Bend** and is a variation of the Figure Eight knot. It is the preferred knot to use when it is necessary to join two ropes together. It is compact and will slide through the larger knot-passing rescue pulleys. It is easy to tie as well as untie. It is visually obvious when tied incorrectly. This knot requires dressing and setting.

Fig. 3-19. Tying a figure eight bend.

Water Knot. Probably one of the most popular knots, the Water Knot (fig. 3-14) is known by many names: **Follow-Through, Overhand Bend, Overhand Follow-Through, Ring Bend,** and **Blood Knot**. It is compact and thus lends itself to many of the needs of the climber. For the most part, many slings (endless loops) are fastened together with this knot. It is an excellent knot for fastening webbing together (fig. 3-20) such as in chicken-loop anklets. The drawbacks are that it can be very difficult to untie in webbing as well as rope after heavy loading and it cannot be tied while under tension. It is important to dress and set this knot, because it can also come untied easily with certain stiff and slippery types of webbing.

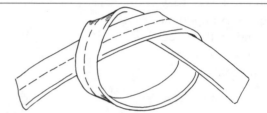

Fig. 3-20a, b, c. Tying a water knot, the preferred knot for joining webbing and forming slings.

PRUSIK KNOT
The **Prusik Knot** is primarily a climbing knot. It is often referred to as a friction knot. A rope, cord or sling (usually of smaller diameter than the main climbing rope) is wrapped around the main climbing rope in such a way that the prusik cord grips the main rope and will not slide under tension.

When there is no tension on the knot, it slides freely up or down. We mention the Prusik knot here because it is one of the most critical knots to learn. It will be discussed again in Chapter 6 when knot climbing systems are discussed. It is important to become familiar with this knot early in the SRT learning curve. There are several varieties of Prusik Knots:

A **Two-Wrap Prusik Knot** is commonly used and seems to work best when using two different rope types. For example, using a laid 5/16" nylon wrapped around a 7/16" kernmantle or 3/8" hardware store solid woven wrapped around a 7/16" laid or 7mm Perlon wrapped around a 7/16" PMI, etc. The combinations go on and on (fig. 3-a).

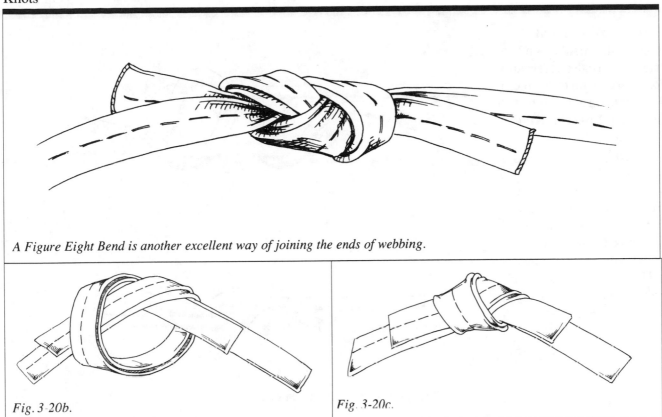

A Figure Eight Bend is another excellent way of joining the ends of webbing.

Fig. 3-20b.

Fig. 3-20c.

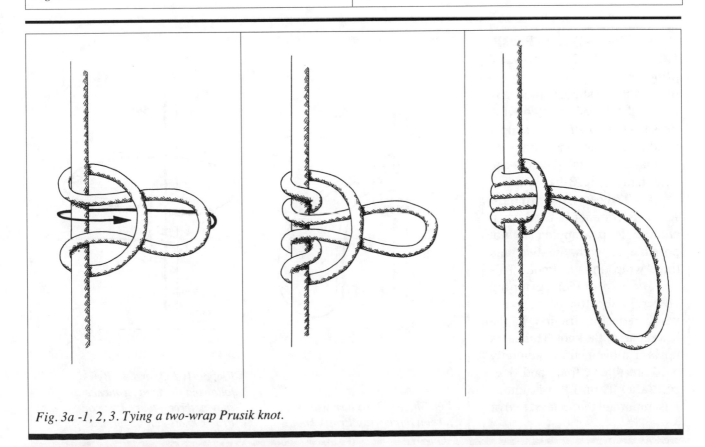

Fig. 3a -1, 2, 3. Tying a two-wrap Prusik knot.

Fisherman's Knot

The Fisherman's Knot (fig 3-21) is also referred to in some texts as the **Englishman's Knot** or **True Lover's Knot** This knot is not that commonly used among cavers or climbers, but its variations are. If the Fisherman's Knot is used for any serious duty, be sure it is dressed, set and backed up several times. It has been known to work loose in slippery nylon.

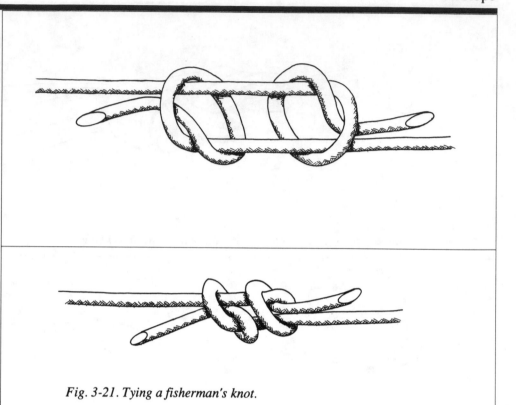

Fig. 3-21. Tying a fisherman's knot.

A **Three-Wrap Prusik Knot** is used when additional gripping is necessary. Sometimes water or slippery mud may cause the standard two-wrap Prusik knot to slip. By simply addding an additional turn, substantial additional friction can be obtained (fig. 3-b).

A **Three Coil Prusik Knot** is commonly used when endless loop-wrapping is not possible as with the two and three-wrap Prusik knot. This variation provides gripping power in the top of the knot while reducing friction in the lower part of the knot. This eases upward movement. Commonly used are three , four and five-coil (after Thrun) Prusik knots. It is important that at least two of

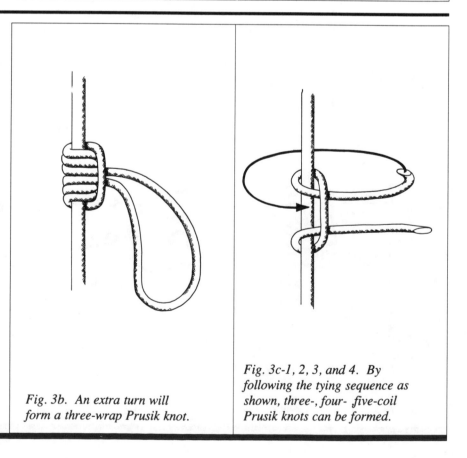

Fig. 3b. An extra turn will form a three-wrap Prusik knot.

Fig. 3c-1, 2, 3, and 4. By following the tying sequence as shown, three-, four- five-coil Prusik knots can be formed.

Grapevine Knot

The Grapevine Knot (also known as the **Double Fisherman's Knot**) is a good knot to use to form endless loops of rope (fig. 3-22). It is compact and is often used when fastening rope to the bottom of a Jumar and particularly when fashioning prusik slings.

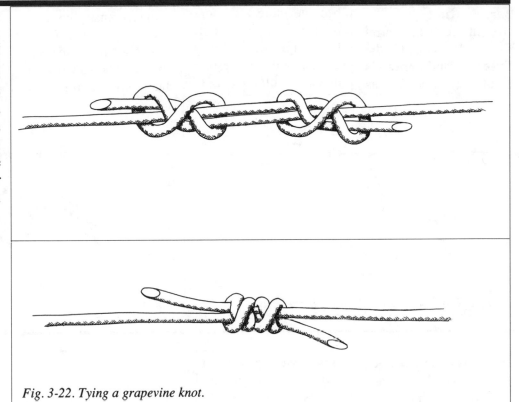

Fig. 3-22. Tying a grapevine knot.

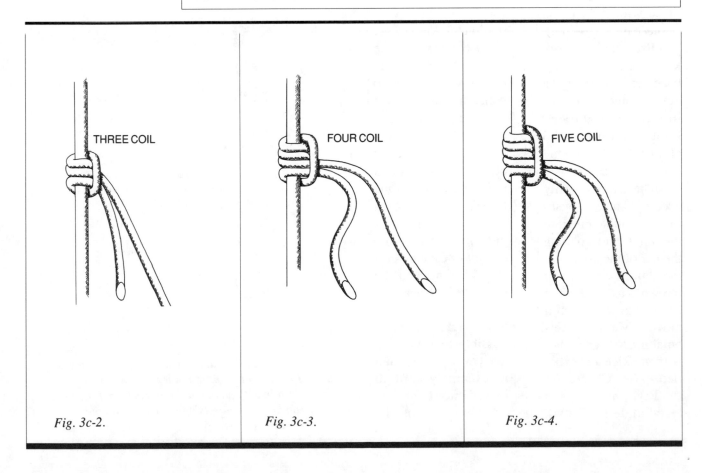

THREE COIL

FOUR COIL

FIVE COIL

Fig. 3c-2.

Fig. 3c-3.

Fig. 3c-4.

Barrel Knot

Over the years the Barrel Knot (also called the **Triple Fisherman's Knot**) (fig. 3-23) has become more and more popular with cavers. It has superior holding power and the testing machine claims it is stronger than the rope itself (Isenhart 1974). It is so good that if loads in excess of 500 pounds are hung on the rope, the knot tightens to the point of impossible release. Untying at times is somewhat troublesome if not impossible. Setting and

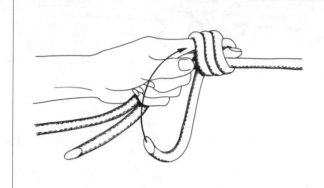

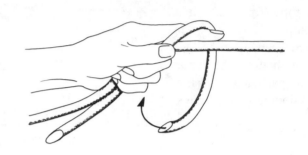

Fig. 3-23a, b, c, d, and e. Tying a barrel knot.   *Fig. 3-23b.*

the turns end up on the "top" of the knot. The primary gripping takes place with the friction in these coils (fig. 3-c).

Breaking a Prusik knot is a common term used to describe the action necessary to loosen a tightened knot, enabling the climber to slide the knots up or down.

The action is easily accomplished by pushing the double line into the knot and rotating the bar of the knot with the thumb or palm of the hand as the knot is being grabbed and moved. Mastering this breaking motion comes with practice and experience. See Chapter 6.

Right-handed and left-handed Prusik knots were a concern when laid mainline ropes were extensively used. With the proliferation of kernmantle ropes there is really no difference in holding power and no need to concern yourself over whether the knot has been tied backwards or not (fig. 3-d). During actual use the left and right orientation of the Prusik knot becomes important to the individual climber as discussed in Chapter 6.

Webbing can be used to fabricate a Prusik knot, although it often takes three and possibly four wraps to get it to grip tightly and is extremely hard to loosen once tight.

The uses of the

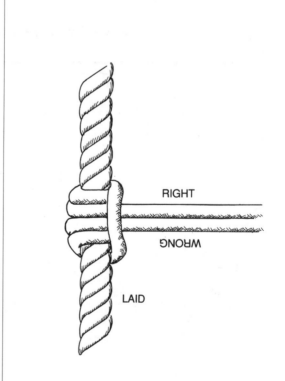

Fig. 3d-1 and 2. On laid rope there exists an upside down Prusik knot. This is not true on kernmantle rope. Movement and operation of each knot by each hand may require tying the knot in a left- or right-handed version.

dressing, as always, are
important here.

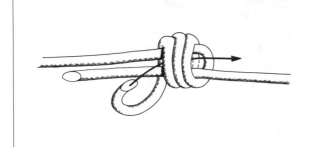

Fig. 3-23c.

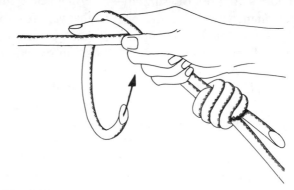

Fig. 3-23d.

Fig. 3-23e.

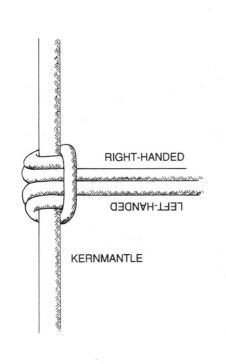

RIGHT-HANDED

LEFT-HANDED

KERNMANTLE

Fig. 3d2. A Prusik knot on a kernmantle rope.

Prusik knots are primarily associated with climbing, but let your imagination run for a minute or two. There are many times during the course of an SRT experience that Prusik knots can be used: a safety line, gear attachment to the main rope, tent stays, scaling-pole guy lines, rescue, and in lieu of any mechanical ascender. The list can get lengthy.

Tucked Double Sheetbend

When it is necessary to join two ropes of unequal diameter the Tucked Double Sheetbend (fig. 3-24) is one of the most popular and safest knots to use. Be sure the smaller diameter rope is the one that takes the double turn around the larger diameter rope.

SUMMARY

Ashley in 1944 presented one of the most complete books of knots ever assembled. For the historian or fanatic, his total effort can surely be appreciated. For the vertical caver or climber a few select knots, thoroughly studied, and well-rehearsed are the key to suc-cessful rigging. For additional information, review the list of references for this chapter.

Too often, high-angle people worry about knot weaknesses or efficiencies, but it is a proven fact that very few ropes ever break at a knot. Usually an old cut, a point of strain or an abrasion will cause a rope to fail. Internal weaknesses caused from a fall or grit inside the fibers can also shorten the life of a rope.

Knots are not the end, but rather the beginning to vertical rope technique mastery. There are a lot of myths and misinformation about knots that experience, practice and good research will eventually make clear.

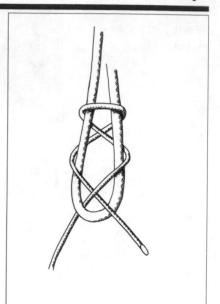

Fig. 3-24. A tucked double sheet-bend for tying together two dissimilar sized ropes/cords.

REFERENCES

Ashley, Clifford W. *The Ashley Book of Knots*, Garden City, New York: Doubleday & Co. Inc., 1944.

Ferber, Peggy, ed. *Mountaineering, The Freedom of the Hills*, 3rd. ed., Seattle: The Mountaineers, 1969.

Montgomery, Neil. *Single Rope Techniques.*, Sydney, Australia: Sydney Speleological Society, 1977, pp. 10-13.

Setnicka, Tim. *Wilderness Search and Rescue.* Boston: Appalachian Mtn Club: 1980, pp. 195-201.

Smith, Bruce. "Knots Used for Caving." *Nylon Highway 4.*, NSS Vertical Section (1975), pp. 13-18.

Smith, Bruce. "Myths." *Nylon Highway 7*, Vertical Section NSS, (1983), p. 20.

Thrun, Robert. *Prusiking*. Huntsville, Alabama.: NSS, 1971, pp. 5-6.

Wheelock, Walt. *Ropes, Knots and Slings for Climbers*. Glendale, California.: La Siesta Press, 1967, pp. 12-16.

Legend:

▲ (solid)	EXCELLENT
◭ (hatched)	VERY GOOD
◇	GOOD
▽ (hatched)	FAIR
▼ (solid)	POOR

	STRENGTH	EASE OF TYING	EASE OF INSPECTION	EASE OF UNTYING	VERSATILITY	KNOT SIZE
END-LINE KNOTS						
BOWLINE	Very Good	Very Good	Very Good	Very Good	Excellent	Very Good
MOUNTAINEERING BOWLINE	Very Good	Good	Very Good	Excellent	Excellent	Good
FRENCH BOWLINE	Very Good	Good	Fair	Excellent	Good	Good
FIGURE 8	Excellent	Excellent	Excellent	Good	Excellent	Very Good
FIGURE 8 ON BIGHT	Excellent	Excellent	Excellent	Good	Excellent	Very Good
MID-LINE KNOTS						
FIGURE 8 ON BIGHT	Excellent	Excellent	Excellent	Fair	Excellent	Very Good
BOWLINE ON BIGHT	Excellent	Very Good	Excellent	Good	Good	Very Good
BOWLINE 3 LOOP	Excellent	Very Good	Good	Excellent	Good	Fair
BUTTERFLY	Excellent	Good	Very Good	Excellent	Very Good	Very Good
END-TO-END KNOTS						
FIGURE 8 BEND	Excellent	Excellent	Excellent	Very Good	Excellent	Very Good
WATER KNOT (WEBBING)	Excellent	Very Good	Excellent	Poor	Excellent	Excellent
FISHERMAN'S	Good	Very Good	Very Good	Fair	Good	Excellent
GRAPEVINE	Excellent	Excellent	Good	Fair	Very Good	Excellent
BARREL	Excellent	Excellent	Good	Poor	Good	Very Good
TUCKED DOUBLE SHEETBEND	Very Good	Good	Fair	Good	Fair	Good

Chart 3-1. Knot Features Chart

Knot Features

The ideal knot should be strong and preserve as much of the original rope strength as possible. It should be as easily untied as tied. It should be readily apparent if the knot is tied wrong. The knot should have a wide range of applications, not just be suited for one job. It is often convenient for a knot to be compact and not bulky.

Comparison Chart Disclaimer

Any rating or comparison is at best an educated opinion. Differing levels of familiarity with an item or differing applications can result in an entirely different rating score. The criteria used and the items rated are intended simply to show general opinions about these items. There will always exist isolated exceptions, and it is the author's intent to avoid such "believe it or not" discussion.

4 Rigging

4 Rigging

Probably the most important group of decisions a caver/climber will make involve the rigging of the main rope. There are many aspects of rigging to consider and there are a few controversies surrounding rigging. One of the major controversies is that Europeans insist on twin tie-off points, while North American cavers and climbers, for the most part, put their efforts into one great tie-off point, with a backup. Another difference is that North Americans go for the long freefall rappel, while Europeans attempt to divide their drops into short segments, changing over at the rebelay point onto the next segment of the drop.

Richard Sewell, a well known British caver, points out four critical criteria that the rigger should attempt to achieve:

1. The rigging should provide for easy as well as safe access to the top of the drop.
2. The rigging should be strong enough to withstand a shock load as strong as the rope's strength.
3. The rigging should allow the rope to hang free to avoid any unnecessary abrasion.
4. The rigging should avoid hazards such as waterfalls, loose and unstable rocks, sharp edges, mud or curved breakovers.

North American cavers/climbers add two more:

5. After rigging, the rope should be long enough to reach the bottom or a step-off ledge.
6. Whenever possible, use a natural rig point to preserve the ecology of our non-renewable resources.

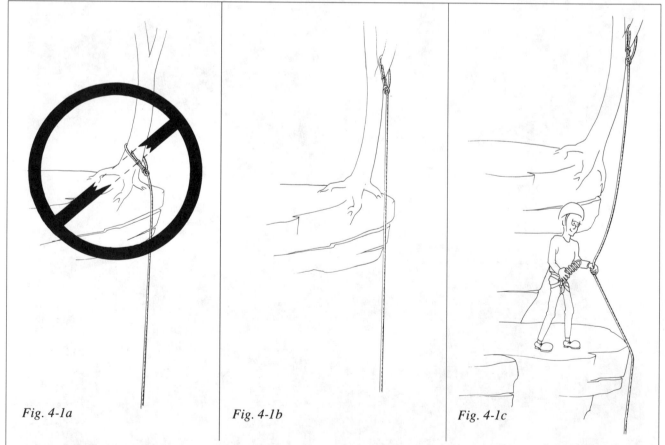

Fig. 4-1a

Fig. 4-1b

Fig. 4-1c

Fig. 4-1. Rig the rope high, enabling easy access by climbers. Avoid rigging situations that result in awkward, off-balance maneuvers when getting on or off the rope. Fig. 4-1c shows how a convenient lower ledge is often useful.

Failure to achieve any of the first five involves reducing the odds of a safe vertical experience for the team. Comparing these criteria to reports published in *North American Caving Accidents* reveals that one or more of these criteria were overlooked in each accident, many of which resulted in death. The sixth criteria should be observed because it is the right and ethical thing to do.

EASY AND SAFE ACCESS TO THE DROP

Criteria number one seems to be the first to be sacrificed when choosing the best of the options available to a rigger. Kyle Isenhart shares this excellent advice, "Rig for the easy ascent, not for the spectacular rappel." Keep in mind that rigging high will eliminate many of the woes of a poorly rigged drop. Look for a place that is at least four feet above the edge of the drop. Ten feet may even be better.

Many Advantages of a High Rig Point:

- The rope can often hang free or at a much reduced angle thus adhering to criteria number three.
- With the rope hanging free and tied off above the drop, a climber can have easy and often safe access to the rope when attaching rappelling gear.
- This same configuration allows for an easy removal of the climber and her gear from the rope even while the next person is climbing.
- Rigging high may reduce the use of pads and other specialized gear: tie-ins, safety Jumars, tether lines or pigtails (Fig. 4-1).

Tether Lines

Sometimes, in order to achieve safe access to the drop-off point or to the main rope, the use of a tether line is required. This is nothing more than a rope that is secured to a fixed object some distance from the pit edge and fastened to the climber with a Jumar safety (which should be attached to the climber's seat sling). Many accidents result from tomfoolery or a lackadaisical attitude at the edge. It is never smart to hand-over-hand down a tether line to the pit edge to look over or toss a rock (Fig. 4-2). Often tether lines must be installed first, so that the rigger can safely secure the main line nearer the edge. A tether line may be part of the main line (Fig.4-3).

Traverse Lines

A traverse line is often rigged from a point of solid ground to a point that is somewhat more precarious—perhaps the lip of a pit. This line, then, becomes a trolley line. Each person traveling to and from the edge of the pit should clip into this line with a cow's- tail, (which is a short sling attached to a seat harness that incorporates a non-locking carabiner, fig 4-4). A non-locking carabiner is preferred because of its ready accessibility. If a safety Jumar is used to traverse, it must be secured with an additional carabiner to prevent disengagement by twisting off the line (Fig. 4-5). After the climber has secured herself to the rope, it is permissible to remove the sling from the traverse line. Traverse lines are convenience lines that let climbers to move safely around a precarious edge (Fig. 4-6).

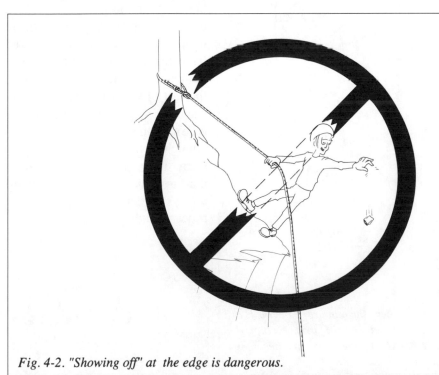

Fig. 4-2. "Showing off" at the edge is dangerous.

Pigtails

A pigtail is nothing more than a secondary line that is rigged next to the main rope. This could very well be a "tether line." Pigtails can facilitate the negotiation of a lip by eliminating the weight of the longer rope. Pigtails usually consist of about 10 to 20 feet of free hanging rope. They always include a figure eight knot at the bottom to prevent someone from inadvertently rappelling off the end of the pigtail (Fig. 4-7).

Pigtails can be used for many purposes during a climb:

• If the rope is too heavy to lift up or would require an inordinant amount of feeding while attempting to negotiate a difficult lip, a pigtail could very well be the answer. Rappel down the pigtail and change ropes after crossing the lip and enjoy the rappel. This may only be applicable in long drop situations. See Chapter 7. Consult Chapter 6 for a complete discussion in the use of pigtails and transferring ropes.

• By adding a loop to the end of the pigtail, it can act as a foothold to facilitate the negotiation of a difficult lip or to clip a pack into to lighten your load when crossing a lip.

• Often the top climber of a tandem duo can transfer to a pigtail and facilitate the end of the climb.

• A pigtail can often be utilized to attach a rope pad as discussed further in this chapter.

• A pigtail has several other uses that involve gear transfer, assistance to an exhausted climber, photographer tie-off, and several others. Pigtails have so many uses and prove to be so handy that a common consideration when rigging a pit or drop should be to hold back enough line at the top for a pigtail.

CAUTION: Upon first inspection a pigtail can appear to be a main rope and invite the next rappeller to unknowingly rig in and begin a possibly gruesome descent. To prevent this a red bandana could be tied to the pigtail and an announcement made to the rest of the party. Some cavers suggest using a different color or type of rope for a pigtail and announcing the difference to the team. It is also worth repeating that a figure eight knot should always be tied at the bottom of all ropes including a pigtail.

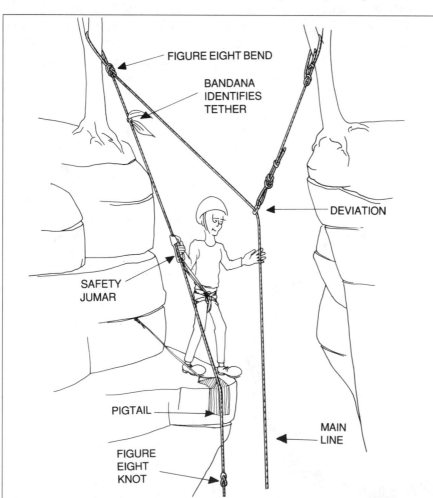

Fig. 4-3. Using a tether line to access the drop where the main rope begins is a safe and wise precaution when negotiating at the edge of the drop. A colored scarf tied to the tether line helps identify it. (NOTE: the tether line becomes a pigtail when it hangs below the overhang.)

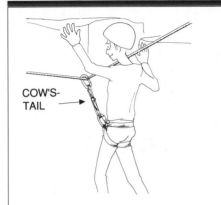

Fig. 4-4. A short sling with carabiner on end (cow's tail) clipped into traverse line is a standard safety practice.

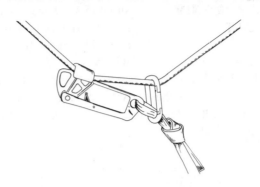

Fig. 4-5. Jumar must be held nearly parallel to rope for it to hold properly and not twist off. When rope is at an odd angle, a carabiner is needed to assist.

Fig. 4-6. Traverse line rigged to gain access to the main rope.

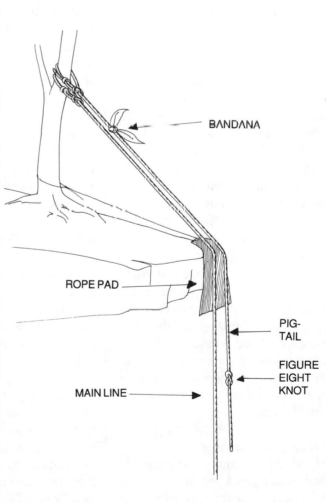

Fig. 4-7. Pigtail.

ONE VERY STRONG RIG POINT

Natural Anchors

The rope should be tied to a solid object, one that is as strong as the rope itself (6,000 to 13,000 lbs.). A first obligation is to find a natural tie-off point, rather than placing an artificial anchor, thus avoiding sabotage of the natural ecology of the drop. There are other significant disadvantages to artificial anchors that will be discussed later in this chapter. Carefully inspect all the options. Look for an object that has smooth rounded faces, with no sharp edges.

Tensionless Anchors

Many times it is possible to wrap a rope around an object a number of times, forming a tensionless anchor. The rope should be tied off, even though the likelihood of a load on the knot is remote (Fig. 4-8). Rigging in this fashion uses rope friction around the object to secure the load. This is probably one of the strongest possible rigging arrangements in that almost 100 percent of the rope's strength is still available. Often a large percentage of a rope's strength is lost in the tight bending of the rope through a knot. Another feature of the tensionless anchor is that it can be untied under tension, allowing the lowering or raising of a disabled climber.

General Rigging

If a tensionless anchor is unavailable, look for an object that will not require the rope to make a sharp bend. There will be many situations where a carabiner will become the only smooth surface available even though the rope will be bent significantly. Testing agencies suggest that a rope, when wrapped around a four-inch diameter drum, will retain most of the original strength of the rope. Many times a good-size, healthy, firmly rooted tree is the best option. Other good tie-off objects include funnel-shaped boulders, natural jughandles, large solid formations or natural rock protrusions (Fig.4-9).

One should be very cautious when rigging onto cave formations. Some are extremely strong, but the average formation that one might rig to is often brittle and will snap like a twig if stressed incorrectly. Before considering rigging to a formation, carefully survey the area to see if there are stronger non-formation rig-point possibilities. If the formation is the last choice, survey the formation area. Are the formations in mud or firmly glued to solid rock? Be sure the formation is not shaped in such a way as to allow the rope to slide off. In addition, it is important to examine any natural rigging points closely for hidden fractures. Experience will be your best instructor when determining formation strength and reliability (Fig. 4-10).

Choosing two anchors,

rather than one, at first glance looks like a favorable option (Fig. 4-11). The concerns start with the fact that one can often find several semi-ok places to rig and be lulled into the belief that two are stronger than one. In fact, if one rig point

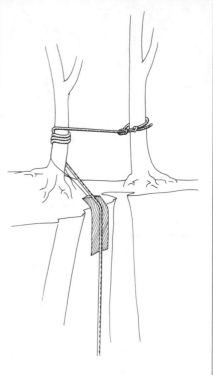

Fig. 4-8. Tensionless anchor.

should fail, all you're left with is a semi-ok rig point to sustain the shock load of the readjusting system. The argument continues: provide equal tension to the two points, thus reducing the load on the anchors. Again, this is not commonly achieved. The average person will only complicate the rigging to the point of confusion and uncertainty. Concentrate all the efforts on one outstanding rigging, eliminating the errors that follow complexity.

Backing up the primary rig point is often a standard practice in North American caving and climbing. After the primary rig point has been chosen and rigged, an excellent question to ask is, "What if this rigging fails?"

Using the tail of the rope, pro-

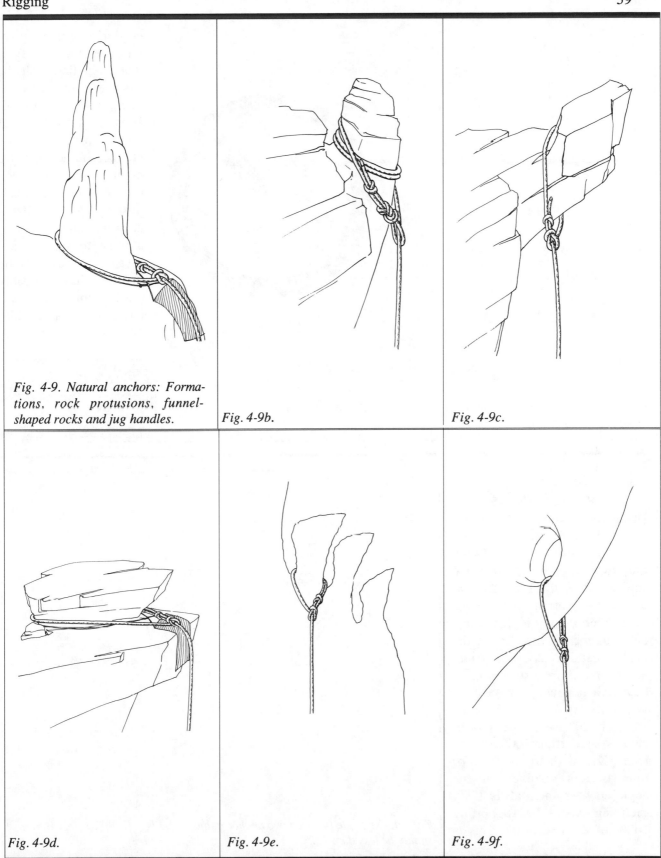

Fig. 4-9. Natural anchors: Formations, rock protusions, funnel-
shaped rocks and jug handles.

Fig. 4-9b.

Fig. 4-9c.

Fig. 4-9d.

Fig. 4-9e.

Fig. 4-9f.

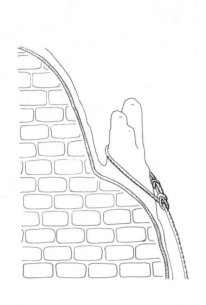

ceed to another rig point (stronger than the first) that is in line with the first. Rig this rope as previously discussed, keeping in mind what will happen to the climber if the main rig point fails and the back up becomes the load-bearing rig point. If the answer is nothing or that a three to six-inch adjustment may occur, then you have probably made an excellent choice for a backup (Fig. 4-12).

Fig. 4-10. A formation used for rigging should be secured solidly into the bedrock and not be sitting on mud or loose sediment.

TWO ANCHORS
Using two anchors to tie off requires special attention. The angle the rope makes between the two anchors can place stresses upon the rope that far exceed the working load of the rope. Even though it seems that the twin anchors are sharing the load, situations may arise causing each anchor to sustain more than the actual weight of the load. When the two ropes form an angle of 120°, each leg of the anchor is supporting 100% of the load. Even if there are three or four anchors involved, if the angle between them all is 120°, each leg would be supporting 100% of the load total. This is

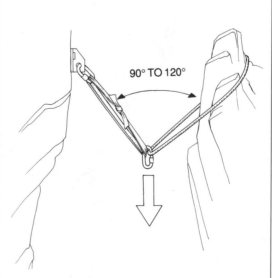

Fig. 4a. The angle between two anchor points should be less than 120°.

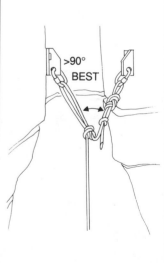

Fig. 4b. 90° or less is even better.

Webbing is often used as an aid to the rigger when securing the rope at the primary rig point. One-inch webbing is probably the most commonly used. Two-inch webbing may do the job more satisfactorily, but it is bulky and usually unnecessary. Webbing and strapping come in flat as well as tubular varieties. Both vary in their general uses but seem to work equally well. Royal Robbins, a California climber, points out that flat webbing holds its shape better, will hug the surface it's wrapped upon without rolling off, and seems to be superior when fabricating etriers (Fig. 4-13).

Webbing may be needed when the rope will not physically slide around the object, or around a thin flake or knob that needs this special attention. Another common and classic use for a webbing-wrapped rig point is when a pull-down rappel is planned. In this case use a small inexpensive Rapide Link or descending ring and sacrifice it. Keep in mind that webbing is about half the strength of the ropes commonly used. To maintain our anchor integrity will require that the webbing be **doubled** (Fig. 4-14).

Do not discount the possible use of trees, logs or beams that can be braced in such a way as to provide for an excellent rig point. Logs can often be jammed in a chockstone fashion. Be sure your choice has not rotted and tie off where the strength is, often, at the end of the log or beam. Only after you have exhausted your search for a natural anchor, should an artificial anchor be pursued.

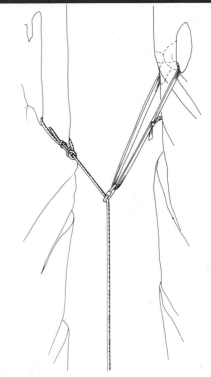

Fig. 4-11. Are two anchors better than one?

because, as the angle increases the legs start pulling against each other. Above 120° the tension begins to increase at an alarming rate. At 150° the load is 200% of the original load on each leg. In actual field work 90° is a safe relationship between the two legs. This concept directly effects tyrolean rigging. See Chapter 10 and figures 4-a, b, c, d and e.

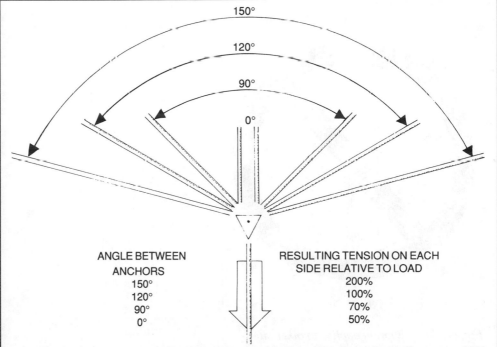

ANGLE BETWEEN ANCHORS	RESULTING TENSION ON EACH SIDE RELATIVE TO LOAD
150°	200%
120°	100%
90°	70%
0°	50%

Fig. 4c. The force on a rope or cable approaches infinity the closer the angle gets to 180°. Due to the elasticity in rope this unlikely event will never happen.

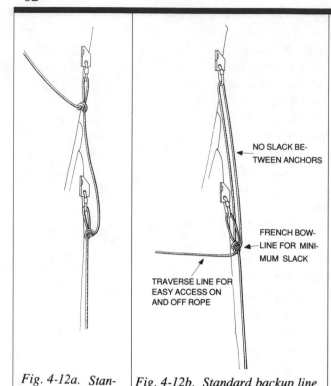

NO SLACK BE-
TWEEN ANCHORS

FRENCH BOW-
LINE FOR MINI-
MUM SLACK

TRAVERSE LINE FOR
EASY ACCESS ON
AND OFF ROPE

NO SLACK
BETWEEN
ANCHORS

ROPE OR
WEBBING
TIED TO
CORRECT
LENGTH

BUTTERFLY
OR FIGURE
EIGHT
KNOT

FIg. 4-12d. Always think what would happen to the climber if the primary rig point were to fail. In this case, the backup anchor would be severely shock loaded and most likely fail.

Fig. 4-12a. Standard backup rig with bolts.

Fig. 4-12b. Standard backup line with a traverse line connecting to lower rig point.

Fig. 4-12c. Using rope as a connection to the backup.

Fig. 4d. This situation applies to other situations that bend and pull the rope at angles greater than 120°.

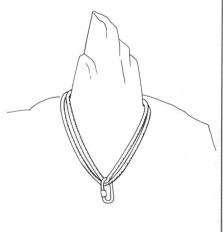

Fig. 4e. The preferred way of using an anchor sling.

SELF-EQUALIZ-ING ANCHORS

When the rig points become tenuous and the need of a strong rig point does not exist a second option would be to choose several points and equalize the tension between them all (fig. f). Self equalizing anchors are very popular among rescue people and alpinists who need to anchor in snow. Belayers occasionally use them when multi-directional anchors or "bombproof" anchors are called for.

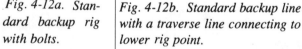

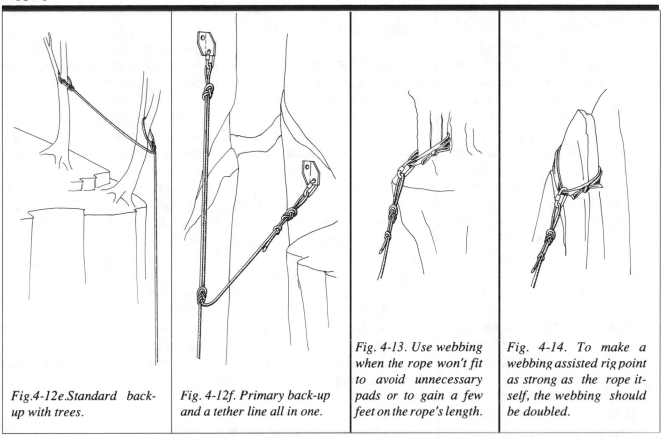

Fig.4-12e.Standard back-up with trees.

Fig. 4-12f. Primary back-up and a tether line all in one.

Fig. 4-13. Use webbing when the rope won't fit to avoid unnecessary pads or to gain a few feet on the rope's length.

Fig. 4-14. To make a webbing assisted rig point as strong as the rope itself, the webbing should be doubled.

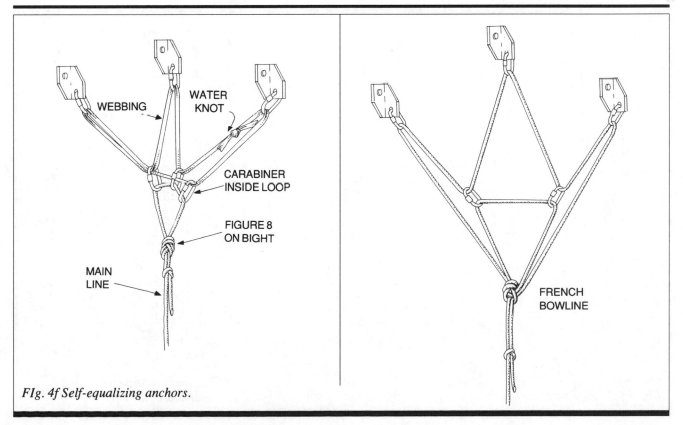

WEBBING

WATER KNOT

CARABINER INSIDE LOOP

FIGURE 8 ON BIGHT

MAIN LINE

FRENCH BOWLINE

FIg. 4f Self-equalizing anchors.

ETRIERS

An etrier (a-tree-a) is a short, fabricated, flimsy ladder made of webbing, rope or metal rungs. They are used for a variety of purposes, most of which have rock-climbing origins. Flat webbing is recommended over tubular webbing because it seems to hold its shape and allows for easy foot insertion. Etriers can come in a variety of lengths from 3 to 15 feet.

To fabricate a typical four step, 60-inch etrier, takes about 14 feet of webbing. Form the eye first, which requires a special knot, known as a Frost knot (fig. 4-g). Each step should be about 10 inches long. Portion the remaining webbing among the four steps, forming each step with an overhand knot (fig. 4-h).

ARTIFICIAL ANCHORS

There is a lot of rockcraft information available that discusses this topic in detail. For outdoor walls of granite and metamorphic rock, these techniques have proven to work well. What most literature forgets to mention when it comes to **cave** rockcraft is that the parameters suddenly change. Caves are formed, in general, through the dissolving of limestone and other minerals to form large hollow passages. Limestone is sedimentary and for the most part tends to be relatively soft; and, if one thinks about it, the inner walls of any cave would have been the next area to be dissolved when the water action stopped (if, in fact, it has).

The bottom line is that cave rock for the most part is soft and is in a state of erosion. Chocks and pitons depend on unforgiving rock to ensure their tightness, especially in the cracks and tapered holes that these items demand. Ironically, cracks and joints, where pitons and chocks are placed, are often the softest parts of limestone. Occasionally a good location for a piton or chock can be found, but more often than not, one will find oneself flirting with death. The sound that a rock makes when tapped with a hammer is an indicator as to the solid nature of the rock. Always use extreme caution when placing and using chocks and pitons. A trained instructor and boltable rock, along with experience, will be the best guides.

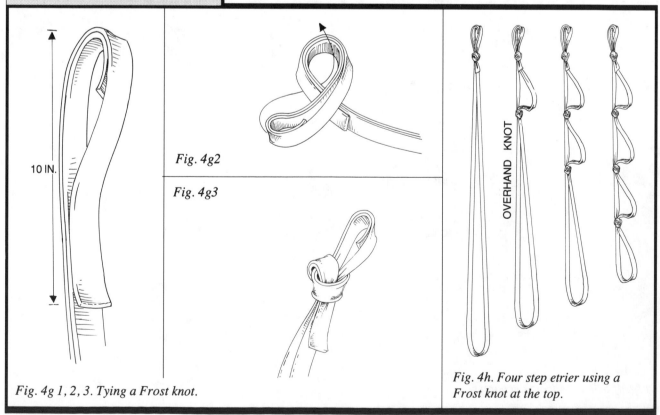

Fig. 4g 1, 2, 3. Tying a Frost knot.

Fig. 4g2

Fig. 4g3

OVERHAND KNOT

Fig. 4h. Four step etrier using a Frost knot at the top.

10 IN.

Bolts

Bolts, then, are the **last resort and alternative** in a rigging. Placement of a bolt requires that a hole be drilled and a bolt device be inserted into the hole. Hammering the bolt into the hole should cause the bolt to expand in the hole and set itself, rendering it secure.

There are many controversies that surround bolts. Once placed, the hole and anchor are usually set forever. At the top of some drops the numbers of bolts and hangers have trashed out the entire area. People tend not to use someone else's bolt for many reasons:

- It's not my brand.
- Its placement wouldn't have been my choice.
- Its placement is loose.
- It looks carelessly placed.
- I don't have that type of hanger with me.

Bolts and anchors comprise the only exception to the NSS motto: "Leave nothing but footprints..." These unsightly pieces of metal that can so often interrupt the natural environment should be the last option to consider. Neil Montgomery writes in his book *Single Rope Techniques*, "Bolts can also remove one of cave exploring's main technical challenges: that of constructing safe, well-positioned anchors using the natural features of the rock. The bolt-oriented caver may never see the inobvious jughandle, or crack which only close scrutiny will reveal. Bolts are the easy way out." He goes on to say, "Ethically, bolts are only justified in the absence of a suitable alternative anchor..."

For the purist, the horror stories of bolt-trashed caves get worse when one is exposed to the European procedures, where almost every anchor involves a bolt and often several. Many of the European drops are rerigged several times throughout the course of one drop with the aid of bolts. David Elliot in his chapter entitled "SRT Equipment" in *Caving Practice and Equipment*, edited by David Judson, states, "It is far more important to stay alive than to rig a cave aesthetically using only natural rock features. Do not under any circumstances be tempted to jeopardize your life for anybody's 'ethics' but your own." The two schools of thought are obvious. The European argument looses its impact on three key points:

- Many bolts are significantly weaker than the rope itself and under a shock load will disintegrate, even when placed well. Assuming that all bolts are placed well is very presumptuous (see chart 4-1).

- Touring popular caves throughout Europe will reveal obvious natural tie-offs with a half dozen bolts placed next to this natural tie-off or drilled into the rig point itself (Montgomery 1977).

- To be a competent bolt-setter one needs to be highly experienced or a competent geologist. Most cavers don't carry these credentials.

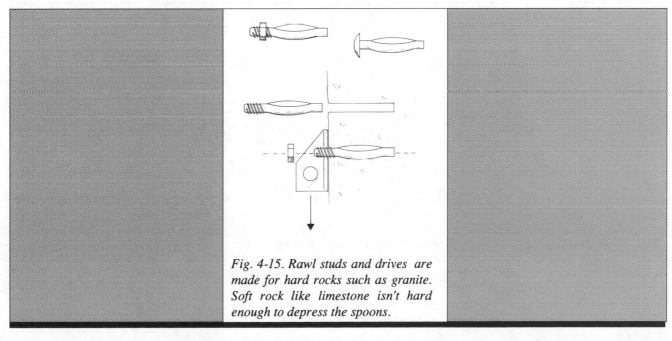

Fig. 4-15. Rawl studs and drives are made for hard rocks such as granite. Soft rock like limestone isn't hard enough to depress the spoons.

Bolt Size	Star Self Drilling [1]				Phillips Red Head Self Drill				Hilti HSL Expansion Anchor				Wej-it			
	Hole Depth	Hole Size	Shear	Tension	Hole Depth	Hole Size	Shear	Tension	Hole Depth	Hole Size	Shear	Tension	Min Depth	Hole Size	Shear	Tension
1/4	1 3/16	7/16	1960	1280	1 1/4	7/16	2713	2103	—	—	—	—	1 1/8	1/4	2316	1760
3/8	1 5/8	9/16	4400	2140	1 7/16	9/16	4200	4500	3 3/4	5/8	15600	9300	1 1/2	3/8	5213	3834
1/2	2 5/16	11/16	6080	3880	1 15/16	11/16	7350	6800	4 1/2	3/4	21900	16800	2 1/4	1/2	10748	5789
5/8	2 3/4	27/32	8640	4960	2 3/8	27/32	10250	9900	5 5/8	1	40200	27500	3	5/8	15583	11185
3/4	3 1/2	1	11720	7340	3	1	13950	12350	—	—	—	—	3	3/4	21000	19299

Bolt Size	Star Wedge Stud				Phillips Wedge				Hilti Wedge Kwik Bolt				Wej-it Ankr-tite			
	Min Depth	Hole Size	Shear	Tension	Min Depth	Hole Size	Shear	Tension	Min Depth	Hole Size	Shear	Tension	Min Depth	Hole Size	Shear	Tension
1/4	1 1/8	1/4	1200	1640	1 1/8	1/4	2161	1346	1 1/8	1/4	2612	1455	1 1/8	1/4	2813	2391
3/8	1 5/8	3/8	4300	3040	1 1/2	3/8	4031	3250	1 5/8	3/8	5107	2355	1 1/4	3/8	4136	3165
1/2	2 1/4	1/2	6240	4300	2 1/4	1/2	6547	5084	2 1/4	1/2	8316	5510	1 3/4	1/2	8018	4339
5/8	2 3/4	5/8	9060	6020	2 3/4	5/8	11984	7744	2 3/4	5/8	11562	6600	2	5/8	11464	6049
3/4	3 1/4	3/4	13100	8620	3 1/4	3/4	16013	9365	3 1/4	3/4	17133	10150	2 5/8	3/4	17724	7596
1	4 1/2	1	25200	17000	4 1/2	1	35778	19234	4 1/2	1	26879	16000	4	1	32494	14629

Bolt Size	Star Sleeve				Phillips Sleeve				Hilti Sleeve				Wej-it Sleeve			
	Min Depth	Hole Size	Shear	Tension	Min Depth	Hole Size	Shear	Tension	Min Depth	Hole Size	Shear	Tension	Min Depth	Hole Size	Shear	Tension
1/4	1	1/4	900	900	1 1/8	1/4	1751	1613	1	1/4	952	1364	1	1/4	1999	1996
3/8	1 1/4	3/8	1600	1600	1 1/2	3/8	2872	2597	1 1/4	3/8	3058	2654	1 1/2	3/8	4535	3280
1/2	1 1/2	1/2	2800	2800	1 7/8	1/2	5582	5385	1 1/2	1/2	5344	3008	1 7/16	1/2	6804	4617
5/8	2	5/8	4200	4200	2	5/8	7435	5708	2	5/8	5625	3404	2 1/4	5/8	11495	8717
3/4	2	3/4	5600	5600	2 1/4	3/4	13071	6470	2	3/4	9413	5062	3 1/2	3/4	15391	14754

All testing data is in inches and pounds   [1] 3000 PSI Concrete

Chart 4-1. Anchor Strength

Anchor strength is a difficult thing to measure. Chart 4-1 is a representation of four companies and three of their comparable anchors. All test results have been supplied by the individual companies. There are two ultimate failure figures: Shear and Tensile. Shear is a direct pull applied at 90° to the anchor and the hole. Tensile is a force applied straight out on the anchor. All tests were performed in 4000 p.s.i. concrete except the Star self-drilling anchor, which was done in 3000 p.s.i. concrete (slightly softer).

By no means can these holding srengths be considered the results someone should expect to achieve in a rock. The irregularities of a rock, the fracture/bedding planes all play a dramatic role on the true strength of an anchor. Realize also that these listed test numbers were achieved with the placement of perfect anchors by experts. These results would have to be the ultimate one could expect to achieve. The field holds many untested variables. Look the test results over. Are the anchors you are using as strong as the rope?

Comparison Chart Disclaimer
Any rating or comparison is at best an educated opinion. Differing levels of familiarity with an item or differing applications can result in an entirely different rating score. The criteria used and the items rated are intended simply to show general opinions about these items. There will always exist isolated exceptions, and it is the author's intent to avoid such "believe-it-or-not" discussion.

If a bolt must be used, make sure that the bolt is made for the proper hardness of rock. For the most part, anchor bolts are industrial fasteners designed for use in concrete. Commonly used Rawl Drives and Rawl Studs are most effective in hard rock. Soft rock such as limestone does not have enough hardness to depress the spoons (Fig. 4-15). For primary anchors, do not choose the quarter inch variety. Three-eighths inch bolts or larger are the best options for a main anchor (the Europeans use 8mm). These larger anchors require time and dedication to place. It may take an hour depending upon the accessibility of the hole you are drilling. It is very important to always wear **safety glasses** when pounding and drilling the hole. These glasses should be secured with a strap. Hot pieces of steel tend to fly in many strange directions. Goggles are not recommended since they tend to fog up.

Placing the hole requires a review of the first four criteria that a rigger must accomplish. Bolt reliability depends on three critical factors (Seddon 1981):

- The quality of the rock that the bolt is being placed in.
- The proper positioning of the final hanger, which is directly dependent upon the anchor placement. The objective: to achieve load directions that are

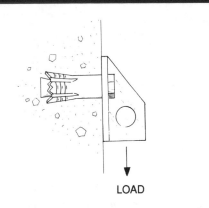

Fig. 4-16. Self drilling anchor properly placed. Load should be in shear (at right angles) with the hole.

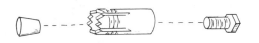

Fig. 4-17. Components of a self drilling anchor.

in shear (Fig. 4-16).

- The quality of the hole, its depth, the final insertion of the anchor and the final setting of the bolt.

The centers of large boulders or flat uncracked walls have proven to be the soundest for primary anchor bolt placement. The most commonly used anchor in limestone is a self-drilling anchor. Brand names include: Phillips Red Heads, Star, Hilti and Petzl (Fig. 4-17).

DRILLING

The procedure for self-drilling anchors, paraphrased from Seddon (1981):

1. Attach the self-drilling anchor to the threaded portion of the driver, making sure that the driver is snugged up tightly against the anchor. This allows the pounding

stress to be on the anchor rather than the threads.

2. A right angle placement to the rock is essential since any other placement angle will cause undesirable stress upon the anchor and the surrounding rock (Fig. 4-18). You may want to chip away any unstable surface rock with a hammer.

3. The first 1/4 inch of the hole is the most important. Take care to keep the teeth of the anchor in exactly the desired position to ensure that the hole will be round and straight with no cone-shaped edges.

4. Use a hammer that is between 1 and 2 pounds. Rapid light to medium blows are ideal. Heavy blows will often damage the teeth of the anchor. Rotate the anchor clockwise to keep it from becoming stuck in the hole (Fig.4-19).

5. Remove the anchor often and tap the end of the driver (not the anchor) to free the teeth of chips and rock dust. Brush, blow out or otherwise clean the hole frequently.

6. Continue drilling until the anchor is flush with the rock surface. At this point continue drilling past any weathered uncertain surface rock. Drill until the anchor is approximately 1/8 inch or 3 mm below the surface where you desire the hanger to hang (Fig. 4-20).

7. Remove the anchor and clean it thoroughly of any rock dust. Clean and inspect the hole.

Blow and brush any dust from the hole.

8. Visually inspect the anchor to insure that no damage or hairline cracks exist on the anchor. If damage has occurred, replace the anchor with a new one.

9. Insert the expansion cone into the end of the anchor. Be sure that the cone is firm, yet not expanding the anchor (Fig. 4-21). Cover the anchor with a water tight sealant such as gasket sealer or Aqua Epoxy. Place a small quantity into the hole as well. A water tight sealant will reduce the chance of corrosion or water action on the rock and anchor (Schindel 1985).

10. Replace the anchor into the hole and do not rotate. Seat it as far

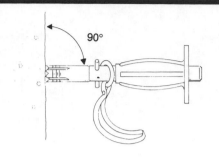

Fig. 4-18. Beginning of the hole is most critical. Drill must be must be held at 90° to the rock surface.

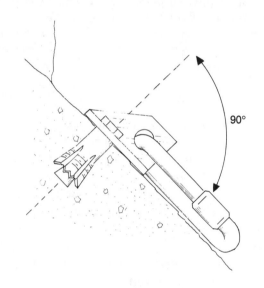

Fig. 4-18b. Final anchor placement must be 90° to the rock surface.

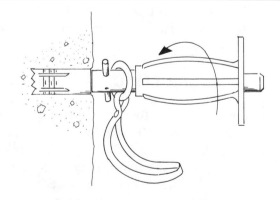

Fig. 4-19. Hammer with light to medium blows. Rotate constantly clockwise and clean the hole often.

into the hole as possible and then drive the anchor home (Fig. 4-22).

DO NOT OVER-HAMMER.

Resist that one last blow for it is that one that may cause a complete shattering of the surrounding rock and hole.

11. Inspect the anchor and determine if it's tight by applying a small amount of pressure back and forth with the driver (which is still attached). If the anchor is loose, three conditions may have occurred:

a. Sloppy drilling has caused the hole to be too large for the anchor.

b. Broken or fractured anchor (unlikely).

c. Conical wedge not driven home due to soft

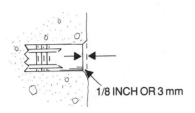

Fig. 4-20. Stop drilling when anchor is about 1/8 inch (3mm) below surface.

1/8 INCH OR 3 mm

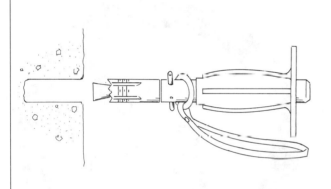

Fig. 4-21. Insert cone in the end.

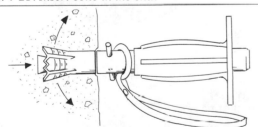

Fig. 4-22. Drive anchor home. After setting, it should be 1-2mm (about 1/16 in.) below surface.

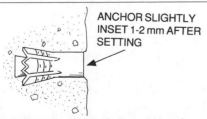

ANCHOR SLIGHTLY INSET 1-2 mm AFTER SETTING

Fig. 4-22b It should still sit below the rock surface after final setting.

rock at the bottom of the hole. If this is the case, attempt to set again by tapping the driver and the anchor gently. If the anchor remains loose, do not use it. Either fill the hole with mud or destroy the internal screw threads.

12. Next, unscrew the driver from the bolt by turning it in a counter-counterwise direction.

13. Inspect the final set anchor. It is critical that it not protrude from the hole, and it should be slightly inset into the hole (Fig. 4-22). Inspect the end of the anchor for cracks or fractures. If the anchor is cracked or protrudes from the hole, **DO NOT USE IT.** Destroy the anchor as outlined in step 11.

14. If the hole flares out as a result of splin-

tered rock, do not use that hole (Fig. 4-24). An anchor such as this will stress the bolt rather than the rock. This situation must be avoided.

15. Align the hanger and high-tensile bolt and screw the bolt into the anchor. A small quantity of heavy-duty grease may be applied to the bolt threads to ward off corrosion.

16. Do not overtighten. Make it finger-tight and then twist it an additional half turn with a wrench. Overtightening will often weaken the placement and in some cases begin to extract the bolt from the hole.

17. Align the hole of the hanger so that the vertical axis of the hanger is the same as the direction of pull of the rope.

OTHER CAUTIONS

There are a few other cautions that should be spelled out with regard to drilling a hole and placing a bolt.

1. Drilling a hole too shallow will cause the stress and load to be placed on the bolt, not the rock, as it is intended. Never use a bolt that protrudes from the hole as in Fig. 4-23.

2. Drilling a hole too deep will not allow the expansion cone to flare the anchor in the hole as the design dictates and will leave a loose anchor (Fig. 4-25).

3. Mushrooming or flaring must be avoided. It occurs when the driver is not held consistently in the same place or at right angles to the rock. Mushrooming can also occur in rotten rock. Once again, the stresses will be in the wrong place (Fig 4-24).

4. A question arises as to how close two anchors can be placed to one another. First reports indicated a 45° cone from the base of the hole outward laid out a pattern on the surface of the rock spelling out the fracture zone. Field testing tells us that the zone of fracture is much more spread out. It is closer to 25° (Fig 4-26). This would indicate that at a minimum there should be four times the hole depth distance between anchors to insure proper separation.

5. Be sure loading is between the outward alignment of the anchor bolt and hanger hole and shear (Fig. 4-27).

6. Be very skeptical as to the stength and soundness of someone else's placement. Discoveries show that bolts over 10 years old, or less under extremely wet conditions, may lose their reliability. As to whether this is due to water corrosion or overuse is uncertain. The NSS suggests that any bolt that is left to be used again, especially those with hangers, be identified with a metal tag stating the date of placement and the person responsible (Fig. 4-28). This will assist in the study of aging hardware and shed light on their reliability.

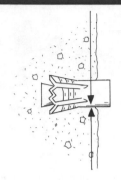

Fig. 4-23. Never use an anchor that is protruding from the hole.

Fig. 4-23b.

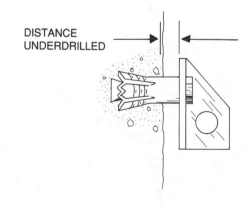

DISTANCE UNDERDRILLED

Fig. 4-23c. When underdrilled, the stress winds up on the bolt, not on the rock.

Fig. 4-24. The hole should never flare out. There is a minimum embedment that each anchor must have to achieve any strength at all.

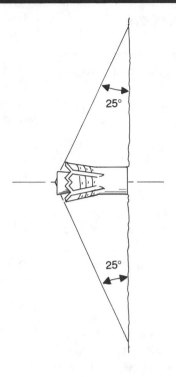

Fig. 4-26. The area of possible fracture around any hole depends on the rock's strata. It may be a very large area.

Fig. 4-25. A hole that is drilled too deep will not allow a self-drilling anchor to seat and will be next to useless.

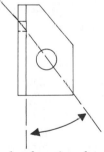

Fig. 4-27. Proper angle of tension should be between shear and the bolt-carabiner hole line.

Fig. 4-28. Tag your bolts if you intend to leave them.

HANGERS

There are many varieties of hangers that deserve some discussion.

Leeper hangers are fine hangers; unfortunately, they only come with 1/4 inch holes for bolts and should not be used on a main rig point (Fig. 4-29).

SMC hangers come in various sizes and can easily accommodate a main line rigging. Made of stainless steel, they will take a lot of abuse and will not rust (Fig. 4-30).

Plate hangers need special attention. Many plates are excellent hangers, while others will actually pry the anchor out of the hole if loaded incorrectly (Fig. 4-31).

Troll MKII hangers are sturdy and also come in a variety of sizes, most of which are metric (Fig. 4-32).

Eye bolts should be avoided. Invariably they end up hanging too far from the rock face causing tremendous torque upon the bolt and hole. Observers have witnessd good 3/8 inch eye bolt placements turn to mush after repeated loading (Fig. 4-33).

Troll Bollard bolt hangers allow for a piece of rope to hang directly from the bolt as close to the wall as physically possible, allowing for maximum strength (Fig. 4-34).

Petzl Clown is another hanger that allows the rope to hang directly from the bolt eliminating the need for carabiners as with the Troll Bollard. The positive aspects of both the Bollard and Clown over previous hangers are superlative and too many to mention here. However, one concern with both is that the rope must be tied and rigged first before the bolt is screwed into the anchor. The view of the anchor becomes obscured by the rope as the hanger is drawn up to the wall. This becomes a disadvantage in that the critical time to view the anchor and its setting is when the assembly is tightened (Fig. 4-35).

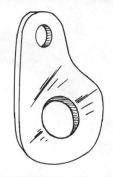

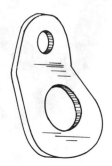

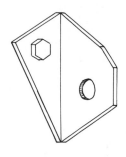

Fig. 2-29 Leeper hanger.

Fig. 4-30. The SMC hanger comes in a variety of sizes.

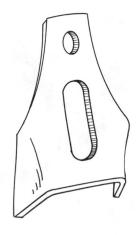

Fig. 4-31a. Plate hangers. There is a large variety available.

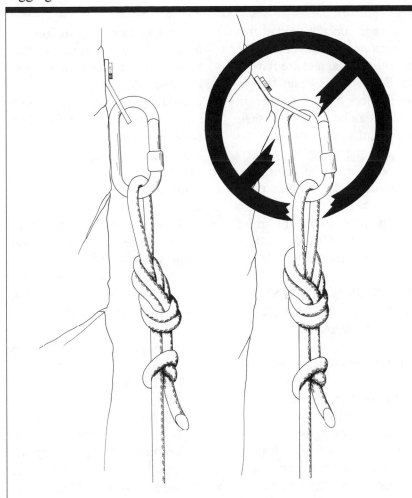

Fig. 4-31h. Beware that loading doesn't pry the bolt out of the hole.

Fig. 4-32. MKII Troll hanger is popular in Europe.

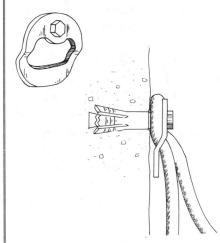

Fig. 4-34. Troll Bollard. No carabiner needed because rope connects directly to anchor. Load bearing elements reduced to minimum. Design ensures optimum anchor loading.

Fig. 4-33. Eye bolts should be avoided. Too often the rope ends up an inch or more from the wall and anchor, causing undue strain on the anchor. A very dangerous situation is depicted here.

Fig. 4-35. Petzl Clown. Contains many features of the Troll Bollard, but its hood prevents anchor inspection. Provides a place to hang a carabiner, which the Bollard doesn't.

Leaving the Hanger Behind

There is a lot of controversy as to whether one should leave the hangers behind. It would be best to look at both sides of the argument.

First Option: It is best to leave the hangers behind.

- With the hanger in place it becomes easy to see. Others will be less prone to drill their own new hole.
- The bolt will keep dirt/mud from entering the threads if the bolt is left in place.
- There are so many different types of anchors and hangers, it is unlikely that the right hanger will have been brought along to match the anchor in the hole.

Second Option: It's best to take the hangers with you.

- The NSS motto states: "Leave nothing but footprints..."
- Hangers and bolts are unsightly and detract from the natural beauty of the cave.
- With the hanger removed it is much easier to examine the condition of the anchor. Whether or not the anchor is cracked, whether the hole is sound and not flared or mushroomed are very important when it comes time to hang your life on the line.

It seems that it is probably best to take the hanger with you. An ample supply of grease can easily protect the anchor from water corrosion. There are several anchors on the market that are as strong or stronger than the self-drilling type and are removable. Some wedge- and sleeve-type anchors (covered later in this text) can be driven into their holes out of sight after use if the setter had the foresight to over-drill the hole in the beginning. Seddon suggests a plastic plug. Veteran bolt-setters seem to come prepared wih the right hangers and bolts that effectively accomplish the mission.

ROPE SHOULD HANG FREE TO MINIMIZE ABRASION

Whenever possible, pursue the rig point that will provide a clear drop for the rope so that it avoids all possible rock contact. There are some contact surfaces that may not be avoidable, such as on the bottom, but experience dictates that where the contact occurs, precautionary measures may be necessary. The primary discussion under this category will focus on what to do when the rock and abrasion points are unavoidable.

To avoid the devastating effects of abrasion, it is necessary to understand abrasion. Abrasion is probably the single worst enemy of a rope. It occurs when the rope is sawed back and forth or up and down on a rock face. The action of a climber as he bounces is the primary cause of this sawing action. A rappeller usually bounces much less. This bouncing action can cause abrasion at every point where the rope contacts with the rock.

Ambient abrasion is another type of abrasion that needs to be understood and avoided. Ambient abrasion is caused by casual contact with rock or abrasives. This often occurs when a rope is being dragged through a cave or snagged on rock chips as it is being coiled. Rope can be protected from ambient abrasion if it is carried in a nylon bag or canvas duffel. Keeping a rope clean while using it will go a long way in extending the rope's life. The severity of the abrasion depends on several factors:

- The angle of the rope bending against the rock face.
- The hardness or mineral content of the rock. Chert, marble, fossils and quartz are often found in rocks commonly rigged upon, which can cause immediate rope damage (Fig. 4-36). Some soft limestones will actually be worn away by the rope, but don't depend on this too much.
- The angle or shape of the rock where the rock comes in contact (Fig 4-37).
- The drop length. Ropes on longer drops will sustain much more sawing action.
- The point of contact in relation to the drop. (Montgomery, see Fig. 4-38). The rope will sustain much more damage toward the top of the drop.
- Waterfalls can slap the rope back and forth across a face causing abrasion.
- On a long drop or tyrolean,

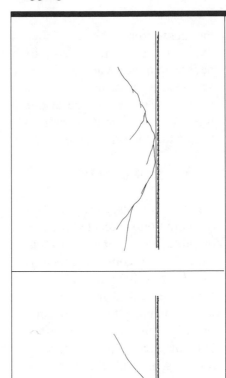

wind can repeatedly slap a rope against a wall, causing severe abrasion.

- The type of rope being used. Some are more abrasion-resistant than others.

With these in mind, one of the rigger's tasks must be to minimize abrasion. There are perhaps three commonly accepted ways of avoiding rub points if the main rig point cannot: deviations, rebelays and rope pads.

Deviations

A deviation is an excellent method of redirecting the fall line of the rope without creating an additional load-bearing rig point. Many times a sling with a

carabiner looped over a knob on the opposite wall or attached to a smaller tree can redirect the fall of the rope into free space where it can be protected from abrasion. A deviation point does not and should not sustain the full load of a primary rig point. Consideration must be made as to the final lie of the rope if the deviation were to fail (Fig. 4-39).

A climber/rappeller should move past a deviation by unclipping the carabiner, not her prusik/rappelling equipment (Sewell 1984).

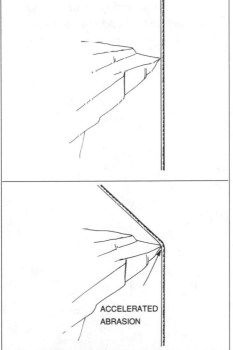

Fig. 4-37. Abrasion can be accelerated if the angle or shape of the rock that it touches bends the rope out of its vertical plane.

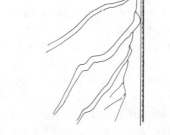

Fig. 4-36. Abrasion cautions: A rounded bulge (top), a sharp lip (center), a mineral vein (bottom).

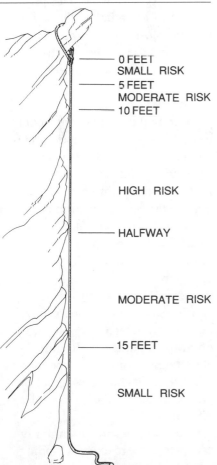

Fig. 4-38. An abrasion risk is dependent upon the position of the rub point.

Rebelays

A rebelay or reanchor is a technique primarily used in European caving in which the rope is reanchored to a wall in the middle of a drop by the use of a bolt or other convenient tie-off point just below the rub point. European style rigging reanchors the rope at any point where it touches the rock. It is common for even a long free drop to be rerigged every 100-150 feet. The techniques involved in rebelaying are detailed and require expertise that the average North American caver is unprepared to handle expeditiously. The positioning of the rebelay, the sag in the rope just prior to the anchor point, and the quality of the anchor are all critical factors in a successful reanchor (Fig 4-40).

Realize also, that the climber will have to change over to a prusik system or incorporate the use of cow's-tails at every reanchor point and maneuver past these reanchor points. These maneuvers are outlined in detail in many European publications. Cow's-tails—European harness connections used for these changeovers—are widely referred to in European literature. North American climbers have universally rejected this method of drop negotiation. Removing equipment from the rope and reattaching it during a rappel or prusik increases the chance of a fatal error.

Reanchors are commonly accepted if there exists a landing where climbers can disengage from the rope and can sit or stand while they reattach their gear for

Fig. 4-39. A deviation: A sling pulls rope aside to avoid possible abrasion.

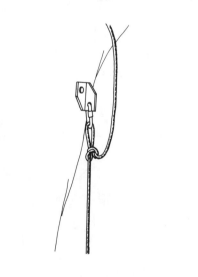

Fig. 4-40. Reanchor or rebelay. At or just below a rub point, another anchor is placed to avoid abrasion (European technique).

the next drop. This can often expedite the movement of people up or down a drop if there are several reanchors. Several climbers can be on rope at one time. This is commonly referred to as a multiple-drop situation.

ROPE PADS

The extensive use of rope pads is the commonly accepted method of protecting a rope from abrasion. All the common concerns by skeptics hold no substance when one has had an opportunity to use and enjoy the freedom and security that rope pads offer. One of the common concerns revolves around the fact that each climber will have to replace the rope on the pad as he passes it. This is a minor inconvenience and surely a less objectionable activity than disengaging one's ascenders to maneuver past a bolt.

Rope Pad Construction

Rope pads should be made of a heavy duck canvas or carpet (wool is best). Nylon carpet can be used, but understand that it is the underside that should be used not the pile side. Nylon rubbing against nylon may overheat and glaze the rope and possibly fuse the rope and carpet together. Carpet also tends to absorb and retain water, rendering it very heavy and impractical for transporting.

Pads can be custom-made in all sizes. A flat pad could be cut to 12-18 inches across. The length depends on the need. A useful length is about four feet but any length ranging from two feet to twenty feet could be necessary. Placing large metal grommets in the corners and along the edges can provide places where small cords can be attached or rope pads can be joined together (Fig. 4-41). On windy days or when there exists a small chance that the rope may come off the pad, simply wrap the pad around the rope and secure these cords to each other (Fig. 4-42). Fastex buckles or other type of clip can be used to speed this securing process.

Rope pads come in a variety of shapes related directly to their use. There are several situations in which rope pads can be used to avoid rope abrasion.

Rope Pads Secured At The Top

Usually the primary breakover or lip of the drop will need a pad. This is often very straightforward. Attach the long cord(s) from the top of the pad to the tie-off point or the rope itself. When tying to the rope, use a Prusik knot, since ascender knots have a tendency to slip. Be

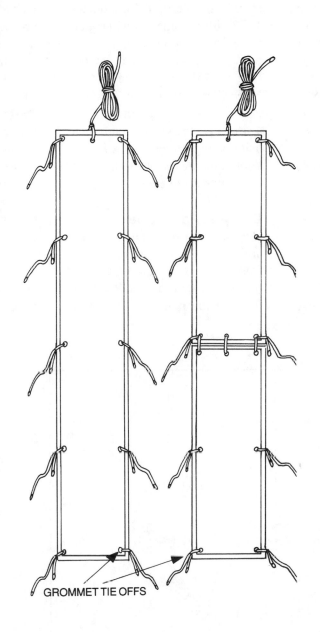

GROMMET TIE OFFS

Fig. 4-41. Rope Pad construction can take many forms. Two smaller ones can be tied together to make one large one.

sure to take into account the stretch of the rope if the pad is secured to the rope and especially if it is rigged a considerable distance from the pit edge. As each person crosses the lip either up or down, it is necessary to check that the rope is replaced on the pad after each pass (Fig. 4-43).

In the staging area, if the rope is bent around any sharp edges, a glove, pack, shirt or jacket could be used to protect the rope at these places.

Rope Pads Secured To The Main Line

Occasionally, there may exist an abrasion point 10-30 feet from the lip. It can be handled several ways:

• **A flat pad** could be secured to the main line with a Prusik knot and taken down to the abrasion spot with each rappeller and brought up with each climber. The pad could then be lowered back into place from the top. Much more than 30 feet from the lip and this method becomes more of a nuisance than freedom.

• **A spiral-sliced hose** could be wrapped around the rope at the point of abrasion, then removed and replaced each time a climber passes (Fig. 4-44). Several problems may occur with a rubber hose protector. If the climber is not careful, the hose could slide down the rope. An internal diameter could be selected to eliminate this problem. Depending on the severity of the bend in the rope and hose, the hose, when stressed, has a tendency to open up, allowing the rope to squeeze out of the protector, resulting in no protection.

• **Circular canvas tubes** wrapped around the rope are the current trend in mid-line padding. The tube is connected along its entire open side with strips of velcro. (Montgomery 1977) Montgomery claims that the velcro does not become muddied if the pad is kept mated (Fig. 4-45). Fischesser (1984 NSS Convention) suggests the use of stick-shaped buttons (Fig. 4-46). Fischesser also adds that using a clip rather than a Prusik knot to secure the pad to the rope is far more convenient.

Using A Pad Rope

One solution that can eliminate unfastening and refastening pads from a rope is the use of a separate rope called a **Pad Rope**. If the abrasion point is a long way down the drop or there are several abrasion points, lower a second rope with the rope pads attached to it. Place the main line on the pads and enjoy the freedom of rappelling and prusiking past these abrasion points without worry (Fig. 4-47).

Pads secured to the Drop Face

Occasionally the drop is so long or so strange that a special pad may need to be bolted right to the abrasion point with the use of bolting equipment. Special brackets may be necessary to hold the rope in place. This pad design was used very effectively on Mount Thor during the 1980 expedition (Fig. 4-48).

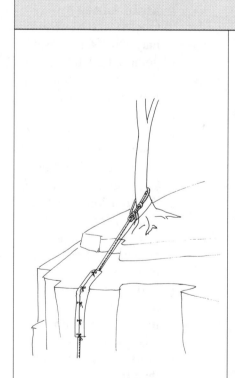

Fig. 4-42. A pad can be wrapped around the rope and secured so the rope won't slip off the pad.

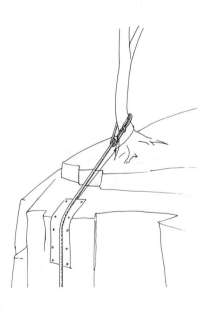

Fig. 4-43. A pad can be secured to the main rope or to another anchor point nearby.

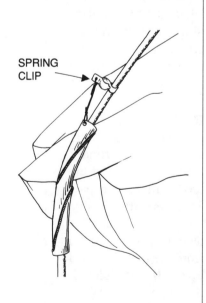

SPRING CLIP

Fig. 4-44. Sliced rubber hose with a spring clip can be used as a pad if the abrasion point is not a sharp bend..

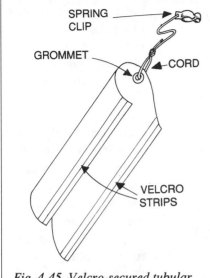

Fig. 4-45. Velcro-secured tubular pad (after Montgomery).

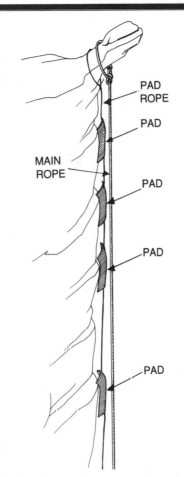

Fig. 4-47. A pad rope provides attachment points for numerous pads, leaves main rope free to rappel or climb.

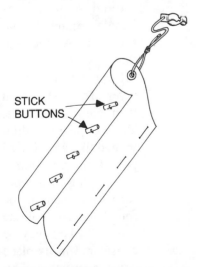

Fig. 4-46. Stick-button tubular pad (after Fischesser)..

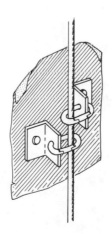

FIg. 4-48. Thor pad. Carabiners keep rope from touching rocks.

A RIGGING SHOULD AVOID HAZARDS

Hazards are non-descript influences that can impede a climber's ability to negotiate through a vertical space with minimal difficulty. Experience tells us that unstable rocks, waterfalls, mud, sharp edges and curved breakovers are among the more common hazards.

The ability to rig a rope in freefall will often allow the climber to avoid many of these listed hazards. Let's look at each one carefully.

Unstable Rocks

When a pit lies at the base of a scree slope or when a virgin pit is encountered, there will often exist many loose rocks that could easily be dislodged and fall on someone. It is critical that all access ledges be cleared of loose rock before a rope is lowered. Throwing the rocks into the pit is dramatic and often the fastest method, but to avoid damage to people or rock formations that may exist at the bottom of the drop, it is best to lift and remove rock debris from the pit edge to a remote area. Above all, if you choose to clean the pitch head, do it before the rope is lowered.

Waterfalls

Climbing or rappelling through waterfalls should be avoided if possible. Hypothermia and very fast out-of-control rappels are both common problems.

The first priority at any drop is to attempt to rig out of the water. Since a large percentage of all vertical death stems from climbers in waterfalls, consider several options:

• If possible, rig the pit out away from the waterfall. This will often require the use of a traverse line (See Fig 4-6). Placing a traverse line can be a most hazardous task when the rigger has to rock climb wet, slippery walls. Once the line is in place, other climbers will need to clip in with a short sling or cow's-tail rather than merely trusting their gripping ability.

Lead climbing over the edge of a pit should not be attempted with gloves. A climber needs every gripping advantage available—advantages gloves are often unable to provide. Exceptions focus around alpine caving conditions where surgical gloves or fingerless mitts may be necessary because of the cold.

• Rappel and climb the drop diagonally. This is often possible and is very effective in avoiding a waterfall. Keeping the first person down and

Fig. 4-49. Angular traverse. This is often necessary when attempting to avoid waterfalls.

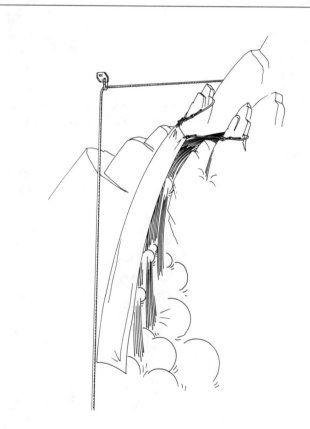

Fig. 4-51. Use a plastic sheet to protect climbers in a waterfall.

the last person up dry challenges even the most experienced climbers (Fig. 4-49).

The first person down may find it feasible to kick off the wall periodically, thus avoiding a close encounter with a waterfall. He can then tie off the rope at an angle for the rest of the party

Traveling up the rope should yield no major problems until the last person ascends. Who holds the rope or unties it from its tie-off? There are two solutions to "the last person up a slanted rope problem."

• Think ahead and use a rope twice the length needed. The second to the last person climbs up the rope carrying the end of the rope, which is wrapped around a log, jughandle, round formation, etc. At the top, this rope is either tied off or belayed by a belayer. The last person then climbs the rope. The rope is then treated like an inverted pull down and pulled up. If a log or smooth formation cannot be found for this pull up activity, a bolt may be considered in its place as an alternative (Fig. 4-50).

• The last person could belay himself up the rope, but as described above an extra-long rope would be needed. This is a very difficult maneuver and should be attempted only by the skilled.

• Though seemingly drastic, an acceptable and very effective way to avoid the frigid spray of an icy waterfall would be to stretch a 6-mil-thick piece of plastic or polyethylene sheet in front of the waterfall. This method has proven most effective in rescue efforts. Simply stretch the sheet above the crest of the falls so that it will float on the water. Tarps or rain flies would do in an emergency (Fig. 4-51).

• By wearing a wet suit, poncho or garbage bags a climber can ease himself into the waterfall. Climbing in a waterfall is very hazardous and all the risks must be weighed, and plans must be made to handle the possible hypothermic climber. Since the last person up a waterfall drop is usually wet, the other members of the party should be ready to leave the moment the wet climber arrives topside. The rope should be quickly coiled and a hasty retreat should be made either toward the entrance or to a point where warmth can be obtained.

Mud

Mud should be considered as dangerous to rope as rock. If a rope must extend over a muddy pitch head, the dirt will be ground deep into the fibers of the rope, causing internal weaknesses. Mud can also obscure sharp rocks. If the mud is allowed to run down the rope it may clog the teeth of ascenders, causing them to slip. Excessive mud gives rise to special climbing procedures. Many ascending knots also slip on muddy ropes. If possible, either move the rope to an area away from the mud or pad the rope and keep it out of the mud.

Sharp Edges

A sharp breakover (Fig 4-52) is a real problem, not so much for rappellers (although rappel devices can easily become snagged on these thin-lipped breakovers), but for climbers. When a climber is

Fig. 4-50. *Last person up an angular drop requires special rigging, To assist in any angular climb, a sliding carabiner between the climber's seat harness and the rope is helpful.*

ROCKFALL ZONES

The rockfall zone is an area defined roughly by the landing area of any item dropped from any point within that drop. Commonly, this term refers to rocks that may be dislodged and arch through space toward this floor area below. Other items such as packs, cameras and equipment must be categorically lumped into this same "rock" category. A safe area away from the rockfall zone is equally difficult to define. If a shaft is narrow, rocks tend to bounce and ricochet back and forth as they fall, complicating our ability to define the rockfall zone. Large open spaces actually provide for more predictable rockfall zones.

Since the largest percentage of vertical accidents are from rock fall, keep clear of the rockfall zone whenever possible:

- After landing from a rappel, remove yourself from the rockfall zone immediately.
- While others are on rope, keep clear of the rockfall zone.
- After a climb has been completed, leave the edge quickly to avoid the possibility of dislodging a rock.
- Be cautious, stay alert, respond to the emergency warning, "Rock!!!".
- Be extra cautious not to dislodge anything during an ascent or descent. If anything is accidentally dropped, immediately sound the alarm, "ROCK!!!" (fig. 4-i).

Fig 4i. A rockfall zone is, at times, difficult to define.

tired, she is required to fight a tough battle with a troublesome edge. First, review the possibility of a high rigging. Are there any other options? If there is no possible alternative, rig the rope over the edge and pad the rope appropriately. Locate logs, rocks or spacers and place them under the rope as close to the edge as possible (Fig. 4-53). The objective is

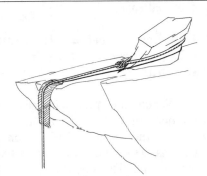

Fig. 4-52. Avoid low angle, sharp breakovers.

to gain places where hands can grip and gear can be clipped when making the difficult edge move.

Many people suggest the use of an etrier at such an edge. An etrier will provide several additional places to grab a hold of while attempting the move. Janet McClurg (1984 NSS Convention) suggests a carabiner be clipped to

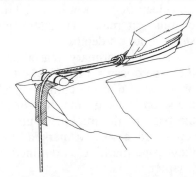

Fig. 4-53. Insert a log or big rock to give climbers a handhold when they come over the top.

the top loop of the etrier and then to the chest harness of the climber so the move can be made without the fear of falling backwards or upside down (Fig. 4-54).

Each climbing system has its own unique features that allow negotiation of difficult edges. The specifics of each system are discussed thoroughly in Chapter 6.

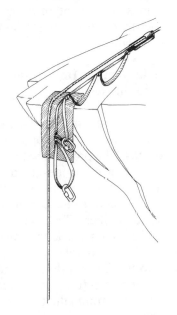

Fig. 4-54. An etrier with a Jumar and carabiners on appropriate loops can help a climber negotiate a tricky lip (after McClurg).

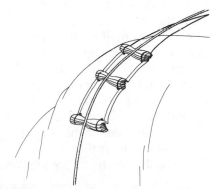

Fig. 4-55. Bunch and roll up a rope pad to provide handhold spacing.

Curved Breakovers

A long curved lip becomes a double hazard. First, there is the possiblility of rope abrasion, and, second, it is difficult to slide some ascending gear up a rope draped across a smooth rock. A very long pad can provide the solution to both of these problems. Bundle the pad at regular intervals forming rolls of padding (Fig. 4-55).

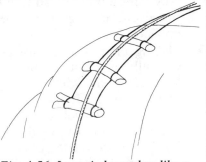

Fig. 4-56. Logs tied together like a ladder can provide necessary spacing between rope and a curved wall.

The rope can lie across these rolls and provide space for sliding ascending gear. Small logs tied together like a rope ladder can offer similar efficiency (Fig. 4-56).

Edge rollers can effectively solve the curved breakover problem. Expense and weight must be considered before toting this solution to the drop in question. Chapter 7 on long drops addresses the use of edge rollers.

Pendulums

Pendulum moves should not be rejected as a solution to avoiding hazards. Repeatedly, pendulums have been effectively used to enter an area of the drop or free space that does not fall in the fall line of the rope. There are three cautions:

- The rigging must be flexible enough to allow a pendulum **without rope abrasion**. Any abrasion point can result in severe cutting and rope abrasion.

- Kicking off the wall must be carefully done so as not to kick off more with one leg than the other. If the pendulum launch is not well balanced, the climber could easily begin to rotate, causing control problems. The landing could easily find the climber smashing on his back against the wall.

- Use a rope that is responsive. Performing a pendulum placement requires skill, technique, balance, experience and a supple rope. Often there is only one chance to make the move. Be sure all elements of a safe pendulum have been considered.

THE ROPE SHOULD REACH THE BOTTOM

Sad, but true, all too often ropes do not reach the bottom and the group is faced with problematic situations. These are only some of the problems that may result from the rope not being long enough: How do you rescue a victim who just rappelled off the end of the rope? How do you tell someone from 180 feet away over a raging waterfall how to get their rack unjammed from the figure eight knot at the bottom of the rope and change over? (See Chapter 6.) How do you climb up a rope when you can't reach it? Does the team rerig the rope on a less than adequate rig point to enable the rope to reach the bottom?

Determining drop length in free space by dropping a rock and listening for the hit, for the most part comes with a lot of experience, but there are a few methods to help us out:

Depth in feet = 16t², where t = time in seconds

For the most part this formula is adequate and will give approximate depths. The problem with the formula is that it was designed to work in a vacuum. There are several other factors to consider. Richard Schreiber (TAG caver), along with several friends, analyzed a large number of pits throughout the southeast and Mexico and carefully measured each pit to determine the exact relationship between any pit's depth and the time it takes an average round rock to reach the bottom. The final results proved revealing.

Chart 4-2 compares the graph of the standard depth curve along side the actual depth as determined by Schreiber. It is important to read the comparisons vertically on the chart. For example, a four-second pit calculates to be 256 feet deep. In reality a four-second pit is 203. A five-second pit calculates out to be 400 feet deep, where in reality it is only 313. The deeper the pit the greater the error as both curves diverge.

Dr. Merrill B. Parker, Associate Professor of Computer Science, along with Dr. Herbert L. Hooper, Jr. Assistant Dean and Professor of Mathematics, both of Chattanooga State Technical Community College, using the method of least squares, processed Schreiber's data and offer this equation as that which describes the depth of a drop as heard from a dropped rock.

Distance in feet = 11t² +8.9t - 7.7, where t = time in seconds

When the rock chooses to bounce against walls as it descends the formulas all become useless. How far away does the rock sound. This could be as good an indicator as anything.

CAUTION: In rigging a drop with an unclear idea of depth it pays to use a little longer rope than your maximum estimate. One often hears the story about the "bottomless" pit where rocks never sounded when they were dropped. After an unbelievable amount of rope was thrown into the pit in preparation for a record-setting rappel, the first rappeller touched the bottom 110 feet later in a 30-foot-deep pile of wet leaves. True or false, it makes an interesting story about pit depths.

Another primary reason that the rope doesn't reach the bottom of drops is that the climbers grab the wrong rope off the shelf or off the back of the truck. Be sure all ropes are correctly marked. Review rope-marking as outlined in Chapter 2.

Drawing 4-1. A pendulum can be used to avoid a hazard or reach an objective. Print of Schoolhouse Cave, West Virginia, by Tom Culverwell (from NSS Bulletin 12, September 1950).

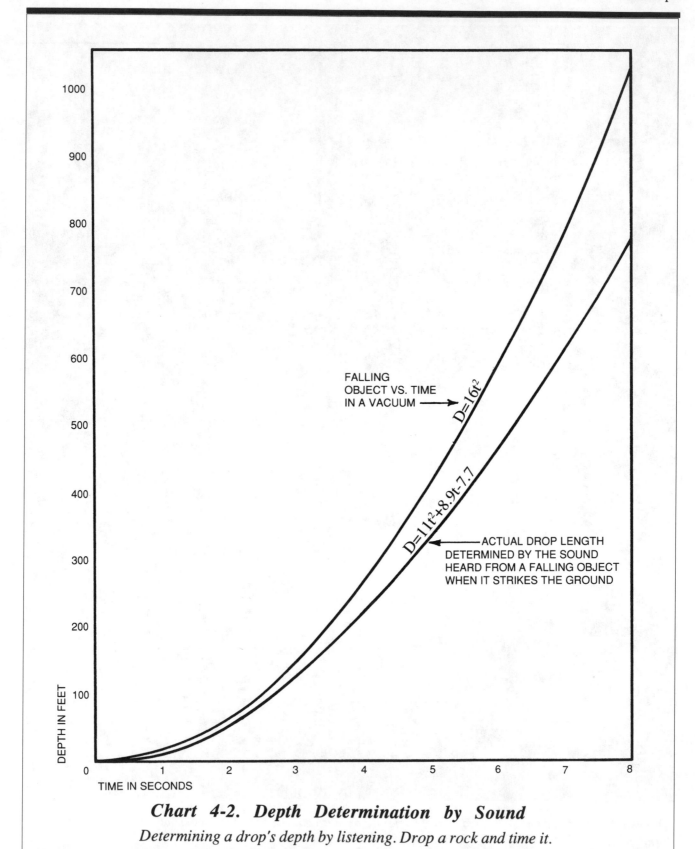

FALLING
OBJECT VS. TIME
IN A VACUUM →

$D=16t^2$

$D=11t^2+8.9t-7.7$

← ACTUAL DROP LENGTH
DETERMINED BY THE SOUND
HEARD FROM A FALLING OBJECT
WHEN IT STRIKES THE GROUND

DEPTH IN FEET

TIME IN SECONDS

Chart 4-2. Depth Determination by Sound

Determining a drop's depth by listening. Drop a rock and time it.

PLACING THE ROPE INTO THE PIT OR DOWN THE DROP

At this point the placement of the rope after it has been tied off deserves mention. It is important to avoid ambient abrasion, rope hang-ups, glazing and many other problems associated with rope-dropping. It is best to lower the rope down a drop or carry it in a rope bag and let it run out of the bag as the first person descends (Fig. 4-57). It is considered permissible to get the rope started

Fig 4-57. Pulling the rope from a bag while rappelling is one way of placing rope in a pit. Be sure of pit depth and rope length when using this technique.

down the drop by throwing only 20 or 30 feet, allowing the weight of the rope to pull the rest of the rope down the drop behind it. Many experienced cavers can relate their own specific horror story of the time they dropped or threw their rope over the edge. One classic tale occurred at Sotono de las Golondrinas (1,100 foot shaft in Mexico) where it took 24 hours to untangle the spaghetti that never made it to the bottom.

PULL DOWNS

A pull down-rappel is one that implies no return. After the rappel, the rope is pulled down and taken with the party. A pull-down usually consists of a doubled rope looped over or around an object (Fig. 4-58). It is important that the object be smooth enough to allow this pull-down activity to happen. There are other methods of pulling down a rope, which incorporate a single rope released or lowered with a string. There are many occasions where a pull-down is necessary, but there are a few parameters regarding each pull-down method.

Double-Line Pull-Downs Equipment. There are only a few rappel devices that work with pull-downs. Double-brake-bar systems and descending racks are two commonly used items that can rappel on two ropes at once. Small figure eights and single-spooled Bobbins can only rappel on one rope. A pull-down situation can be accomplished, but only with teamwork. One person can tie one end

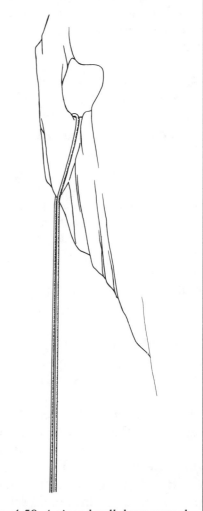

Fig. 4-58. A rigged pull down rappel.

of the rope, either at the top or bottom, while another rappeller descends (Fig. 4-59).

Cautions It is critical that the ropes never become twisted or the rope will not pull down. As the last rappeller descends, it is imperative that ropes remain separated and untwisted. This can be accomplished by holding the rope with your rappel control hand like you would a horse's bridle reins. It is also critical that the rope be allowed to pull through. To achieve this may require the use of a doubled sling that extends the pull-down point to a place of least friction (Fig. 4-60).

Single-Line Pull-Downs

Equipment. Any single-line pull-down requires the use of a retrieval cord. Using a Fiffi Hook (Fig. 4-61) one can rappel down and, by pulling on the retrieval cord, release the Fiffi Hook from its anchor. It is important not to accidentally entangle the retrieval cord or remove one's weight from the rope during the rappel. Since the Fiffi Hook results in a heavy falling piece of metal, it is important to be cautious during its pull-down.

Another single-line pull-down incorporates a small chain link. (See Fig. 4-62.) A simple grape-vine knot may need the assistance of a strong metal washer. After rappelling, the retrieval cord can pull the rope through a descending ring, effecting a safe pull-down.

Pull-down trips commit the party to a well defined route either off the cliff or through a cave. Be sure the team members have done their homework and are absolutely sure of their abilities.

There is one more important point to a pull-down that needs to be mentioned. Often, there is a good anchor, but it is too far from the lip to allow an easy pull down. With the aid of a sling, this pull-down can take place. Be sure to always use a descending ring or Rapide link between the sling and the rope. Nylon rubbing on nylon will surely severely damage the webbing (Fig. 4-63).

Fig. 4-59. If the rappellers come equipped with single rope rappelling devices (figure 8), careful improvisation will be necessary. Once the first climber is on the bottom, she can secure the rope and the others can rappel down the other side of the rope.

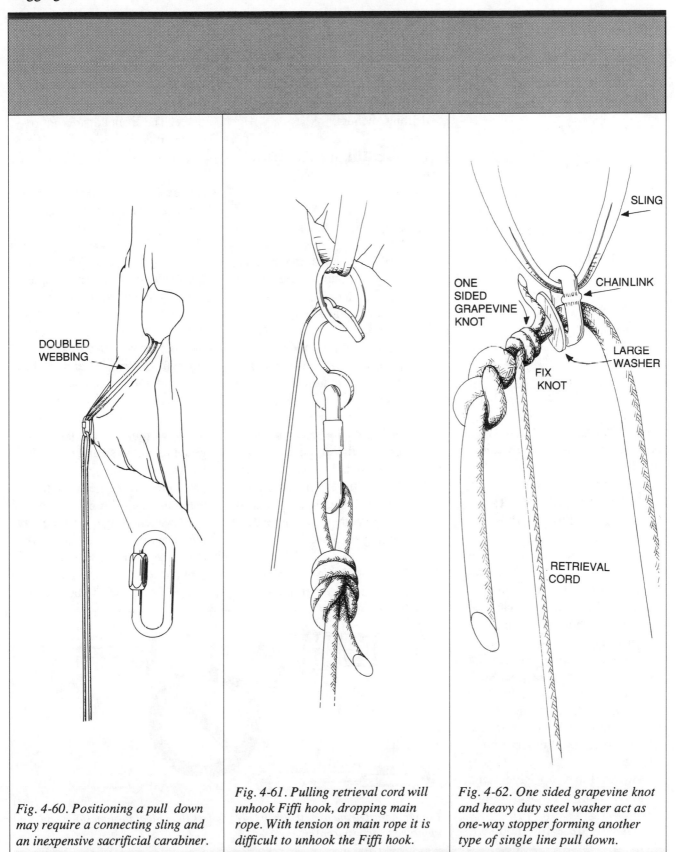

DOUBLED
WEBBING

ONE
SIDED
GRAPEVINE
KNOT

SLING

CHAINLINK

LARGE
WASHER

FIX
KNOT

RETRIEVAL
CORD

Fig. 4-60. Positioning a pull down may require a connecting sling and an inexpensive sacrificial carabiner.

Fig. 4-61. Pulling retrieval cord will unhook Fiffi hook, dropping main rope. With tension on main rope it is difficult to unhook the Fiffi hook.

Fig. 4-62. One sided grapevine knot and heavy duty steel washer act as one-way stopper forming another type of single line pull down.

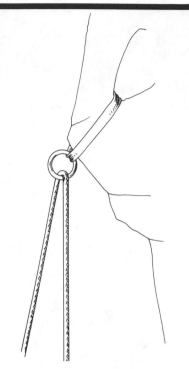

FIg. 4-63. On any pulldown always slide the nylon across a metal device (descending ring, carabiner, chain link). Pulling a piece of rope directly through a sling will severely damage the sling.

OTHER ANCHORS AND HANGERS
Anchors

There is a vast assortment of anchors and hangers that deserve some attention. In surveying the field of available hardware, the self-drilling anchor comprises only a small percentage. Many anchors are not suited for limestone, such as lead anchors or the Star Stazin. For a multitude of reasons, these anchors are not the best choice for climbers. Experience has shown that Star Dryvins, Pin Grip Rivets and Plastic Plugs fall within this same category (fig. 4-j).

There are a few non-self-drilling anchors on the market that have great potential for primary anchor application and in many ways show superior setting attributes over the self-drilling anchors.

Self-drilling anchors have at least these primary drawbacks:

- The depth of the hole is critical.
- Setting requires the precision of a pounding hammer.
- Case-hardened bolts are pre preferred and often difficult to find.
- During drilling, teeth are often broken off and several anchors are required to place just one.
- The shaft that is finally inserted into the hole and which supports the weight is considerably smaller than the hole. Besides the shaft being considerably smaller, it is also scored with threads, rendering it even weaker.

There are at least two other widely available anchors where the hole depth is not critical. They are set with a wrench, which enables the anchor setter to feel the firmness of the set as it tightens down and hardens in place. These anchors do not require bolts.

Sleeve type stud bolt anchors require a separate drill for the hole, but install easily and are very appropriate for limestone work. After drilling the hole, secure the hanger, attach the nut and screw the bolt tight. The hole could be as much as an inch too deep and the anchor will develop the full strength of the bolt and/or the rock in which it is installed. A nice feature about this bolt is that it is removeable. Simply unscrew the nut on the end, give the bolt a tap and the locking sleeve disengages. Another plus comes from the strength of these anchors. Some stud and sleeve anchors can provide as much as four times the strength that a self-drilling anchor can provide for the same diameter drilled hole. With the age of

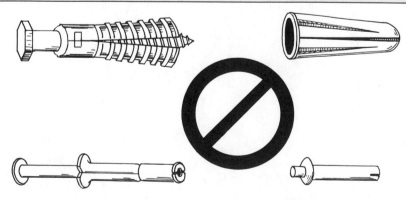

Fig. 4j. Assorted anchors that have proven less than ideal for limestone and climbing anchor purposes.

portable power drilling equipment the sleeve-type anchors appear very attractive (Fig. 4-k)

The Wej-it company manufactures an amazingly strong anchor which, at first appearance, looks like it has two arrowheads fastened to the anchor shaft (Fig. 4-l). The feature that allows this anchor to be so strong centers around the fact that the shaft of steel which slides into the hole and holds all the weight is exactly the same size as the hole that was drilled. Self-drilling anchors, for example require a 9/16 inch hole to secure a 3/8 inch hex bolt. With the Wej-it, drilling that same 9/16 inch hole will allow a 9/16 inch solid steel shaft to be inserted to the desired depth.

The Wej-it also tightens down with a wrench so the anchor setter feels the "hardening" of the anchor. The Wej-it company also boasts a line of sleeve anchors as well.

Other popular brands of drop-in anchors include Hilti, ITT-Phillips, Ramset, Rawl, and Star. Look closely at the anchor comparison charts. The shear and tensile strengths of many of these manufacturers' anchors are superior to the self-drilling anchor.

The one major drawback with these anchors is that the setter would need to transport a drill, when before the drill was part of the anchor. This could very well be a blessing. Battery-powered drills and gaso-

line-powered drills have reached an evolutionary point where their use on big domes and walls will soon be a common reality. European climbers use power drills routinely.

Bosch Power Tools happens to be one of those progressive companies with a battery-powered hammer drill—model no. 11213. On a full charge, Bosch claims that this hammer drill can drill 21 holes 3/8 inch diameter and 1 3/4 inch deep in 17 seconds each or 40 holes 1/4 inch diameter 1 3/8 inch deep in 10.5 seconds each. Normal battery-powered drills will not last due to the necessary push from the user. This push often bogs down the drill, rapidly draining the battery.

Fig. 4k. Sleeve anchors.

Fig. 4l. The Wej-it. The size of bolt becomes the actual size of the hole necessary to drill.

Fig. 4k. Sleeve anchors.

Fig. 4k. Sleeve anchors.

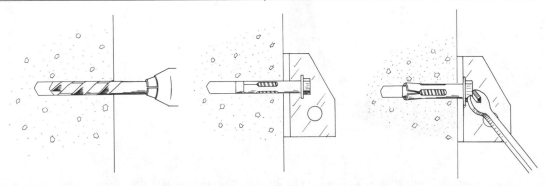

Fig. 4j. Sleeve type anchors are removable after use, eliminating hardware clutter that collects at top of many drops. To install, drill desired hole, insert anchor assembly through hanger into the hole, then tighten nut with a wrench.

Hangers

In addition to anchors, there is a vast assortment of hangers that remain to be mentioned. Unlike anchors, most of the remaining hangers fall within the "second choice" category. Many of them, such as the ring hangers, eyelet hangers and the home-made varieties, lack dependability studies and can often be attached to the anchor

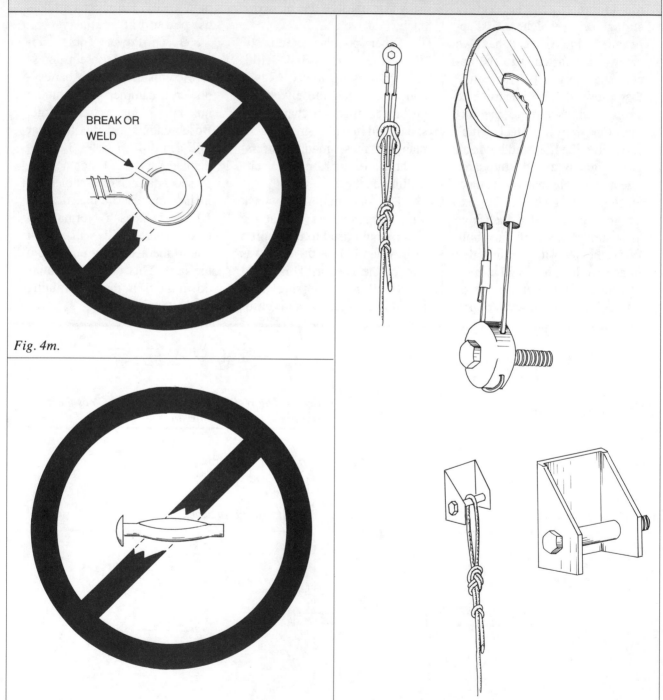

Fig. 4m.

Fig. 4m. Many hangers and bolts that for one reason or another have proven less than ideal for limestone and primary anchor utility.

incorrectly, providing a suicide rig point. Look over some of the examples in fig. 4-m and realize the risks if you choose to use one of these for a primary rig point.

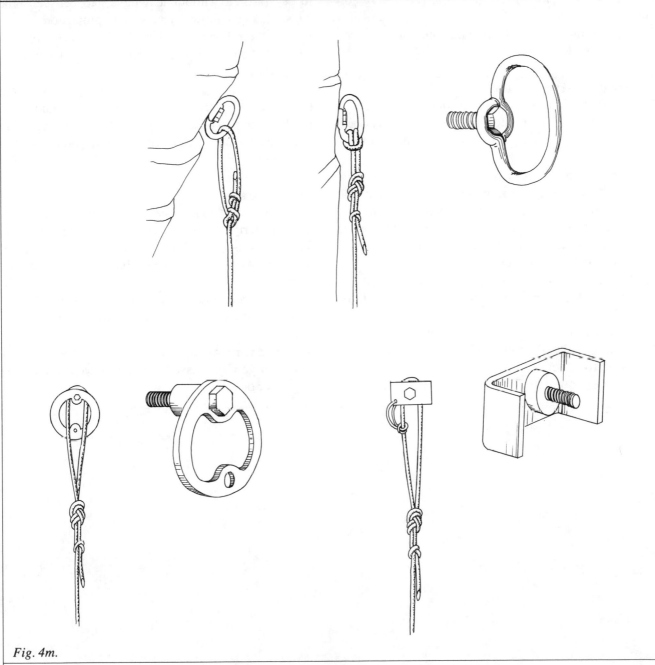

Fig. 4m.

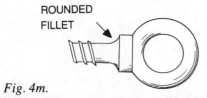
ROUNDED FILLET

Fig. 4m.

MAKING A ROPE PAD

Materials List
1   24 inch x 36 inch Piece of fabric (i.e. heavy cotton, denim or canvas).
1   10 foot piece of 1/4 inch parachute cord.
4   1/2 inch Grommets.

Cutting Instructions
1. Cut fabric into two pieces 12 inch x 36 inch.
2. Cut parachute cord into one 2 foot piece and one 8 foot piece. Seal the ends with a flame or hot knife.

Construction Details
1. Sandwich the two pieces of fabric together and sew a single seam on both sides and at the bottom of the fabric. The finished sewn seams should be 1/2 inch from the edge of the fabric.
2. Turn the pad inside out.
3. Fold the top edges of the pad to the inside and sew a 1/2 inch double seam. This closes the open end of the pad.
4. Sew two seams lengthwise 4 inches in from either side. This devides the pad into 3 equal parts and holds the fabric together.
5. Set the grommets. The top grommets should be 1 inch from the top edge and side. The bottom grommets should be 1 inch from the side but 4 inches from the bottom. This spacing will allow another rope pad to be attached without leaving a gap between the pads. This can allow for maximum protection.
6. Tie the bridle string. Use the 2 foot piece of cord and tie it to the top two grommets. Bowline knots work well.
7. Attach the rigging cord (8 foot piece) to the bridle string with a square knot finished off with a bowline.
8. Roll the pad up and wrap it with the rigging string to make package small enough to transport to the rigging point.

To Use Pad
1. Unrole the pad and place it over the edge.
2. Attach rigging cord to an object to hold it in place.
3. If there is no object available, tie the cord to the main rope with a prusik knot. (Never use an ascender knot)
4. If a longer pad is needed, attach another pad to the lower grommets with the rigging cord from the second pad.
5. **Caution**: Always verify that the rope is on the pad after you've crossed it, whether you're travelling up or down.

Rope Pad Construction

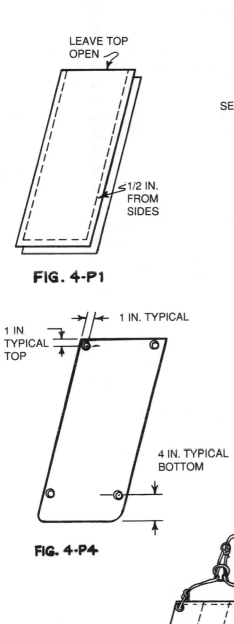

LEAVE TOP
OPEN

≤ 1/2 IN.
FROM
SIDES

FIG. 4-P1

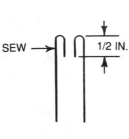

SEW → 1/2 IN.

FIG. 4-P2

TOP

4 IN. 4 IN.

FIG. 4-P3

1 IN. TYPICAL

1 IN
TYPICAL
TOP

4 IN. TYPICAL
BOTTOM

FIG. 4-P4

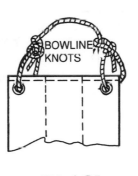

BOWLINE
KNOTS

FIG. 4-P5

BRIDLE

FIG. 4-P6

FINISHED PROJECT
A ROPE PAD

FIG. 4-P7

REFERENCES

Brindle, D. & R. A. Smith. "Strength of Rock Anchors." *Caves and Caving 20*, BCRA (1983).

Elliot, David. "Petzel 'Clown' Bolt Hangers." *Caves and Caving 24*, BCRA (1984), p. 29.

Fischesser, Mike, "Loose Bolts at the top of Fantastic Pit." Paper presented at 1984 NSS Convention.

Judson, David, Ed. *Caving Practice and Equipment*..:London: David &Charles Ltd., 1984, pp. 52-83.

Martin, Tom. *Rappelling*. Mt. Sterling, KY.: Search, 1985, pp. 7-9.

McClurg, Janet. "Negotiating Tricky Lips." *Nylon Highway 19*, NSS Vertical Section (1984) p. 20.

Montgomery, Neil. *Single Rope Techniques*. Sydney, Australia, Sydney Speleological Society, 1977, pp. 15-44.

Robbins, Royal. *Advanced Rockcraft*. Glendale, CA.: La Siesta Press, 1973.

Schindell, Gary. "Bolts" Paper presented at 1985 NSS Convention.

Schreiber, Richard. "Pit Depths by Rock Drop," Investigative Study. Unpublished paper, Vertical Section NSS, 1985.

Seddon, Paul. "Bolts Belays for SRT." *Caves and Caving 12*, BCRA, (1981), pp. 20-25.

Sewell, Richard. "Basic SRT Pitch Rigging Techniques." *Caves and Caving 25*, (1984), pp. 6-7.

Smith, Bruce. "Rope Pads." *Nylon Highway 1*, NSS Vertical Section, (1974), pp. 6-8.

Williams, Kathy. "Mount Thor." *Nylon Highway 15*, NSS Vertical Section, (1983), pp. 17-21.

Williams, Toni, Ed. *Manual of U.S. Cave Rescu Techniques* 1981, ed., Huntsville, AL. NSS, p. 81.

Zelenka, Antonin. "Lezeni Velkych Vertikal." *Stalagmit*, Vol. VII, No. 3, Czechoslovakia: Speleologicky Klub, 1985, p. 9.

5 Rappelling

5 Rappelling

appelling, quite simply, is the skill of sliding down a rope at a speed safe enough to prevent injury. In order to rappel, a counter force to gravity must be applied (Fig.5-1). During descent, the controlled application of friction determines the rate of descent. The by-product of controlled friction is heat. Dealing with these forces and by-products has led to many different ways of rappelling.

Body Rappels

On a short drop of less than 30 feet, just about any rappel device or method will work. For short distances, friction devices designed for large drops will work well, but the reverse is not true. Devices or methods designed for short drops will not work safely on long drops (over 200 feet).

The most primitive rappel device is the human body with the rope wrapped about it for friction. The short drop method of body rappel (classic dulfersitz Fig.5-2) is especially useful if another rappel device fails. The body rappel is also convenient on those short drops where it is a nuisance to rig in with normal gear or where no equipment is available or necessary.

There are two obvious drawbacks to this method:

- The rope is attached to nothing; it is merely wrapped around the body. A hazard, especially on steep rappels, is the possibility of the rope coming unwrapped from the body. This possibility is reduced by keeping the wrapped leg slightly lower than the other. If ANY slip or mishap were to occur, the rope could come loose, resulting in a fall (Fig.5-3).

- As with any rappel, heat is generated. With body rappels the heat is transferred through the clothing and burns are common.

Fig. 5-2a. Body rappel or classic dulfersitz: Face anchor straddling rappel rope. A right hander passes rope behind right thigh to outside.

Fig. 5-2b. Next pass rope back up across chest over left shoulder and down across back to right waist.

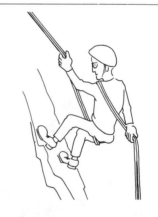

Fig. 5-2c. Right hand acts as brake on rope tail. This hand draws rope across front of body to increase friction or stop. To prevent upset, keep right leg low.

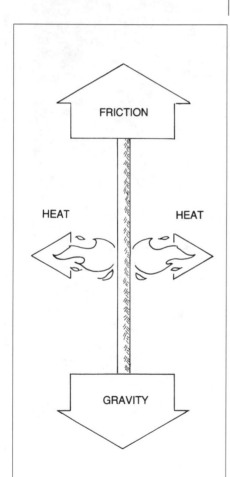

FRICTION

HEAT   HEAT

GRAVITY

Fig. 5-1. Forces present in rappelling

A hasty rappel is handy on short sloping drops when a handline seems appropriate.

Fig. 5-3. Right handed rappeller experiencing unwrapping. To prevent this, keep the right leg low and straight.

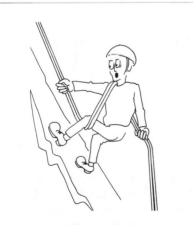

Fig. 5-3b. Reverse view of unwrap.

The Chain

Body rappels are limited in their application and, as vertical drops became longer, a whole new technology of rappelling came into being. This complex technology has many dependent component pieces. This component system is like a chain with each link dependent upon the others, the whole system being only as strong as the weakest link (Fig. 5-4).

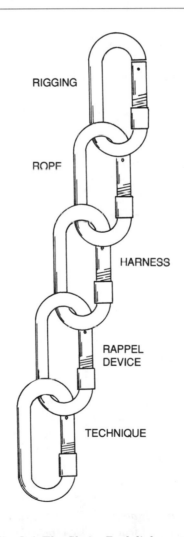

RIGGING

ROPE

HARNESS

RAPPEL DEVICE

TECHNIQUE

Fig. 5-4. The Chain. Each link must be strong, connected, and secure.

THE HARNESS

A harness is used to attach the rappel device to the body; commonly a seat sling and locking carabiner. There are four essential requirements of a good harness:

* Strong and secure.
* Attached to the climber's center of gravity.
* Possess an accessible attachment point for a rappel device.
* Comfortable.

There are two primary component parts to a harness, the seat sling and the locking harness carabiner (Fig.5-5).

Seat Slings

To obtain a seat sling that satisfies the four criteria there are two avenues available. A rappeller can make his own or purchase one of the many commercially made harnesses.

Fig. 5-5.The harness has two primary components: seat sling and locking carabiner. Note low center of gravity with "diaper seat" type of harness.

Homemade Seat Slings:

The G.I. Rig

1. Take 12 feet of 1/2 inch rope or 1 inch tubular webbing. Place the sling across the back so that the midpoint (center) of its length is on the hip opposite the brake hand.

2. Bring the ends around front, looping them twice, forming a double overhand knot around the waist (fig 5-6a).

3. Take the ends and drop them down between the legs, bring them up across the hips from behind, and tightly pull them up through the inside of the waist loop (Fig.5-6b).

4. Tie the ends together with a square knot. Back up the ends with half hitches (Fig.5-6c). A better choice of knot to join the ends may be a water knot backed up with overhand knots.

5. Clip a locking carabiner through both rope loops in the front.

This rig, (Fig.5-6d), though rather uncomfortable, is adjustable, but must be readjusted often during use. It is a single loop, so a break at any point would cause the failure of the entire rig. The rig cannot be sewn and must be tied with each use. However, the advantage is that it is probably the cheapest harness available, using only 12-15 feet of 1 inch or 2 inch tubular webbing or serviceable rope.

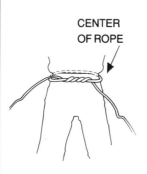

Fig. 5- 6a. The GI Rig. Rope around waist and secured by double overhand loop.

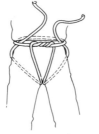

Fig. 5-6b. Drop ends down through legs, around seat and up through rope at each hip.

Fig. 5-6c. Tie a square knot (or a water knot) on side opposite the control hand.

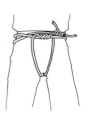

Fig. 5-6d. Back up knot with half hitches. Clip a locking carabiner through both rope loops across the front.

The Diaper Sling

A diaper sling is commonly attached by two methods: an endless loop, and an adjustable buckled strap.

Endless Loop

Using between 10 and 15 feet of 2 inch seatbelt webbing, make an endless loop by tying the ends off with a water knot. To put the diaper seat on:

1. Place the endless loop behind one's seat. Put the knot in the small of the back. Let the other side of the loop hang below the buttocks (Fig.5-7a).
2. With the locking carabiner in the right hand, place the ends of the loop over each forearm, which allows freedom of the hands to pull the loops together when attaching the seat-sling carabiner (Fig.5-7b).
3. With a downward motion, clip the carabiner through the left side first. Reach between the legs and pull the loop forward. Clip this loop next and finish up with the right side (Fig.5-7c).
4. When finished it should look like figure 5-7d.

If the harness is fitted with a buckle, at this point the rig can be tightened to a comfortable snug fit. If no buckle is present, wrap a carabiner in the webbing to take up any slack.

FIg. 5-7a. Diaper seat: hold the endless loop behind your back.

Fig. 5-7b. Hold the locking carabiner in the right hand.

Fig. 5-7c. Clip loops together in the proper sequence: left, center, then right.

Fig. 5-7d. Harness ready to use.

The Oversized Diaper

By using a slightly larger sling, a variety of benefits can be achieved over the traditional diaper (Fig.5-8).

- The fixed loop fits almost anyone

without the use of buckles.
- It is more comfortable in the crotch for men.
- It orients the seatharness carabiner up and down along the major axis, while avoiding stresses against the

gate.
- It is easy to fit onto a clinging-for-his-life victim from the back.

An Adjustable Buckled Strap

With a similar length of 2 inch strap, sew a high quality parachute buckle onto one end of the webbing. The stitching should overlap about 6 inches.

1. Insert the buckle and about 4 inches of strap through a locking carbiner. Position the carabiner in front of the pelvis (Fig.5-9a).
2. Wrap the long end of the strap around the seat, bringing the end back through the carab-

iner (Fig.5-9b).
3. Reverse the strap back around the leg, bringing it back through the carabiner and forming a loop around the leg (Fig.5-9c). Wrap the strap around the other leg forming another leg loop.
4. Buckle the strap together and tighten up the seat sling until comfortable. Back up the buckle with an overhand knot in the strap end (Fig.5-9d).

The diaper sling is easy to put on, especially on narrow ledges, because one does not have to step through leg loops. However, it is a single loop and a break at any point will cause failure of the entire rig.

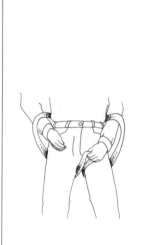

Fig. 5-8. Oversized diaper has many advantages.

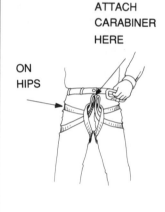

ATTACH CARABINER HERE

ON HIPS

Fig. 5-8b.

Fig. 5-9a. Starting diaper using 2 in. buckled strap.

Fig. 5-9b. Around the waist and back through the buckle.

Fig. 5-9c. Reverse back around leg and up through crotch.

Fig. 5-9d. Reverse back down through crotch, around other leg, and cinch buckle tight.

If made with a buckle, the diaper sling is adjustable for a wide variety of sizes and uses. The strap is also convenient for other rigging jobs, as the sling can be unbuckled and passed around large rocks or other objects for rigging.

Sewn Leg Loop Harness

Using between 12 and 16 feet of 2 inch webbing, follow the directions in the do-it- yourself project at the end of this chapter. A double-loop system makes the rig safer, because a break at any one point will not cause a failure of the entire rig. Putting the seat sling on is simple:

1. Orient the seat sling with the opening to the front, holding the sling by the sides behind the knees (Fig.5-10a).
2. Step into the leg loops (Fig. 5-10b).
3. Pull the harness up and secure the two carabiner-attachment loops with the seat-harness carabiner (Fig.5-10c).

With the incorporation of a buckle in the rear strap, the system now becomes somewhat adjustable. There are a lot of variations on this type of seat sling, and many designs and patterns exist to satisfy just about anyone's preferences. See the do-it-yourself project at the end of this chapter. See also Chart 5-1.

Fig. 5-10a. Putting on a sewn leg loop harness (after Gibbs).

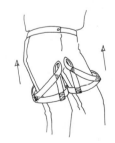

Fig. 5-10b. One leg at a time.

Fig. 5-10c. Clip the locking carabiner into place, thus securing the harness.

HOMEMADE	SECURE ON CLIMBER	REDUNDANT	CENTER OF GRAVITY LOW	COMFORT	EASE ON-OFF CLIMBER	SIZE/BULK	BUCKLE CONFUSION POSSIBLE	ACCESSORY LOOP POSITION	ACC.LOOP CONFUSED W/MAIN RIG	ADJUSTABILITY	MULTIPURPOSE	AVAILABILITY
GI	EXCELLENT	Y	Y	POOR	FAIR	EXCELLENT	N	N	N	EXCELLENT	EXCELLENT	EXCELLENT
DIAPER SEAT	VERY GOOD	N	Y	FAIR	VERY GOOD	EXCELLENT	N	N	N	FAIR	EXCELLENT	EXCELLENT
DIAPER SEAT W/BUCKLE	EXCELLENT	N	Y	GOOD	EXCELLENT	EXCELLENT	N	N	N	EXCELLENT	EXCELLENT	EXCELLENT
SEWN LEG LOOPS	VERY GOOD	Y	Y	VERY GOOD	GOOD	VERY GOOD	N	N	N	FAIR	GOOD	EXCELLENT
SEWN LEG LOOPS W/BUCKLE	EXCELLENT	Y	Y	VERY GOOD	GOOD	VERY GOOD	N	N	N	GOOD	GOOD	EXCELLENT
DIAPER SEAT VARIATION	EXCELLENT	N	Y	GOOD	EXCELLENT	EXCELLENT	N	N	N	EXCELLENT	EXCELLENT	EXCELLENT

Chart 5-1. Rappel Harnesses

HARNESSES

The ideal harness remains securely on the climber during a variety of applications. It should load at the approximate center of gravity of the climber and must be strong enough to withstand shock-loading. Comfort is an obvious plus as it is occassionally necessary to sit in a harness for hours. A good harness is lightweight, not bulky and is adjustable for clothing or climber-size variation. If buckles are incorporated there should be little opportunity for a mistake when putting the harness on or during use. A good harness has accessory attachment loops that do not get confused with the primary harness attachment point.

Some harnesses can be unbuckled to allow the webbing to be used for a number of purposes. Rescue personnel find this feature most useful.

COMPARISON CHART DISCLAIMER

Any rating or comparison is at best an educated opinion. Differing levels of familiarity with an item or differing applications can result in an entirely different rating score. The criteria used and the items rated are intended simply to show general opinions about these items. There will always exist isolated exceptions, and it is the author's intent to avoid such "believe-it-or-not" discussion.

▲	EXCELLENT
◣ (hatched)	VERY GOOD
◇	GOOD
▽ (half)	FAIR
▼	POOR
Y	YES
N	NO

COMMERCIAL

	SECURE ON CLIMBER	REDUNDANT	CENTER OF GRAVITY LOW	COMFORT	EASE ON-OFF CLIMBER	SIZE/BULK	BUCKLE CONFUSION POSSIBLE	ACCESSORY LOOP POSITION	ACC.LOOP CONFUSED W/MAIN RIG	ADJUSTABILITY	MULTIPURPOSE	AVAILABILITY
A16 MAXIMA	▲	Y	Y	▲	△	△	Y	Y	N	▲	◇	▲
A16 SIT	▲	Y	N	△	△	△	N	Y	N	▲	◇	▲
CMC RESCUE	▲	Y	Y	▲	△	◇	Y	Y	N	▲	◇	▲
ROBERTSON PELVIC	▲	Y	N	△	△	◇	Y	Y	N	▲	◇	▲
CHOUINARD SIT	▲	Y	Y	△	△	△	N	N	N	▲	◇	▲
TROLL-WILLANS SIT	▲	Y	N	△	△	◇	Y	Y	Y	▲	◇	▲
WILD COUNTRY LITTLE JOHN	▲	Y	N	△	△	△	Y	N	N	▲	◇	▲
IME VILLAN	▲	Y	Y	◇	△	△	Y	Y	N	▲	◇	▲
REI PINNACLE	▲	Y	N	▲	△	◇	Y	N	N	▲	◇	▲
REI BASIC	▲	Y	N	◇	△	◇	N	Y	Y	▲	◇	▲
PETZL VERCORS	▲	Y	N	▲	△	◇	N	Y	Y	▲	◇	△
PETZL RAPID	▲	Y	Y	◇	△	△	N	Y	Y	▲	◇	△
PETZL CROLL	▲	Y	Y	◇	△	◇	Y	N	Y	▲	◇	△
LIRAKIS RAPPEL	▲	Y	Y	▲	△	▽	Y	Y	Y	▲	◇	◇
RSI SYMPLEX SLOT	▲	Y	Y	△	△	◇	N	N	N	▲	▲	▲
RSI QUICK-FIT	▲	Y	Y	△	▲	△	Y	N	N	▲	◇	▲

The Harness Locking Carabiner

An integral part of the harness is the locking carabiner that attaches the rappel device to the harness. This carabiner should be large enough to hold all of the necessary harness webbing attachment points plus the rappel device. A locking carabiner should be the only type used. Most commonly used are the oversized locking D-shaped carabiners, (Fig.5-11), because of the odd direction of pressures and bumps that would open a non-locking carabiner. It should be noted that a locking carabiner is not necessarily stronger than a non-locking carabiner, but it comes equipped with a gate safety to prevent unexpected detachment. When placed in the harness, the carabiner should not be loaded sideways on its gate by the rappel device, as the gate is the weakest point on the carabiner. The threads on the locking gate should not be of the sharp kind, with pointed peaks (Fig.5-12). These threads will quickly rub and cut harness webbing.

Maillon Rapide Links

These inexpensive strong carabiner-like links are available in most hardware stores. However, the hardware store links have smaller gate openings than sport shop varieties. They are exceptionally strong and should be loaded like carabiners, along the major axis. Maillon rapides (sometimes called quick links) come in two basic varieties (Fig.5-13). One looks like a stan-

dard oval carabiner, while the other is triangular-shaped. This "Delta" variety seems to be an ideal alternative to a seat harness carabiner, in that it can be loaded in multiple directions. Whenever any rapide is used, it is important that the gate be screwed shut to ensure security. A small wrench may be necessary to loosen a jammed gate.

It is important to double-check the gate of the carabiner to make sure all components are inside and properly hooked together. An all-too-common occurrence, while standing around a pit or walking to it, is to wear the rappel device clipped to a carabiner hanger through a belt loop or a gear loop on a harness. In a moment of distraction or fatigue the device can be rigged in, leaving the rappeller hanging only from a belt loop on a pair of blue jeans. All the essential parts were present, but the links of the chain were not properly connected.

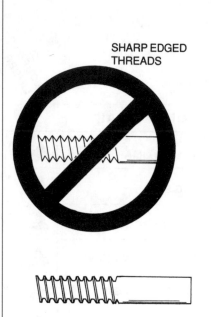

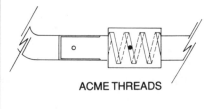

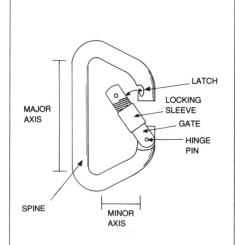

Fig. 5-11. Locking carabiner parts.

Fig. 5-12. Carabiner locking sleeve threads. Acme threads have proven unreliable although they eliminated the weak threaded carabiner gate.

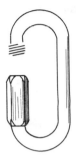

REGULAR

DELTA

Fig. 5-13. Maillon Rapide links. Must only be loaded with the sleeve closed.

RAPPEL DEVICES

The next link in the chain is the rappel device. There are two broad categories of rappel devices. First are the fixed friction devices, which, when placed on the rope, give essentially the same amount of friction from the top to the bottom of the drop. On some of these devices, you can change the available friction by the manner of attachment before you start the rappel. Second are the variable friction devices. These enable the user to add or subtract friction while descending without detaching the device from the rope. This friction change should be such that any amount of friction large or small can be added or subtracted. There are several semi-variable friction devices. These can add and subtract friction, but usually only in stepped amounts with little or no variation between steps. Within these categories, there are seemingly hundreds of different varieties. The basic design premise of a rappel device is to create a piece of hardware that attaches the rope to the climber and provides friction to the extent needed for a safe descent. Conditions vary greatly in ropework and because of this there is no one perfect rappel device.

Caution: Realize that rappelling is inherently dangerous and all the pictures, descriptions, warnings and coachings will not guarantee a safe rappel every time. Falling rock, the elements, weather, rope condition and skill all contribute to the uncertainty of each rappel. There are far more recorded accidents when rappelling than when prusiking. There is no "bomb-proof" safe rappelling system that will guarantee a safe, controlled descent every time. With this in mind, enter into rappelling with caution.

FIXED FRICTION RAPPEL DEVICES

The Figure 8

The figure 8 rappel device named for its obvious shape is an extremely strong lightweight piece of equipment (Fig.5-14). If offers an excellent level of control and is simple to use. To rig into a figure 8, simply take a bight of rope and pass it down through the larger loop of the 8 and then loop this bight around the smaller loop. The free end should come off the 8 on the control-hand side. Then attach the 8 to the seat sling carabiner. This is one of the drawbacks of the 8, in that to rig it in, it must be removed from the harness. Another problem with the figure 8 is that if any slack is allowed in the rope above the rappeller, the bottom loop of rope in the figure 8 can move upward, forming a girth hitch (Fig.5-15). The climber in this situation will be locked in place until he can take his weight off the device.

To alleviate this problem, manufacturers developed a figure 8 with "ears" (Fig.5-16). This model has two small projections on the upper part of the 8. These ears prevent the rope from form-ing a girth hitch (Fig.5-17). Due to the route the rope takes around the 8, the device imparts spin to the rappel and can, at times, kink the rope badly. To quickly stop and lock off while using the 8, take the free end side of the rope (Fig.18) and slide it in between the mainline and the device. To fully lock off the device for any work or maneuvers while on rope, take a bight of rope and pass it up through the top of the 8 and tie this bight off to the mainline (Fig.19).

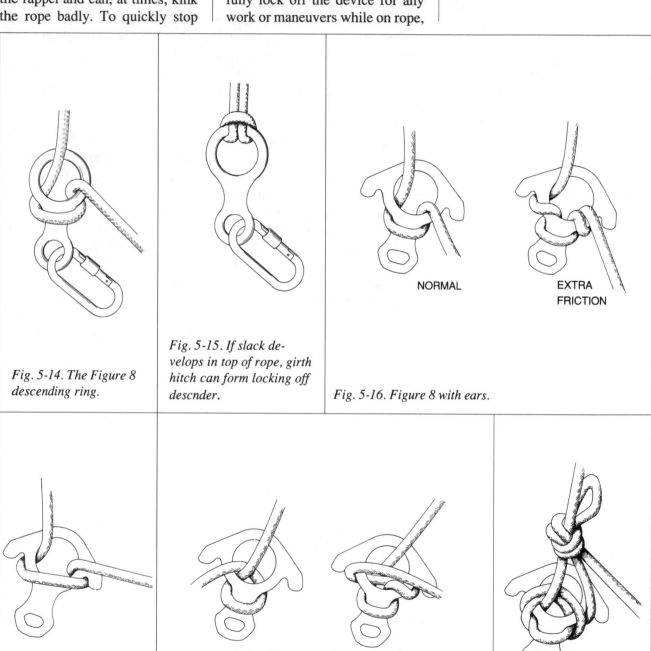

Fig. 5-14. The Figure 8 descending ring.

Fig. 5-15. If slack de-velops in top of rope, girth hitch can form locking off descnder.

NORMAL   EXTRA FRICTION

Fig. 5-16. Figure 8 with ears.

Fig. 5-17. "Ears" eliminate forming of girth hitch.

Fig. 5-18. Figure 8. Two quick stop techniques.

Fig. 5-19. Figure 8. Full lock off.

The Bobbin

The bobbin is the leading rappel device in Europe and is becoming popular in North America. The bobbin is light, strong and compact. It consists of fixed pulley wheels inside an aluminum frame (Fig.5-20). The rope is inserted by swinging open one side of the frame and is locked into place by clipping the catch back onto the seat-sling carabiner. This is an advantage over the figure 8 in that you can rig in while still attached to the device. Most commercially available bobbins have rope-threading instructions stamped on their sides. Control is good and can be made even better by passing the rope through an offset carabiner (Fig.5-21). If one is very familiar with the device, long drops can be done; however, it tends not to rappel smoothly at

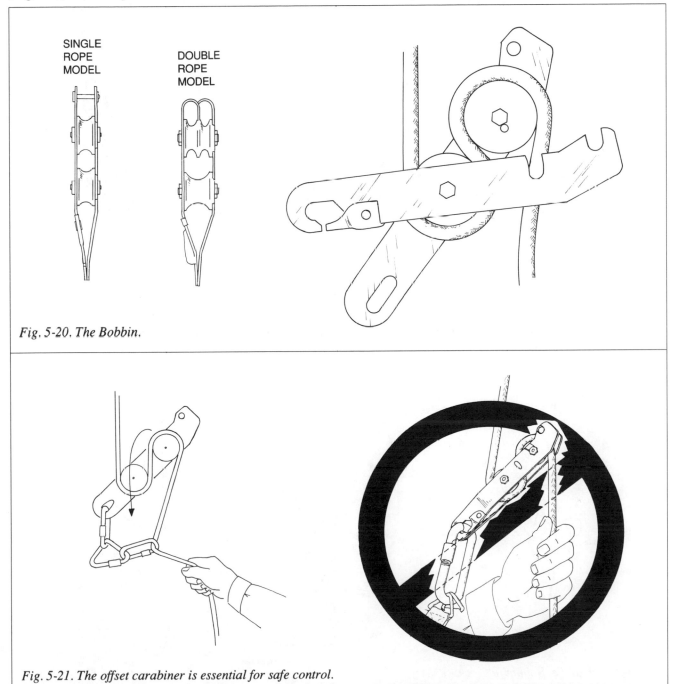

SINGLE ROPE MODEL

DOUBLE ROPE MODEL

Fig. 5-20. The Bobbin.

Fig. 5-21. The offset carabiner is essential for safe control.

the top because of rope weight, tight bends in the rope and inconsistent friction. To add friction, simply loop the rope over the top of the device (Fig.5-22). A full lock can be achieved by passing a bight of rope through the seat carabiner and then looping it over the top of the device (Fig.5-23). The bobbin is a reliable, easy-to-use rappel device. It does not kink the rope or impart spin to the rappel. A bottom belay remains very effective, even though the device pivots during application.

Petzl Stop

An excellent modification of the bobbin is the Petzl Stop (Fig.5-24). A handle on the back of the device operates a cam arrangement just like a parking brake. Pushing in on the handle allows the device to function like a nor-

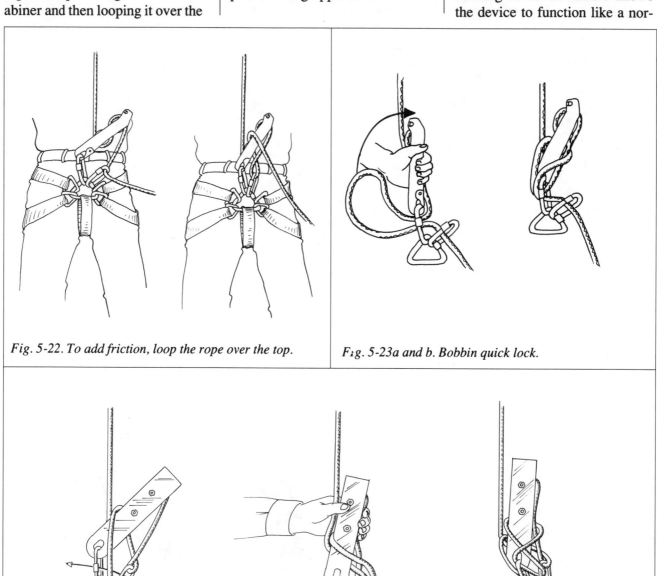

Fig. 5-22. To add friction, loop the rope over the top.

Fig. 5-23a and b. Bobbin quick lock.

Fig. 5-23c, d, and e. Bobbin full lock.

mal bobbin, while letting go of the handle results in the device stopping. It should be noted that the handle is strictly an "ON-OFF" feature and never meant to be the friction-controlling mechanism. The improved 1985 model of the Stop has a different cam arrangement that does not allow it to creep down the rope after stopping as the older model sometimes did. The Stop arrangement can be disabled by inserting a carabiner in a provided hole in the frame. The Stop is a great device, especially for someone needing to start and stop often while on rope. The device has a self-belay feature built in, making it unique. Stiff dirty rope retards the effective use of this rappel device. The Stop and the classic bobbin are both very useful rappel devices.

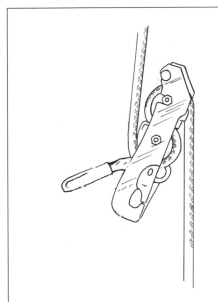

Fig. 5-24a. Petzl Stop in stop position.

Fig. 5-24b. Stop mechanism locked out with carabiner.

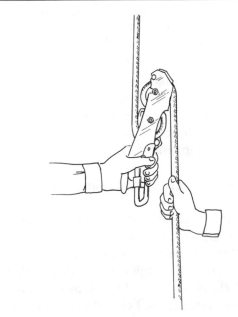

Fig. 24c. Correct hand positions.

Fig. 4-24d. The stop handle is an on-off function only. The control hand should remain in contact at all times.

VARIABLE FRICTION RAPPEL DEVICES

As people began to rappel longer and longer distances in caves, on buildings and off cliffs, they realized that friction needs during the descent change with the length of the rappel. The answer to this need for a practical variable friction device was met by John Cole in 1966 with the invention of the rappel rack (Fig.5-25).

The Rappel Rack

The rack, very popular among North American cavers, enables the rappeller to begin descent with one amount of friction, and add or subtract friction during a rappel, thus retaining precise control and a safe rate of descent. Bill Cuddington, noted vertical cave explorer, says, "The rack is the best all-around rappel device ever invented." There are two ways to vary friction in a rack:

- Changing the number of bars in contact with the rope will adjust friction.
- Changing the distance between the bars will also adjust friction (Fig.5-26).

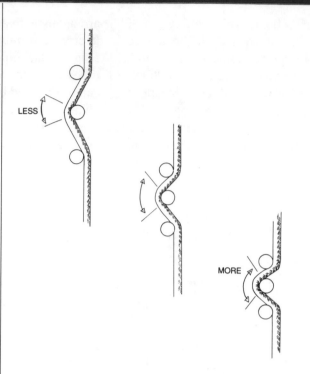

Fig. 5-26. Friction adjustment: Spaced out bars provide less friction, while bars positioned close together provide more friction.

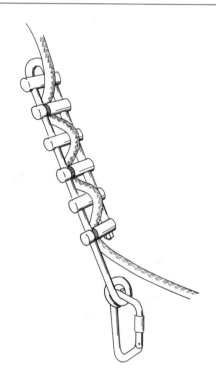

Fig. 5-25. The Rappel Rack.

Basically, the closer the bars are squeezed together, the more rope comes in contact with the bars, resulting in more friction.

The rack and its correct use are often overlooked and misunderstood. It has been described improperly in several published works and most users are unaware of the two methods of varying friction and how these can complement each other. It can be properly placed on the rope by most, but many seemingly experienced people have no comprehension of how to use the features of the rack to its full design potential. To learn to utilize the rack to its fullest, it is important to start with the basics.

Definitions (Fig.5-27a, b, and c)

Rack —A U-shaped piece of equipment consisting of a frame and a number of brake bars attached to it.
Brake Bar—A piece of cylindrical metal used as a friction surface in conjunction with a rack frame.
Control Hand—The hand that provides braking action on the standing line below the rappel device. The

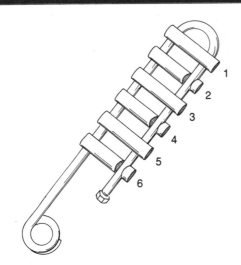

Fig. 5-27a. The rappel rack. The bars are commonlly referred to by number.

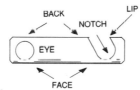

Fig. 5-27b. The brake bar.

- There is a natural tendency for the rope to track sideways.
- The groove will protect the steel frame of the rack from wear.
- The wear point on the brake bars should be on the face of each bar between the notch and the eye.
- A center pull or friction on the bar does not torque the bar and hence locks it in position on the frame.

It is best to groove the top two bars, since the rope is guided by these grooves and will stay in the center. In reality a deep groove in the second bar alone will sufficiently guide the rope around the rest of the bars. If one rappels a lot, especially on dirty ropes, the upper bars wear out faster but can be easily replaced. Alternating new smooth bars with older grooved bars will eliminate the need for filing. Commercially available pregrooved bars are available if you do not desire to modify your own.

The next step is to place the brake bars on the

control hand's usual position is at the hip. The control hand is often referred to as the braking hand.

Cradling Hand—The hand that holds and moves the bars up and down and/or off and on to add and subtract friction with the rack. On other devices this hand is often the balance hand that is held above the rappel device.

Fine-Tuning a Purchased Rack

The rack frame should be purchased from a reputable manufacturer. There are many aspects of metallurgy, metal forming, machining and design that are best left to the experts. Purchase the desired number of bars, usually six, that fit the manufacturer's rack frame.

Before using a new rack, some fine-tuning may be necessary. A small round file to groove the bars and a wrench to tighten the locknut will be needed. The first step in fine tuning is to file a rope groove in the first two bars (Fig.5-28). This groove will form a channel so that the rope will run down the center of all the bars. There are several reasons for this:

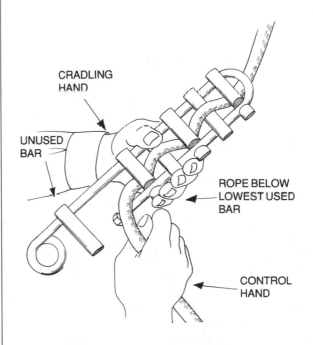

Fig. 5-27c. The cradling hand controls friction within the bars while the control hand provides friction by pressing and releasing the rope against the hip.

rack frame (Fig.5-29). To allow for the maximum spread of bars on the rack, it is best to carry the bars on the long leg of the rack. Bar number six goes on first with its notch facing away (Fig.5-30).

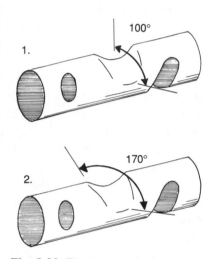

FIg. 5-28. Fine tuning the first and second bars before use will ensure prolonged life.

Put all the bars on and replace the locknut finger-tight for now. Snap the bars into place starting with bar number one. The bars will go on easier toward the bottom. Next slide each bar upward.

To test the rack, take it by the eye and turn it upside down. All six bars should easily slide downward by their own weight as the rack is inverted. If they do, consider yourself lucky. If they don't slide freely, unclip all the bars except bar number one. Invert the rack and see if this bar slides freely. If it slides a bit, but not all the way, the sides of the rack may not be parallel. If this is the case, unclip bar number one and check again. If a bar fails to slide freely, it may be shorter between the eye and the notch than the other bars. To fix it, take the round file and remove a little metal from the

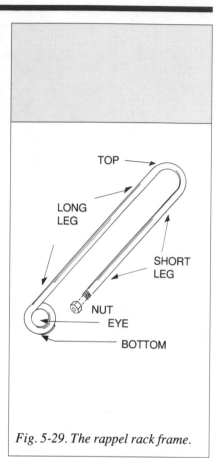

Fig. 5-29. The rappel rack frame.

VARIATIONS ON THE RACK

The rappel rack, as described by Cole in 1967, is a very versatile rappel device. As with any device, there are ways to fine-tune the design based on personal preferences.

Length
The length of the standard Cole Six Bar Rack is 14 inches overall. The need for a smaller device that easily fits into a cave pack influenced the design of a five bar rack which is only 12 1/4 inches long. Shorter racks, primarily designed for short drops, are of-ten mistakenly purchased by light adults and small children. It is true that a small person needs fewer bars, but it is more important to have a long traveling space to spread the bars out to reduce friction. The shorter racks are a poor option when needing less friction. Five bars on a longer traveling space can often safely take care of the needs of most small rappellers.

Super-long drops (approximately 1500+ feet) require custom-made long racks. Commonly, 24 inches has been chosen as a desirable length that often accommodates eight bars (fig.5-a). The long rack allows the bars to be spread further apart to compensate for very heavy rope weight at the top of the super drops. The standard rack will rappel with extreme ease any drop from 1 to 1500 feet. It will work on drops longer than 1500, but a longer rack is easier to use. Super-long racks often tend to distort in shape during the rig-in process, which has become a concern to many. Care should be taken when attaching to the rappel line. Friction adjustment is difficult to judge when dealing with the lengthy extremes.

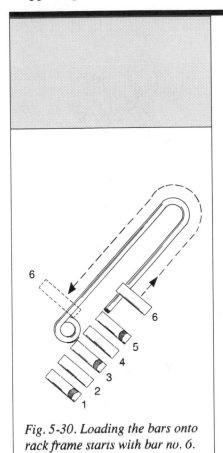

Fig. 5-30. Loading the bars onto rack frame starts with bar no. 6.

outside edge of the notch (Fig.5-31).

Test the bar often and repeat the process on each bar until all six bars slide freely. Next, check the seating of the number one bar against the end of the rack (Fig.5-32). The bar should sit square to the frame and not at an odd angle. To fix any angle, file the upper inside edges of the eye and notch. Test often and repeat until the bar sits square. When this is done, check all of the bars and make sure that the gaps alternate, one facing left, one facing right. Take your wrench and tighten down the locknut on the frame. Most commercial racks now use a nylon insert locknut so it is only necessary to tighten the nut so that the rack frame threads engage all of the nut.

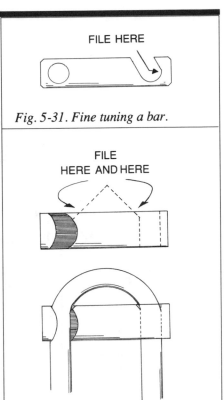

Fig. 5-31. Fine tuning a bar.

Fig. 5-32. Seating bar no. 1 requires careful filing.

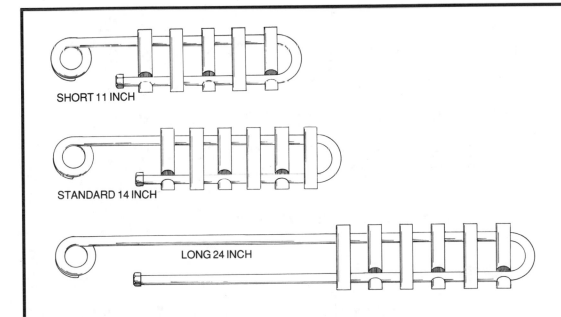

SHORT 11 INCH

STANDARD 14 INCH

LONG 24 INCH

Fig.5a. Racks come in different sizes: 5-bar 11 inch rack, 6 bar 14 inch rack, and 6 bar 24 inch rack for the super drops.

	FRICTION VARIABILITY	EASE OF ATTACHMENT TO ROPE	EASE OF INSPECTION	STRENGTH	WEAR RESISTANCE	REPLACEABLE PARTS	HEAT ABSORPTION/DISSIPATION	TWIST/KINKS ROPE	SIZE	KNOT PASSING ABILITY	DOUBLE ROPE CAPACITY	DIFFERENT ROPE SIZE CAPACITY	AVAILABILITY
FIGURE 8 STANDARD ALUMINUM	N	◇	◇	△	▽	N	▼	Y	▲	N	Y	▲	▲
FIGURE 8 EARED ALUMINUM	N	◇	◇	▲	◇	N	▽	Y	△	Y	Y	▲	▲
CARABINER WRAP WRAP	N	▼	▼	▼	▼	N	▼	Y	▲	N	Y	△	▲
POMPIER FIREMAN'S HOOK	I	◇	△	▲	▲	N	▲	Y	▼	Y	Y	▲	▽
SKY GENIE	N	▼	▼	▼	▼	N	▽	Y	▽	N	N	▼	▼
RACK STANDARD	C	△	▽	△	◇	Y	◇	N	▽	N	Y	▲	▲
RACK 5-BAR	C	△	▽	△	◇	Y	▽	N	◇	N	Y	△	▲
RACK EXTRA LONG	C	△	▽	△	▲	Y	◇	N	▼	N	Y	▲	▼
WHALETAIL	I	◇	▼	◇	▽	N	▲	N	▽	N	N	△	▼
SUPER RACK	I	◇	◇	▲	▲	Y	▲	N	▽	N	N	△	◇
PETZL CLASSIC BOBBIN	N	△	◇	△	△	N	▽	N	▽	N	N	△	△
PETZL STOP BOBBIN	N	△	◇	△	△	N	▽	N	◇	N	N	△	△
TANDEM CARABINERS, BARS	I	▼	▼	▽	◇	Y	▼	N	△	N	Y	◇	▲
BRAKE PLATE MACGREGOR	C	▼	▼	△	◇	N	◇	N	▼	N	N	▼	▼
BRAKE PLATE ESCAPELINE	C	◇	▼	▲	◇	N	▼	N	◇	N	N	▼	▽

Chart 5-2. Rappel Devices

▲	EXCELLENT
◭	VERY GOOD
◇	GOOD
▽	FAIR
▼	POOR
Y	YES
N	NO
I	INCREMENTALLY
C	CONTINUOUSLY

RAPPEL DEVICES

The ideal rappel device should be like the transporters on the starship Enterprise, however, techology has not reached that point yet. Devices that enable a person to control his descent on a rope are inherently dangerous because they slide rather than grab the rope. Any good descent device incorporates an easy stop and lock position. A good rappel device has a wide continuous range of friction variabiltity. It should be easily and correctly attached to the rope, with little opportunity for error. Strength and wearability are important. If wear occurs, parts should be easily replaced. Because heat is generated in rappelling, the device should readily absorb and dissipate heat. The rope should pass through the device without being twisted or kinked. Overall, the rappel device should be compact, small and lightweight. Other useful features include the device's abilities to accept different sizes of rope as well as multiple ropes.

COMPARISON CHART DISCLAIMER

Any rating or comparison is at best an educated opinion. Differing levels of familiarity with an item or differing applications can result in an entirely different rating score. The criteria used and the items rated are intended simply to show general opinions about these items. There will always exist isolated exceptions, and it is the author's intent to avoid such "believe-it-or-not" discussion.

Attachment to the Seat Sling

With the rack fine-tuned, it is ready to be attached to the seat-sling carabiner. Attach the rack so that the locknut side of the frame is on the outside and away from the body. This will allow travel of the rope from side to side when adjusting friction. Many climbers insist that a linking locking carabiner be used between the rappel device and the seat harness. During more complicated rope maneuvers it may be helpful to be able to remove the rappel device from the seat harness without opening the seat harness carabiner. At this point, all of the bars except number one should be unclipped. Step up to the rope, safely away from the edge of the drop. Face the anchor point. The rope should be on your right side (reverse if you are left handed).

Attachment to the Rope

Take the rope and lay it over the front of bar number one in the filed groove made earlier. (It is wrong to have the rope lying on the steel frame.) Clip in and slide up each bar as you thread the rope back and forth over the alternating bars (Fig. 5-33).

CAUTION: It is essential that the bars be loaded correctly on their faces. Failure to load the rope properly will result in the bars coming unclipped when loaded. This usually occurs after the rappel has begun. It can result in serious injury or death. Double-check (See Fig. 5-33).

There are idiot-proof bars on the market that have a straight notch instead of a lipped notch. If these bars are rigged backwards they will simply fall away making the fact obvious that the rack has been rigged wrong. However, use this type of bar in position two only because during use of the rack, the lips on the lower bars need to hang on the frame of the rack to prevent their accidental disengagement.

Gloves

After the rope is rigged in to the rack, put on your gloves. A light-weight pair of leather work gloves will do fine. There is no need for heavy welding or fence-stringing gloves. The use of light gloves will enable a rappeller to feel what she is doing yet protect her hands from hot bars and the simple abrasion of the rope passing through them. Also the gloves allow a back-up system by enabling the addition of friction by gripping the rope. For maximum effectiveness, the control hand should hold the main rope at all times. With a light grip, allow the rope to run on the right hip; reverse if left-handed. (Do not allow the rope to run over the seat harness. Nylon rubbing nylon will glaze and melt the seat harness.) On long drops it may be more comfortable to let the rope run between the legs. The other hand should cradle the lowest engaged bars on the rack as this controls the amount of friction and, ultimately, the rate of descent (Fig. 5-34).

VARIATIONS (Cont.): RACK EYES

Another variation is whether the eye of the rack is flat (in plane with the rack), offset or rotated 180° (Fig.5-b). The flat configuration allows the rope to swing freely when changing bars. The offset allows better visual examination of the bars. A 180° rotation can provide a longer short leg and thus more bar traveling space. Ultimately this variation can provide the greatest rappel speed control with any length of rack. A locking linking carabiner between the seat harness and the rack will reorient the rack 90°. Final orientation of a rack will also depend upon the seat harness and the way that the seat harness carabiner clips into it.

Because of the moisture and mud in caves, a rack's frame used in these wet environments should be stainless steel. To form the **eye** of the rack requires bending or welding (Fig.5). If welded by an expert stainless metal welder, the welded eye is by far the strongest. The spun eye can also be welded. The wrapped eye bends the metal sharply and causes weakening by bending. Most commercial racks now have welded eyes.

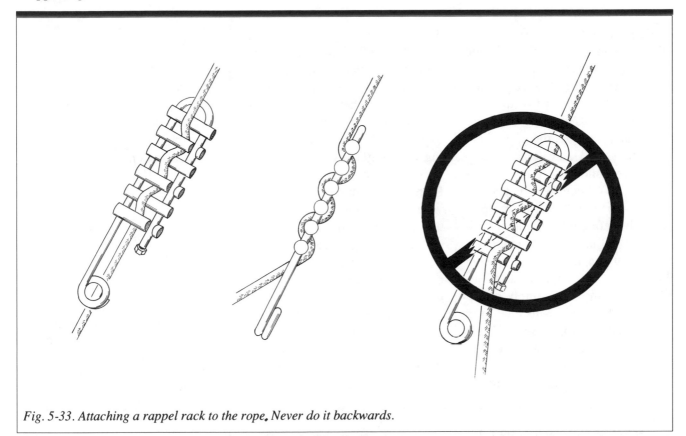

Fig. 5-33. Attaching a rappel rack to the rope. Never do it backwards.

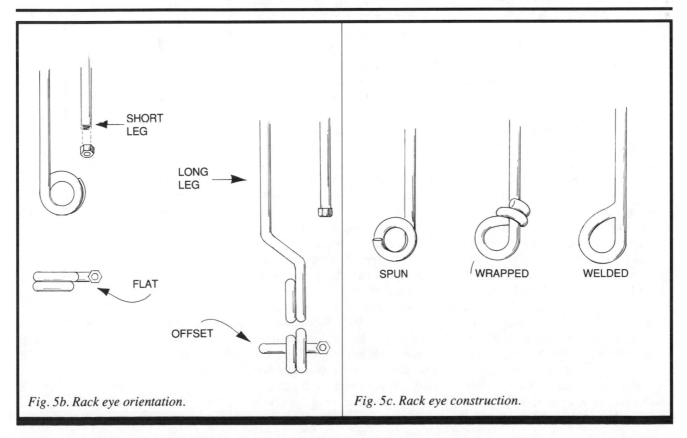

SHORT LEG

LONG LEG

FLAT

OFFSET

SPUN

WRAPPED

WELDED

Fig. 5b. Rack eye orientation.

Fig. 5c. Rack eye construction.

Friction Adjustment

With a correctly tuned rack, the cradling hand can easily move the bars downward to reduce friction or slide them upward to increase friction. Often, after getting over the edge of a drop, the upper bars (numbers 2, 3 and 4) are sometimes crammed up to the top of the rack. To decrease this friction just reach up and pull them apart with the left hand. The other rack friction adjustment is made by changing the number of bars in contact with the rope. To add friction while moving, simply swing the rope to the opposite side, lift a bar with the left hand and swing it under the rope and clip it to the frame. Slide it up and you have added a bar while still moving. To decrease friction just reverse the procedure. All of these operations should take place while you are moving down the rope. Rappelling generates heat and to stop on rope allows one point on the rope to become heated. Surface heating causes glazing, a melting of the outer nylon layers of the rope. If one can add or subtract bars and vary the spacing between them, the full potential of the rappel rack can be appreciated.

In normal usage the average person will alternate between five to six bars; however, on a dirty rope, four bars may be all that is necessary. There should never be less than four bars engaged with the rope at any one time. In certain rescue situations or unusual

Fig. 5-34a. Correct hand position when using a rack. Cradling hand adjusts friction by moving bars up and down or adding and subtracting bars. Control hand gives additional friction against hip. Rappeller should never have to feed rope into rack with control hand.

VARIATIONS (CONT.): BRAKE BARS

The standard brake bar is a solid 3/4 inch aluminum bar with a hole and lipped notch. These provide excellent control and function on the rack. A variation is to machine a straight notch and use this bar in the second position **only** to guard against rigging the rope in backwards. Aluminum bars tend to wear and leave a black aluminum deposit or streak on the rope. To slow down bar wear and keep a clean rope, stainless steel bars were developed. These bars were made hollow to reduce weight and to increase the bar surface area to form an excellent heat dissipater. Acting like a radiator, this hole keeps the bar cool. Aluminum bars are better heat sinks than steel bars. This means they can absorb more heat away from the rope, but once the bar is hot the heat cannot be dissipated further. The steel bar cannot grab as much heat, but it can get rid of it better. Steel bars do not offer as much friction as aluminum bars. This offers lightweight rappellers an attractive option. Steel bars are also available in a straight notch version. To aid in heat sink ability and wear resistance, a 1 inch solid aluminum bar is available. This bar should be used as a top bar and serves to aid in heat dissipation. Some climbers feel that because the second bar gets the hottest during a rappel that this larger bar should be used as the second bar. This added diameter may easily give too much friction, causing a control problem. It's important to note that this bar will still get much hotter than a hollow steel bar (Fig.5-k).

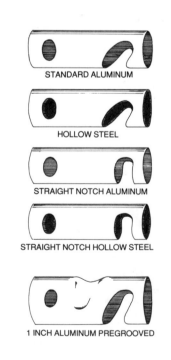

Fig. 5d. Brake bar types.

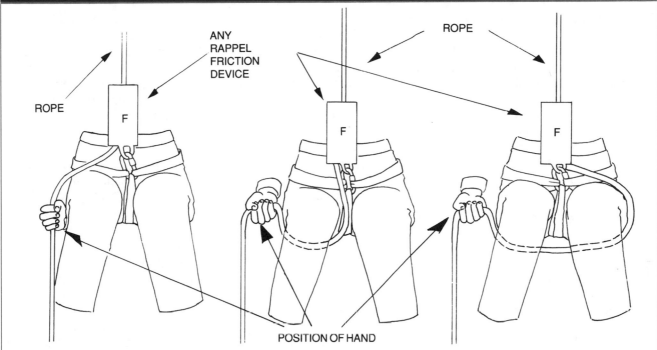

ROPE

ANY RAPPEL FRICTION DEVICE

ROPE

POSITION OF HAND

Fig. 5-34b. Various amounts of friction can be achieved with the control hand by holding the rope against the legs at different points.

circumstances three bars might be used.

CAUTION: Keep a positive grip on bar number three since, if the rope is swung to the side and the bar falls away, it can unclip itself resulting in a two bar situation. If this occurs, the rack acts only as a guide for a fall down the rope.

In summary, the rack is an excellent variable friction device capable of varying friction in two ways—by changing the number of bars and by changing the distance between the bars.

STYLE

Regardless of the device used,

there is a certain technique or style to rappelling properly. Surviving the rappel does not necessarily mean it was done correctly. One may have just been lucky. Knowing what to do and the reasons for doing it are the essence of style. Research has shown that a smooth technique puts less strain on all components in the system. Less strain means greater safety. How is this style achieved? As a pilot has a pre-flight checklist so should rappellers have a pre-rappel checklist:

1. Check for loose clothes or hair that might get snagged in a rappel device.
2. Place any packs on your off-side (The side opposite the control hand/hip side).
3. Helmet on? Chin strap tight?

4. Check the Chain:
   • Rope: Is it in good shape?
   • Rigging: Safe and sound? Pads OK?
   • Harness: Seat carabiner screwed tight?
   • Rappel device: Rigged in properly?
   • Technique: How will the lip be negotiated?
5. Signal the appropriate intentions to others.
6. Begin to rappel.

Going through this checklist sequentially will highlight key aspects of each section.

Loose Clothing and Long Hair

As the rappeller is descending the drop, he leans over to look down and touches his long hair or coarse beard to the rappel device. Instantly, the hair is drawn into the device and the rappeller becomes painfully aware of the predicament. It is difficult to think while in extreme pain. The first option at this point is to attempt to continue by just pulling out the offending hair and rappel on down the drop. But what if there is too much hair to pull out? What about clothes? Often, gear and other body parts get caught. Can these be just pulled out? If not, the next option is to reach into the pack and pull out an ascender and stand in it in an effort to relieve the pressure on the rappel device long enough to remove the stuck hair. Another option is to have a climber come up the same rope or an adjacent rope to assist in freeing the stuck rappeller. The final option and a very hazardous one is to pull out a knife and start cutting.

Whoa!!! Back Up!!! Stop!!!

The rappeller is hanging from one rope. That rope and the hair are stuck together. The rope is under tension. Rope under tension cuts like hot butter (Fig.5-35). If the rappeller's head is stuck against the rappel device it becomes impossible to see what he is about to cut. Also, there is a scalp nearby that deserves some concern. The possibility of cutting flesh or rope is very real. If it comes to this option, place a seat harness attached ascender well above the reach of the knife. Cut carefully in a direction away from the rope and any attachment slings. Prevention is the best option, so just be aware that rappel devices have an affinity for hair, clothes and body parts.

Gear Bag on the Off-Side?

Place any pack with ascending gear on the off-side. Ascent is difficult without this important cargo. Even if one does not intend to climb the rope, it is a wise idea to carry ascending gear anyway in case of an emergency. If the pack or gear is heavy it can be hung from the seat carabiner. Any load should not upset the rappeller's center of gravity. See Chapter 10 for more on gear transfer.

Helmet Secure?

Next, check and secure the helmet and tighten down the chin strap. The most common cause of injury during vertical work is rockfall. A quality climbing helmet should be used. See Chapter 10 for a full discussion on climbing helmets.

The Chain

Make sure the links of your chain (see Fig.5-4) are strong and are connected. Examine the rope. Is it in good shape and is it the proper rope for the drop? Is it long enough? If you have any doubts about this, is there a knot in the end? Is the anchor strong and is the rope connected to the anchor? Is the harness secured properly with all the buckles tight? Check the carabiner and make sure the rappel device is locked inside and the device is properly rigged to the rope. Double-check here!! Notice the position of the rope and the rope pads and plan how to negotiate the lip. Think through the

Fig. 5-35. The final option. To free caught hair or clothes, never try to cut the slings or rope supporting you. Rope under tension cuts like hot butter!

proper technique. Focus your thoughts and concentrate on the business at hand.

Signals

In check point number five, signal the others in the party so that they will know what is going on. Use voice communication if possible to prevent confusion. Sometimes, however, whistle signals must be used because of echos, waterfall noise, or distance. It is important that signals be discussed before a trip to be assured that everyone understands. No standard truly exists. Some utilize the universal three whistle blasts for emergency, but this system requires the ability to discern a count in difficult situations. See Chapter 10 for a fuller discussion of signals.

Voice Signals

ON ROPE   Rigged in; ready to descend or ascend.

OFF ROPE   Derigged and **out of the danger zone** at the top or bottom.

ON BELAY   Response to on rope (rappelling) meaning ready to apply a bottom belay if needed.

ROCK!   Warning that **ANYTHING** is falling down toward those below.

OK   Obvious acknowledgement.

Whistle Signals

1 Blast   Stop! Used to stop all movement, especially in hauling systems.

2 blasts   Up.

3 blasts   Down.

4 blasts   OK or rope free, off rope.

Sustained Blast   Emergency, Help, Rock!

Negotiating the Edge

After signalling "On rope!", begin to rappel down the drop. Before trying to negotiate the lip, make sure there is sufficient friction in the rappel device. When moving backward toward the edge, be careful not to dislodge any rock or debris that could fall and injure those below or the rope. To begin a rappel over an easy lip, simply keep your feet comfortably apart (for balance), lean back, and walk backward over the edge (Fig.5-36). As the rappel begins, make sure the rope stays on the pad. A common novice error is to begin to walk backward into the pit, freeze his feet and continue to rappel. Soon he is almost upside down in a very awkward position. Not all drops have a nice easy lip at the top. Many, if not most, are awkward at best. Good rigging can solve some problems, but not all.

Undercut Edges

A tough common problem is the narrow undercut ledge. This problem can often be solved by approaching the edge, lying on one's off side, extending the off-sided leg into the drop and easing over the edge (Fig.5-37). This method isn't pretty, but it works. Possibly the toughest lip is one that is undercut and must be rigged at a sharp angle (Fig.5-38). Here the previ-ous technique does not work because the rappel device wants to hang up on the edge. In this situation the easiest solution is to rig a pigtail/etrier to act as a foothold just below the edge to allow the rappeller to ease over without getting the rappel device hung up. If a pig tail/etrier is not rigged, try this alternative method. Approach the edge, get down on the knees and crawl backwards towards the edge. When the breakover is reached, do like the frozen novice (Fig.5-39). After leaning back far enough to clear the rappel device, ease into the rock face with the off side leg and continue on down.

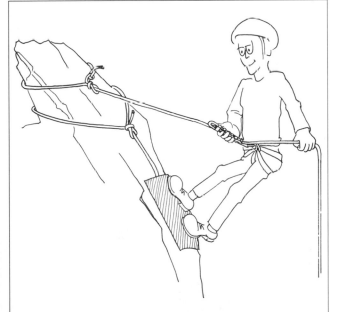

Fig. 5-36. Beginning rappel. Legs spread apart and relatively straight for balance. Avoid rappelling on knees. Hold rope tightly with control hand during first few moments of neitherspace.

Fig. 5-37 Negotiating an undercut edge.

Fig. 5-37b.

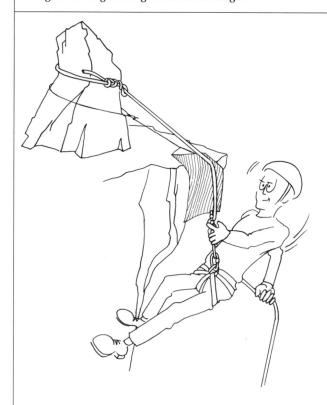

Fig. 5-37c.

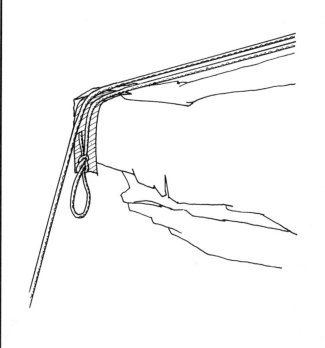

Fig. 5-38. An etrier or a pigtail with a loop can assist when negotiating an undercut edge.

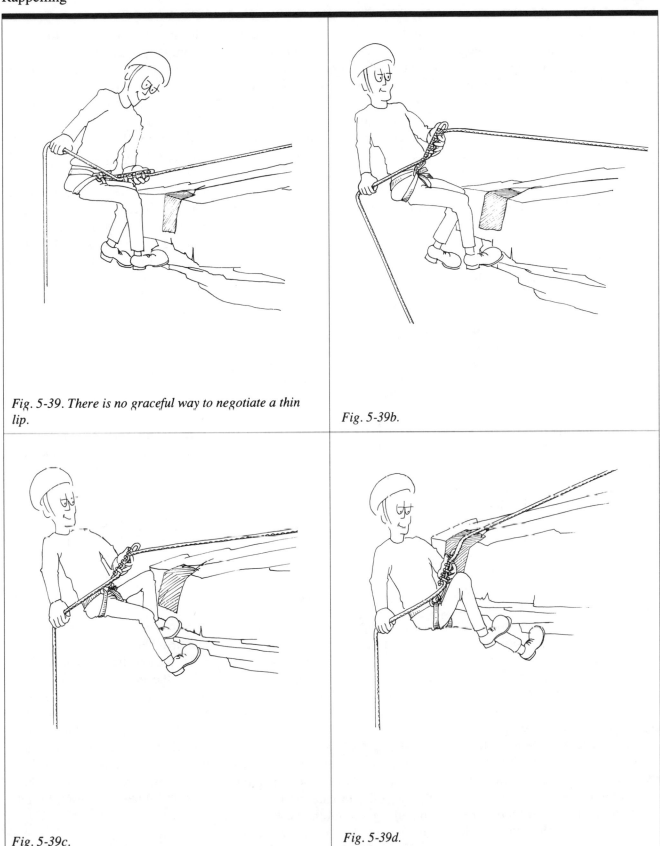

Fig. 5-39. There is no graceful way to negotiate a thin lip.

Fig. 5-39b.

Fig. 5-39c.

Fig. 5-39d.

Rate of Descent

The rappeller is now over the edge and hanging in the drop with her full weight on the rope. The harness should be comfortable and the rappel device should have sufficient friction to control the rappel. The question now becomes how fast or slow should descent be? True, one can easily go too fast, but too slow can also be a problem. Probably the key is smoothness. The rate of descent should be the same from top to bottom. A smooth rappel is best. Bouncy rappels may load a rope beyond its working limits, causing shock-loading and unsafe situations. A rappel device is used to create friction. The by-product of friction is heat. Going fast or going slow, over the same distance, generates the same **total** amount of friction and heat.

However, the thermal conductivity (the ability of the device to absorb heat and not get superhot at the friction surface) of the rappel device determines the safe rappel rate. If a person rappels too fast there is little friction developed while descending, but as she nears the bottom, friction must be added rapidly to slow down. This generates heat quickly and, often, faster than the device can radiate the heat. If this happens, the surface temperature of the device becomes so hot that it can easily glaze the outer surface of the rope, especially if the rappeller comes to an abrupt stop on the rope. If the rappeller keeps moving, the nylon rope keeps passing by and does not get too hot.

A good rule of thumb is not to rappel any faster than you could land without getting hurt. A moderate rate seems best, because the heat build-up plus the movement of the rope seem to strike a useful balance. Remember: rappelling is supposed to be fun.

On long drops the rappel device is going to heat up regardless of the speed. Again, a moderate rate is best. Remember to keep moving while changing friction in order to keep the nylon in contact

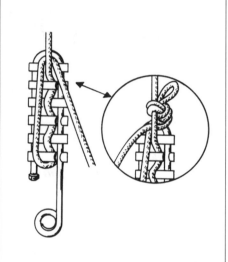

Fig. 5-40. Rope in locked off position. Simplest position shown in A. More secure configuration shown in B. Bight of rope (2 to 3 feet) had been brought up and knotted around standing rope.

with the rappel device from heating up to the damage point. One technique on longer drops, say over 1500 feet, is to take a water squirt bottle and cool the device during rappel.

Locking Off

Occasionally there will be a need to lock the system off, enabling the rappeller to take pictures, get something out of a pack, assist another climber, install a pad or change over. Being able to stop is as important as being able to go. Be sure the device is cool enough to avoid rope damage. The easiest way to lock off the rack is to pull the trailing end of the rope over the top of the rack frame and wedge the rope between the rack frame and tensioned rope (Fig. 5-40). Another less popular way to lock off a rack, because it takes more time and effort, is to tie the trailing rope around the rope above the rack. This method may be less popular but it is more secure and should be used anytime serious control is required such as in rescue, bolting or photography.

Landing

When you reach the bottom, land squatting with the feet spread apart. Then stand up. This will take the tension off the rappel device and allow for quick and easy removal. Be cautious, because rappel devices can get very hot, sometimes over 300° Fahrenheit. Close the bars of the rack and with rope in hand, move to a position of relative safety and out of the rockfall zone. Give the "Off rope" signal and prepare to belay the next rappeller. Usually, the most experienced climber rappels first and then belays the next rappeller. Each person then stands ready to belay the next person down. By doing this, the belayer remains attentive and knows she has only one person to watch all the way down. The bottom belay is a back-up for proper rappelling style and, if done with respect to other hazards, it can be a very useful safety measure.

Bottom Belays

During a rappel, one back-up system is the bottom belay, in which a person at the bottom of the rappel line simply pulls down on the rappel rope. This force applies additional friction to the rappel device and allows for bottom control of the speed of rappel. A bottom belay is the margin of safety for the rappeller who gets out of control due to insufficient friction, and allows the belayer to lower an injured climber. The bottom belay can prevent accidents, but it has a serious drawback. There is a very real threat of rockfall. The belayer must be underneath the rappeller to be effective and must, therefore, enter the rockfall zone. A place of safety near the bottom can often be found to allow for an effective belay out of danger from above. It should be noted that the longer the drop, the more directly beneath the rappeller the belayer needs to be to properly effect a belay. If a belay is applied from an angle on a long drop, it merely pendulums the climber, rather than exerting pressure on the rappel device. Rope stretch amplifies the problem, resulting in the belayer frantically trying to take the slack out of the rope in time to be effective. Chapter 9 for further discussion.

Rappelling Sequence

To enable an entire team to safely rappel a drop, everyone should be experienced and should have practiced beforehand on smaller, less consequential drops. Regardless of the precautions, experience levels will vary within a group. It is critical to have at least two voices of experience with the team. The most experienced should be on the bottom in the event of a needed bottom belay. The second most experienced should be at the top ensuring that equipment is attached properly. The only exception to the experience-down-first rule would be that time when a moderately experienced person wants the honors of first plunge. Deep in a dark cave this single experience can be exhilarating as

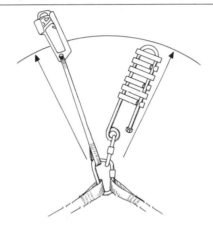

Fig. 5-41. A safety Jumar should be a standard piece of attached descending gear. The Jumar should be just long enough to reach above the rack if both are to be attached to the same rope. An extra linking carabiner on the rack is vital during changeover (see Chapter 6). A linking carabiner on the Jumar adds versatility of use.

well as humbling.

Up to this point, everything that has been discussed has gone right. How about a little pre-planning for things that might go wrong, those unexpected surprises, those things that lead to accidents?

WHAT IF?

What if the rope is too short? Correct rigging with a knot tied in the end of the rope will prevent this from happening. One of the most common accidents in rappelling is descending off the end of a rope that does not reach the bottom. However, suppose the "What If" has occurred, and luckily you noticed it in time, but you are now faced with the prospect of a rope ending nowhere near the bottom of a drop. First, lock off the rappel device and perform a changeover maneuver. This is a critical skill that involves a knowledge of prusiking. Be sure to become thoroughly familiar with this changeover maneuver, which is discussed in detail in Chapter 6.

Safety Jumar

A normal precaution that helps in the changeover maneuver and many other situations is to wear a safety Jumar, which should be clipped into the seat harness on a short sling (Fig.5-41).

Note: Any ascender that can be attached easily with one hand can be substituted and used in place of a Jumar. Over the years the term safety Jumar has become the generic reference. When wearing the safety Jumar, one already has an ascender in place should a changeover become necessary. One use of a safety Jumar includes staying clipped in at the top of the drop while getting ready for a rappel to prevent a slip before being fully rigged in. Another situation might include a gradual failure in the rappelling device. Here a climber could avert the impending doom. Occasionally a climber will need to wear an entire ascending system in addition to the safety Jumar because of hazards and problems that may occur during a rappel.

Rappelling While Wearing Full Ascending Equipment

Indeed, there are times when it would be wise to wear the entire ascending rig, so that quick changeover could be possible. Such situations are:

1. Heavy water falls.
2. The possibility that the rope does not reach the floor.
3. The uncertainty of the condition of the drop zone.
   - Unstable breakdown or shifting boulders.
   - False floor—thin crust of mud or rock.
   - Fragile formations that may be destroyed if you land.
   - Smelly animal carcasses
   - Raging river where you had expected to get off rope.
   - Ferocious beasts.

In any circumstance, your ascending gear should be in your pack with you and it should be packed in that bag in the order in which it would be attached to the rope. In an emergency it is tough to fumble through a gear bag looking for the correct piece of gear.

Self-Belay

A rappel that is speeding out of control can be arrested by raising the running end of the rope above the rappel rack. If the rope is heavy, this becomes difficult. This motion cinches the bars and the rope tightly together, arresting the rapid descent (Fig. 5-42). If this fails, or if you are using a device other than a rack, kick your leg in a circular motion wrapping the rope several times around the leg. This maneuver is called a **Leg Wrap** and can be used for a variety of situations other than an out-of-control rappel (Fig. 5-43).

A secondary solution to an out-of-control rappel is to use a self-belay system. The basic problem with a self-belay system is that the rappeller must overcome a panic reaction and then do something positive. Many self-belay systems require the rapeller to maintain them while rappelling, rather than tending to the business of rappelling.

Prusik Knot as a Self-Belay

The earliest self-belay rig was the tag-along Prusik knot, rigged above the rappel device and held with the upper hand (Fig. 5-44). It was learned through several bad accidents that if a problem occurs, instead of letting go, the natural reaction is to grab. Grabbing a Prusik knot allows it to slide down the rope, traveling faster every instant. If a person is actually able to come to his senses long enough to let go of the knot, the sling material may disintegrate, allowing the climber to descend even more rapidly than before. In actual usage, the prusik safety has proven to be troublesome and dangerous.

Spelean Shunt

In an effort to design a better system, Petzl built a self-belay action into the bobbin. It still requires the positive action of letting go in a time of crisis. Another self-belay system compatible with any rappel device is the spelean shunt (Fig. 5-45). A Gibbs ascender, with an intertwined carabiner, rides above the rappel device. However, the shunt sometimes inadvertently engages itself. This often occurs at the top of the drop

Fig. 5-42. Lifting the mainline upward should arrest the descent.

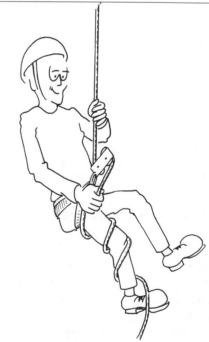

Fig. 5-43. In an emergency, a fast leg wrap can arrest the fall.

or upon brushing against a wall. For the most part, it does not need to be held during a rappel. Effective use of a rappel safety requires a slow rappel. It does require a positive reaction in a time of crisis. The Gibbs spelean shunt rig, however, will not melt or slip once engaged.

To release a locked shunt, take your weight off the sling for an instant and pull down sharply on the outside end of the carabiner. A short sling tied there can help. If it is really jammed, attach a foot loop there and kick down to free the device. It may also be helpful to use another ascender, ena-bling you to step up to release the shunt.

A complex variation on the spelean shunt is the safety rappel cam (Davidson 1976, Fig. 5-46). It is a modified Gibbs cam less prone to false triggering and can actually be triggered by the passive action of simply falling backward. It need not be grabbed or held to operate. The rig, though workable, is complex and is not commercially available.

The Petzl Shunt is a popular commercially available rappel device. It can be released once loaded and the manufacturer claims it will hold well on icy or muddy ropes (Fig. 5-47).

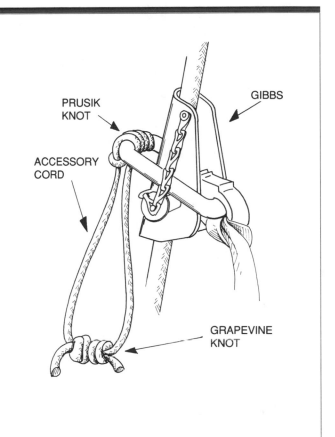

Fig. 5-45. The Spelean Shunt.

Fig. 5-44. A prusik safety in the hands of the inexperienced does not work.

No self-belay device should interfere with rappelling technique. If it does interfere, it is counterproductive in that it exists to help control a problem, but instead it tends to create one. The best solution here is prevention. See Chapter 9 for more on belays.

What If a rappeller's seat harness begins to disintegrate before her eyes? Remember the bodywrap rappel? (Classic dulfersitz, See Fig. 5-2.) This would be an excellent time to use a variation on the body-wrap known as the leg-wrap, not necessarily to finish the drop but to keep from falling. She can add extra wraps around her body, arresting the descent, then rig in her ascending gear. Once the situation is stabilized, partner rescue techniques can be employed (see Chapter 11).

There are many other "What ifs?." Examine possible emergencies with a problem-solving attitude before they happen. This may avert many nasty situations. With a buddy, rig

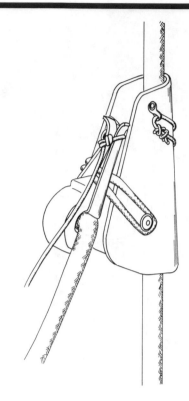

Fig. 5-46. Safety rappel cam (after Davison).

a rope in a backyard tree and practice close to the ground to build confidence and work on solving problems.

Rappelling is dangerous, so you must know what to do and do it well. A little bit of learning can be a dangerous thing. Know **WHY** something is done, not only that it needs doing. Seek quality training and practice.

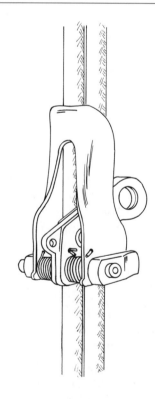

Fig. 5-47. Petzl shunt.

	EASE OF ATTACHMENT	SELF ACTIVATING BY SPEED	SELF ACTIVATING BY UPSET	RESIST FALSE TRIGGERING	RESIST HUMAN ERROR	AVAILABILITY
PRUSIK KNOT	▽	N	N	◇	▼	▲
RAPPEL SAFETY CAM	◇	N	M	◇	◇	▲
SPELEAN SHUNT (GIBBS)	◇	N	Y	◮	◇	▼
PETZL SHUNT	▽	N	M	◇	◇	◮
TRAILING GIBBS	◇	N	M	◮	◮	▲
PETZL STOP	◮	N	Y	◇	▼	◮

▲	EXCELLENT
◮	VERY GOOD
◇	GOOD
▽	FAIR
▼	POOR
Y	YES
N	NO
M	MAYBE

SELF BELAY DEVICES

The ideal self-belay device should probably attach above the rappel device, run freely and engage instantly when trouble with the rappel is sensed. It should trigger automatically and should also resist false triggering. If engaged, it should hold solidly. The rappeller should not have to hold or touch the device during descent. After engagement, the ideal self-belay device should be easily released.

COMPARISON CHART DISCLAIMER

Any rating or comparison is at best an educated opinion. Differing levels of familiarity with an item or differing applications can result in an entirely different rating score. The criteria used and the items rated are intended simply to show general opinions about these items. There will always exist isolated exceptions, and it is the author's intent to avoid such "believe-it-or-not" discussion.

Chart 5-3. Self Belay Devices

CARABINER DEVICES

Carabiners were designed and manufactured to be used by climbers to hold things together. Someone discovered a use for which they were not intended: as a rappel device. There are two basic fixed friction rappel modes that use carabiners: the carabiner wrap and the brake-bar rig.

The carabiner wrap is probably the world's most popular rappel method. Thousands of GIs have survived its drawbacks. To rappel with a carabiner wrap, take a carabiner hooked to the harness. Lay the rope across the gate, which should be up, with the hinge pin toward the climber. Wrap the anchor end of the rope around the carabiner and bring it back to the gate. Repeat this wrapping for at least two turns (fig.5-e). This is a fixed friction set up. Once a climber is on the rope, it cannot be changed. The U.S. Army uses a non-locking carabiner, but in any life support mode a **locking** carabiner should be used. The carabiner-wrap rappel will wear out carabiners rapidly, impart tremendous spin to the rappeller and will kink the rope. When used with a non-locking carabiner it tends to come off the rope. Its advantages are that it is simple, inexpensive and uses already available hardware.

The carabiner wrap often would not have enough friction, so early rappellers tried to overcome this problem along with the spin problem by developing the **carabiner brake-bar** rig. However, one was not enough; two in tandem were necessary (fig.5-f). As with the wrap rigs, the carabiner was again used in a way it was not designed. Carabiners are designed to load on their long axis, never to be loaded sideways. The two carabiners were often joined together with a piece of chain or another carabiner. The brake bars were clipped onto the carabiner gates and the entire assembly was fastened to the rappeller's seat har-

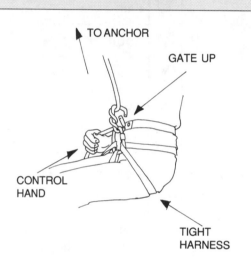

Fig. 5e. Carabiner wrap rappel. Hard on the rope, and often the rappeller, as he finds himself spinning down the rope. Laid rope works best with this.

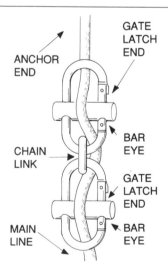

Fig. 5f. Tandem-carabiner brake-bar rig. If a carabiner is ever used as a connecting link between barred carabiners, be sure the gate is opposite the side the rope is passing over.

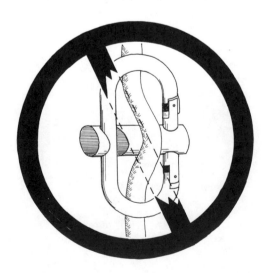

Fig. 5g. Failure mode. The rope will pull the bar away from the carabiner.

ness. To begin rappelling, the individual would push a bight of rope through the brake-barred carabiner and swing the bar shut entrapping the rope. This process was repeated for the second brake-barred carabiner.

WARNING If the rope is placed backwards, it will pop the bars open when loaded, causing a fall (Fig. 5-g). Numerous accidents and injuries have resulted from using just one bar/biner rig. Another problem which causes accidents with the rig is angled rope pressure, which when applied can cause the carabiner's gate to open, allowing the bar to slide off or the gate to bend, or both. The bars must be mounted so that the gate openings are up. The natural tendency is for the rope to pull rope and bar upwards, locking the gate and bar in place against the rest of the oval.

In a survey of U.S. cavers in 1971, it was found that 63 percent used this method of rappelling. Realization of the inherent design weaknesses of this system

the percentage has dropped to 18 as revealed in a 1986 survey. Mountaineers often use this rig as a **six-biner rappel** rig (Fig. 5-h). It may solve the problem of the brake-bar gate, but it still loads the weakest axis on the carabiner. If carabiners are used to connect the two braking carabiners, the gates should be positioned opposite the side the rope travels to avoid the possibility of the rope crossing the carabiner, depressing and opening the gate, causing complications.

SEMI-VARIABLE RAPPEL DEVICES

A semi-variable friction rappel device is one that has the ability of friction change while on rope, but only in stepped amounts with little or no variation between steps.

The **Super Rack** (Isenhart 1974) was designed to have a very strong frame and excellent heat sink properties. It has four or six massive aluminum bars with rope grooves for friction. (Fig. 5-i). Between the top bar and second bar

there are 3/4 inch spacers on the frame to prevent rope pinch as it bends around the large bars. To rig the Super Rack, swing back the two slotted bars, and place a bight of rope through the frame. Engage the first bar and remove the rope slack. Repeat this procedure for the second slotted bar. With all four bars in use at all times, the device is varied only by changing the distance between the bars. Having the spacers in place limits the variance range and control problems have been experienced by some rappellers. With the Super Rack, the spacer length is critical and as factors such as rope slickness and rappeller weight change, the friction variability of the device cannot sufficiently cope with the change. The Super Rack is super strong and a super heat sink, but because of its configuration it is only semi-variable as a rappel device.

The **Whaletail** (Wood 1967) is another semi-variable device, which works on a differ-

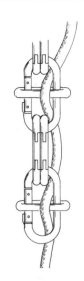

Fig. 5h. Mountaineer's six carabiner rig.

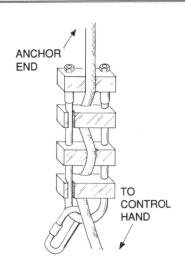

Fig. 5i. Super Rack.

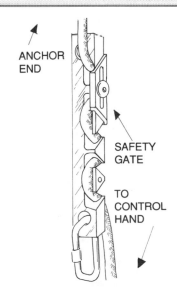

Fig. 5j. The Whaletail.

ent principle—the bars are fixed in place and only the number of bars can be changed. It is machined out of a solid aluminum bar (fig.5-j). The device is an excellent heat sink and when new the device is strong. However, with use the rope wear weakens the bar posts. Because it is machined out of a solid piece of metal, the bars are not replaceable. An essential part of the whaletail is the added safety gate. Early usage, especially on long drops, showed that the rope had a nasty habit of popping out of the device. The safety gate prevents total failure, but the possibility of the rope popping out of the gates is still cause for concern.

To use the device, slide the safety gate down and insert the rope into the slot path. Slide the gate in the opposite direction. Continue weaving the rope and reposition the gate to cover the top through the slots. To change friction on the rope, lift the rope and either place it in an angled slot or remove it from an angled slot. There is no friction adjustment other than the ability to change the number of friction points. There are several combinations of wrapping the rope around the various slots in a whaletail (Montgomery 1973) (fig.5-k).

As with any friction rappelling device, additional friction can be obtained, fined-tuned or adjusted with the control hand. If a rappeller relies too much on her control hand for control and braking the rappel, the rappel turns into a body rappel or an out-of-control rappel.

SQUEEZE BRAKES

An offshoot technology for rappelling is the squeeze brake. This device works by applying compression forces to the rope as it passes through the device. Because of the slightly uneven diameter of rope, squeeze brakes needed in addition to the compression brake, an additional method of instantaneous control. The MacGregor Squeeze brake (fig.5-j) uses a nutcracker device to apply quick compression to the rope. The Escapeline device (fig.5-m) uses a friction bend point thus becoming a hybrid device (compression and bend friction).

Pure squeeze brakes have a design problem in that they could not support a rappeller's weight if the load were to double, as might occur in a rescue situation. With Escapeline the sharp bend the rope takes when threaded through the device could control the descent, but the margins of control are minimal. The Escapeline, because of its small size and mass plus the use of a friction point, has the potential of significant

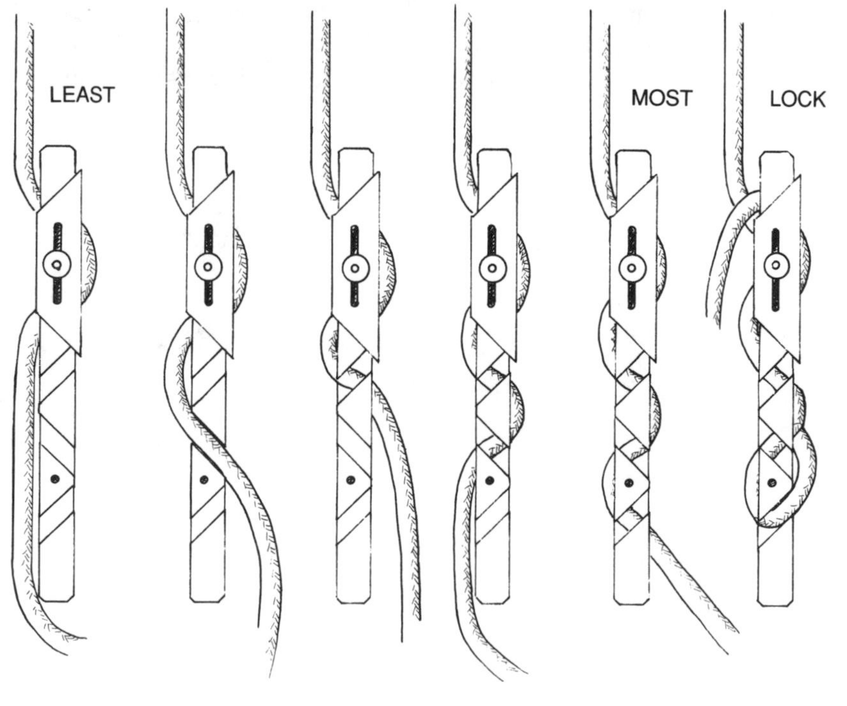

Fig. 5k. Six friction positions of the Whaletail.

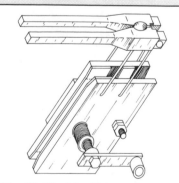

Fig. 5l. The MacGregor Squeeze Brake.

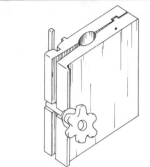

Fig. 5m. The Escapeline.

overheating on medium size (200 feet-300 feet) drops or with a heavy load. It is possible to rappel with two or three of these devices in tandem, using only one or two at a time. When one becomes overheated, simply engage a cool device and disengage the hot device.

The major unresolved question at this time is whether squeeze brakes significantly damage rope. No scientific test has been conducted, but circumstantial evidence indicates the possibility that the compression forces damage the nylon mechanically. The jury is still out. Probably more design work needs to be done on squeeze brakes and related descending devices. Studies of rope damage may make the whole technology a moot point or it may start a new way to rappel.

TOP BELAY

The use of a seperate belay line gives a back-up system to the life-supporting mainline. To be a true independent system, the belay should be rigged to a separate anchor system and tied to the climber with an independent harness. In training sessions, the top belay can be an excellent confidence builder and allow the instructor independent control of the rappeller (fig. 5-n). The training belay should be used in a carefully structured environment.

There are several serious drawbacks to the use of a top belay. Besides the extra equipment (separate rope as long as the first), it requires that someone know how to belay a falling climber. To better understand the technique of belaying, see Chapter 9. Communication between belayer and climber is essential to keep slack out of the system. However, the most serious problem related to a top belay is that of the entwining of the rappel and the belay line. This results in a climber being unable to descend due to the friction between the two ropes above him. It does not seem possible that two ropes rubbing together could create much friction; however, they are not crossed, rather entwined for their length creating a very large friction surface (fig. 5-o). This rope twist is most severe when using laid ropes, but even one turn on a braided rope on a moderate drop is sufficient to lock a rappeller in place. Even though a braided rope may be perfectly spin-free, the rappel device may

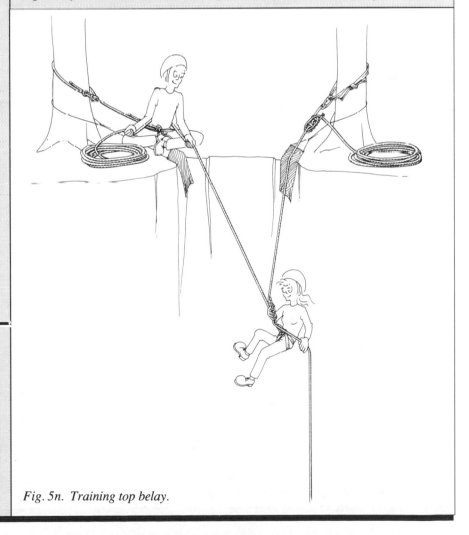

Fig. 5n. Training top belay.

track down the rope at a path that results in spin. One revolution may lock the climber in place.

What do you do if a climber becomes hopelessly entwined in the two ropes (Fig. 5p)? In the first place let's understand that the "safety" measure (belay) has developed into a victim/rescue situation. There are several options:

1. All the people at the top could pull the victim up, untangle the rope and start all over.

2. The victim could untie the belay, but chances are it is wrapped very tightly or support-ing the rappeller, in which case the victim could cut the rope. This option is extremely dangerous and should be avoided at all costs. A third rope could be lowered with a set of climbing equipment attached to it so that the rappeller could attach him/herself to the new rope, climb up a few feet, remove the tension from the first and second ropes, remove the gear from the first two ropes and finish the prusik or changeover again to a rappel and finish the drop without a belay.

Looking at the options, one could conclude that they all look very grim. The first takes man-power; the second is more than risky. Even if the rappeller is successful in removing the be-lay, he is now faced with a situation of no belay. The third option takes a lot of equipment, which may not be available, and a lot of technical know-how. It seems apparent that if the rappeller knew how to change over and change ropes, he would be experienced enough not to have used a top belay in the first place.

On a drop that is predominently against the wall to pre-

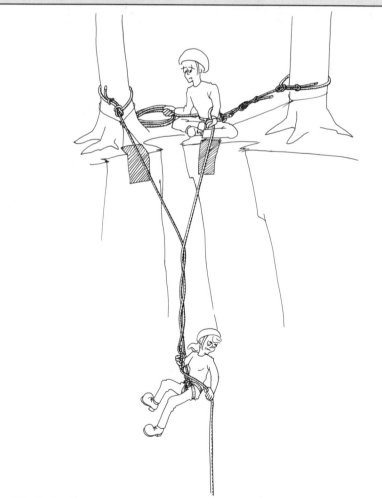

Fig. 5o. The 'safety" rope caused problems.

Fig. 5p. Rope twist or rappeller twist over a long distance generates extensive friction. Contact over the entire length of rope on a 100 ft drop will often be too much for rappeller or belayer to overcome.

another problem. As the rap-peller moves down, the belay line acts as a snowplow above him and can dislodge rocks and debris.

Trying to overcome prob-lems in a rappel-belay setup by widely separating the rappel and belay anchor points can create another hazard. If the climber's mainline breaks, instead of crashing onto the rocks below, he will be pendulumed to the side to crash into the rocks across the rock face (Fig. 5-q).

The top belay is limited in its use and application, but it is truly the only way to protect against a mainline failure. SRT evolution has ruled out the top belay as a standard practice, for it causes more problems than it pre-vents. See Chapter 9 for more on top belays.

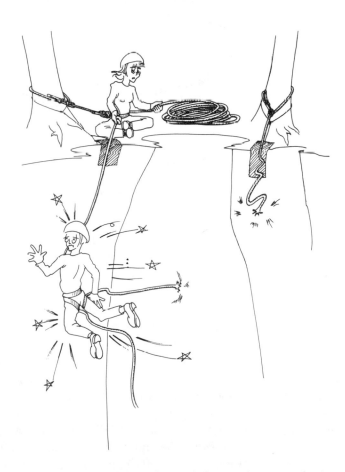

Fig. 5q. A pendulum generated from the top belay can be just as detrimental as an encounter with the rocks below.

DIAPER SEAT

Materials List

12 ft. of 2 inch Seat belt webbing. 2000 lbs. min. tensile.

1 Heavy Duty buckle. Size—1 23/32 inch quick fit adjustable cinch buckle. 2500 lbs. min tensile.

Cutting Instructions

Melt the ends of the piece of webbing with a flame or hot knife to prevent fraying.

Construction Details

1. Place webbing through the buckle off side (see the illustration). Fold the webbing back overlapping at least 6 inches.

2. Sew webbing together using longitudinal stitches. Make at least 12 passes back and forth. Be sure to use only nylon thread for both top and lower bobbins. (See illustration)

3. Thread opposite end of webbing through buckle in the manner shown and adjust to size. Back up the end of the webbing with an overhand knot.

To Use Harness

Consult the beginning of Chapter 4 for a full discussion of its proper use.

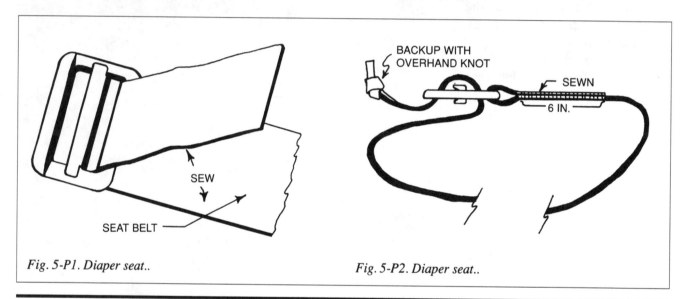

Fig. 5-P1. Diaper seat..

Fig. 5-P2. Diaper seat..

SEWN SEAT HARNESS

Materials List

12 feet of 2" seat belt webbing. (2000 lbs minimum tensile)

1 foot of 1" tubular webbing.

6 large pins or a stapler may be used during fitting.

Cutting Instructions

Cut the 1" webbing into two 6" pieces. Melt the ends to prevent fraying. Melt in such a way as to keep the ends of the tubular webbing open. No cutting of the 2" material is required prior to fabrication.

Construction Details
Fitting Process

1. Wear the clothes that will be used with the harness. Fitting is best done in a sitting position because the position while rappelling is also a sitting one.

2. Place the middle of the 2" webbing in the small of the back.

3. Wrap the webbing forward around the hips, down through the crotch and back around the legs and up over the hips.

4. The webbing should cross just in front of the hip bone with the lower part of the webbing supporting the hip/cheeks instead of the thigh.

5. Using large straight pins or a stapler, fasten these crossing points. We'll call them "A" and "A."

6. Bring the ends of the webbing inward (toward the belt buckle/belly button area).

7. Take a 1" tubular webbing piece and thread the

2" webbing through the 1" webbing. Slide this piece down to the belt buckle area. These are wear protectors for the attachment point.

8. Make a loop for the seat harness carabiner attachment point. Don't make this too long. The attachment point should be **low**. Pin or staple this crossing and repeat for the opposite side. This crossing we'll call "C" and "C'".

9. Bring the free end of the two inch webbing downward and thread it through the leg loop as close to the crotch as is comfortable.

10. Bring the free end back up toward the attachment point.

11. Pin the crossing at the leg loops. This webbing joint is called "B" and "B'", and will be three thicknesses if done properly.

12. Adjust all the pinnings for smooth angles. The attachment loops should be low. The top of the connecting carabiner (Delta Maillon) should be no higher than one's belly button.

Stitching

13. Using a temporary tacking stitch pattern begin sewing at junctions A and A'. All finished stitching should be pointed towards the strain at the seat harness carabiner attachment loops.

14. After tacking A and A', refit the harness to make sure of the angles and the comfort.

15. Temporarily tack junction B and B'. Note that these junctions are triple thick for strength. The webbing comes down from the attachment loop, across the leg loop and is passed back on the inside. Leave any excess for now in case of a fitting error.

16. Refit the harness and make sure of the angles once again.

17. Sew junctions C and C' with a diamond shaped pattern being sure to have the wear protectors inside the attachment loops. This junction is not a load bearing junction so it is not imperative to stitch it heavily. It should be sewn in such a way as to provide equal pull from junctions A and B and A' and B'.

18. Once again, refit the harness and check to see that all is correct. Pull on the attachment loops with the seat harness carabiner in place.

19. After you are sure everything fits properly, remove the harness and trim all the excess 2" webbing from junctions B and B'.

20. **FINISH THE HARNESS BY ADDING THE NECESSARY LOAD BEARING STITCHES.**

Either with an awl, harness sewing machine, or down at your local shoe cobbler, sew the A, A', B and B' seams with all the sewing talent that can be mustered. Don't neglect C and C' for if either A or B seams fail, C becomes load bearing.

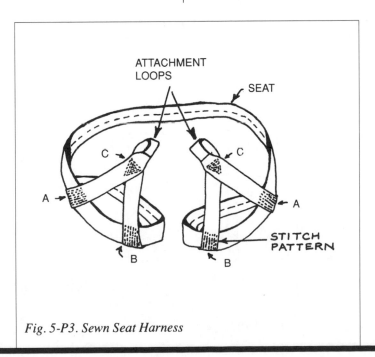

Fig. 5-P3. Sewn Seat Harness

SAFETY JUMAR

Materials list

1 handled cam ascender with one hand operation capabilities such as a Jumar, Petzl or CMI.

3 feet of 1 inch tubular webbing.

Cutting Instructions

No cutting is necessary prior to assembly. Melt the webbing ends to prevent fraying.

Construction Details

1. Loop the webbing through the eye of the ascender overlapping six inches and sew up tight to the ascender.

2. The finished length of this device can be critical to efficient climbing and during rope negotiations. It should be fitted with the seat harness on while hanging from a locked off rack suspended on a piece of rope. There should be one linking carabiner between the rack and the seat harness carabiner.

3. While hanging attach the ascender just above the rack.

4. Thread the loose end of the strap through the seat harness carabiner. Pull the 1 inch webbing tight while overlapping the webbing by at least six inches.

5. Mark the points to be sewn together with a pen, pencil stapler or large pins.

6. After removing yourself from the suspended rope, cut off any excess webbing and melt the end to prevent fraying.

7. Sew using strong nylon thread and with a longitudinal stitching patern

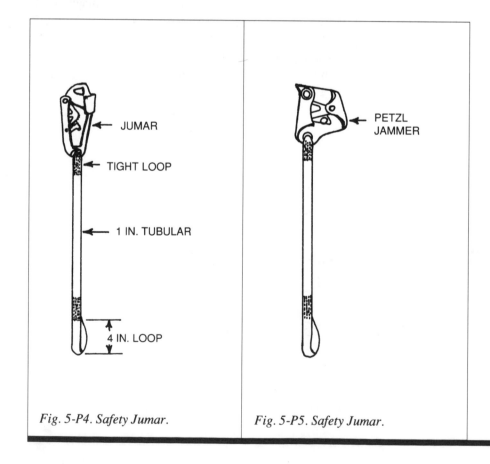

Fig. 5-P4. Safety Jumar.

Fig. 5-P5. Safety Jumar.

REFERENCES

Cole, John. "A new Rappel Device." *NSS News*, Vol. 24, No. 6, 1966, pp. 154-155.

Davison, Don. "Safety Rappel Cam." *NSS News*, Vol. 34, No. 8, 1976, pp. 140-143.

Ferber, Peggy, ed. *Mountaineering, The Freedom of the Hills*. 3rd. ed., Seattle, WA.: The Mountaineers, 1974.

Frank, James A. and Jerry Smith. "Figure Eight Descenders." *Nylon Highway 16*, NSS Vertical Section, (1983), pp. 1-4.

Howie, Wil. "In Search of a Better Seat Sling." *Nylon Highway 4*, NSS Vertical Section, (1975), p. 2.

Hudson, Steve and Toni Williams, "Using the Rappel Rack." *Nylon Highway 16*, NSS Vertical Section, (1983), pp. 5-14.

Isenhart, Kyle. "The Super Rack." *Nylon Highway 1*, NSS Vertical Section, (1975), pp. 20-23.

Isenhart, Kyle. "Temperature Studies of Rappel Devices." *Nylon Highway 4*, NSS Vertical Section, (1975), pp. 20-23.

McClurg, David. *Exploring Caves*. Harrisburg, PA., 1980.

McClurg, David. *Adventure of Caving*. Carlsbad, NM.: D & J. Press, 1986, pp 235—261.

Meredith, Mike. *Vertical Caving* Kendal, England: Westmoreland Gazette, 1980.

Montgomery, Neil. *Single Rope Techniques*. Sydney, Australia: Sydney Speleological Society, 1977.

Montgomery, Neil. "A New Look At The Whaletail Descender." *Nylon Highway 7*, NSS Vertical Section, (1977), pp. 2-7.

Padgett, Allen & Karen Padgett. "A Guide to Rappelling." *Nylon Highway 4*, NSS Vertical Section, (1977), pp. 2-5.

Padgett, Allen & Karen Padgett. "An Analysis of Vertical Caving Accidents." *Nylon Highway 17*, NSS Vertical Section, (1983), pp. 13-15.

Para-Gear Equipment Co. *Product Catalog. Number 42*, Skokie, IL.: Para-gear, 1985, pp. 112-134.

Petzl Manufacturing Co. *Technique Pamphlet*, Brignoud, France: Petzel, 1983.

Pigeon Mountain Industries Inc. *Catalog & Equipment Guide*. Lafayette, GA. PMI, 1984.

Rushin-Bell, C.J. "Selecting Brake Bars for Your Rack." *Nylon Highway 18*, NSS Vertical Section, (1984), pp. 1-3.

Sam, Uncle. *Military Mountaineering* Training Circular No. 90-6-1, Washington, DC.: Dept. of the Army, 1976.

Smith, Bruce. "Carabiner Problems." *Nylon Highway 3*, NSS Vertical Section, (1974), pp. 6-9.

Sprouse, Peter. "Figure Eight Descenders—Shop Wisely." *Nylon Highway 17*, NSS Vertical Section, (1983), pp. 6-8.

Steele, Bill. "On The Ups And Downs of Vertical Caving. "*Caving Basics*, Jerry Hassemer, Ed., Huntsville, AL.: NSS, 1982, pp. 62-67.

Storey, J. Welborn, et al. *American Caving Illustrated*, Atlanta, GA.: Dogwood City Grotto, 1965.

Vittetoe, Marion. "A Safety Hint." *Nylon Highway 17*, NSS Vertical Section, (1983), pp. 8-9.

Wood, G. A. "The Whaletail Descender." *NSS News*, Vol. 25, No. 12, 1967, pp. 215-216.

6 Prusiking

6 Prusiking

It takes a lot of effort to climb a rope. The amount of effort depends heavily on the system that one chooses to climb with and the distance that one needs to climb. Ropes have been climbed for years by simply grasping the rope and pulling oneself up it. However, this hand-over-hand technique is inefficient, requires superhuman strength over a great distance and is often closely associated with tragedy (Fig. 6-1).

Climbing a rope with a more dependable method is a more attractive option. "Prusiking", the common name for climbing a rope using grasping knots or grasping devices, involves the transfer of the climber's weight between at least two attachment points on the rope. When weight is placed on an ascender, it is possible to move another ascender or knot up the rope. By transferring one's weight to the newly positioned ascender or knot, the first ascender is free to be lifted up the rope and locked into a new position. Repeating this sequence allows upward movement. This technique makes possible the practical and safe climbing of ropes.

Each climbing system offers a different level of safety and redundancy. Many competent climbers suggest that a system incorporate three points of ascender contact. In actual use during the movement of one point, two are left to support the climber's weight. In the event of a failure of any one of the remaining two, the climber remains on the rope supported by the last locked ascender. During the discussion of each different system note the points of contact and determine which systems fall within this special umbrella of safety. These points of contact introduce the safety aspect of prusiking. See Chapter 9 for a further discussion on the third ascender.

In theory, the minimum amount of work required to raise a climber will always be equal to the energy necessary to lift a climber's weight a given distance against the force of gravity. While rappelling, friction is used to control gravity, producing heat as the energy by-product. Ascending requires the reverse of the equation; the use of energy to over-come the force of gravity. It is important for a climber to be able to apply a force downward exactly opposite the direction he desires to ascend (Fig. 6-2). Properly directing the

Fig. 6-1. Hand-over-hand is often closely associated with tragedy.

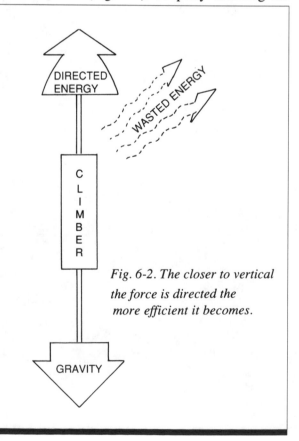

Fig. 6-2. The closer to vertical the force is directed the more efficient it becomes.

climbing force can result in minimum wasted energy. The closer to vertical a climber can direct his energy, the more efficient the climbing system.

The basic design criteria for any prusik system are:

- It must grasp the rope and allow for upward movement.
- It should enable the climber to stop and rest while on rope.
- It should use applied energy efficiently.
- It must be safe by having strength and enough compo-

nent redundancy to prevent catastrophic failure.

- It should never allow a climber to fall or invert.

SIT-STAND CLIMBING SYSTEMS

Classic 3-Knot Climbing System

To meet these criteria two basic prusik methods have evolved, the sit-stand method and the ropewalker systems. The earliest climbing system that met the de-

sign criteria was the **classic 3-knot** climbing system (a sit-stand method). To hold the rope, a self-tightening knot was used called a Prusik knot (after Dr. Karl Prusik who described it in 1931). This knot wrapped around the main climbing rope and slid up or down the rope until tension was applied to the trailing knot cords. At this point it would grasp the rope and lock into place. A system was fashioned whereby the climber could **sit** while hanging from a chest knot, and then move two independent foot knots up the

Fig. 6-3a. Standing in the two foot loops while hanging from chest prusik. 6b: While supported upright by chest, one leg prusik is advanced. 6c: Second leg prusik is advanced bringing us back to beginning again. 6d:Kick heels inward and stand. 6e: Quickly move top knot upward.

	HOLDING ABILITY	UPWARD MOVEMENT EASE	ATTACHMENT TO ROPE EASE	EASE OF INSPECTION	STAYS ON ROPE	STRENGTH	WEARABILITY	REPLACEMENT PARTS AVAILABLE	WORKS IN MUD	WORKS ON ICY ROPES	SIZE	ACCEPTS VARIED ROPE SIZES	DOWNCLIMB ABILITY
PRUSIK KNOT	◇	▽	▽	△	▲	▲	▽	Y	▽	▽	▲	▲	◇
PRUSIK KNOT EXTRA WRAP	△	▼	▽	△	▲	▲	▽	Y	◇	▼	▲	▲	▽
ASCENDER KNOT	▽	△	▽	▽	▲	△	▽	Y	△	▼	▲	▲	△
GIBBS	▲	▲	▽	△	▲	△	△	Y	▲	△	◇	△	▼
GIBBS SPRING LOADED	▲	▲	▽	△	▲	△	△	Y	▲	△	◇	△	▼
JUMAR YELLOW	▲	▲	▲	▲	▲	△	△	Y	◇	▽	▽	▲	▲
JUMAR OLD GRAY	▲	▲	▲	▲	▲	◇	◇	Y	◇	▽	▽	△	▲
PETZL JAMMER	▲	△	▲	▲	▲	◇	◇	N	◇	▽	◇	△	△
PETZL EXPEDITION	▲	▲	▲	▲	▲	◇	◇	N	◇	▽	▽	△	△
PETZL CROLL	▲	▲	▲	▲	▲	◇	◇	N	◇	▽	◇	△	△
CMI 5000 SERIES	▲	▲	◇	▲	▲	◇	△	Y	◇	▽	▽	△	◇
CMI SHORTI	▲	△	◇	▲	▲	◇	△	Y	◇	▼	▽	▲	◇
BONAITI HANDLED	▲	▲	▲	▲	▲	▼	◇	N	◇	▽	▽	△	◇
CLOG BASIC	▲	△	▲	▲	▲	◇	◇	N	◇	▽	◇	△	◇
CLOG EXPEDITION	▲	▲	▲	▲	▲	◇	◇	N	◇	▽	◇	△	◇
SALEWA HEIBLER	▲	△	▲	◇	▼	▼	▽	N	▲	▲	△	△	◇
PETZL SHUNT	◇	△	▽	◇	◇	▽	◇	N	◇	◇	△	▼	△

Chart 6-1 Ascenders

▲	EXCELLENT
◮	VERY GOOD
◇	GOOD
▽	FAIR
▼	POOR
Y	YES
N	NO

ASCENDERS

The ideal ascender device will hold the rope tightly when loaded and easily release when desired. Good ascenders should slide up a rope effortlessly. They should also easily move down a rope when desired. Their attachment to the rope should be easy, take place quickly, and be obvious if attached incorrectly. A good ascender should be strong, resist wear and those parts that do wear, should have available replacement parts. They should be able to function under adverse conditions such as mud, ice or subzero temperatures. Being lightweight and compact are desirable features. Another desirable feature is an ascender's ability to accept a wide range of rope sizes. It is always helpful if the cost is reasonable, however as with other specialized equipment, ascenders can be expensive.

COMPARISON CHART DISCLAIMER

Any rating or comparison is at best an educated opinion. Differing levels of familiarity with an item or differing applications can result in an entirely different rating score. The criteria used and the items rated are intended simply to show general opinions about these items. There will always exist isolated exceptions, and it is the author's intent to avoid such "believe-it-or-not" discussion.

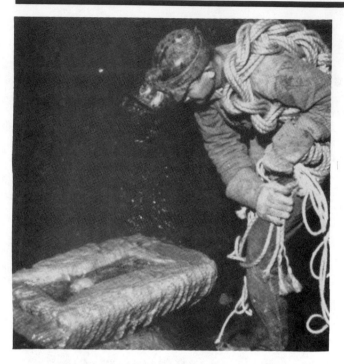

Fig. 6-4. Bill Cuddington was a significant influence during the vertical caving developmental years. (From Caves of Tennessee, *by T.C. Barr, Jr. Used with permission.)*

too long, while their associated harnesses were painfully uncomfortable. Comfortable chest harnesses were later developed. Some climbers have chosen to connect the chest harness to the seat sling to make sitting more comfortable (Fig. 6-5). See the workshop project 6-1 at the end of this chapter for proper system fabrication.

Prusik Knots Must Hold Properly

Variations on the gripping knot make the system more versatile. The standard Prusik knot (Fig. 6-6) has several factors that influence its holding ability. The smaller the diameter of the prusik cord in comparison to the mainline diameter, the better the knot will hold. By using "slick" material for a knot sling, efficient tightening and loosening can be achieved. Polypropylene, for example, has the ability to conform to the shape of the main line while grasping it tightly and will release easily because of its slippery nature. Stiffer rope makes knots that are easier to loosen and slide, while supple rope tightens and grabs better. The knot material needs to be non-stretch so that the climbing knot will not contract and tighten, which

rope, **stand** and move the chest knot up the rope. Repeating the cycle accomplishes ascent (fig. 6-3).

This system, popularized by Bill Cuddington in 1952 (Fig. 6-4) for exploring deep caves, spread throughout the cave exploring world. Prior to this innovation, all vertical work was done by block and tackle hauling, or simple hauling without the aid of mechanical advantages and ladders. The sheer bulk and weight of block and tackle rigs as well as the bulk of ladders became a significant limiting factor in the successful exploration of deep caves. Bill Cuddington and explorers like him, took readily to rappelling and prusiking with its comparative minimal gear requirements. See Chapter 13 for a more complete history of North American ropework. The National Speleological Society, formed in 1941, provided an organization to help spread the new climbing technology through its publications and national meetings.

The classic 3-knot system is the standard of comparison for all other ascending rigs. It is still a popular and useful system—a testimony to its functional ability. As with any system, refinements have been made. Early descriptions showed Prusik knot slings entirely

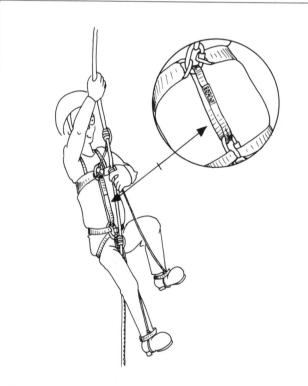

Fig. 6-5. A short tether between chest girth and seat harness makes sitting and resting more comfortable.

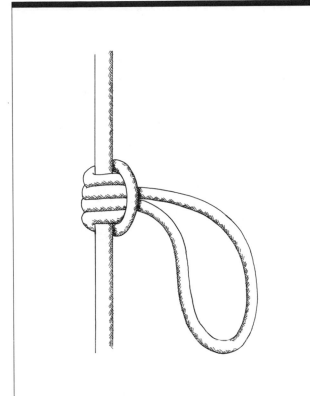

Fig. 6-6. Standard Prusik knot.

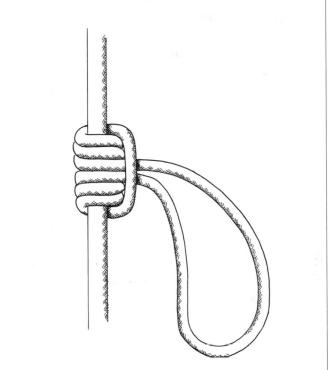

Fig. 6-7. An extra wrap can provide additional holding power.

would prevent its loosening and ultimate movement upward. To achieve more holding power, additional wraps can be added (Fig. 6-7).

Breaking a Prusik Knot

Breaking a knot describes the loosening of that knot. To move a Prusik knot properly and with efficiency, the correct grip is important (Fig. 6-8). After lifting all weight from the knot, move the hand that is going to break the knot (breaking hand) toward the knot. First, grasp the sling with the ring and little fingers and push the sling cords inward slightly. Almost at the same time, pull on the bar portion (called thumbing the knot) of the knot. These two actions should open the knot so that by bringing the middle and index fingers together under the barrel portion of the knot and lifting upward, knot movement can easily be achieved.

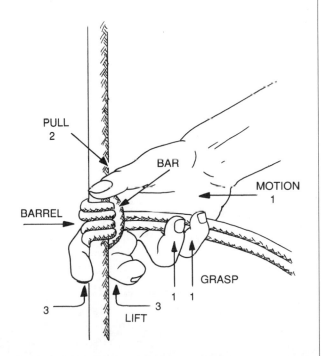

Fig. 6-8. One method of breaking and moving a Prusik knot. 1). Push the rope into the knot. 2). Pull the bar—called thumbing the bar. 3). Grasp and lift the knot.

CABLE LADDERS

Cable ladders, long the standard method of ascending all pits, still have their uses. Ladders are an excellent technique for moving a large group of people up and down a small drop. They are also useful for certain awkward climbs too tight for prusik systems.

All ladder work requires the use of a standard top belay or self-lining procedure. When using a ladder the belay line should always be a static line.

Using a ladder requires practice and technique (Fig.6a-d).

Though the basic idea of climbing a ladder is simple, the details and finer points come with research and instruction. For further information, consult many of the fine European publications such as *Caving Practice and Equipment* by David Judson.

The sheer bulk of laddering equipment precludes its use in extensive vertical systems. Rolls of metal ladders plus coils of belay rope convince small groups to consider other methods of pit negotiation.

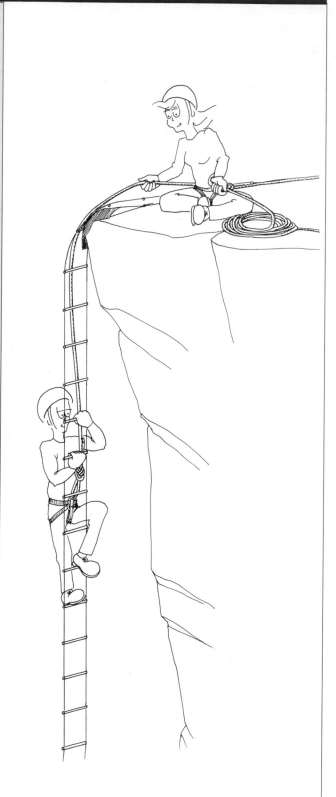

Fig. 6a. Ladder climbing requires a belay and proper body positioning on the ladder.

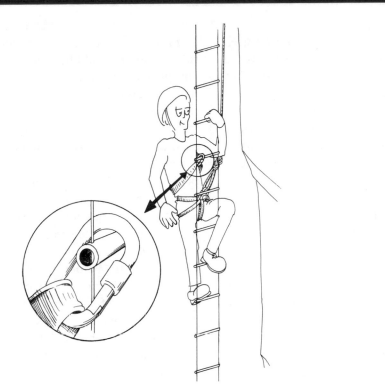

Fig. 6c. Clip carabiner around both cable and rung when resting.

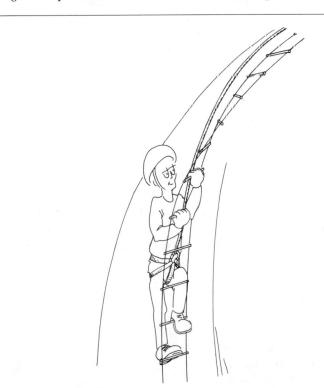

Fig. 6b. Self lining has many advantages: faster, uses less rope, reduced communications, doesn't depend on belayers's skill.

Fig. 6d. When against a wall, rotate ladder 90° to give climbing clearance between ladder and wall.

Ascender Knot

A different knot commonly used in the classic 3-knot system is the Ascender Knot (Fig. 6-9). This knot has several advantages over the traditional Prusik knot, such as: it is easier to move and wraps can be added or subtracted without removing the sling from your harness. This knot almost breaks itself when lifted upward. This makes it much easier to move upward than the standard Prusik knot, although it remains somewhat more difficult to tie.

There are at least three parts of the knot that need careful attention. First, the correct number of wraps necessary to tightly hold the main rope must be incorporated. Second, the correct amount of slack must be left between the wraps and the tie-off knot. Experience has shown that minimal slack is best. Finally the ascender knot should be tied off using a proper knot, usually a version of a bowline. Perfecting these three knot criteria requires experience and patience. For slippery muddy rope, extra wraps can be added.

The one caution with ascender knots is to avoid any downward pressure on the top of the knot (Fig. 6-10). Pressure from above will open the knot and allow it to slide down the rope. If it contacts another knot below it as it is sliding, it too will open and begin sliding. Tragedy could result.

Sling Wear

As with any rope sling a caution about wear is necessary. This is especially important in prusik slings that are continually slid up ropes. Any climber using the clas-

sic 3-knot system should carry an extra sling at all times. A rough rule of thumb would be to replace any prusik sling when 20 percent of the fibers are worn. The life of climbing knot slings can be extended by moving the wear point each time the sling is tied. Reducing sling wear can be achieved by perfecting the knot breaking motion and moving the slings properly. Forcefully jamming knots up the rope will shorten sling life.

Novices can be especially rough on slings before the proper technique is learned. If using 1 inch webbing for foot stirrups, doubling up on the webbing will avert excessive abrasion. Careful inspection of all slings before and after use is highly recommended. With any method of climbing, chicken loops are a must. See the sidebar on chicken loops.

Many climbers find that a useful adaptation of the classic-3 knot system is to substitute a mechanical ascender for the top knot. The hybrid system adds ease in upward movement, less hassle in moving the top knot, and the ascender does not wear out like a prusik knot.

The classic 3-knot sit-stand climbing method brought about many other versions that have proven functional and reliable.

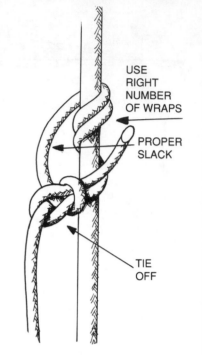

Fig. 6-9. Ascender knot needs proper number of wraps, proper slack, and proper tie off.

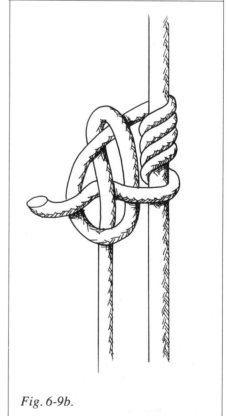

Fig. 6-9b.

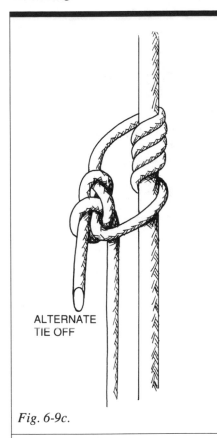

ALTERNATE
TIE OFF

Fig. 6-9c.

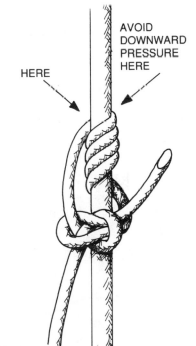

AVOID
DOWNWARD
PRESSURE
HERE

HERE

Fig. 6-10. Downward pressure on the top can cause the knot to slide down even if weight is on it.

Texas System

The Texas System is a very basic climbing system utilizing only two knots or ascenders (Fig. 6-11). The top ascender is rigged off the seat sling. This ascender often doubles for the earlier mentioned safety Jumar. The climber should be balanced from his hips. This allows the climber to lift his legs together without needing superhuman abdominal strength.

A variation of the Texas climbing system often utilizes only one foot sling to the lower ascender (Fig. 6-12). This allows the unattached leg to be swung forward when standing thus balancing the center of gravity and allowing efficient vertical movement. The free leg also becomes the body's wall feeler and during a climb is often used to properly position the body against walls or faces so as to avoid unwanted swinging or loss of balance.

Note: The strap lengths for the Texas System are often the same length as many found in more complicated climbing systems such as the Mitchell System. If a failure should occur in one of the ropewalking systems, it is often easy to salvage the components and rig up a simple Texas System and finish the ascent.

Texas Sling Lengths

The stand-up motion during a Texas climb can be tiresome, in that one leg often does all the lifting and the stomach and back muscles must work together to attain efficient progress. When lifting the upper ascender it is important that the elbow remain snug against the side of the climber's body (Fig. 6-13). The additional strain on the climber's shoulder muscles necessary to push an ascender a little bit higher is not worth the effort. The critical length of the upper ascender is such that it can be moved up the rope while the climber is balanced without allowing slack when the balance is lost.

The upper ascender has additional length requirements as well. It should be long enough to reach over the top of a rappelling device to effect a changeover. A standard rack is 14 inches long and if attached to a seat harness must not end up higher than the attachment point of the upper ascender.

A problem with many commercial harnesses is that they will not allow a low enough attachment point on the body to satisfy all the variables. The attachment point needs to be between the climber's waist and crotch. Any attachment above the waist as those found in REI's, some Petzl harnesses, Troll's, Robertson's and others are designed for rock climbing and are inappropriate for single rope techniques if one desires to have a multi-purpose seat harness and do more than just rappel.

The lower ascender's length will determine the upper movement for each cycle. The shorter the lower sling(s), the greater the possible distance during each cycle. Fourteen to 18 inches per cycle is considered a good stroke. Body length and leg length all enter into this sling's length and the best way to determine it properly is to get on a rope and climb using

CHICKEN LOOPS

In the event of a failure of one part of any climbing rig, the remaining parts must remain securely fastened to the climber. If an upper attachment point fails, the system will be shock loaded as the climber drops or inverts. It is essential that the foot attachment points remain attached. Chicken loops, as they have come to be known, prevent the foot loops from coming off of the foot. There are two basic methods of chicken looping. First is a endless sewn loop or sling that is placed around the climber's ankles before the climber's boots are put on. The loop should be snug over socked feet. The climbing stirrup runs inside this loop (Fig.6-e). A variation on the sewn loop is the Ganter loop which utilizes a Rapide link (Fig.6-f). The second is to sew a chicken loop onto the foot loop assembly (Fig.6-g). Then after the foot is inserted into the foot loop, the chicken loop is tightened. It is important that the buckle be heavy duty enough to take the possible shock loads of a falling climber. Realize the dual function of the chicken loop. It does keep the foot stirrups on the climber's feet while climbing, but even more, it acts as a safety for the climbing system. A third chicken loop design is the Smart loop where by an endless loop is secured to the climbing stirrup, around the ankle and around over the ascender. As soon as the ascender is secured to the rope, the Smart loop acts as a redundancy feature of the foot stirrup (Fig.6-h). The cinch-knot foot loop will not act as a back up in the event of failure. If a climber becomes inverted, the knot and/or boot will simply snap off the foot (Fig.6-i). To be effective, the chicken loop must remain snug behind the heel and must be in use on each and every ascent.

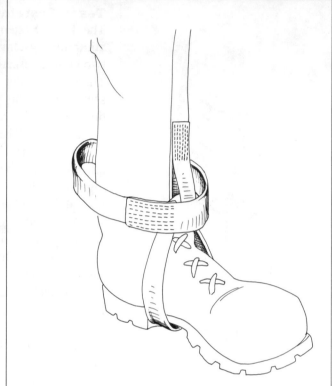

Fig. 6e. Sewn chicken loop.

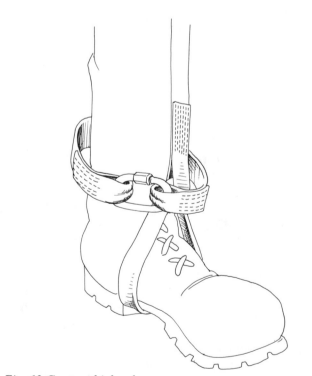

Fig. 6f. Ganter chicken loop.

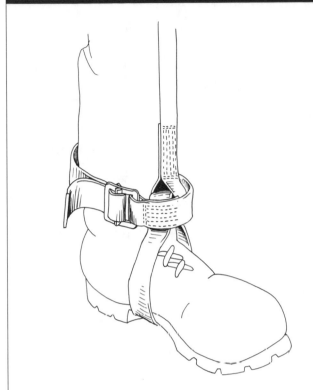

Fig. 6g. Chicken loop sewn onto foot loop assembly.

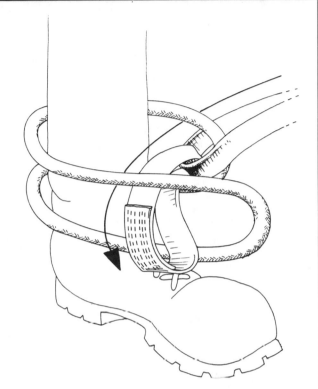

Fig. 6h. The Smart loop has many attractive features.

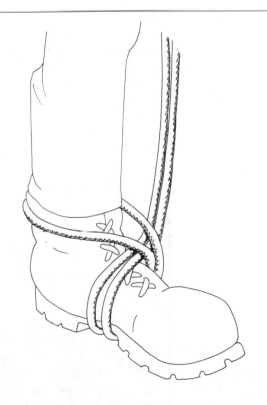

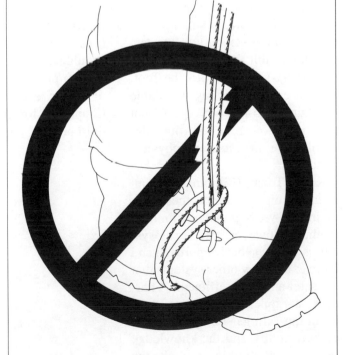

Fig. 6i. Cinch knot chicken loop—proper way and improper way to secure.

Fig. 6-11a. Texas Prusiking. While sitting in seat harness, grasp the main rope below lower knot.

Fig. 6-11b. Raise the lower knot.

Fig. 11-c. Standing up and pulling the top knot up at the same time is difficult to master at first.

an ascender with adjustable sling lengths. There was a small school of Texas high steppers in the late 1960s that felt the lower ascender should be very close to the foot. During each cycle they were able to attain 4 to 5 feet of progress, but this variation required that the climber be in excellent physical condition.

The Texas Climbing System, because of its compactness, remains a very popular climbing method. However, the Texas system is simply a basic approach and there exist many other systems that are safer and more efficient. A harness, a rappel device, two short climbing slings complete with chicken loops, and the knowledge of knots and climbing can take the vertically oriented person any-

where he wishes to go. It should be noted that the Texas System only uses two points of contact and should be tethered to the seat harness to prevent heel hang in case of upper ascender failure. See Chapter 9 for the addition of a third point of climbing contact.

HIEBLER ASCENDERS

Hieblers are early European-made mechanical ascenders (Fig.6-j). Over the years they have been the cause of many "hits and near misses." The most glaring problem with Hieblers is that the same motion you use to move the clamp upward is also used for removing it from the rope. The two motions differ only by a slight twist. Climbers have inadvertently removed the ascender from the rope while ascending. Other problems also exist:

• The rope has been known to come out from between the cam surfaces when weight is applied (the chances are likely that the the rope was not completely in the ascender before the weight was applied).

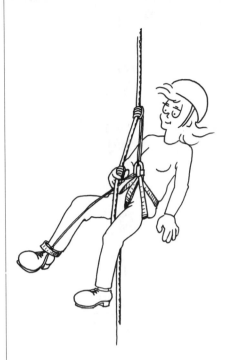

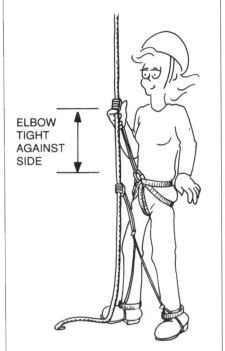

Fig. 6-11d. Completely raise the knot as high as it will go. Sit back down and you're ready to begin again.

Fig. 6-12. Many Texas prusikers prefer just one foot ascender.

Fig. 6-13 Shoulder fatigue can occur quickly if the upper Texas sling is too long so that it allows the ebow to move away the from climbers side.

- The ascender was modified with a paper clip-size wire safety gate, which didn't prove to be practical
- The pivot pin seems to be the weakest part of the ascender and has failed at as little as 450 pounds.
- Because of the large arm pivot there is a lot of wasted motion.

On the positive side, since the clamp functions by squeezing and bending the rope, Hieblers will work when it seems nothing else will. They work extremely well on ice and mud if you can keep them on the rope. Hieblers should only be used by careful, experienced climbers and even then with appropriate backup ascenders attached to the rope.

Fig. 6j. The Hiebler has proven to be somewhat problematic.

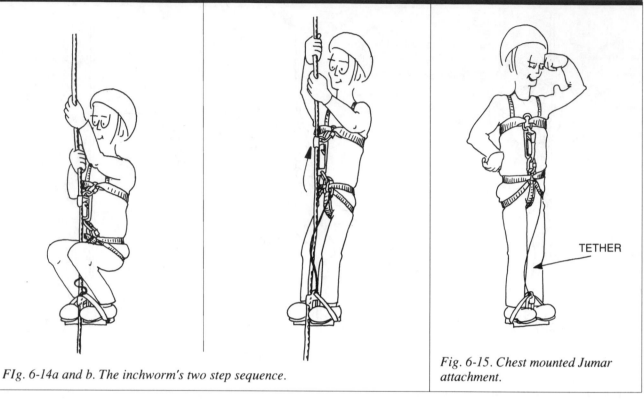

FIg. 6-14a and b. The inchworm's two step sequence.

Fig. 6-15. Chest mounted Jumar attachment.

TETHER

Inchworm

The inchworm method was developed by Charles Townsend and popularized by Pete Strickland. It uses the large muscles of the legs to power the upward movement (Fig. 6-14). The system consists of a chest-mounted ascender fixed in place both top and bottom (Fig. 6-15) and a bar-mounted ascender (Fig. 6-16), called a Mar-bar, to give the climber a step platform.

The climbing motion consists of a stand-up motion, setting the top ascender and then lifting both legs up the rope. The climber's position is nearly vertical, rendering the system very efficient in energy conservation and upward movement. It does require some abdominal strength to lift the legs, but they are being drawn directly upward so abdominal bending is not needed. An advantage to the inchworm system is that the arms are generally not needed and are

free for other tasks.

To pass lips or overhangs, the arms simply push the upper body away from the rocks and the lower ascender is pulled over by foot pressure and a pull on the tether strap. The tether strap is the back-up system to keep the climber attached in the event of an upset. The Mar-bar does not have chicken loops, which allows the climber to step out of it and reattach it above an obstacle or ledge. An easy chin-up will pull the climber up over the obstacle. The tether line should always remain securely tied to the seat harness (Fig. 6-17). Any failure with the upper ascender will result in one hanging from the Mar-bar and an easy recovery. Chapter 9 discusses a third point of ascending contact.

Portly Prusik

Designed for the overweight climber, the portly prusik system utilizes a shoulder mounted ascender to help balance the heavy climber and a double-footed sling that allows the climber to use all the available leg strength (Fig. 6-18). This system would also allow a physically fit climber carrying or hauling a heavy load to effectively move this load up a rope. A benefit for the out-of-shape climber is that the rig is comfortable to rest in. This system is the back-up mode for a Gibbs ropewalker system that experiences foot-cam failure.

Bill Cuddington, noted vertical caver, states that he and his associates have had success getting overweight people up a rope using a ropewalker method with Gibbs when a Simmons roller and chest plate are incorporated into the system. These ropewalker methods will be discussed later in this chapter.

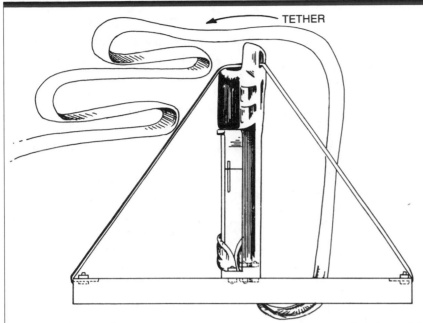

TETHER

Fig. 6-16. A Mar-Bar is constructed with a sturdy step plate and a piece of 1 inch webbing stretched between the two ends of the step plate and through the lower hole of the Jumar. A tether strap made of 1 inch webbing should be fastened securely to the climber's seat harness.

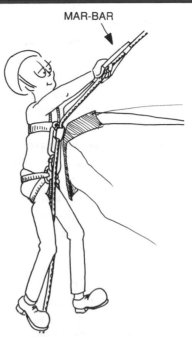

MAR-BAR

Fig. 6-17. Difficult lips can be easily maneuvered past using the Mar-Bar as a chin-up bar.

SPUD

Fig. 6-18. Portly prusik, an excellent system when it becomes necessary to get very large people up a rope.

LARGE-CHESTED WOMEN

The amply endowed woman faces a problem in ropework. Large breasts, besides getting in the way, upset the balance of the climber. The systems that work best are those that allow the rope to follow a path between the breasts. The Simmons Roller-Gibbs rig is useful, as is a sit-stand system where the rope tracks up the middle. Caution is advised to keep ascenders from gripping baggy clothes or flesh. While rappelling, the large chested woman may find balance a problem. Attempting to keep close to the rope is the very activity that can cause clothes and flesh to snag in a rappel device. Be extra cautious.

Frog System

The frog system best gives the maneuverability required by the intricate rigging styles of European cavers. As a sit-stand system, it allows the foot ascender to be moved above the chest ascender to pass obstacles. With the frog system, it is important to move the heels inward before standing to bring the body into a more vertical plane to increase efficiency. The length of the foot sling attached above the chest ascender tends to make the system an inefficient energy user. The system also requires a tether line from the foot ascender to the seat harness as a back-up safety. If this tether is the proper length of an upper Texas ascender (safety Jumar length), it will only afford about six to 14 inches per cycle.

Fig. 19a. Frog system, the dominant climbing system used by Europeans.

Getting started seems to be somewhat difficult, but about 40 feet or so off the floor the system works well (Fig. 6-19). Getting started can be facilitated by trapping the rope with the feet just prior to standing up. This will prevent the rope from riding up with the chest ascender. The Europeans augment the system with two cow's-tails that are utilized to maneuver past reanchor points. The ability to pass reanchor points is a key feature of this system. Even though the system is heavy, bulky and relatively slow, it is an essential part of the European style of ropework and has become the dominant climbing system used by an entire continent.

ROPEWALKING SYSTEMS

Ropewalking systems are named for the motion necessary to make them work. Unlike the somewhat choppy sit-stand methods, a ropewalker need only stand and walk up the rope utilizing his legs to accomplish most of the work. It's quite similar to the motion used to climb stairs.

Jumar System

The first ropewalking system was a 1960 Jumar rig shown on the instruction papers included with the ascenders. Though crude, many people began to use this system. The two Jumars (or other handled ascenders) are attached to long foot slings that pass behind a chest sling, or through a chest harness carabiner to keep the climber upright. As with many of the current systems, the main rope does not pass through the chest harness.

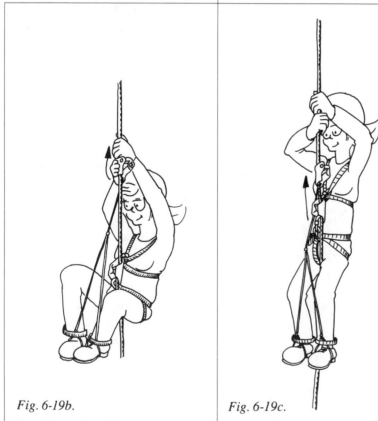

Fig. 6-19b.

Fig. 6-19c.

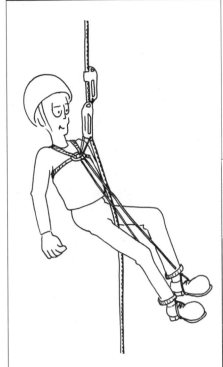

Fig. 6-20. The original Jumar system left the climber hanging at an uncomfortable angle.

ing the knees and standing erect for a few moments. This only rests some muscles but continues to tax others. Finally, you could crouch down in a fetal position and rest.

This early Jumar rig has a significant safety drawback in that there are only two attachments to the rope. If the chest sling fails, the climber inverts and swings a long way from the ascenders attached above (Fig. 6-21). Also, with the seat safety Jumar as long as it must be, modification of the system into a sit-stand back-up rig is inconvenient.

The system has several drawbacks. Due to the chest sling or chest harness carabiner being high, the weight of the climber swings underneath, resulting in a loss of efficiency (Fig. 6-20), as the climber is not standing up straight. The two long slings also restrict the step length, for the lower sling bumps into the upper sling during each step cycle. The step cycle also becomes awkward, for it seems as if one leg is constantly doing all the work while the other plays catch-up. Resting can be achieved any one of three ways. Probably the best way is to attach a third Jumar with a relatively long sling to your seat harness and attach it to the rope above the uppermost Jumar. You only need to sit down. A second resting method can be achieved by lock-

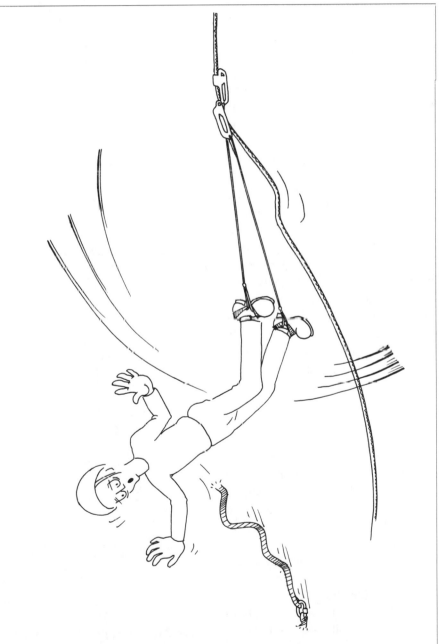

Fig. 6-21. A chest harness failure would cause the climber to invert leaving him a great distance from his ascenders.

Mitchell System

The Mitchell system, the second major Jumar system to appear, was first developed and written about by Dick Mitchell in 1967. It modified the early Jumar system and cured many of its problems (Fig. 6-22). By passing the main rope through a high chest harness the climber is held in a more efficient vertical climbing position. Sling and ascender arrangements (any handled ascenders work with this system) allowed the legs to climb in a more natural way, similar to that of climbing stairs. In the event of an upper sling failure the lower ascender merely jams into the ascender box arresting any possible fall (Fig. 6-23). See Chapter 9 for tether attachments that will prevent upset. The Mitchell system is the fastest and best climbing system ever developed using Jumars. Resting can be accomplished by using a safety Jumar or by standing up and locking the knees. This is somewhat more restful than the early Jumar system because the rope is attached to the chest harness and the climber tends to hang more vertically.

The original Mitchell system used a chest harness consisting of two inch webbing and a carabiner. The main rope and upper sling were passed through the carabiner (Fig. 6-24). This was convenient but resulted in a great deal of friction entering the system, along with a loss of efficiency. Some climbers used a webbing strap with an adjusting buckle, but they soon discovered that nylon slings rubbing on nylon straps abrade at an alarming rate.

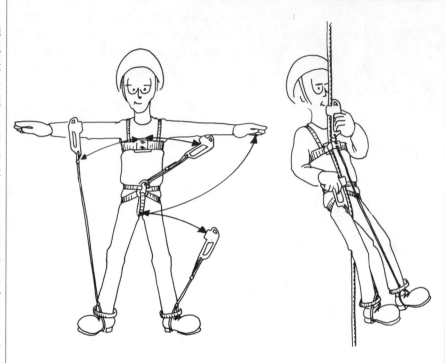

FIg. 6-22a, b. Mitchell System. Proper sling lengths can provide a very efficient climbing system. The Mitchell System is sometimes called Phase One.

Fig. 6-23. If the upper sling fails, the lower ascender jams into the box arresting the fall.

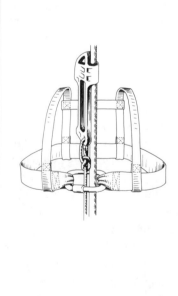

Fig. 6-24. The original Mitchell System chest harness used a carabiner.

THE MITCHELL SYSTEM PHASES

In the late 1960s and early 1970s Bill Cuddington used and preached the three-phase Mitchell climbing system. Sling lengths are critical for all phases.

Phase One This is the primary Mitchell System (Fig.6-22a). It is useful on drops longer than 50 feet. It is considered an efficient way to climb. It can be quickly rigged and derigged. On drops of less than 50 feet, it becomes inefficient because of the time it often takes to put on and take off the chest box (See Fig. 6-22b).

Phase Two. By using the lower Jumar and seat sling Jumar (safety Jumar), a secondary system can be utilized. This is none other than the Texas System and uses a sit-stand motion (Fig.6m) to make it work. To change from Phase One to Phase Two on rope, you may need to switch the foot Jumar from the left foot to the right to take advantage of a stronger leg. Phase Two is excellent for short drops or a difficult lip. Phase Two can be relied upon as a back-up if an ascender box or an upper Jumar sling fails. Phase Two makes the rig redundantly safe

Phase Three. In Phase Three, the ascender box is not used The safety Jumar is attached to the long upper Jumar sling just below the Jumar. This attachment allows you to vary the limit of your backward lean. The Third Phase is best used on slopes of 60° to 85° which are often encountered at the top of drops, mountain slopes and building roofs (Fig.6n). On a long phase three climb, the long upper Jumar sling must be shortened with a carabiner wrap so that a good advance can be achieved with each step.

Ascender Box

The next step in the system's evolution was the elimination of this friction point. The ascender box, which was first developed by Keith Wilson in 1969, was inserted into the chest harness in place of the carabiner, allowing the ropes and slings to roll over the independent roller wheels, reducing friction (Fig. 6-25). It is important that the box ride as high on the chest as possible so that the climber maintains a vertical orientation. There are many commercial designs available (See chart 6-2), most of which have originated with the home machinist. The ascender box may require some maintenance prior to use.

Begin by examining the box closely and eliminate any and all sharp edges from the ascender box with a file and emery cloth as this piece of equipment is a central control and attachment point for many pieces of rope and webbing. The tightening bolts on the standard Blue Water Box should be checked for wear, as gritty ropes tend to abrade the bolt shafts. To eliminate this problem, a thin piece of tubing (metal or hard plastic) can be fitted over the bolt shafts to act as a protector and as an internal roller wheel (Fig. 6-26). To prevent wing-nut loss after the rig is assembled, take a hammer and lightly peen the ends of the tightening bolts. For any ascender box designs, periodic disassembly and cleaning is warranted, especially if muddy conditions have been encountered.

With any Mitchell system rig, it is important to use the proper upper sling material and replace it as wear occurs, as it wears four times faster than the lower sling.

Fig. 6m. Phase Two can be recognized as the Texas System.

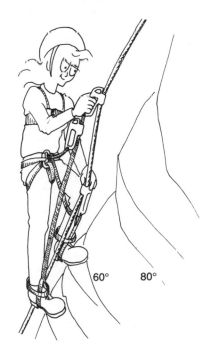

Fig. 6n. Phase Three uses all three ascenders. Best on sloped walls.

The best material is 5/16 inch or 3/8 inch static nylon rope that has a high abrasion resistance. Do not use polypropylene ropes or any rope not suited to endure abrasion. At times, this sling rope is subjected to extreme wear. Webbing is not recommended, as it tends to jam in some boxes, won't work in many others, can stretch, or can catch in the teeth of the lower Jumar during actual use. Pre-shrinking webbing and rope by soaking or washing them prior to rig fabrication will assure a good fit. When measuring climbing slings be sure to measure them with tension on the slings to ensure accurate sewing or tying. It is also best to have the upper ascender very close to the top of the box when both feet are together as shown in Fig. 6-22. The lower Jumar/ascender needs to be within

reaching distance and should be pulled up with a finger (Fig. 6-27).

Jumars have proven best as the lower ascender because of the ease in which the cam may be released with the thumb. See Fig. 6-38. This facilitates not only ascending off the bottom when there is no tension below on the rope, but also aids downclimbing, which becomes necessary from time to time.

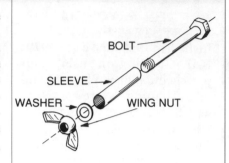

Fig. 6-26. Blue Water chest box modifications.

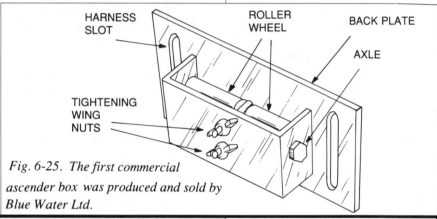

Fig. 6-25. The first commercial ascender box was produced and sold by Blue Water Ltd.

THE GOSSETT SYSTEM

A modification of the 1960 Jumar method is the Gossett System (Fig.6-o). Incorporating a well manufactured ascender box (See Fig.6-p), the Gossett System differs from the Mitchell System in that the ascender box is worn at or just above the waist. Both Jumars ride above the box. By having the box tight around the waist it is possible to hold the rope much closer to the climber. Chest harnesses tend to be loose because of chest expansion and contraction, causing the climber to hang 10° to 30° from vertical. On the other hand, with the box attached to the midsection, the climber tends to feel unstable. People heavy in the upper body should avoid this rig, for it may leave the climber hanging upside down. A climber with a back-

pack could easily wind up in the same situation. Because of the tenuous balance of the system, any climber using this method should be thoroughly familiar with the more traditional Mitchell System.

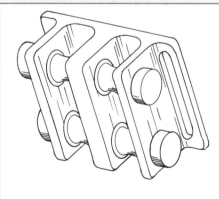

Fig. 6p. The Gossett box is a rugged, finely tooled chext box.

Fig. 6o. Gossett system features a waist level ascender box.

COMPARISON CHART DISCLAIMER

Any rating or comparison is at best an educated opinion. Differing levels of familiarity with an item or differing applications can result in an entirely different rating score. The criteria used and the items rated are intended simply to show general opinions about these items. There will always exist isolated exceptions, and it is the author's intent to avoid such "believe-it-or-not" discussion.

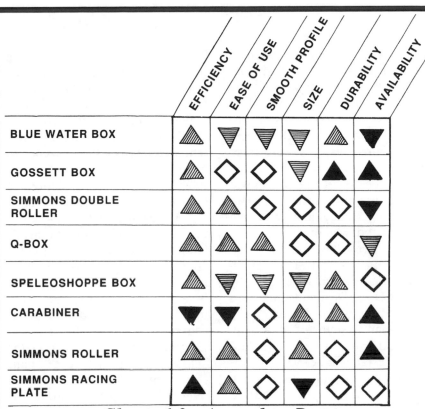

	EFFICIENCY	EASE OF USE	SMOOTH PROFILE	SIZE	DURABILITY	AVAILABILITY
BLUE WATER BOX	VERY GOOD	FAIR	FAIR	FAIR	VERY GOOD	POOR
GOSSETT BOX	VERY GOOD	GOOD	GOOD	FAIR	EXCELLENT	EXCELLENT
SIMMONS DOUBLE ROLLER	VERY GOOD	VERY GOOD	GOOD	GOOD	GOOD	FAIR
Q-BOX	VERY GOOD	VERY GOOD	VERY GOOD	GOOD	GOOD	FAIR
SPELEOSHOPPE BOX	VERY GOOD	FAIR	FAIR	FAIR	VERY GOOD	GOOD
CARABINER	POOR	POOR	GOOD	VERY GOOD	VERY GOOD	EXCELLENT
SIMMONS ROLLER	VERY GOOD	VERY GOOD	GOOD	VERY GOOD	GOOD	EXCELLENT
SIMMONS RACING PLATE	EXCELLENT	VERY GOOD	GOOD	POOR	GOOD	GOOD

Chart 6-2. Ascender Boxes

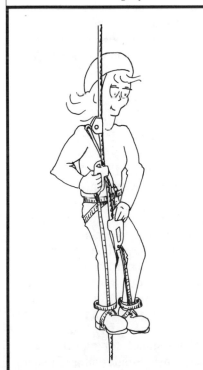

Fig. 6-27. Lower Jumar should be lifted with finger. Secure webbing as shown with older gray Jumar.

Fig. 6q. Pygmy system keeps both arms low, allows arms and shoulders to maintain efficiency longer.

The primary function of an ascender box is to provide a smooth frictionless guide for ropes to pass through. It should hold the climber as close to vertical as possible. Ropes should be securely held inside the box, but inserting ropes into the box should be easily accomplished. The box should be smooth on the outside to allow for crossing difficult lips. Compactness and light weight are desirable features, and the box should be able to withstand tortuous treatment and still function properly.

▲	EXCELLENT
◮	VERY GOOD
◇	GOOD
▽	FAIR
▼	POOR

PYGMY PRUSIK SYSTEM

The Pygmy Prusik System uses parts of both the Jumar Mitchell System and the shoulder mounted Gibbs Ropewalker system. The shoulder cam is used for the upper body stabilization point. This allows for both arms to ride below this upper point. With both arms working below shoulder level, the climber's arms and shoulders retain their strength much longer. The upper shoulder Gibbs allows the body to hang at its maximum vertical angle. The system was designed for long drops where a Mitchell motion is desired and energy needs to be rationed (See Fig.6-q).

Gibbs

As the Jumar systems were beginning to evolve, a new design of ascender came forth. Experimenting in 1965 with cam action gripping the rope, Robert Henshaw and David Morehouse developed a climbing cam (Fig. 6-28). These "Iowa Cams," as they were often called, were sold primarily to cavers. The method of attachment was to strap a cam to each foot. This awkward arrangement was the first cam ropewalker rig. An early variation was the "infernal machine" (Fig. 6-29), which was actually a modified cam designed by Dwight Deal. Deal substituted his modified cams for Jumars using the Jumar system of climbing. Pete Lindsley later modified Deal's design (Fig. 6-30).

The big breakthrough in cam climbing came from Charles Gibbs. Looking for a better way to ascend, he obtained a model of a homemade cam. He redesigned it, changing the rate of cam closure and cam face shape (Fig. 6-31). The real innovation was the method of attachment. Charles Gibbs placed a cam low on one foot and another at the knee, which created an efficient cam climbing system. The original system used a Prusik knot attached to a chest harness (Fig. 6-32). Almost instantly the evolution of Gibbs climbing systems began.

A developmental revolution in the early 1970s saw dozens of harnesses and rigs devised to utilize the new Gibbs cams. The chest harness Prusik knot was replaced by a shoulder-mounted cam making the climbing system a three-cam rig (Fig. 6-33). The most significant development was in the "floating" of the knee cam (MacGregor). The knee strap was removed and replaced with rubber bands, surgical tubing or bungie cords, all utilized to pull the knee cam up the rope.

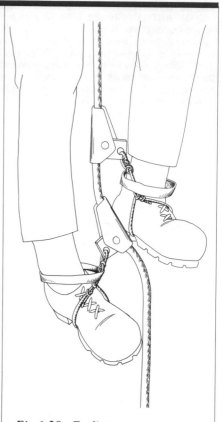

Fig.6-28. Earliest cams were commonly referred to as "Iowa Cams."

DOUBLE-BUNGIE SYSTEM

The Double-Bungie System differs from the normal Gibbs Ropewalker System in that it eliminates the attachment of the foot cam directly to the instep. The system requires a shortened version of the knee cam arrangement for the foot (Fig.6-r). This arrangement prevents ankle fatigue from off-center foot cams and makes the system efficient by removing the sometimes sloppy action of the foot cam. One of its finest advantages is the conservation of energy it provides. The downward movement of the right foot directed through the pulley tends to pull up the ascender on the left knee and the downward movement of the left foot pulls up the ascender on the right foot (Fig.6-s). Single-bungie systems tend to force the climber to stretch the bungie cord each cycle, thus taxing the very muscles the climber needs the most in order to climb.

An efficient method of attaching the elastic cord is to use a single piece and pass it through a small pulley attached to the chest harness or chest roller. Elastic cord attachment to each Gibbs could either be at the top of the shell or with the aid of a connection plate snapped into the quick-release pin (Fig.6-t). Both of these connection methods are adequate, yet can produce drag in the system. See the single bungie attachment. It would be unwise to ever attach the bungie cord around or in the eye of the cam, since that would prevent the ascender from locking (Fig.6-u).

SINGLE-BUNGIE

Many single-bungie systems are too tight, causing the overtaxing of the leg muscles as mentioned earlier. If single-bungie is the system preferred, the cord should be extended over the shoulder and attached to the back of the chest harness or seat harness. To test the tension of the shock cord, grasp the cord near your midsection with your thumb and forefinger and stretch the cord up and down. It should move easily with minimal resistance for one inch either way. Single-bungie users have found that placing the cord inside a piece of tubular webbing protects the soft flesh atop

Improvements to this three-cam rig took the form of better sewing techniques and redundant harnesses. Most of these improvements took the slop or play out of the system, creating more climb-

ing efficiency (Smith 1974, Davison 1974, Fischesser, 1977). The foot-cam attachment was a critical part of this evolutionary process. The developers agreed that it was best to have the foot cam attached

to the strongest leg. Any play in this small foot harness can slow a climber down considerably (Fig. 6-34).

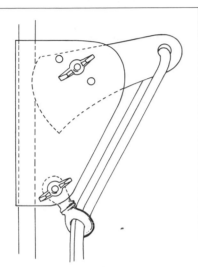

Fig. 6-29. Dwight Deal built the infernal machine.

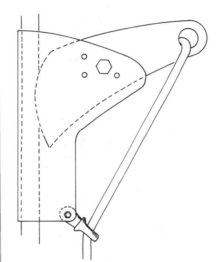

Fig. 6-30. Lindsley later improved upon Deal's model.

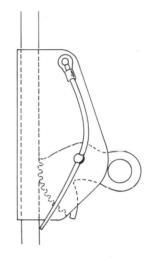

Fig. 6-31a. Early Gibbs ascender (1968) used wire to retain center pin.

the shoulder where the cord passes. The attachment of the bungie cord to the cam has proven to be critical. Attachment to the shell has proven to cause drag, making the system less efficient than if the cord were attached directly to the top of the cam itself. The attachment should be directly over the pivot pin hole and in many models a screw and threads have already been provided.

ROLLER CAM
When using a standard ropewalker rig with Gibbs shoulder suspension, there is noticeable friction in the upper or shoulder cam. Inefficiency in climbing and premature cam shell wear has prompted a solu-

tion. Kyle Isenhart in the early 1970s modified existing Gibbs by adding a roller. During climbing, rope friction was reduced by as much as 70 percent.

The alteration is simple (Fig. 6-v).

1. Using a hacksaw, cut vertically down the center of the curved end of the shell for 1/2 inch.
2. Cutting horizontally at the 1/2 inch mark, cut through all the curved portions of the aluminum.
3. Bend out and flatten these two tabs.
4. Drill 1/8 inch holes in the center of the two tabs.
5. Prepare a roller 5/8 inch long, 3/8 inch diameter with a 1/8 inch hole.
6. Bolt or pin the roller in place.

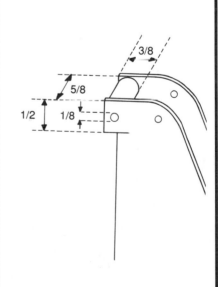

Fig. 6v. The roller cam modification.

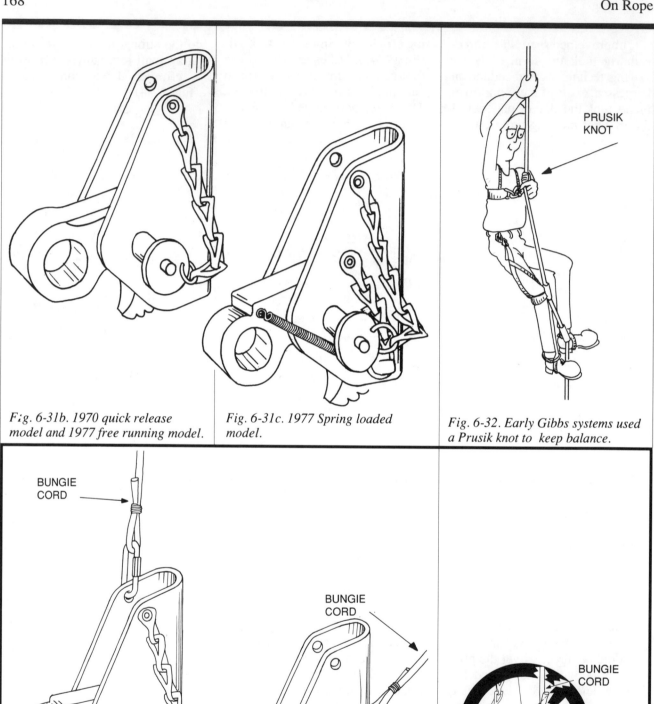

Fig. 6-31b. 1970 quick release model and 1977 free running model.

Fig. 6-31c. 1977 Spring loaded model.

Fig. 6-32. Early Gibbs systems used a Prusik knot to keep balance.

PRUSIK KNOT

BUNGIE CORD

BUNGIE CORD

Fig. 6t. Bungie cord attachment points.

BUNGIE CORD

Fig. 6u. Attachment through eye of cam will not work.

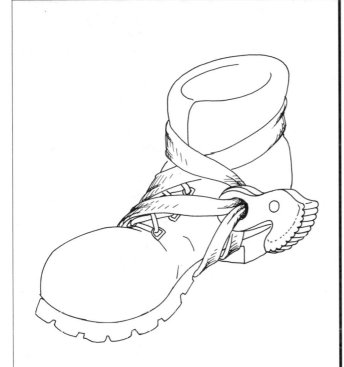

Fig. 34a. An early sloppy method of tying the foot cam evolved into more efficient forms.

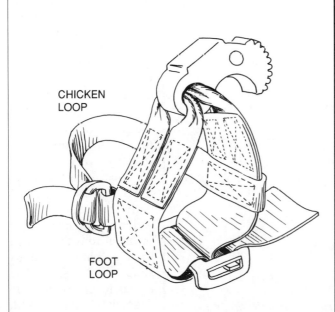

Fig. 6-34b. Modern efficient method.

CHICKEN
LOOP

FOOT
LOOP

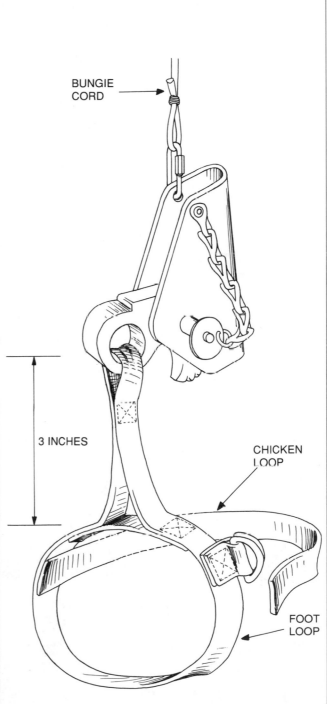

BUNGIE
CORD

3 INCHES

CHICKEN
LOOP

FOOT
LOOP

Fig. 6r. The floating foot cam is a shortened version of knee cam.

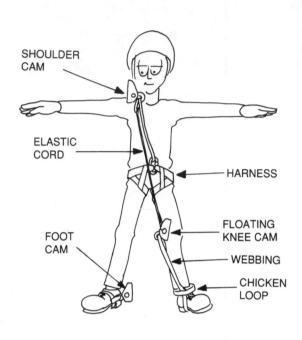

Fig. 6-33. Many Gibbs systems float the cam away from the knee and use elastic cord to pull the knee ascender up during each cycle.

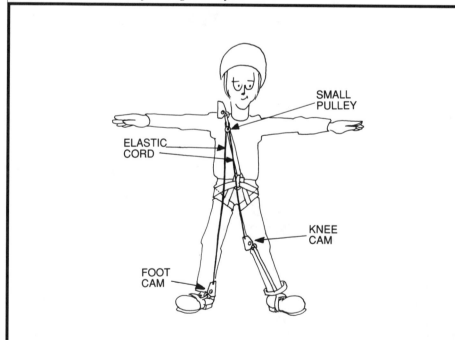

Fig. 6s. Double-bungie system. Movement of bungie cord through the pulley assists with each step. Can be rigged with traditional foot cam that does not incorporate the three-inch space.

Chest Roller

Another innovation that improved the efficiency of the Gibbs Ropewalking System, was the chest roller. It took many forms during its development, mainly being of the homemade variety. Ron Simmons was the first to make and market a single chest roller on a large scale (Fig. 6-35). His roller, placed high in the center of the chest, allows the climber to be oriented vertically instead of being tilted to one side by a shoulder cam. The roller holds the climber tight to the rope without the friction of a shoulder cam. To increase efficiency and comfort by holding the roller tight against the chest, Simmons developed the racing roller: a Simmons roller bolted or welded to an aluminum back plate 9 1/2 inches wide (Fig. 6-36). This wide plate keeps the harness from restricting the breathing process and crushing the ribcage. The plate also applies the pressure to the back to hold the climber comfortably, very close to the rope. John Ganter in 1986 proposed an alternative two-ounce lightweight "I" shaped frame of metal rods that attach to the chest harness straps (Fig. 6-37). The actual length of the "I" depends on the breadth of the climber's chest. In climbing use, the Gibbs should be positioned above the roller. The Gibbs should be tethered to one's seat harness and the strap positioned behind the chest harness.

Ropewalking systems have evolved greatly since the early primitive Jumar system. Efficiency and speed allow for rapid progress during cave trips and comfort when climbing awesome long drops. A Gibbs rig used by Rossano Boscarino currently holds the World Record for the 100 ft/30 m rope climb, which he set in 1987. His record time is 25.7 seconds. The 400 ft/120 m record was also set with Gibbs in 1987 by Boscarino at 4:10.7. Actual drops of over 1000 feet have been climbed in under 33 minutes. Not everyone has such stamina, but proper technique can go a long way in making everyone a faster, more efficient climber.

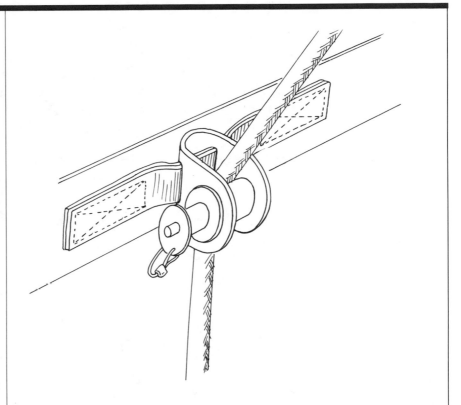

Fig. 6-35. Ron Simmons was the first to make and sell single chest rollers.

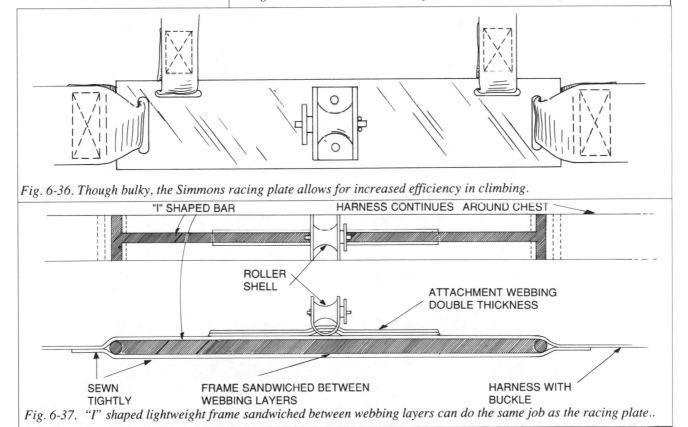

Fig. 6-36. Though bulky, the Simmons racing plate allows for increased efficiency in climbing.

"I" SHAPED BAR   HARNESS CONTINUES AROUND CHEST

ROLLER
SHELL

ATTACHMENT WEBBING
DOUBLE THICKNESS

SEWN   FRAME SANDWICHED BETWEEN   HARNESS WITH
TIGHTLY   WEBBING LAYERS   BUCKLE

Fig. 6-37. "I" shaped lightweight frame sandwiched between webbing layers can do the same job as the racing plate..

	CLIMBING EFFICIENCY	EASE OF FITTING TO CLIMBER	ON-OFF CLIMBER EASE	EASE OF RIG BUILDING	ON-OFF ROPE ASSEMBLY EASE	ON ROPE SECURITY REDUNDANCY	VERSATILITY	DURABILITY	WEAR PARTS RE-PLACEMENT ABILITY	LIP CROSSING ABILITY	KNOT PASSING ABILITY	USE ON SLOPES	DOWNCLIMBING ABILITY	BULKY/WEIGHT
CLASSIC 3-KNOT	◇	△	◇	△	▽	▲	◇	▽	Y	▽	▼	◇	◇	▲
TEXAS PRUSIK W/KNOTS	▽	△	△	▲	◇	◇	◇	▽	Y	▽	▼	◇	△	▲
TEXAS PRUSIK W/JUMARS	◇	△	▲	△	▲	◇	△	▲	Y	◇	▲	◇	△	△
MITCHELL W/JUMARS, BOX	△	◇	◇	◇	△	◇	△	▲	Y	◇	▽	◇	▲	◇
MITCHELL PHASE 3	◇	◇	◇	◇	△	◇	△	▲	Y	◇	▽	▲	▲	◇
INCH WORM	◇	◇	◇	◇	▲	◇	▼	▲	Y	◇	▽	◇	▼	▽
FROG SYSTEM	◇	◇	◇	▽	▲	◇	◇	△	Y	△	▽	◇	△	▽
GOSSETT SYSTEM	◇	◇	◇	◇	△	◇	◇	▲	Y	△	◇	◇	△	◇
PIGMY	△	◇	◇	◇	△	▲	◇	△	Y	△	▽	◇	▽	◇
GIBBS FLOATING/SHOULDER	△	▽	◇	▽	◇	▲	△	△	Y	△	▼	△	▼	◇
GIBBS FLOATING/CHEST ROLLER	▲	◇	△	▽	◇	◇	△	▲	Y	◇	▼	◇	▼	◇
GIBBS DOUBLE BUNGIE	▲	◇	△	▽	◇	◇	△	▲	Y	◇	▼	◇	▼	◇
GIBBS BUTTSTRAP HARNESS	△	△	▽	▽	◇	▲	△	△	Y	△	▼	△	▼	▽
PETZL JAMMER FL/CHEST ROLLER	▲	◇	△	▽	△	◇	△	▲	N	◇	◇	◇	▼	◇

Chart 6-3. Climbing Systems

▲	EXCELLENT
◭	VERY GOOD
◇	GOOD
▽	FAIR
▼	POOR
Y	YES
N	NO

CLIMBING SYSTEMS

The ideal climbing system should enable the climber to move comfortably and efficiently up the rope. It should provide a secure attachment to the rope, yet be easily removed as well as attached. It should fit the climber properly, be easily taken on and off with ease. It should be lightweight and not bulky. A good system is versatile, able to accomplish a variety of tasks such as being transformed into a rescue haul system. It should be redundant so that any failure will not place the climber in immediate danger. After a component failure, it should have the versatility to be transformed into a system enabling the climber to continue up or down safely. A system should be durable and incorporate interchangeable replacement parts. A good system climbs a wall as well as a free drop and allows a climber to ascend over difficult lips. Systems that fit climbers of different sizes are useful during rescues and training seminars. A great system incorporates the ability to downclimb.

COMPARISON CHART DISCLAIMER

Any rating or comparison is at best an educated opinion. Differing levels of familiarity with an item or differing applications can result in an entirely different rating score. The criteria used and the items rated are intended simply to show general opinions about these items. There will always exist isolated exceptions, and it is the author's intent to avoid such "believe-it-or-not" discussion.

PRACTICAL USE

The rope-climbing systems described so far are very useful, but only if one understands their features and, most important, how to use these systems effectively. Climbing rigs are an extension of the body to enable it to climb and thus must be fitted to the climber. To accommodate varieties in the thickness of clothing that a climber wears, the harness should be made adjustable. For example, a climber in a wet suit would require a substantially larger harness than if the same climber were wearing shorts during a practice session. When engaging in rope-work each person should have his or her own complete climbing system. This means **everything** necessary for safe descent and ascent.

Preparing To Ascend

In preparing to ascend, it is important to remember all the necessary equipment. Vertical gear should be with a climber, not left at the top of a drop or in the trunk of the car. Assuming that all the necessary gear is present, pull it out of its pack and repack any descending gear. It may be necessary to remove heavy or warm clothing to prevent overheating during physical exertion. Tightly secure the pack so there is no chance of any gear or clothing falling out during ascent. Make sure there is sufficient light available to make the climb (Will the sun set before the climb is over? If using a carbide light, is recharging in order? Does the electric headlamp need fresh batteries?). Put on chest and seat harnesses, chicken loops, foot

slings and the safety Jumar. Make sure the pack is secured to a lower torso clip-in point. Snug up the chin strap on your helmet. Confirm plans with the rest of the group still waiting to climb.

When the drop is free of rockfall danger and the previous climber is up and is away from the top of the drop acknowledge his or her "Off Rope!" signal with a "Thank You" or "OK". Move to the bottom of the rope and attach ascenders or knots to the rope. Begin with the lowest attachment point and work up. If done in the opposite manner it is often difficult to bend over to adjust a foot cinch buckle or to make other lower adjustment.

Because getting the system properly attached is very important, it is helpful that a routine that is almost ritualistic be observed in preparing to climb. If the process is completed in an identical progression each time (that is doing things in the same order, holding things the same way), fatigue, cold, distraction or emergency will not interfere with the process. Because of this, the safe climber finds a versatile system and sticks with it. Total and complete familiarity with a system prevents the careless moment that could lead to an accident. The novice might even prepare a written checklist until he is completely familiar with his system.

Many experienced climbers ask themselves a series of questions and complete a total system checkout of their gear. Do I have all the gear necessary to attach my harness(es)? Can I descend safely? Can I ascend safely? Am I

able to change over and cross a knot? Gloves? Chicken loops? Safety Jumar? Do I have appropriate footwear? Are the helmet and

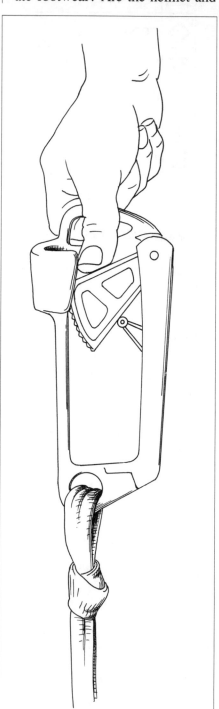

Fig. 6-38. Thumbing the cam eases Jumar movement especially during the first few feet of an ascent.

chin strap in place? Do I need a light? What will I need when I arrive at the other end of the rope? Sandwich? Compass? Surveying gear? Rain gear? Warm clothing? Am I taking with me everything I brought? Trash? Dead batteries? Questions such as these, if asked every time, can be a major step towards being prepared to climb.

Getting Started

Make sure that the point chosen to begin the ascent is directly beneath the rope. If not, a pendulum swing will result the instant one's weight is transferred from the floor to the rope. If a pendulum results, rocks could be dislodged and the rope could abrade while sliding past a sharp rock. After proper positioning, signal to all those present, "On rope." Remove as much slack from the rope as possible and begin to climb.

Sit-Stand

With sit-stand methods, pull the rope through the seat harness knot or ascender until taut above the top knot or ascender. Sit back into the seat harness and raise the appropriate leg ascender(s) up the rope. Continue this cycle until the stretch is out of the rope and the climber is hanging free and is ready to climb. Before the weight of the rope increases below the climber, it may be necessary to move the lowest knot/ascender with one hand while holding the rope taut from below with the other hand. As the climber gains altitude, (10 to 50 feet) the weight of the rope hanging below the climber is often enough to counteract the upward force of the ascenders during each cycle. If the climber is ascending with knots it may be necessary to break those knots throughout the entire climb.

Fig. 6-39. The traditional way of self starting.

Mitchell System

With the Mitchell system, hold the lower Jumar with one hand and pull the slack in the rope through it. The ascender box and upper Jumar will follow. When the rope becomes tight, grasp the upper Jumar and hold the lower Jumar with the index finger or middle finger through the eye hole. Other brands of handled ascenders will also allow this "lifting" motion. Take short steps until you hang free. To ease the start with the lower Jumar, use the thumb to push the cam open before lifting the Jumar (Fig. 6-38). Thumbing the cam will be necessary, until the rope weight below the climber is enough to offset the drag of the cam mechanism within the ascender. It may be necessary to thumb the cam for the first 10 to 50 feet of a climb.

Gibbs.

With the Gibbs ropewalker systems, pass the rope under the instep of the knee-cam foot and back up to the hand on that side. As short steps are taken the climber should pull upward on the tail of the rope (Fig. 6-39). As progress is made upward, the rope can be dropped when its weight is sufficient to allow the cams to function properly. David McClurg suggests passing the end of the rope through a carabiner attached to the chest harness somewhere and pulling down on the tail rather than up (Fig. 6-40).

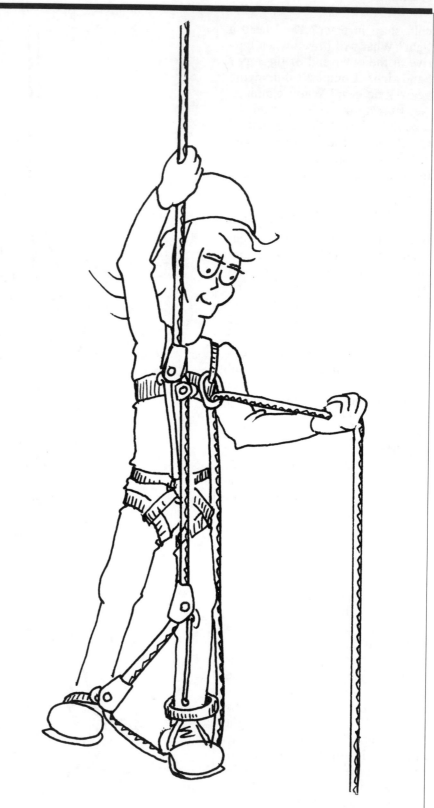

Fig. 6-40. An improved self start method incorporates a chest carabiner (after McClurg).

CLIMB AT
STEADY
PACE

TAKE A
BREATHER

CLIMB AS
FAST AS
POSSIBLE TO
AVOID WATER

Fig. 6-41. Unusual conditions such as a waterfall will dictate an abnormal but necessary climbing rate.

CLIMBING

How fast should one climb up the rope? There is no ideal speed. The pace should be above all else, steady. The number of steps per minute should remain fairly constant for the length of the climb. The exception here would be in a waterfall room where spray blows onto the bottom of the rope (fig.6-41). In this case the climber would ascend as rapidly as possible to escape the spray blown about by the waterfall. He would then rest for a moment and ascend at a steady rate the rest of the way.

The experienced climber climbs at a steady pace and is not jerky, bouncy or awkward. Remember, any jerking or flailing about is using energy that is not directed. If the climber aims for a smooth climb, efficiency will follow. A smooth climber is inherently safer as rope will abrade less, anchors will be stressed less, and she will arrive at the top of the drop sufficiently fresh to negotiate the lip and move to a place of safety.

The large, powerful leg muscles do the primary job of advancing a climber. There exist efficient as well as inefficient methods of using these powerful muscles. Ergonomics shows the best way to utilize one's various muscles efficiently. Tests have shown that the **maximum** horsepower produced by a leg movement, can be achieved at a rate of 65-90 cycles per minute. To reproduce this rate of cycle or rhythm, a step size of 18 to 22 inches is ideal. However, there is no way to sustain this rate for any distance.

The average climber's step size is 12 to 14 inches. Those who climb long drops claim that it is more important to maintain ones climbing rhythm on the rope than to climb at a rate that necessitates stopping to rest. They suggest even shorter steps of six to nine inches be used (Fig. 6-42) in an effort to maintain a rhythm. Regardless, because of the way the human machine works, fewer moderately long steps are more efficient than a lot of small steps. This is one reason ropewalker systems are so fast. Other systems cannot utilize the horsepower as efficiently.

Not all climbers are finely trained athletes. In fact, very few are. An efficient method is to climb 5-10-20 cycles/steps or some set number and then stop for a breather, not a rest. A rest is a total stop, which may include setting the system up for comfort for an extended stop at some point on the rope.

To pause for a breather is simply to stop climbing momentarily, assume a reasonably comfortable position and breathe deeply for less than one minute; preferably less than 30 seconds, resume climbing and go the same number of cycles/steps before stopping again. One should aim for the goal of not having to stop at all. The pace should feel like the step frequency of walking. It is harder, however, going up than simply going forward. As technique and physical condition improve, a quickening of the pace to a quick jog-like rate should occur.

No one should attempt a difficult climb if he can't keep up a walking frequency on rope with occasional pauses. Physical conditioning to improve horsepower output is desirable. The energy re-

quired to climb a certain distance is approximately equivalent to the energy required to climb a similar height of stairs. For instance a 200-foot prusik requires the same approximate effort it takes to climb 20 staircases.

Keep in mind that fear and nervous energy can sap a climber's energy reservoir as fast or faster than the climb itself. It has been

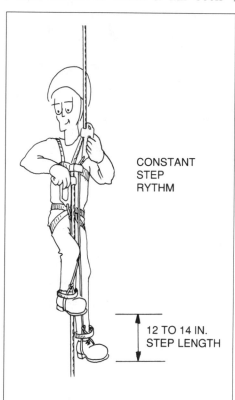

CONSTANT STEP RYTHM

12 TO 14 IN. STEP LENGTH

Fig. 6-42. Climbing efficiently calls for 12-14 inch steps and constant rhythm.

suggested that if one cannot ropewalk an average of 100 feet in five minutes under good conditions, there exists a problem with the climbing system and its fit.

While climbing, there are many things one must be aware of. Do not blindly move ascenders, rather think about which ascender is holding which leg. It is a common mistake to attempt to lift the Jumar one is standing in. It is a

good idea to keep prusik slings between the climber's legs. This will reduce the possibilty of the slings getting snagged and help to establish the three-dimensional balance a climber must maintain.

It is easy to get so involved in climbing that your head bumps into a forgotten ledge. Caution should be exercised anytime the climber is close enough to the walls of the drop to touch them. A careless foot or backpack could dislodge a rock onto unsuspecting people below. Rockfall is the leading cause of injury in ropework. Remember, if something is dislodged or dropped, yell **"ROCK!"**

Tight Climbing Areas
If the drop being climbed gets tighter so as to make it a narrow crevice, special considerations must be made. Packs should be adjusted carefully or slung on a tether beneath the climber (Fig. 6-43). Caution should be exercised and slow deliberate moves made. Often, one must flatten out into a crack and climbing steps must be taken at odd angles. This stresses gear and muscles. It is important to climb either the rope or the rock. Don't try to do both: don't prusik a step, step up onto a rock, then prusik another step. Do one or the other.

Trying to establish a rock-climbing balance and a rope climbing balance will waste time and tremendous amounts of energy. Wasted motion is wasted energy. It is best to relax and enjoy the climb. If you do get snagged on a rock protrusion, it may be necessary to downclimb a step or two and reassess the situation.

Chest ascender boxes and chest rollers may protrude in a manner that will prevent a climber from maneuvering through a crevice. In this case it may be necessary to remove the chest box and replace it with a temporary tight chest strap (Fig. 6-44). With the ropes and slings sliding inside the chest strap, friction will increase, but the chest size will be reduced two to three inches.

Fig. 6-43. Maneuvering a pack through a tight place may call for a tether line.

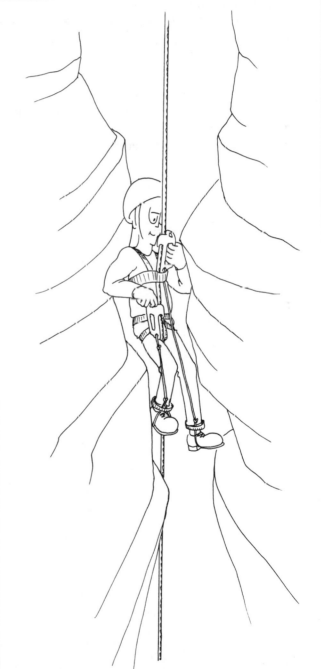

Fig. 6-44. Narrow areas may require a flat strap rather than a protruding ascender box.

THE LIP

Often, the hardest part of a climb is not the long haul up the rope, but rather the effort required to get over the lip. Careful rigging can eliminate many problems with lips, but often the drop dictates the climbing system. There are two major factors that quickly increase lip negotiation difficulty. If the rope drops over the edge at a sharp 90° angle or if there are no natural projections or ledges below the ledge to aid in coming up over the edge, the climber has problems.

The worst case would be a 90° rope bend over a narrow undercut ledge (Fig. 6-45). This worst case could be compounded if the rope is wedged deep into a three or four foot vertical crack that extends all the way through the lip.

Each system requires a slightly different approach and the approaches get more technically complex as the lip is more difficult to overcome.

3-Knot System

Climb up within inches of the contact point. Take a breather and look things over. If the lip does not appear too difficult, stand up, push off of the rock with one hand and slide the top knot up. If the lip is slightly more difficult, try lying to one side of the rope. Push out with your feet and stand up and then ease the top knot up past the ledge. Watch that fingers do not get pinched. If this doesn't work, employ the safety Jumar and extend the Jumar above the obstacle and move on. If you don't own a safety Jumar, take out an extra Prusik knot and attach it above the obstacle. Stand up and

Fig. 6-45. The worst case: Rope rigged low over a sharp breakover with a severe undercut ledge.

Fig. 6-46. Jamming your elbow between rope and rock provides space to move knots or ascenders.

clip the sling into your seat harness with an extra carabiner. Never unscrew a seat harness carabiner while hanging in it.

If the knot sling is too short, remove the lower foot knot (it's much longer) and retie it above the ledge. Stand up and clip it to your seat harness. Again, an extra carabiner will greatly assist with this maneuver. Once one knot is over the obstacle it is often easy to get the rest over the tough spot. If the lip is a long arc, the knot climber can assume the sideways position, swing outward and jam his elbow beneath the rope (Fig. 6-46). The rope laying on the fleshy part of the arm gives some space to move a Prusik knot.

The Mitchell System

Jumars tend to slide over lips fairly well. However the ascender box frequently gets stuck. On an easy lip, move the Jumars until both feet are even and the knees are slightly bent. Place both hands on the lip and push outward while standing up. Repeat this process if necessary. If the ledge is very bad, consider attaching the safety Jumar and removing the main rope from the box. The Texas system with two Jumars is excellent for passing difficult ledges. Depending on the arc or angle of the edge, it could be helpful to attach the safety Jumar to the long Jumar sling, converting to the useful Cuddington Phase three.

The Gibbs Ropewalker

The Gibbs systems represent probably the best rig for passing a difficult ledge. Because the hands are not needed to move the cams on most lips, the climber merely

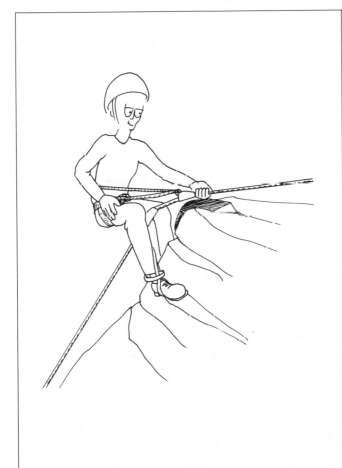

Fig. 6-47. Sliding the shoulder cam off the shoulder can assist in overcoming a difficult ledge.

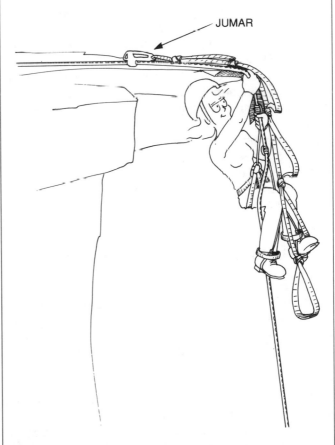

JUMAR

Fig. 6-48. Lowering an etrier to a climber may be just the assistance needed to get over a difficult lip.

pushes away and crawls over. If the drop is sloped, the shoulder cam can be slipped off, (Fig. 6-47), and the climber can lean back (as with the Cuddington Phase 3) to pass the obstacle. If using a Simmons Roller rig, the roller can be released and the climber can utilize the cam or Jumar that is riding above the roller. If the lip is really bad, the upper cam can be removed from the rope and replaced above the lip. A safety Jumar should be attached to the rope above the lip prior to removing the shoulder cam from the rope.

If the climber is frustrated by a difficult lip, help can come from above. An ascender on a sling can be positioned above the lip and a carabiner attached to the ascender sling can be lowered. An etrier (fig. 4-48) could be lowered to give a handhold or foothold to a climber who normally has none. The rope pigtail as shown in fig. 4-7 can be attached to the climber and he can simply be hauled over the edge by willing strong arms from above. The "haul the climber over" method may be the best course of action if total exhaustion exists.

Completing the Climb
When moving over the lip, caution should be taken since this is where most rocks are dislodged and fall into the drop zone. Before moving away from the edge, make sure the rope is back on the rope pad. Continue to move ascenders up the rope until a position of safety is reached. Remove the ascenders, starting with the lowest if possible. The signal "Off Rope" is to be given only when there is no danger of rockfall from the movement of a tired climber and the rope pad is in place. If the rigging

permits, it is possible to be "off rope" while ascenders are still attached. Remember, it is **not** a signal that the climber has reached the top, **rather,** it is a signal that means it is safe for the person below to move out of a sheltered spot and begin his climb.

TANDEM

There are many drops that lend themselves to tandem climbing. A tandem climb is one in which two people ascend the same standing rope at the same time. There are special problems with this method, and at least three considerations are necessary when climbing tandem.

First, is it worth the bother? The main advantage of tandem climbing is time. For long drops where a party must wait on others to exit, tandem climbing cuts the waiting time in half. However, this time can be lost due to the complexities of two people crossing the lip and getting on and off the rope. Second, the combined weights and stresses will amount to approximately 600 lbs. If the rope rubs on any ledges unprotected, it will abrade quickly. In fact, it will abrade much quicker than if the rope is supporting the weight of just one climber. Third, is the lip suitable for crossing with the weight of another climber below the top person?

If it is decided to climb tandem, let the other members of the party know so that a foul-up of signals will not result, such as a third person rigging onto the same rope. The two climbers should move at about the same speed. The more experienced climber should be on top because the top climber has the task of crossing the lip with an extra person's weight be-

low her. To begin, the top climber should rig her ascending system onto the rope and ascend about 20 feet. The bottom climber should get on and climb up to the top climber. After a breather, they can both climb at the same time or alternate climbing. In either method the two climbers should stay within 30 to 40 feet of each other (Fig. 6-49). When approaching the lip the climbers should be close together so that if a rock were to be dislodged the lower climber, who surely cannot escape, would not be hurt due to the momentum of a falling rock.

The top person may have a difficult time getting over the lip. An alternative to this difficulty would be for either the top or bottom climber to transfer over to a pigtail. Other solutions are discussed in Chapter 7.

Many people enjoy climbing tandem. Others hate it. If two people have a rhythm and step that complement each other, the bounce in the rope can make the climb easier. If they bounce and shake each other, it can feel like small ships on a big ocean. Pity the lower climber if the top person gets seasick on the rope. One of the nice things about climbing tandem on a long drop is that there is someone nearby to talk to and it makes the work go by quickly.

Prusiking is a skill and like any skill, takes practice and thought to master. It is easier to learn if one will concentrate on style and form, rather than brute strength and speed. There are climbers who can climb faster and more efficiently with three Prusik knots than others can climb on a Gibbs rig. Without style or the ability to use a system properly, a lot of energy, effort and time are often wasted.

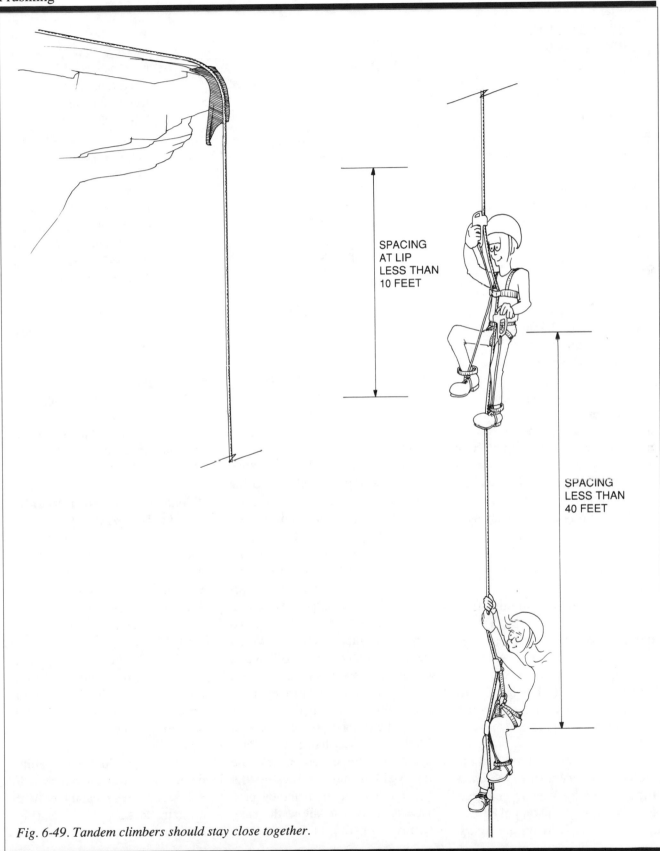

SPACING
AT LIP
LESS THAN
10 FEET

SPACING
LESS THAN
40 FEET

Fig. 6-49. Tandem climbers should stay close together.

CHANGEOVER, DOWNCLIMBING AND CROSSING A KNOT

Changeover

Changeover is the changing from rappel to prusik or from prusik to rappel depending on the climber's current mode. Changeover is a critical skill and is basic to many other activities associated with prusiking and rappelling. Regardless of the system being used, a safety Jumar is essential and must be long enough to reach the rope above any descending device (Fig. 6-w). but not too long to be out of reach. Other ascenders can be substituted for a Jumar, but it becomes important to be able to attach and detach the safety Jumar with one hand, as you will surely discover during a changeover practice session.

Changeover from Rappelling to Prusiking

To successfully execute this procedure, there should be a connecting locking carabiner between the rappel device and the locking harness carabiner. This will allow the slack necessary to remove the rope and rappelling device from the person.

1. Stop descending and attach the safety Jumar to the main rope. Allow the rope to continue to slide through the rappel device until full weight is on the safety

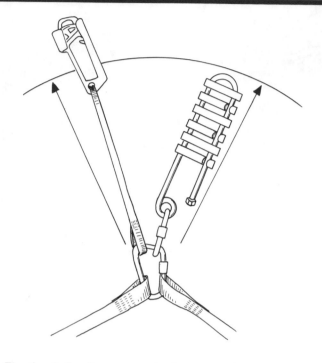

Fig. 6w. Safety Jumar must be long enough to reach above rappel device and include a second locking carabiner to enable changeover.

Jumar.

2. Attach all foot and knee ascenders appropriately, securing all chicken loops and buckles.

3. Attach any and all foot and knee ascenders to the rope.

4. Completely remove the rappel device from the rope and unclip it from the seat harness carabiner. Clip the rappel device to a secure place—not a belt loop. To remove a rappel rack it would have been necessary to have a locking carabiner between the seat carabiner and the rappel rack (Fig.6-w). An alternative method would be to incorporate two delta Maillons as seat-harness carabiners. Attach the seat ascender to the top Maillon and the rack to the bottom. The pivot that they provide is enough to allow the easy removal of the rack (Fig.6-x).

With this method, no linking carabiners are necessary and the rack maintains a low connection, providing several other advantages.

5. Attach any chest harness, chest rollers, boxes and shoulder cams in place and connect them to the rope.

6. Attach bungie cords, tethers or redundant safety buckles, and secure appropriately.

7. Stand up in the foot sling(s) of the system. This will allow slack to form in the safety Jumar. Remove the safety Jumar and secure it conveniently to one's side.

8. Changeover is now complete and the climber is in position to climb.

Changeover from Prusiking to Rappelling

1. Assume a resting (sitting) position or attach a safety Jumar to the rope, allowing the climber to be in a sitting position. If a box or chest roller is present, the safety Jumar should be attached above it.

2. Remove bungie cord tension and rope and cords from ascender box roller(s) if appropriate. Remove the rope from any box or chest attachment device.

3. Take out a rappelling device and securely attach it to the seat harness carabiner with an extra locking carabiner (Fig. 6-w).

4. Lower foot and/or knee ascender about two feet. This slack will allow the attachment of the rappel device to the rope. Properly attach the rappel device to the rope and securely lock it off.

5. Remove the lower foot ascender if using Gibbs or the long upper Jumar if using one of the Jumar rigs.

6. Stand up in the remaining foot ascender and slide the safety Jumar down the rope to where it no longer experiences tension.

7. (*See also alternative method*) Sit back down placing all your weight on the rappel system. If the system is attached incorrectly the safety Jumar will prevent a mishap.

8. Remove the lower ascender from both the rope and your foot and pack it away.

9. Remove safety Jumar.

10. Unlock the rappel device and enjoy the rappel. Changeover is complete.

Alternative method for last five steps:

6. Stand up in the one remaining short knee-length Jumar or knee cam and disconnect all other ascenders including the safety Jumar. Before placing weight back onto the rappel device, grasp the rope with the control hand.

7. Sit back down allowing the rappel device to hold all the weight.

8. Remove the foot ascender from the rope and then from the foot itself.

9. Secure all prusik gear tightly in a gear bag or clip securely. Gloves on?

10. Unlock the rappel device and enjoy the rappel. Changeover is complete.

In all cases, when **attaching** ascending systems,.it is important to work from the bottom up (foot, knee, chest and shoulder). But, when **detaching** ascending systems, you work from

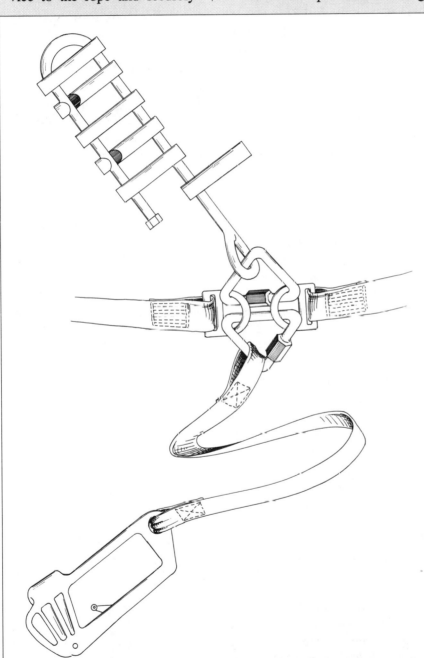

Fig. 6x. Another changeover solution is to use two delta Maillon links. As you apply weight to the seat harness ascender, the rack is allowed to pivot down making room for the rope to be removed.

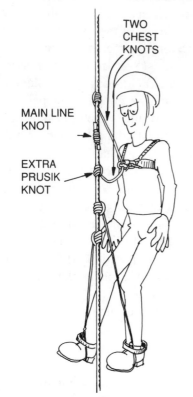

Fig. 6y. Crossing a knot requires an extra prusik sling.

the top down (shoulder, chest, knee, and then foot) . Knot systems tend to be simpler, because there is less to connect, yet it often takes two hands to tie the knots, which complicates the process.

DOWNCLIMBING AND CROSSING A KNOT

To move downward past an obstacle on rope requires a skill called "downclimbing." Rappel hardware will not pass knots or anchors. Prusik systems are designed to move easily upward. Downward motion is awkward at best. Each system has its own peculiarities.

3-Knot Downclimb and Knot Cross

Move the bottom knot a moderate distance downward and pull the knot tight to set it. Move the second foot knot down the rope so it is even with the first knot and set it. Stand and release the top knot and squat and set the knot. Repeating this process will accomplish downclimbing.

To cross an obstacle, remove each foot knot (one at a time) and replace them both below the obstacle. Take out the spare Prusik knot or safety Jumar (Fig. 6-y). Tie/clip it to the rope below the obstacle with an extra locking carabiner. Clip it into the seat harness. Remove the upper prusik sling from the harness carabiner, being careful not to unhook harness. Remove from the rope and continue to downclimb. Reverse the process to pass a knot going upward.

Mitchell System Downclimb and Knot Cross

Using a thumbing motion as shown in Fig.6-38, release the Jumar cams and step downward similarly to backing down a set of stair steps. A very rapid rate can be achieved. This is the most efficient downclimbing system available.

To pass a knot, shift into phase two (Texas system with Jumars). Keep the long foot Jumar on. Move the lower foot Jumar down below the knot first (unclip and reclip). Even up the long sling with the short sling just to keep an extra contact point. Release the safety Jumar and quickly move it below the knot. Reattach the main

rope into the ascender box below the knot. Reattach the long foot Jumar, (Fig.6-z), below the knot as well. Remove the safety Jumar and continue to downclimb. Reverse the process to pass a knot when going upward.

Gibbs Rig Downclimb and Knot Cross

Downclimbing with a Gibbs is extremely difficult due to the foot cam being out of reach. To ease the situation, convert to a Texas system; knee cam and shoulder cam or knee cam and safety Jumar by removing the foot cam from the rope. Gibbs cams must be set as weight is applied or the shell will slip down the rope. To cross a knot, downclimb to the obstacle. Place the foot cam on the rope below

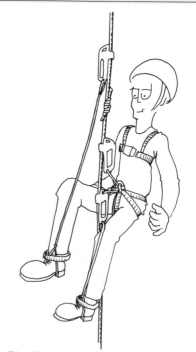

Fig. 6z. After the safety Jumar is attached, move the long foot sling down as you sit.

the knot. By pulling up some rope, setting the foot cam, then lowering the leg back down, some downward distance can be gained (Fig.6-aa). Next, move the knee cam below the knot. Because Gibbs require two-handed assembly, quick movement is impossible. The shoulder cam/chest roller must remain attached to keep the climber upright. The safety Jumar should be attached below the knot. The shoulder cam/chest roller should now be moved below the knot. Remove the safety Jumar. To ascend past an obstacle, reverse the process.

GENERAL COMMENTS

Any system used needs to maintain two points of contact at all times, even the inchworm and frog systems. A safety Jumar or simply a carabiner on a sling hooked into the knot can substitute for an extra ascender. These special maneuvering procedures take practice and refinement. Changing over, downclimbing and passing a knot are all skills that the competent climber should be well versed in.

POWER ASCENDING

For those who do not view vertical work as an end in itself, but instead only wish to traverse the distance to accomplish another task, a motorized ascender may be for them. The MAD (Motorized Ascending Device), built by Nevin Davis in 1969 was the first successful powered ascender and most probably the only motorized device in use. It has unexplored applications with regard to rescue work. The device was successfully used to pull a heavy rope out of a deep Mexican pit during derigging. Using a small gasoline engine, the device powers a "Vee" drive pulley to winch the climber up the rope. A cam assembly acts as a safety in case of engine failure. The MAD weighs 21.5 lbs., will carry 400 pounds up a rope at a rate of 37 ft/min. and gets 2 miles/gal. of gas. It is custom—built, but detailed plans are available (Fig.6-bb).

Fig. 6bb. MAD (Motorized Ascending Device).

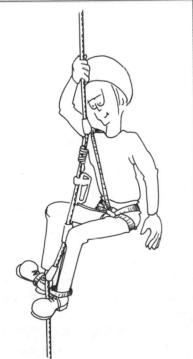

Fig. 6aa. Pull up the slack in the rope to attach the lower foot cam.

3-KNOT PRUSIK RIG

Materials List

16 feet of suitable Prusik knot material.
12.5 feet of 1 inch webbing.
8 feet of flat 2 inch seat belt webbing.
1 heavy duty buckle suitable for 2" webbing.
1 heavy duty buckle suitable for 1" webbing.
2 locking D-ring carabiners of standard size.
(1 delta maillon and 1 locking D carabiner may prove to be best)
3.5 feet of 1/8" to 1/4" cord (non-load bearing for shoulder straps).
32" X 4" X 1/4" closed cell foam padding (non-load bearing).
33" X 9" durable fabric for covering the foam padding (non-load bearing).
1 seat harness.

Chest Harness Assembly
Construction Details

1. Take the 8 feet of flat 2" webbing and attach the heavy duty 2" buckle to the end, overlapping by 6 inches. Sew securely.
2. Take 2 six inch pieces of 1" tubular webbing and insert the end of the 2" strap through the 1" webbing pieces sliding them into place as shown in Fig. 6-p1. Place these wear protectors at approximately the 1/3 and 2/3 length of the strap.
3. Take the piece of closed-cell foam and cover tightly with the fabric.
4. Take a 9 inch piece of 1 inch tubular webbing and fold it over double. Place it in the center of the pad and sew it first at the bottom connecting the two ends of the 9 inch piece of webbing and forming a loop at the top. Sew to the top of the pad as well, leaving a small loop extending above the pad. This loop will be used for the shoulder pad cord.
5. Eleven inches on either side of this center piece place two 4" pieces of 1" tubular webbing. Sew at the top and the bottom of the foam padding. See Fig. 6-p2.
6. Thread the Fig. 6-p1 assembly under the keepers as shown in Fig. 6-p3.
7. Position the wear protectors at either end and thread the buckle so its final position is in the back as also shown in Fig. 6-p3.

8. Take the 3.5 feet of light shoulder strap cord and thread through the center loop.
9. Tie off one end on one wear protector with a bowline.
10. Connect one of the locking carabiners to the loop formed by one of the wear protectors.
11. Put on the harness. 12. Connect the 2" buckle and adjust so that the shoulder cords hold the harness high on the chest. The chest strap should ultimately be snug around the chest, but not too tight for it to restrict breathing.

Chicken Loop Assembly
Construction Details

13. Cut two 17" pieces of 1" tubular webbing.
14. Form two endless loops with a 5 inch overlap.
15. Sew these loops securely. These loops will need to be placed onto the ankles prior to the climber's boots being put on. See Fig. 6-p4.

Adjustment Strap Assembly
Construction Details

16. Take 30 inches of 1" tubular webbing and place a 1" heavy duty buckle on one end overlapping 5 inches.
17. Sew very securely.
18. Thread the buckle to make an endless loop as shown in Fig. 6-p5.

Foot Loop Assemblies
Construction Details

19. Take 54 inches of 1 inch tubular webbing and lay it out flat for measuring and marking.
20 On one end keep 18 inches of webbing and fold it back so that the webbing is double thickness for 18 inches.
21. On the closed end of this flat loop measure 8 inches. Pin, staple or mark this point.
22. On the opposite end measure 8 inches from where the open end of the double piece is in step 20. Fold and mark the webbing back over forming a 4 inch long loop. Lay the excess webbing along the double webbing forming a triple thickness. If this piece extends past the point marked in step 21, cut off the excess.
23. Sew the triple thickness webbing securely. This sewing area should be 10 inches long. The eight inch loop is the foot loop. The four inch loop is used to attach the Prusik knot material. Repeat steps 18 thru 23 to make the second loop.

Three Knot Prusik Rig

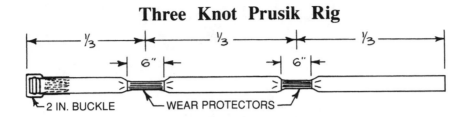

Fig. 6-P1. Chest harness strap

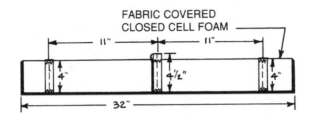

Fig. 6-P2   Foam padding

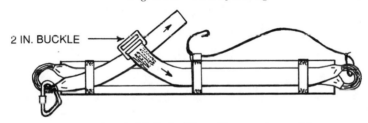

Fig. 6-P1, 2, 3. Chest Harness Assembly.

Fig. 6-P4.

Fig. 6-P5.

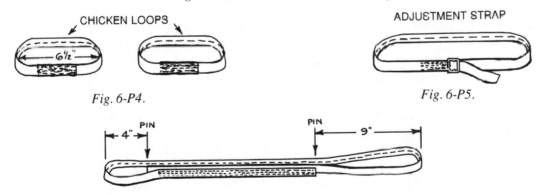

Fig. 6-P6. Foot Loop.

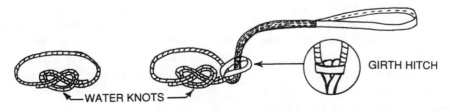

Fig. 6-P7. Foot Loop Assembly.

Three Knot Prusik Rig

(Continued)

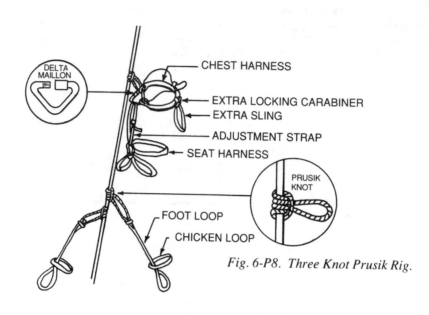

Fig. 6-P8. Three Knot Prusik Rig.

24. Take the 16 feet of Prusik knot material and cut it into 4 equal 4' lengths.

25. Using water knots, tie all four pieces into endless loops.

26. Pass the 4" loop end of the 6-p6 foot loops through two of the endless Prusik knot slings and form a girth hitch as shown in Fig. 6-p7. The remaining two slings become the chest knot and the emergency back-up knot.

Final Assembly: Fig. 6-p8

Construction Details

27. Put the chicken loops on and secure your climbing boots.

28. Put on a seat harness.

29. Put on the chest harness and connect to the seat harness with the adjustable strap. Tie the second side of the shoulder loop cord to the wear protector loop.

30. Tie the chest knot Prusik onto the main rope.

31. Tie the foot knot Prusiks onto the main rope.

32. Place the foot loops down through the chicken loops and over the feet. 33. Attach the chest prusik sling to the chest harness carabiner.

34. Clip the extra prusik sling to the climber with the extra locking carabiner. Attach to a convenient point, but out of the way.

35. Snug up the chest harness and seat sling.

36. Climb off the floor by raising each knot sequentially and come to rest in a sitting position.

37. Tighten the adjustment strap until weight is distributed comfortably between the seat and chest harness.

38. Continue climbing.

Fine Tuning the System

39. The chest knot, when tied correctly, should be at forehead level when the climber is in a sitting position on the rope.

40. Foot knots should be adjusted so that when the climber is in a sitting position, the climber's arms stretch out parallel to the ground when grasping the two foot knots. The climber's heels should be able to swing under the climber's buttocks.

Mitchell System

Materials List

One pair of handled ascenders (Jumars, Petzl expedition, CMI, etc.)

One ascender box.

2" cinch buckle (2500 lbs. minimum tensile).

9 feet of 2" seat belt webbing (2000 lbs. minimum tensile).

14.5 feet of 1" tubular webbing.

5 feet of 5/16" static kernmantle, no stretch, hard abrasion-resistant rope.

2 one inch load-bearing heavy duty buckles.

2 one inch non-load-bearing light duty buckles.

Optional: One 5/16" cable thimble, nylon or aluminum.

Cutting Instructions

Cut the seat belt webbing into three pieces:

> One 60" chest loop.
>
> Two 24" foot loops.

Cut the 1" tubular webbing into the designated lengths as the construction details indicated. Remember to fuse the ends after each cut.

Foot Loops

Construction Details

1. While wearing climbing boots, take one 24" piece of 2" webbing and form a loop around the instep of the boot. This loop should be large enough to slip on and off your boot, but not so big as to hit the climber's shin above the boot.

2. Overlap at least 4" and trim the excess. Melt the ends and sew securely.

3. Place the loop on the foot with the sewn seam on the inside of the foot.

4. Above the seam, high on the inside, attach an 18" piece of 1" tubular webbing securely forming three layers for strength as shown in Fig. 6-p9.

5. Place a heavy duty 1" buckle low on the outside of the foot loop. Take a 5" piece of 1" webbing and thread the buckle in place as shown in Fig. 6-p9. Again, notice there are three layers to sew through for strength. Sew securely.

6. Remember to make both a left- and right-hand model.

Chest Box Assembly

Construction Details (Fig. 6-p10)

7. Thread the 60" piece of 2" webbing onto the 2" buckle and sew one 5" piece with the non-load bearing 1" buckle about 12" from the edge of the buckle. Sew this 1" buckle keeper strap in place along with the secure sewing of the 2" webbing to the 2" buckle.

8. Slide the ascender box onto the 2" webbing to within 3/8" of the 1" buckle keeper, checking to be sure that there are no sharp edges where the webbing comes in contact with the metal box.

9. Measure approximately 3/8" on the other side of the box and sew your second 5" piece with the other non-load bearing 1" buckle.

10. Fold over the end of the chest straps twice and sew to form a stopper for the buckle.

Shoulder Strap Assembly

11. Find the 4.5 foot piece of 1" tubular webbing and fold this in half.

12. Measure up from the looped end 2 1/4", mark, and sew the webbing together together.

13. Slide this piece onto the long end of the 2" strap and the chest harness will be complete.

Fitting the Chest Harness

The chest harness should never be so tight that it restricts breathing and yet it needs to be tight enough to hold the climber tight up against the rope. The box should be positioned high on the chest. This positioning becomes a careful three-way adjustment between the chest buckle and the two shoulder straps.

Lower Jumar Assembly

Construction Details

14. Take the 24" piece of tubular webbing and thread a 3 inch long wear protector piece onto each end of the sling.

15. Place the webbing through the eye of the bottom ascender.

16. Position the wear protector as shown in fig. #6-p11.

17. Overlap the webbing 4" and sew securely.

18. To determine the proper sling length, place the foot loop on the left boot and hold the ascender with the left index finger through the top eyehole.

19. Stand up straight with your back slightly arched.

20. While holding the ascender in your index finger, have someone thread the loose strap through the foot

loop, position the wear protector, allow for a 4 inch overlap and staple or mark.

21. Cut the excess and fuse the ends to prevent unravelling. Sew securely. **Add an upset protector**.

22. Take the 36 inch piece of 1" tubular webbing and thread it through the lower eye of the Jumar with the foot sling strap.

23. Overlap 4 inches and sew securely.

24. On the other end, overlap 8 inches leaving 4 inches open for a loop and 4 inches for a securely sewn seam.

25. This loop is attached to the seat sling carabiner. In the event of catastrophic failure of the chest box during a climb, a heel hang can be prevented with this simple attachment.

Upper Jumar Assembly
Construction Details: Fig. 6-p12

26. Take the 5 foot piece of 5/16" rope and thread it through the lower eye on the ascender.

27. Tie-off with a bowline as snug as possible to the Jumar frame.

28. To keep the knot from coming untied, melt a button on the rope end. This can be done with a hot knife or electric stove eye.

29. For ascenders with thin frames, such as Petzls, a 5/16" cable thimble can be placed through the ascender eye to prevent sharp rope bends and possible cutting.

30. For proper fitting, place the right foot loop on the boot.

31. Put the chest box assembly on tightly, high on the chest.

32. Thread the sling rope down through the box and through the foot loop. 33. Arch your back sightly and have someone tightly tie-off the sling rope to the foot loop with a bowline.

34. Put your full weight on the long cord to stretch and set the knots. You may find a tightening adjustment may be necessary. The most efficient length of the long strap is obtained by adjusting the sling so that the knot just below the Jumar rests right on top of the chest box with a minimum of space between the box and the ascender. However, a slightly longer sling is required when using the Cuddington switch. An even longer sling is needed if a safety cam is employed as an ascending belay.

35. Adjust any knots accordingly and cut off any excess. Melt a button and secure the knot.

NOTE: In conjunction with the seat harness and a safety Jumar as shown in Chapter 5 the three phases of the Mitchell system can be utilized with the design shown here.

Mitchell System Rig

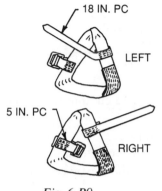

18 IN. PC

LEFT

5 IN. PC

RIGHT

Fig. 6-P9.
Foot stirrups

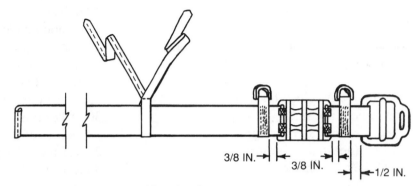

3/8 IN. → | ← 3/8 IN. → | ← 1/2 IN.

Fig. 6-P10   Chest box harness

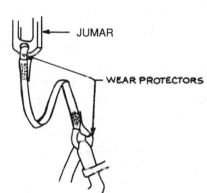

JUMAR

WEAR PROTECTORS

Fig. 6-P11
Lower Ascender Assembly

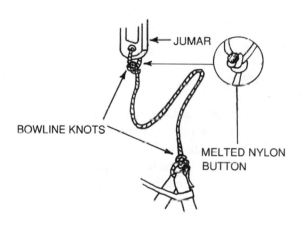

JUMAR

BOWLINE KNOTS

MELTED NYLON
BUTTON

Fig. 6-P12
Upper Ascender Assembly

Gibbs Rig

Materials List (overall)

9.5 feet of 2" seat belt webbing (2000 lbs. minimum tensile).
16.5 feet of 1" tubular webbing.
3 Gibbs ascenders.
1 Simmons chest roller or similar type of roller.
2 two inch heavy duty cinch buckles.
2 one inch heavy duty cinch buckles.
2 one inch light duty cinch buckles.
1 Maillon rapide link small, 1" long.
1 spring snap (non-load bearing).
1 3/4" D-ring (non-load bearing).
8 feet of 1/4" elastic shock cord.

Foot Cam

Materials List

26 inches of 2" seat belt webbing.
36 inches of 1" tubular webbing.
1 two inch buckle.
1 one inch buckle.
1 Gibbs ascender.

Cutting Instructions

Cut the tubular webbing into five pieces:

one 18" piece for the chicken loop.
one 5" piece for the buckle holder.
two 6" pieces for the cam attachment.
one 1" piece for a wear protector in the eye of the cam.

Construction Details

1. Take the 26 inch piece of 2" webbing and insert it into the 2" buckle. Fold back for 3 1/2" and sew securely.
2. Take one of the 5" pieces of tubular webbing and insert it into the 1" buckle. Fold the webbing and position as shown in Fig. 6-p12.
3. Take both 6" pieces of 1" webbing, slide the 1" long wear protector onto them and slide them both into the eye of the cam. Make sure the cam is correctly oriented and sew one of the cam holders as shown in 6-p12.
4. Sew the other 6" piece of webbing onto 2" wide foot strap and sew securely.
5. Place the 18 inch tubular webbing chicken loop onto the seat belt webbing and sew securely.

Knee Cam

Materials List

24 inches of 2" seat belt webbing.
5 feet of 1" tubular webbing.
1 one inch heavy duty cinch buckle.
1 Gibbs cam.
1 Maillon rapide link, 1" long.
1 spring snap.
8 feet of 1/4" elastic shock cord.

Cutting Instruction

Take the tubular webbing and cut into five pieces:
30 inches for the sling.
18 inches for the chicken loop.
2 three inch pieces for wear protectors.
5 inches for the buckle. Cut the elastic cord in half (4' lengths).

Construction Details

6. While wearing climbing boots, take the 24" piece of 2" and form a loop around the instep of the boot. This loop should be large enough to slip on and off the boot but not so big as to hit the climber's shin above the boot. Overlap at least 4", trim the excess, fuse the ends and sew securely.
7. Place the loop on the foot with the sewn seam on the inside of the foot. Above the seam high on the inside, attach securely the 18" piece of tubular webbing. Add strength by extending the webbing behind the foot loop webbing to form three layers.
8. Place the 1" buckle on the 5" piece of webbing and secure it to the foot loop as shown in Fig. 6-p13. Sew securely.
9. Take the 30 inch piece of webbing and thread a 3 inch wear protector onto each end.
10. Thread one end through the eye of the Gibbs cam and positon the wear protector.
11. Overlap the webbing for 4 inches and sew securely.
12. Place the foot loop on the boot.
13. Making sure that the cam is facing the right direction, thread the tubular webbing through the foot loop.
14. The eye of the knee cam should be 3 to 4 inches above the knee cap. Position the wear protector and overlap the seam by four inches. Trim the excess, fuse the ends and sew securely.
15. Take one of the 4 foot pieces of shock cord and tie

Gibbs   System   Rig

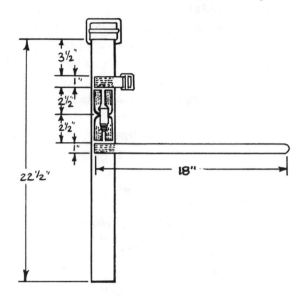

Fig. 6-P13.
Foot cam

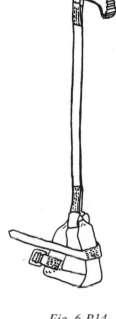

Fig. 6-P14
Knee cam

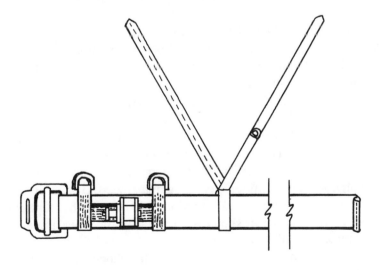

Fig. 6-P15
Chest roller assembly

Fig. 6-P16
Third cam

a small bowline in one end.

16. Take the small Maillon rapide link and pass it through the hole in the Gibbs cam shell in the upper corner. It may be necessary to drill this hole larger depending on the size of the Maillon one is using.

17. Attach the bowline end of the shock cord to the rapide link and close the gate on the link.

18. Tie a figure eight knot on the other end of the elastic cord and clip the spring snap into it. The best final length for this elastic cord will be determined after the chest roller harness has been completed.

Chest Roller Assembly

Materials List

5 feet of 2" seat belt webbing.

8.5 feet of 1" tubular webbing.

1 chest roller. 1 2" cinch buckle.

1 Gibbs ascender.

1 1" light duty cinch buckles.

1 D-ring 3/4".

Cutting Instructions

Cut the 1" webbing into 5 pieces:

4.5 feet.

2 six inch pieces to attach a roller.

2 five inch pieces for buckle attachments.

2.5 feet for the third Gibbs attachment.

Construction Details

19. Thread the seat belt buckle onto the seat belt webbing, overlap 5 inches and sew securely.

20. Check slots on the chest roller for sharp edges. Use a fine flint paper and buff the metal edges of slots to prevent cutting or excessive wear of the webbing.

21. Thread both 6" pieces of webbing through the slot of the roller and position one set of ends right next to the buckle. This will put the edge of the roller about 3" from the edge of the buckle.

22. Sew these six inch straps securely to the center of the harness as shown in Fig. 6-p14.

23. With the two 5" pieces of webbing, insert the buckles into each, fold and stitch into place about 2" from each side of the chest roller.

24. Position the buckles at the top of the chest strap and sew securely.

25. Take the 4.5 foot piece of webbing and fold it in half. Measure up 2 1/4" from the folded end, mark and sew a bar tack.

26. Slip it on the end of the 2" strap, put the chest harness on centering the shoulder strap in the center of the back.

27. Pull the straps over the shoulders and secure to the front buckles.

28. On the back of the right shoulder strap (assuming the knee cam goes on the left knee) sew the small 3/4" D-ring in place using a stitch similar to a bar tack.

29. Remove the harness and trim any excess, but not too much as to not allow for bulky jackets, wet suits or other variable clothing. Fuse the ends. 30. Fold over the end of the 2" strap and provide a stopper to prevent the harness from disengaging.

Third Cam Ascender

31. Thread the 2.5 foot piece of webbing through the eye of the third and last cam.

32. Overlap 4 inches and sew securely as shown in Fig. 6-p15.

33. Put on the chest harness you have just completed and the seat harness you'll be climbing with.

34. Thread a rope through the chest roller and attach the Gibbs just above the chest roller.

35. The Gibb's strap should pass behind the chest harness strap and extend down to the seat harness.

36. The third ascender should be snug but not sloppy. Form a 4" overlap through the seat harness carabiner, trim any excess, fuse and sew the loop securely.

Attach the Elastic Cord

37. Place the knee Gibbs on the foot, thread the elastic cord through the spring clip and secure it in place with a small bowline.

38. Clip the spring clip to the D-ring.

39. As you raise your right foot, the cam should be forcefully pulled up. It should not be so tight that it becomes difficult to extend your left leg straight.

40. The proper tension on the elastic cord can be determined by grasping the shock cord at the climber's mid-section and flexing the cord up and down. It should stretch easily for at least one inch in either direction.

41 Make adjustments to the shock cord length if necessary.

42. Place the extra piece of shock cord in your pack so you always have a ready replacement when necessary. Invariably, the shock cord will be the first item to show age on your system.

REFERENCES

Cuddington, William F. "Let's Talk Prusiking." *Nylon Highway 22* Vertical Section NSS, (1986), pp. 9-10.

Deal, Dwight. "The Infernal Machine." *1965 Speleo Digest*, Huntsville, AL.: NSS, 1965, pp. 3-33 to 3-38.

Fischesser, Mike. "The Butt Strap Harness." *Nylon Highway 15*, Vertical Section NSS, (1983), pp. 12-16.

Ganter, John. "A Quick Installation Chicken Loop." *Nylon Highway 17*, Vertical Section NSS, (1983), p. 16.

Ganter, John. "A Lightweight Frame for the Simmons Roller." *Nylon Highway 21*, Vertical Section NSS, (1986), pp. 1-2.

Gibbs, Charles. "Exclusive Interview With Charles Gibbs." *Cleve-O-Grotto News*, Nov. 1980. 28-31.

Gibbs, Peter. "A Short History of Gibbs Products, Inc." *Nylon Highway 15*, Vertical Section NSS, (1983), pp. 5-7.

Graham, Dick. "Ergonomics and Efficient Climbing Systems." *Nylon Highway 7*, Vertical Section NSS, (1977), pp. 15-21.

Halliday, William R. MD. *American Caves and Caving*, New York: Barnes & Noble Books, 1982.

Halliday, William R. MD. *Depths of the Earth*. New York: Harper & Row, 1976.

Henshaw, Robert & David Morehouse. "The Climbing Cam: A New Ascender." *NSS News*, Vol. 23 No. 11, 1965, p. 158-60.

Isenhart, Kyle. "Roller Cam." *Nylon Highway 1*, Vertical Section NSS, (1974), p.13.

Judson, David, ed. *Caving Practice and Equipment*, London: David and Charles Ltd., 1984, pp. 68-74.

Jumar Company. *Jumar Techniques and Methods*. Pamphlet, Jan, 1981.

McClurg, David. "An Improved Gibbs Self-Start Technique." *Nylon Highway 18*, Vertical Section NSS, (1985), p. 6.

Mitchell, Dick. "Fastest Method With Jumars." *NSS News*, Vol 25, No. 12, 1967.

Montgomery, Neil. *Single Rope Techniques*. Sydney, Australia: Sydney Speleological Society, 1977, pp. 73-99.

Padgett, Allen. "The Mitchell System." *NSS Caver Information Series*, 1972.

Schindel, Geary. "The Use of Knives in Vertical Caving." *NSS News*, Vol. 43, No. 11, 1985, pp. 349-351.

Simmons, Ron. "A Versatile Ropewalker: The Development." *Nylon Highway 15*, Vertical Section NSS, (1983), p. 3-5.

Smith, Bruce, W. "Rigging the Floating Cam System," *Nylon Highway 1*, Vertical Section NSS, (1974), p. 10-13

Smith, Bruce. "Efficiency with Versatility: Jumars," *Nylon Highway 1*, Vertical Section of the NSS, (1974), p. 14-16.

Smith, Bruce. "Chicken Loops: A Must," *Nylon Highway 1*, Vertical Section NSS, (1974), p. 17.

Smith, Bruce. "The Pygmy Prusik System." *Nylon Highway 2*, Vertical Section NSS, (1974), p. 19.

Smith, Bruce. "The Critical Length for the Long Texas." *Nylon Highway 3*, Vertical Section NSS, (1974), p. 19.

Smith, Bruce. "Inchworm Climbing." *Nylon Highway 5*, Vertical Section of the NSS, (1976), pp. 8-10.

Smith, Bruce. "The Ascender Knot." *Nylon Highway 17*, Vertical Section NSS, (1983), p. 19.

Smith, Bruce. "The Portly Prusik." *Nylon Highway 16*, Vertical Section NSS, (1983), pp. 15-17.

Thrun, Robert. *Prusiking*. Huntsville, AL.: NSS, 1971, pp. 17-23, 29-42.

Tomer, Darrel. "Climbing With the Gossett System." *Nylon Highway 11*, Vertical Section NSS, (1979), p. 2.

Weisbrod, Richard. "An Alternate Inchworm Technique." *Cal Caver,* Vol. 22, No. 5, Oct. 1971.

Williams, Kathy. "Boing! The Double Bungie Gibbs Ascent System." *Nylon Highway 14*, Vertical Section NSS, (1981), pp. 12-14.

7 Long Drops

7 Long Drops

By Dan Twilley, D.C.

A long drop is defined for this discussion as any vertical expanse over 500 feet. Such drops not only include mountains, caves and cliffs, but also bridges, buildings and other manmade structures. The drop should be able to be rigged with one rope. If it is possible to get off the rope during a climb or descent and walk around (on a ledge for instance), then two drops probably exist. Most long drops take special preparation, special equipment and special resources and may fall into the definition of an "expedition."

Prior Planning

It is vital to be prepared when attempting a long drop, and a lot of prior planning is required. Maps of the terrain or cave should be obtained, and even aerial photographs may be helpful. Thought should be given to the arrangement of special transportation, special food and other needs. Knowledge of the weather, vegetation, insects and animals may need to be included in the preparation phase. A talk with a resident of the area or with someone who has done the drop could be helpful. A reconnaissance trip to the drop by one or two members of the party prior to the trip may be helpful, especially if the drop has never been done or if adequate information is unobtainable from other sources.

Special Equipment

There are several necessary pieces of specialized equipment that are usually not required for shorter drops. Many of these items are used during high-angle rescue work and are available from some of the better mountaineering shops.

Two-Way Radios

Radios are extremely useful during long drops. There is a variety of radio equipment available to solve almost any communication need.

When determining the best radio system for an expedition, the following questions need to be answered:

- What is the physical nature of the site? Is it off a cliff, across a valley, in a cave, or from one side of a mountain to another? This will determine if line-of-sight transmission is possible.

Fig. 7-1. It takes all three: frequency, antenna, and power.

- How many base units and portables are needed?
- How long will these units be in service and under what climatic conditions? The answer to this last question will determine battery requirements.

Regardless of all the physical restrictions, the radios must be powerful enough and clear enough to do the job. There are several ways to improve the effectiveness of any radio system. The right power, the right frequency and the right antenna configuration will provide a clear top-to-bottom talk line (Fig. 7-1). Low-powered, head-set mounted Easy Talker type radios are too weak and fragile to be of much use on long drops. For difficult around-a-corner situations a repeater system can be employed. Each separate radio talks to the repeater, which then automatically retransmits the signal. These devices, though somewhat expensive, can solve communication problems on many big walls (Fig. 7-2). For assistance with communications planning, consult local experts engaged in the sale and service of business radios.

Other Means of Communication

Radios are often expensive and, even though they may be the best option, there are others. For small drops many of the following have merit, but on long drops, the drawbacks outweigh any advantages (Fig. 7-3):

- An airhorn or small trumpet could provide a limited supply

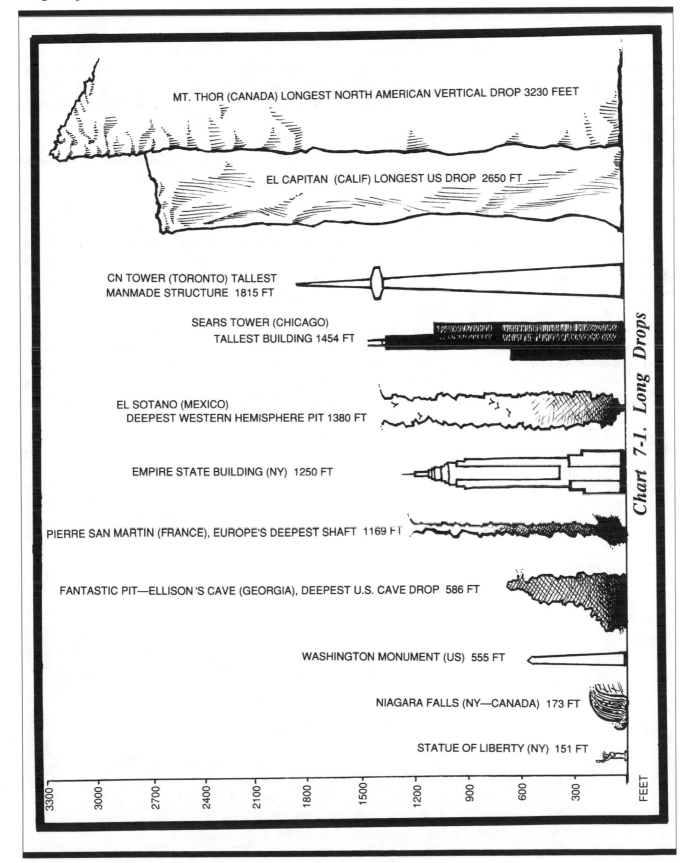

MT. THOR (CANADA) LONGEST NORTH AMERICAN VERTICAL DROP 3230 FEET

EL CAPITAN (CALIF) LONGEST US DROP 2650 FT

CN TOWER (TORONTO) TALLEST
MANMADE STRUCTURE 1815 FT

SEARS TOWER (CHICAGO)
TALLEST BUILDING 1454 FT

EL SOTANO (MEXICO)
DEEPEST WESTERN HEMISPHERE PIT 1380 FT

EMPIRE STATE BUILDING (NY) 1250 FT

PIERRE SAN MARTIN (FRANCE), EUROPE'S DEEPEST SHAFT 1169 FT

FANTASTIC PIT—ELLISON'S CAVE (GEORGIA), DEEPEST U.S. CAVE DROP 586 FT

WASHINGTON MONUMENT (US) 555 FT

NIAGARA FALLS (NY—CANADA) 173 FT

STATUE OF LIBERTY (NY) 151 FT

3300 3000 2700 2400 2100 1800 1500 1200 900 600 300 FEET

Chart 7-1. Long Drops

of long and short blasts. However, codes such as this can often be misinterpreted due to echos. Also horns are often as bulky as radios.

- Whistles are certainly compact, but lose their volume in the wind of long drops. Around a corner their volume is often lost entirely.

- Flares may accidentally burn the rope, and one is never sure anyone else is watching. At night, however, they may be useful in getting attention.

- A note attached to a carabiner and slid down the rope will not arrive if there are attached rope pads. Even if the carabiner does arrive at the bottom, the piece of paper rarely does. Sliding a note up the rope results in even greater challenges.

- A message attached to a dropped rock should not be considered, for obvious reasons.

- Yelling over great distances is probably the most unreliable method of all.

Long drops underground offer special problems, because narrow shafts can interfere with and distort the signal. Sometimes an antenna lowered over the top of the drop will solve this problem. At best, the topside radio antenna needs to be extended over the edge. For extra communication problems where line-of-sight is unavailable, consider wired communications. Field phones, though awkward, provide a reliable communications link. When using phones, the wire must be away from the rope to prevent entanglement. Field phones are discussed further in Chapter 10.

Telescopes and Binoculars

On drops of 1000 feet or so, binoculars can provide adequate viewing of the climber. However, for much over 1000-foot drops, binoculars often fall short in providing adequate magnification. Telescopes are the best option. Realize of course, that all these viewing instruments become useless in fog, darkness and heavy rain. There should be at least two telescopes: one for the summit team and one for the base team. Prior testing with several sizes of

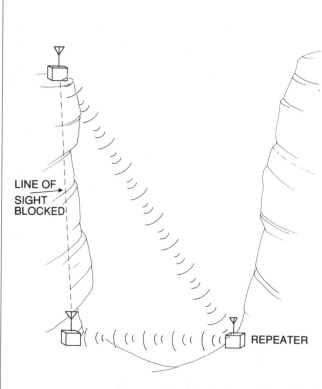

Fig. 7-2. Repeaters help when line of sight isn't possible.

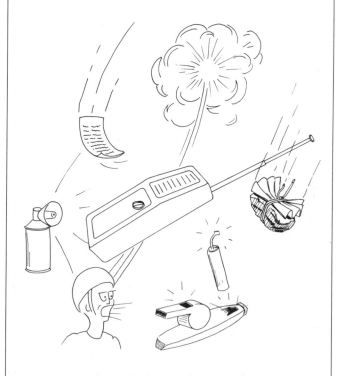

Fig. 7-3. Of all the options, radio is best.

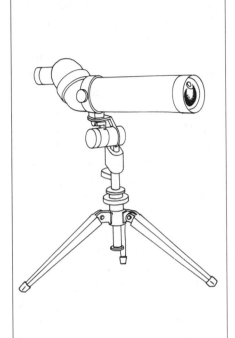

Fig. 7-4. Spotting scopes are light-weight, rugged, and powerful.

telescopes to determine the best one for the job may be necessary. Spotting telescopes (Fig. 7-4) used by sportsmen, are rugged, compact and powerful.

SPECIAL RIGGING EQUIP-MENT

Edge Rollers

On a long drop where the bending of the rope may be a critical factor, an investment in edge rollers will work far better than a rope pad. There are several varieties available for various types of edges (Fig. 7-5). It is easy to attach several edge rollers together to overcome any unusual rope/rock contact situation. Edge rollers also greatly reduce the friction a team will encounter when hauling up the rope or hauling up and down

food and equipment.

Haul Cord

If the team decides to pull the rope up the face of the drop, a haul cord will be necessary. It should have a tensile strength of at least five times the maximum anticipated weight of the rope. It should also be somewhat longer than the drop. During hauling, the pull of gravity, the friction generated from the rope and cord rubbing the rock, combined with the upward pulling can put excessive strain on the haul cord. On the second El Capitan trip these stresses broke the 1/8 inch haul cord, seriously endangering the success of the expedition.

Summit Rope

There may be a need for at least one additional rope at the summit that should be 10 to 20% of the length of the main rope. This rope can be used for a hauling system to pull up the main rope, allowing rappellers and climbers to get on and off the rope without the cumbersome weight of the rope. This summit rope can also be used to scout below the lip to view areas on the face out of sight from above before the final rigging point is selected. This rope can also be used as a pig-tail or a tether line for non-climbers, while they assist other climbers over the lip. Photographers may find the best shooting angle to be over the edge and down the drop some distance. This rope may be useful in the unlikely event of a rescue either as lacing for a makeshift litter or as part of a staged rigging during a

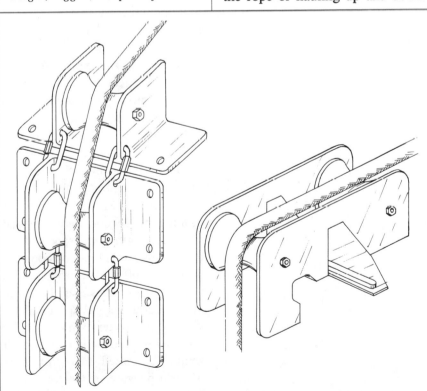

Fig. 7-5. Edge rollers, though expensive, are a fine alternative to rope pads.

victim evacuation. Take stock of the summit needs and determine how many additional ropes will be helpful.

Summit Equipment
Besides edge rollers and haul cords, there is a variety of additional equipment that must be transported to the summit, such as pulleys, large steel carabiners, padding, tethers, straps, webbing, haul system hardware, duct tape, first aid kits, shelter, cold/wet weather gear, cooking stove and community food. The logistics of any expedition are very involved and should never be taken lightly.

SPECIAL DESCENDING EQUIPMENT

Long Racks
Long drops require special descending devices because of the extreme rope weight. Longer racks seem to provide the ultimate in control and smoothness. Longer drops require longer racks. Experience on drops over 2000 feet shows that racks with overall lengths of 18 inches, 21 inches and 24 inches have all worked to the advantage of the rappeller. With racks this long, spacers need to be added between the first and second bars, as well as the second and third bars. For example, a 21 inch rack requires two-inch spacers between the 1st and 2nd and 1 1/2 inch spacers between the second and third (Fig. 7-6).

Long Rack Use
The longer racks, even though they provide more control, can be

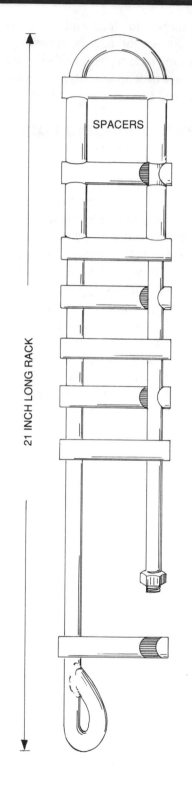

SPACERS

21 INCH LONG RACK

Fig. 7-6. Long (21 inch) rack showing spacers between top bars.

awkward when negotiating a lip. Their length requires a lip which is easy to get over. Another minor concern with the long racks arises when they are stressed with excessive weight. They tend to distort and bend, which effects the smoothness and responsiveness of the rack but in no way endangers the rappeller. Another drawback is the inability of a standard Jumar safety to reach above the rack enabling the rappeller to rest or change over. Most of these are measured and presewn for a climber using a standard 14-inch rack. Even if extension cords were attached to a safety Jumar, the likelihood that a climber could reach the rope above a long rack is remote. As mentioned in Chapter 6, a low-attachment sit harness may put the top of the long rack low enough for a safety Jumar to reach over (Fig. 7-7).

Hollow Steel Brake Bars
Hollow steel brake bars, because they remain cooler, are the best option for racks used on long drops. Aluminum bars act as heat sinks, and on long drops they tend to overheat because they cannot dissipate heat effectively. It is reported that on Mount Thor speeds of 8 feet per second were achieved over the length of the rope and yet the hollow bars remained cool. On drops of 500 feet to 1500 feet a normal-length rack can be used, but moderate rappel speeds along with squirt water bottles can be used to keep the equipment cool. It should be noted that aluminum bars do provide better control on nylon ropes due to their higher friction. Steel bars are slippery

and inexperienced rappellers may have control problems. However, practice using a long rack with steel bars is easily accomplished. On a shorter drop, attach a person or a duffle bag full of rocks to the bottom of the rope. This added weight will simulate the rope weight on a long drop.

Group and Personal Gear

Base Equipment

The equipment at a base camp will depend entirely upon whether the trip originates from the bottom of the drop or the top. If the trip originates from a valley and a percentage of the team hikes to the top to set up a summit camp, the base camp should include the bulk of all the personal gear. It should have shelter for everyone, spare parts, equipment hauling bags, the majority of the food and the bulk of any emergency gear that may be necessary.

If the expedition originates from the top of the drop, then the top of the drop is "base camp." The bottom camp, if one even exists, will have few supplies.

Personal Gear

There are a few items that every person should carry with him whether he is at the top, on rope, or at base camp. When a rappeller starts over the edge or starts a climb from below, he is essentially, separating from the team and exploring alone. Besides climbing and rappelling gear, he should go prepared to survive in that particular terrain for at least 24 hours.

This should include appropriate weather gear, a space banket, rain shell or poncho, 24 hours worth of food, water, a back-up signaling device, compass, possibly a map of the area, a flashlight, small first aid kit, dry matches or equivalent, toilet paper and a pocket knife or a survival knife. In the unlikely event that the lone climber should get separated from the group, some or all of these items may prove to be life-sustaining.

On one long drop expedition, all the members were expected to rappel the drop and either climb back up or walk out by an obscure trail. When a portion of the party, after leaving their climbing gear at the top, finally completed the rappel, the group had run out of daylight and was unable to find the trail in the dark. The majority of the group crawled under a cold rock and waited out the frigid night without proper protection. This one true story points up the need for prior planning and personal gear. Most of the deaths that have occurred on big walls are from exposure and/or an adverse weather change, not spectacular 3000-foot screamers.

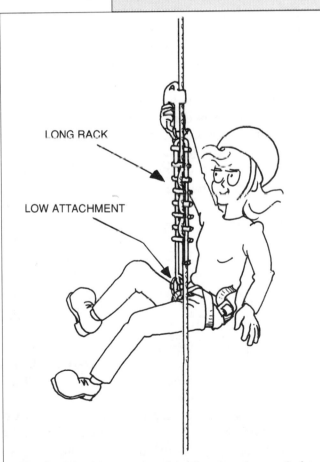

Fig. 7-7. Seat harness must have low attachment. Safety Jumar should be long enough to reach over top of long rack, but still be within reach.

RIGGING THE ROPE

How the rope must be transported is a decision that must be made. Will it be carried to the top of the drop or to the bottom of the drop and be hauled up with a haul cord? Each drop holds its own set of circumstances, and getting the rope in place will require special planning. Carrying a long rope to the top of a high place requires a tremendous amount of work and in most cases will not be practical or even possible. The rope was driven to the top of Toroweap Point, Grand Canyon and Snake River Canyon. It was carried to the top of Stone Mountain, Golondrinas, El Sotano and Long's Peak. The trip to Long's Peak was the only unsuccessful attempt because the team suffered such physical abuse and energy expenditure during the climb up the mountain with the rope that neither energy, stamina nor time allowed the team to successfully rig the drop. It is important to review both situations.

Transporting the Rope to the Top

There are several proven ways of transporting a long rope to the top of a drop. Some of the options include:

- Some drops allow vehicle access.
- It is possible to helicopter personnel and equipment to the top. This is often a very expensive option.
- Closely associated with the above, it would be possible to airlift equipment and possibly parachute the equipment to the site. This has been done extensively during many military operations. It has not been extensively experimented with by the private sector.
- Renting burros or horses has been used successfully during repeated trips to Mexico and other deep pit areas.
- Putting the rope in several duffle bags or coils with about 15 feet of line between each bag or coil allows each member of a hiking party to carry his share of the load to the drop site.
- Chaining the rope as described in Figure 2-22 allows each team member to carry his share over his shoulder as he hikes to the drop site.
- Spreading the hiking party over a long distance and carrying the rope up the mountain in a single strand is a solution and has been used when derigging caves of great depth. The drawback to this method is the severe ambient abrasion that the rope will suffer prior to its use. The rope would probably suffer enough damage during such an ascent that experienced climbers would probably decline the privilege to ride the rope.

HAULING THE ROPE TO THE TOP

Hauling Rope Up the Drop Face From Below

To haul the rope up the drop face, the assault team should divide themselves into two teams: the **base team** and the **summit team.** The summit team should make its way to the top with all the appropriate equipment, including the haul cord, while the base team makes its way to the approximate landing zone at the base of the drop. The base team should stay away from the rockfall zone until it becomes time to attach the rope to the haul cord. The possibilities of falling rock, packs and debris are highest just as a summit team arrives and begins clearing the lip area.

Selecting the Rig Point

When selecting the rig point, among the least of the concerns should be the drop length. First and foremost consider the cleanest, smoothest, safest rocky place available. Look for a place that may provide rigging freedom, as well as a rock face that appears unshattered; a place where the rope will have minimum rock contact; a place where the rope will bend gradually and enter free space 15 to 20 feet below the lip. Avoid a place where there seem to be a lot of pebbles and small rocks that could be easily kicked off by accident. It may be necessary for someone to drop over the edge, rappel down, and scout the drop below the lip. This will allow close scrutiny of problems that may not be visible from the top.

CAUTION: Rockfall is an ever-present and tremendously dangerous part of long drops. This danger cannot be overemphasized. One of the objectives of each member should be to allow no rocks to fall once the rope is in place. It may be necessary to clear upper ledges prior to rigging. If this is the case, consider moving the rocks back away from the edge. Dropping the rocks should be the last resort. Radio warnings to the base team should be made prior to any ledge cleaning.

Lowering the Haul Cord

Lowering the haul cord begins some very tense moments that could determine the success or failure of the entire mission. To assist the cord in finding its way to the bottom, 30 to 50 pounds should be placed into a haul bag tied to the cord. High winds during a long drop may cause the haul bag to drift and float away from the vertical. The bag being lowered should be free of buckles, straps or any item that may allow the bag to snag. As mentioned earlier, the base team should be clear of the rockfall zone and under substantial shelter.

At least two summit team members should lower the weighted bag. One should control the rappel device while the other feeds and manages the haul cord, preventing it from snarling and kinking. It should be lowered smoothly and at a moderate speed in one smooth complete descent. This will allow the summit crew the best opportunity to feel a weight loss if the bag were to hang up. Lowering the bag in a jerky fashion may allow the bag to snag. If the cord snags and is later freed, there will be no opportunity to inspect any abrasion points that may have occurred on the haul cord before the hoisting of the rope. Obviously, it is important to maintain the integrity of the haul cord.

The anticipated length of the drop should be marked on the haul cord and hopefully the loss of haul cord weight will occur about the same time the marked spot is payed out. Base team members should enter the drop zone only after the bag has touched down.

Hauling Up the Rope

After the haul bag completes its descent, the rope should be transported to the rockfall zone and prepared so that it will pay out easily and continuously. The haul cord should be tied to the main rope with a knot that offers the least strength loss. Simply wrapping the cord around the main rope several times and securing the bundle with duct tape works well; however, to best secure the haul cord to the main line requires a multi-wrap Prusik knot coupled with an overhand knot at the end of the main rope (Fig. 7-8). Duct tape all loose ends and knots to smoothness.

Hauling the rope up the drop should be done in one smooth straight one-to-one pull. Except for edge rollers, and one edge pulley, avoid pulley systems and mechanical advantage systems. A straight one-to-one haul will heighten the hauler's sensitivity to the stresses being experienced by the haul cord. Heavy rope on the long drops rigged in North America with a haul cord were discovered to be quite manageable. However, it is felt that the mechanical advantage system contributed to the failure of the haul cord on the second El Capitan Expedition. Mechanical advantage systems provide the leverage that allows the haulers to exceed

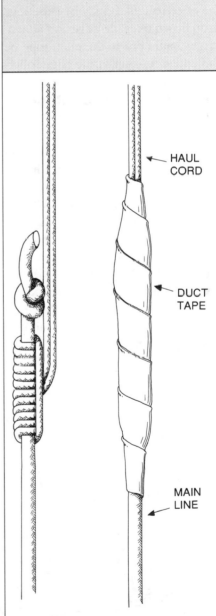

Fig. 7-8. Attach the haul cord and the main rope with as smooth a knot as possible.

the haul cord's breaking strength. In addition, hauling systems become time-consuming; A two-to-one haul system will require more than twice as long to haul up the rope due to resetting and loss of efficiency.

Bringing the rope over the edge is often a very tense moment. If the haul cord is to fail, it will probably happen there. It is at the top that the haul cord experiences the added weight of the entire rope as well as the friction of the bumpy knot as it rolls over the edge rollers. It may be beneficial to have someone drop down over the edge and attach an ascender and a larger haul cord to the main rope before it encounters the added tension of the edge rollers.

Tying Off the Main Rope

After the end of the main rope arrives at the top, it is best to pull up all excess rope, leaving only zero to 20 feet of rope on the ground at the bottom of the drop. At the top the rope should be draped across the edge rollers and wrapped around a smooth padded object such as a tree or a smooth rock. Take special precautions to ensure that the rope encounters no sharp bends. If it is possible, place a large anchor. Three-quarter-inch studs shear between 13,000 and 18,000 pounds. On Mount Thor a metal four-inch cylinder (Fig. 7-9) was bolted into the rock with four bolts. The rope was wrapped around this metal "tree" and then backed up with a couple of larger anchors. To avoid sharp rope-bending consider the use of rope or cable

thimbles (Fig. 7-10).

The top of a long drop may involve many important elements of which tying off the main rope is only one (Fig. 7-11). Padding, hauling systems, ratchet-cam placements and pigtails may all be other important elements in a long drop setup.

It may be advantageous to be able to tie the rope off in such a way that it could be untied while someone is on the rope. This could allow the summit team to raise or lower a climber if the situation calls for it. A mechanical advantage raising system could be set up and placed on the ground ready to use if needed to lift a climber. Some experts suggest rigging the main rope with a rack already on the rope at the top and secured to an anchor in the event it becomes necessary to rappel someone or something down the rope quickly. If this situation occurs it is necessary to have enough rope at the top for a victim to safely reach the bottom.

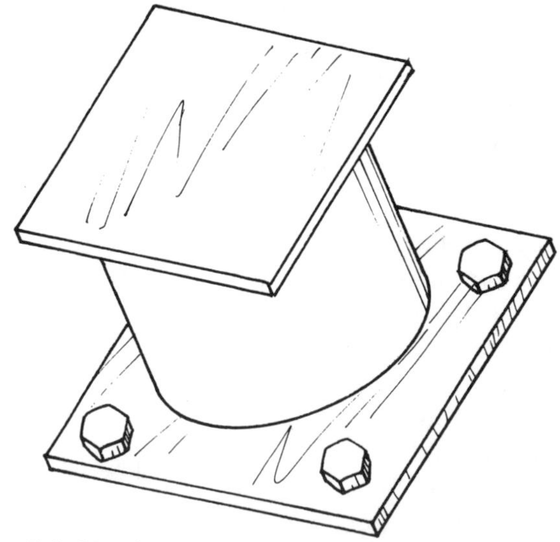

FIg. 7-9. Metal tree, used on Mt. Thor, utilized four rock expansion bolts.

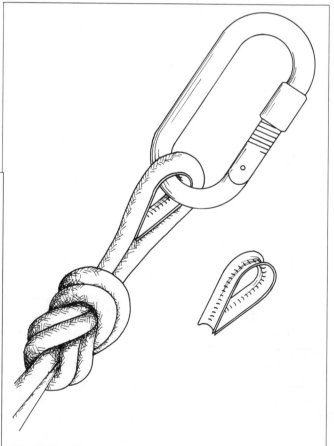

Fig. 7-10. The use of rope and cable thimbles can eliminate the sharp bending of a rope.

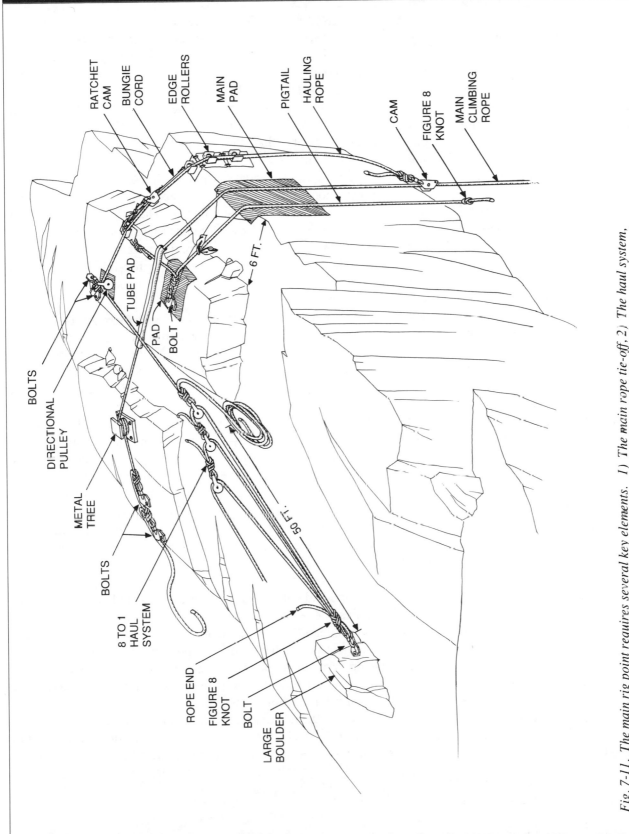

RATCHET CAM
BUNGIE CORD
EDGE ROLLERS
MAIN PAD
PIGTAIL
HAULING ROPE
CAM
FIGURE 8 KNOT
MAIN CLIMBING ROPE

BOLTS
DIRECTIONAL PULLEY
METAL TREE
BOLTS
8 TO 1 HAUL SYSTEM
ROPE END
FIGURE 8 KNOT
BOLT
LARGE BOULDER

TUBE PAD
PAD
BOLT

6 FT.
50 FT.

Fig. 7-11. The main rig point requires several key elements. 1) The main rope tie-off, 2) The haul system, 3) Pigtail(s) and 4) Ratchet cams.

Haul System

A haul system should be included in the summit rigging. It should be used primarily to lift the rope so rappellers and prusikers can get over the edge without the inhibiting weight of the rope. The summit rope should be used with this mechanical advantage system. See Chapter 10 for diagrams of several helpful systems.

The haul system purchase line should pass over edge rollers at the lip and then be directed down a cleared path, lane or runway where the haulers can attach an ascender to the haul cord and walk the entire length of the runway pulling the purchase line as they walk. Between the runway and the edge rollers, an ascender should be secured to capture progress (ratchet cam). This could be a Gibb, a Jumar, a CMI, a Petzl or any reliable ascender. A person should be designated as the "ratchet minder" who ensures progress is adequately captured after each cycle of the hauling team. Typically, the haulers attach an ascender to the rope, space themselves out and on command of "Haul" they pull and walk together the length of the runway. When they reach the end of the runway, someone yells, "Set." The ascender minder sets the ascender, ensuring that the progress has been captured and yells, "Slack." The haulers release the tension and their ascenders and walk back to the start of the runway, reattach their ascenders and start the cycle all over again.

RAPPELLING A LONG DROP

Getting Started

The easiest way to get over the lip with a long rack is to rappel over the lip with a standard rack on the pigtail. It is necessary that the standard rack be connected to the rappeller's harness at a secondary point of connection. A better option may be to incorporate a secondary diaper harness over the rappeller's primary harness and attach the standard rack to it. After transfer is complete, the rappeller should remove this temporary harness. Once in a comfortable spot below the lip, lock off the standard rack and attach the long rack to the main rope. Unlock the standard rack and slowly descend until the long rack can be attached into the seat harness with a connecting locking carabiner. Screw the carabiner shut and continue to rappel until all the rappeller's weight is hanging from the main rope. Unclip the standard rack from the seat harness, leave the rack for the next rappeller, and continue the rappel on the main line. A safety Jumar is not needed for this procedure.

Another method of getting started requires the assistance of other party members. Using the haul system, the rope can be lifted below the lip providing the rappeller with easy attachment. The rappeller should take a quick inventory of the gear he is carrying, verifying that it is attached to his harness properly. A safety measure calls for a safety Jumar being attached to the rope before attaching rappelling equipment. After easing over the edge, the rope is carefully placed on the edge rollers, and all the rappeller's weight is placed on the rope. After the rappel system is checked out, the haul system should be lowered, putting full tension of the rope on the rappeller and the rappelling device. The Jumar safety can then be unclipped to start the descent. It may be necessary to adjust the rack with the full weight of the rope hanging below.

The First Person Down

Descent, rather than ascent, should be the first activity to take place on the rope. A rappeller can check and verify the safety of the drop from the rigging point down. On the way up, a climber may discover a problem such as an abraded rope against a sharp rock. It would be too late to save the rope for future one rope rappels. The first person down must go prepared for almost anything. Her equipment should include bolts and bolting equipment, rope pads, and deviation equipment such as short slings and carabiners. Any time the rope hints at lying against a rock, it should be protected if at all possible. Pads may need to be bolted to the side of the wall and then clipped to the rope as discussed in Chapter 4. It may be necessary to avoid ambient abrasion with a deviation. Wind, again, may be the rope's worst enemy on a big drop. The wind can cause the rope to constantly slap the rock, destroying the rope. It may be helpful to secure the rope to the rock wall with a bolt, chock or sling. The group may consider derigging the rope when it is not in use.

If there is an excessively long expanse of rock which comes in contact with the rope and is obviously too large to pad, the rope could be raised or lowered 30 or 50 feet after each climb to minimize the abrasion in any one spot. It is possible to walk the rope out a short distance from the drop face and tightly secure the rope to a point that will keep the rope from touching the rock. No face pads would be necessary, thus simplifying the rigging. Long racks may be needed with this type of rigging.

During a Rappel

After a rappeller has overcome the initial difficulties of the lip, carefully placed the rope onto the edge rollers, set the brake bars for movement, positioned the control and cradling hand, she should be ready to move down the rope. Speeds should be kept in control and reasonable. When the rappeller feels the descent may be getting out of control, it is probably the time to add another bar. Waiting too long to add another bar could be devastating, since a runaway rappel on a long drop becomes an uncontrolled slide to serious injury or death.

Adding bars may appear diffi-

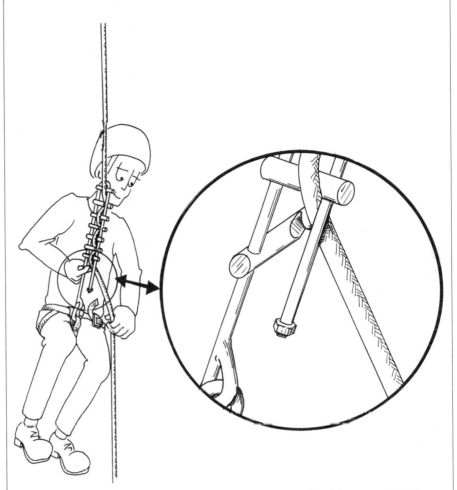

Fig. 7-12. Forcing the heavy rope to ride on the outside of the rappeller's leg (the rope often runs between the legs on a long drop) will provide just enough gap for the bars to be opened and closed permitting the adding and subtracting of those bars.

cult because of the weight of the rope; however, simply rotating the body to one side of the rope and placing the rope on a hip, will provide the necessary gap to slide a bar into place (Fig. 7-12). It is preferable to change bars on a long rappel without stopping, because the bars may have accumulated enough heat to damage the rope.

When the rappeller encounters rope pads that are not attached to the rope, she must be careful to make sure that they are replaced on the pad. Maneuvering past an attached rope pad or deviation will require the rappeller to:

• Unclip the attached carabiner.
• Slide past the attachment point.

- Reconnect the rope after passing. Depending on the length of the rack, speed of rappel, wind and other conditions, this maneuver can be physically difficult. As unimportant a maneuver as this may seem, the entire success or failure of the expedition may rest upon the reattachment of the rope after a deviation.

Relief straps may be necessary to keep the rappeller's legs from going to sleep (Fig. 7-13). By simply standing in these straps, one can take the pressure off spots that the seat harness may be constricting. These straps have proven extremely helpful during long tyroleans and during some of the first-person-down rappels in deep Mexican pits. In addition to relief straps, simple flexing of the legs can assist in regaining some circulation.

Upon landing, it is important to detach from the rope quickly because the rappel device may be quite hot. The rappeller should close the bars of her device, secure her gear and rapidly move away from the rockfall zone. It is then appropriate to signal to the top, "Off rope!"

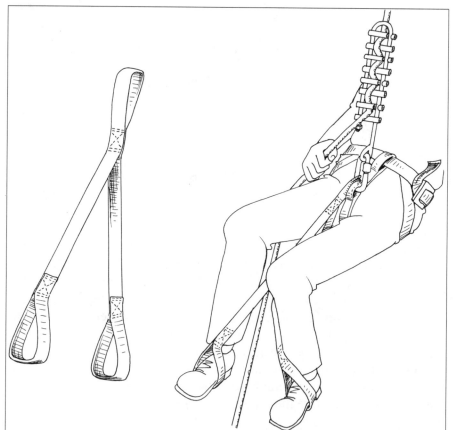

Fig. 7-13. Relief straps can provide a way to allow blood circulation to return ro a rappeller's legs on a long drop. Sitting in a harness for long periods of time can cause this condition.

Climbing a Long Drop

An important part of accomplishing any great feat is the strong belief that it can be done. The negative physiological effects of a lack of confidence have been well documented. Every first-time big drop climber needs to be aware that upon first gazing skyward at a disappearing rope he will experience the strong belief that he may not be able to climb that far. Climbing a rope is not difficult **IF** the climbing rig fits and works well. The hard part about climbing rope is maintaining a pace that doesn't exceed cardiac abilities.

Most people climb too forcefully. A climber should attempt to climb with an easy stride that involves the least amount of wasted motion, does not stress the joints or push the muscular system. This is accomplished by establishing a beneficial rhythm. The right rhythm can actually assist the heart in its effort to feed the body. A hard-climb/long-break rotation is not the best for any climber. Timed periodic breaks can also be useful for photography and meditative experiences. Any climber can have a good or a bad day and he should listen to his body as he climbs and climb accordingly.

Preparing For a Long Climb

Prior to the event it would be wise to climb the same distance elsewhere. This can be done by using pulleys or climbing a shorter drop repeatedly. Aerobic exercise beginning two to three months before the trip will ensure a much easier climb. A schedule that eventually involves 30 to 40 minutes of workout three to four times a week will usually provide adequate training.

To prepare for endurance activities, a person should follow these nutritional guidelines: Eating should take place at least two hours before a long climb and should consist of simple, easy-to-digest foods such as fruit, rice or yogurt. Foods that should be avoided are those that contain sucrose (table sugar) such as peanut butter and candy bars and also difficult-to-digest foods such as milk, eggs or grains. The meal should not be a large one, since digestion involves the use of blood, thus depriving the priority muscles of the needed attention and nutrition.

There are several substances commercially available from local health food stores that can increase endurance. On the day of a big climb, it may be helpful to ingest several of these supplements even while climbing. Read and follow the directions carefully.

On the other hand, except for high-sugar drinks, a climber can drink any healthy liquid. On long drops a climber may need as much as two or three quarts of water. A climber should slightly overdrink before climbing and drink frequently during the climb as the sensation of thirst occurs after the affects of water deprivation have occurred. If a climber oversaturates with water he/she should be prepared for the normal biological functions of elimination. Seat harnesses and other restrictive devices may require innovation.

When to Climb
On a dry hot rock face the sun is absolutely merciless and the air near that rock can be motionless. Climbing during times such as these should not be attempted. Most people prefer to climb in the morning, evening or at night, when the sun is off the wall. Keep in mind that rock will often retain sun heat for a couple of hours after becoming shaded. Weaker climbers should climb during the coolest times. Nevertheless, if the trip is managed properly, the rope will rarely be free and will almost always be in use. Rain and wind can be problems that require advance preparation as weather conditions can change dramatically. See the section on personal gear.

If a chance storm surprises the group, it is important to remove all climbers and rappellers from the rope and its vicinity. Wet rope attracts lightning and becomes a conductor.

Climbing Gear
There are many climbing methods, as Chapter 6 explains. Mastery of many of these systems may be very helpful on a big drop. The body suffers stresses that need to be alleviated. Regardless of the climbing system, on a very long drop, the straps will become painful and the climbing system may often seem inadequate. A good custom fit is essential. A climber's system should be made with 3 inch inch webbing at points of high stress. It is most helpful to be able to adjust the system several ways in an effort to alter the stress points. For example, if the upper arm gets tired when using the Mitchell system, change hands. Bill Cuddington proposed such a movement in the early 1970s, and it became known as the "Cuddington Switch". It may be helpful to have a rig that could be converted from a shoulder Gibb to a chest roller in an effort to reduce the fatigue on one part of the body. In any event, it is helpful to have a harness and a system that allows a climber to hang motionless for hours without pain and without areas of the body falling asleep. On a long drop the use of both arms and legs for upward movement is preferred.

CAUTION: Polypropylene ascender knots should not be used as they will most likely deteriorate substantially after only 1000 feet.

MOVEMENT AND TANDEM CLIMBING

Tandem climbing requires that both climbers ascend at a very constant pace and an even rhythm. Two concerns seem to be common among all tandem climbers:

- The climbers should never become separated by any more than about 50 feet. If a loose shattered section of wall is encountered, it is important that tandem climbers are separated only by inches. This ensures that if a piece of equipment were to be dropped or a rock knocked off the wall by the upper climber, the falling object would not kill or seriously injure the lower person.

- Either climber can be affected by the bounce of the other; and a rope-bounce form of sea sickness is very possible due to the distances involved. Smooth climbing comes with technique and practice. It takes a pro to climb smoothly while a common mistake of a less experienced climber is to bounce his muscles and weight up the rope. Try to pair tandem rope-walkers and sit-stand climbers that climb at the same rate. See Chapter 6 for more on tandem climbing.

Changing Ropes on a Long Drop

It would be rare, but the possibility of needing to change to another rope while on a long drop could happen. The dominant problem arises from the stretch that a long rope sustains when a climber is hanging by it. For example, if a climber were to quickly attach to an unloaded 600-foot rope, it can stretch as much as 20 feet. To safely change ropes and avoid getting torn in half, the climber should follow these steps:

- Change over to a rappelling mode.
- While hanging in

the rappel device attach all the climbing gear to the second rope. It is easiest if the feet or lower ascenders get attached first.

- After full attachment of the climbing system to the second rope, rappel off of the first rope until all weight is now hanging from the second rope.
- Disengage the rappel device from the first rope and the transfer is complete.

An alternate method would involve hanging in a safety Jumar while climbing the stretch out of the second rope until all of the climber's weight is transferred. Disengaging the safety Jumar, the climber is now free to continue up the second rope.

Coming Over the Lip

At the lip the crew should always be prepared to deal with the overly fatigued climber. Most people will easily have the energy to finish, but the safety of fatigued individuals in either a windy, wet, cold or combined situation could quickly become a priority. Fast action in the form of a rope haul,

already in place, an etrier with carabiners on the two lower loops (see Fig. 4-54), or a couple of

strong friends attached to a tether should always be available on short notice. It would always be

Fig. 7-14. When tandem climbing on a troublesome lip, have the lower climber remain below the hauling device, thus retaining part of the rope weight that the hauling team then proceeds to eliminate for the top climber.

possible on a tandem situation for the lower person to stay below the haul system ascender while the summit team hauls up the weight of the rope along with the second climber, allowing the top climber to ascend over the top with minimal problems (Fig. 7-14).

A long drop is a perfect place to use a pigtail. Here a climber can transfer over to a rope with no weight below and come over the edge with minimal problems. The top person during a tandem climb will often find that using a pigtail is the best option. It would be best if the person doing the transferring had quick clip-on ascenders such as Jumars, CMIs or Petzls. Climbers can become too fatigued to align and insert the pin associated with a Gibbs.

Derigging

Derigging can easily be accomplished by two people. The rest of the summit crew should carefully pack up all the summit supplies, connect them to their harnesses and rappel to the bottom. It would be helpful if the summit ropes could all go down with the rappellers leaving as little gear as possible to be walked out.

A mininum of two racks should be placed in tandem (Fig. 7-15), providing the necessary friction on the smaller diameter haul cord, which will provide for the safe lowering of the main rope. Once the main rope is on the bottom the haul cord should be pulled up and packed out. A final collecton of gear and a cleanup of the rigging area should precede the

long walk to base camp.

If the drop has been rigged from above such as at El Sotono, Golondrinas or Toroweap, Grand Canyon, the haul system could be used to pull up the rope, or perhaps a winch or windlass on a vehicles could be used in a similar manner.

Long-drop assaults involve a vast amount of planning, money, time and human resources. The leadership has proven to be the key to the degree of success or failure these ventures have enjoyed. Chapter 10 discusses leadership. The thrills and overwhelming intensity of participation in a long-drop expedition make for a life-fulfilling experience and seem to be among some of the greatest memories of vertical rope people.

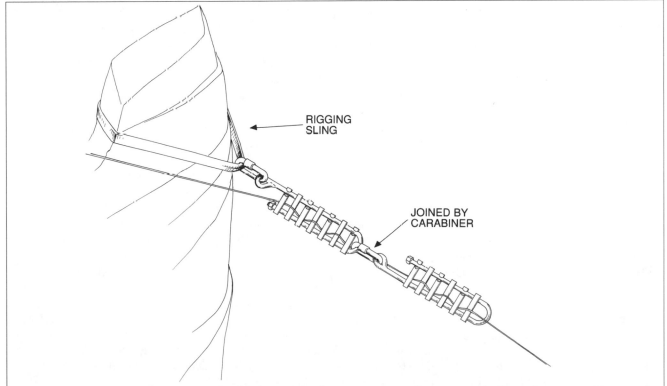

RIGGING SLING

JOINED BY CARABINER

Fig. 7-15. Since haul cords are smaller diameter, it is often necessary to place two racks in tandem to provide enough friction.

LONG DROPS AS A COMPETITIVE ACTIVITY

Many individuals over the years have assaulted long drops competitively. Some rappel a drop for speed, some climb it for speed, some see how many vertical feet can be climbed in a specified amount of time, while some just set themselves up as critics and judges as to what qualifies or counts as a long-drop challenge.

Most big drop climbers agree on three long-drop criteria:

- A long drop should contain as much free space as possible and shouldn't drape across slopes. Simply tying a long rope to the top of some Himalayan mountain and hand-over handing up the slope would not qualify in this arena, but a rope dropped from a balloon, blimp or helicopter could qualify.
- To go on record the drop must be climbed, not just rappelled.
- The drop should be climbed without the assistance of a motorized ascending device. For the most part, prusik times are recorded, not rappel records. It is considered unsafe and dangerous to attempt rappel speed records.

Bridges, Towers and Buildings

Bridges, towers and buildings, while often providing an attractive alternative for the long-drop enthusiast, are the main back-drop for fire, rescue and S.W.A.T. exercises. If climbing a man-made structure for the challenge or enjoyment, permission should be obtained.

Permission

An absolute requirement, before rappelling off the top of any structure is to obtain permission from the proper authorities. These people can go a long way in providing important information that can facilitate the execution of the drop. They are the people that often determine if other groups will be provided similar opportunities. It is advisable to carry a legal drafted waiver absolving the owners or authorities of liability.

It is an important mental exercise for the climbers to imagine themselves as the owner or controlling authorities and imagine what they expect as appropriate behavior. Language, manners, attire, courtesy and professionalism are all important considerations. This becomes especially important in national parks or in front of crowds. Businesses tend to lose money and popularity if crudeness or tragedy shroud a vertical event.

Not obtaining permission may result in committing criminal trespass which may result in a stiff fine or a jail term. This in turn may jeopardize future trips by other groups.

Precautions

All man-made structures seem to have sharp corners. Carefully placed edge rollers at the corners of girders or stone capstones should be an important precaution. Some railings can be adequately padded with wrapped canvas pads. Framing structures that have been exposed to the elements may have developed coarse rusty surfaces and rope will quickly become abraded if left unprotected. The tie-off on any framing member of a structure should be carefully reviewed before the final decision as to where to rig is determined. It is unwise to attempt to place a bolt in any concrete structure. One rarely knows the density or holding power that the concrete may provide.

Vertical work in a public place may invite tampering from bystanders. A member of the climbing party should be at the top and at the bottom at all times to protect the rigging and other expensive gear. In short, some members of the party may need to become in charge of crowd control.

Buildings may have large expanses of glass that require extra precautions during a rappel. Bounding down the side of a glass structure may result in building as well as rope damage.

The Elements

As a general rule, heat and wind become the dominant influencing elements during structure climbs and on big walls. A rope hanging over many hundreds of feet can act as a sail and billow into a defined arch, resulting in a lifting sensation to the rappeller even during descent. In the midst of several tall urban skyscrapers the air movement seems to exist in extremes. Either the stale air and trapped heat quickly dehydrate a climber, in which case extra water may be an important consideration, or a wind-tunnel situation buffets the climbers randomly against the windows and walls, in which case, it may be necessary to pack it up and choose another day.

REFERENCES

Ballew, Kent. "SRT on Half Dome." *Nylon Highway 24,* NSS Vertical Section (1987), pp 23-24.

Halliday, William R. M.D. *Depths of the Earth.* (Chapter 14, "Surprise! Fantastic! Incredible!."), New York: Harper & Row, 1976, pp. 294-316.

Johnson, Brad. "El Capitan." *Nylon Highway 15. ,* NSS Vertical Section. (1983), pp. 20-21.

Schreiber, Richard. "Grand Rappel—Toroweap Point, Grand Canyon, Arizona." *Nylon Highway 17,* NSS Vertical Section (1983), pp. 22-23.

Strickland, Peter. "Leaning Tower; Yosemite." *Nylon Highway 21,* NSS Vertical Section (1986), pp. 19-20.

Williams, Kathy. "Mount Thor." *Nylon Highway 15,* NSS Vertical Section (1983), pp. 17-19.

Williams, Kathy. "Old and New Vertical Techniques used at Mount Thor." *NSS News,* Vol. 40, No. 11, 1982, pp. 289-290.

Williams, Toni. "El Capitan 1981." *Nylon Highway 16,* NSS Vertical Section (1983), pp. 21-24.

PROFILE OF THE AUTHOR

Dan Twilley (NSS 16411).

Twilley began caving in 1970 with a group of unaffiliated cavers and quickly earned the nickname of cave rat. He joined the NSS in 1974 as a founding member of the Athens Speleological Society. Three terms as the Director of District Three of the Tennessee Chiropactic Association and four terms as President of the Southeast Chiropractic Association has not kept him from being one of TAG's most active vertical cavers. He is a member of the Vertical Section of the NSS, as well as numerous professional organizations associated with his profession.

His long drop experience is significant. In 1980 he was the first to climb and rappel El Capitan in Yosemite National Park, Califorrnia In 1982 he co-lead the Thor Expedition which established the current rappel and prusik record. He was the first to climb that 3250 foot drop. In October of 1986 he organized a return to El Capitan which also included an 1800 foot virgin rappel and prusik of Half Dome.

Twilley resides in Chattanooga, TN with his wife Stella and their two children.

8 Domes and Walls

8 Domes and Walls by Mike Fischesser

One of the more advanced and specialized techniques of underground exploration is the ability to ascend, or traverse, sections of domes and walls within caves to gain otherwise inaccessible passage. Underground rock climbing is the technique used to carry out this exploration. The technique is borrowed from our aboveground counterparts, the mountaineers. For years ideas have been traded back and forth between the caving and mountaineer/rescue communities as each group has discovered or perfected new equipment and techniques. Underground rock climbing, while based on aboveground principles and methods, has evolved into its own distinct brand of exploration. Since the conditions for rock climbing underground are often less than ideal, a variety of tricks and specialized techniques have been developed in order to deal with cold, water, mud, loose rock, darkness and remoteness unique to caving.

The objective of reaching high virgin passage that can actually be seen or imagined, but not easily gained, has intrigued many cavers over the years. The enthusiasm for actually undertaking such challenges usually diminishes when such factors as time, equipment, fun and boldness diminish. The group must be totally committed to the undertaking in order to attain its goal. Gaining access to "seen" or "hoped for" passage could necessitate scaling distances as far away as 400 feet. The determination, skill and cunning of the group will be a major factor in the success of the project. However,

the dome or cave walls themselves will sometimes have the last word.

The intent here is not to deal with rock climbing as a sport, but deal directly with the practical problems of risks, equipment, systems, strategies, ethics, clothing and safety in very specialized exploration techniques of underground rock climbing.

Experience Needed

The potential for serious accidents will increase if the group does not have proper training and judgment. Of course the same warning holds true for the entire area of vertical exploration. However, underground climbing does require another whole realm of knowledge and training, in addition to that which is known about SRT (Fig. 8-1). In addition, the team should have training in first and second aid techniques due to the added seriousness of injuries that might occur in a cave. Like cave diving, both disciplines are pushing the limits of extreme cave exploration and participants must ensure that their training and experience are thorough.

One of the factors to be considered before tackling a climbing project is to determine the degree of risk involved. The risk must be evaluated not only for the safety of the actual climbing team members, but for the potential rescuers should outside resource assistance be required. The team usually discusses such issues as:

- Is the objective of new passage worth the risk to reach it?
- Is our team self-sufficient enough to deal with our own

emergencies?
- Do we have the proper abilities to attempt the climb or are we simply going to be a burden on the rescue community if we get in over our heads?

While up on a wall each member (usually two people make up a team) must know techniques to rescue himself and his partner. Once the umbilical cord has been cut from the cave floor and climbers are no longer within easy reach of others, the climbing team is on its own. Most underground climbing situations do not allow the luxury of having would-be rescuers position themselves overhead to provide assistance. The only alternative if the climbing team needs help is for rescuers to re-climb the route or for a rope to be lowered from the climber's stance. This is one of the factors that makes underground rock climbing a serious proposition, not to be taken lightly by cavers or climbers who are not prepared. In aboveground rock climbing or mountaineering, assistance can usually be given by bringing in rescuers from above. It would be helpful to maintain a standing rope from the belayer's position to the floor throughout the climb. Underground climbing has the potential of becoming a life-threatening situation made worse by the ever-constant, total darkness, cool temperatures and moisture present in most caves.

The cave climber needs to have some understanding of cave geology. Since the medium being scaled is not always dependable in terms of predictable stability, the team members, especially the lead climber, need to know how to deal with mud-covered limestone, flowstone-covered mud, bands of shale, and extremely loose areas.

Before setting off on an underground climbing mission, the team members must be advanced rock climbers in aboveground situations. Of course, if a very simple, short climb near a cave entrance is the goal, then perhaps climbers possessing basic or intermediate skill levels would be OK. Since direct aid (using artificial means, such as pitons, chocks, or bolts, to hang from or advance up or down a rock face) techniques will more than likely be employed during the climb, the team must really have their aid climbing act together. Just as underground rock climbing is another whole realm to vertical caving knowledge, so is artificial or aid climbing to normal, free rock climbing. Probably every climber who has ever attempted to learn aid on his own has become hopelessly tangled up trying to figure out the smoothest system. The team should practice direct aid climbing in an out-of-cave situation first.

PREPARATION

After the goal is chosen, careful planning is the next step. As almost everyone who has gone caving, climbing or backpacking knows, carrying extra weight can take a lot of fun out of the experience. The gear required to support and execute the climb must be trimmed to a minimum. Ounces of climbing gear, as well as caving equipment, have a way of adding up to burdensome pounds in a hurry. While one goal may be to go as light as possible, another balancing goal is to "be prepared." Hence, an age-old dilemma. To many cavers and climbers, half the work of the trip is planning what to take.

Key parameters that should be carefully considered:

- First aid items, wall gear, food, water, lights, camping gear, and other vertical climbing gear will need to be scrutinized carefully.
- People should take fitness and nutrition seriously when planning adventures.
- Personnel and back-up plans need to be carefully considered.

- The decision to camp underground can greatly increase the odds for a successful climb, while making preparation more important.

Ethics and Conservation

During the planning stages of the climb, the team will need to discuss a couple of issues surrounding ethics and conservation.

The style of climbing underground is a bit different than that of above ground. The cave climber is more concerned with the safest, most direct method and route of reaching the goal, much as were the early mountaineers. Cave climbers have not stopped thinking about the style of their ascent and the conservation of the

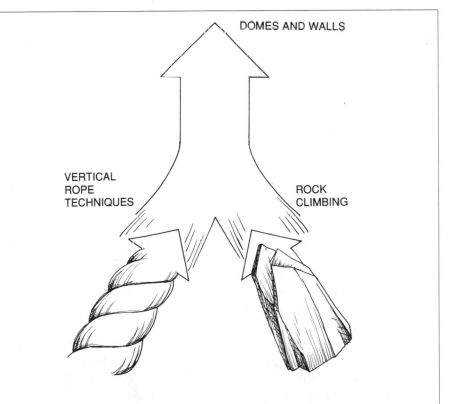

Fig. 8-1. Dome and wall assaults require expert skill in both rock climbing and vertical rope techniques.

cave, but sometimes the two issues take a back seat to the goal of just getting up. Taking an extension ladder is against the ethics of most aboveground rock climbers. Cave climbers, however, would be delighted if they could reach their goal with an extension ladder. Although the style of the ascent is considered important to some cave climbers, the passage above is the purpose of the climb with less emphasis or concern on "how" it is done.

If other teams will attempt to repeat the first ascent, then the style of the first-ascent team comes under more scrutiny. Some feel strongly that bolt hangers, bolts and pitons should be removed after the first ascent to leave the cave as natural as possible. However, widespread acceptance of any one set of values does not exist at this time, due to underground rock climbing's relative infancy in North America.

One thing that most everyone does agree with, though, is to do as little damage to the cave environment as possible. Formations and other sensitive areas should be protected from debris that may fall during the climb. It is the prevailing view that large amounts of human waste and trash should be removed from the cave.

While frowned upon in mountaineering circles as cheating, the use of a practical, cordless, electric hammer drill for placing bolts on the lead is winning favor among underground alpinists. Bolts are definitely permanent disfigurations of the natural cave environment. The issue becomes a matter of principle and a question

of values because, even if the hangers are left on, most future cave visitors would never spot the bolts on the wall above. The fact remains that the part of the bolt still there is considered a piece of trash left in a cave. Most people in North America accept the fact that artificial protection is often required to further certain areas of cave exploration. However, the climbers should be discreet and conservation-minded.

Some cave climbers will use chocks and natural cave features as often as they can because it is faster than placing a bolt. However, surface weathering of limestone in a cave environment often makes chocks unsafe, particularly in the smaller sizes. It seems to be the tendency for most cavers to set "bombproof" anchors to compensate for their lack of understanding of geology or the confidence in their ability to use chocks. Once set, these anchors remain.

PROTECTION

Most of the equipment carried by the cave climber is the same gear used in aboveground rock climbing. Pitons, bolts, chocks of various designs, etriers, hooks, hammer, Friends, slings and Jumars are often useful in the cave environment.

The French have used a small platform to stand on (Fig. 8-2) when placing long stretches of bolts for aid. This platform allows for greater distances between holes. Most North Americans use etriers (or aiders) made from stiff nylon webbing. See Chapter 4. Some climbers have found a nail

apron tied behind the back handy for locating the various pieces of bolts when free climbing. They have also managed to speed up the aid climbing by drilling shallow holes for sky-hook moves (Fig. 8-3), or by simply "hooking" a few moves before reaching or placing a solid multi-directional anchor (good for a pull in any direction).

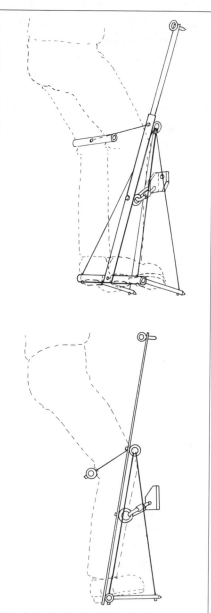

Fig. 8-2. A platform lets a climber reach well above his last anchor point.

If a section of stiff clay or hard mud must be negotiated, sometimes long 14 inch bolts or even longer (2 foot) pieces of steel rod can be used to provide enough purchase to support body weight. They are called mudstakes or mudpitons (Fig. 8-4).

Cordless, electric hammer drills have been successfully used to speed up bolt-drilling time. Regular cordless electric drills have proven somewhat ineffective, due to the fact that drilling rock drains battery life quickly. It is also difficult to maintain enough pressure behind the drill while hanging in etriers. Cave rescue groups have successfully modified available drills by adding outrigger batteries to increase usable drilling time.

The belayer's stance needs to be in an area where rockfall either isn't likely to occur or in an area out of the rockfall zone. The belay anchors for each pitch must be absolutely unquestionable, for this is the key

to the whole safety system while climbing. If the leader falls, the belayer must be securely anchored in order to arrest the leader's fall (Fig. 8-5). When setting up a belay station multi-directional anchors should be established whenever possible.

A good rule of thumb is to use at least two 3/8 inch bolts for a belay anchor. If using chocks or natural tie-offs, consider three points, self-equalized together as a safe minimum. Of course, the competent leader will use her own judgment in determining the best combinations of natural and artificial anchors.

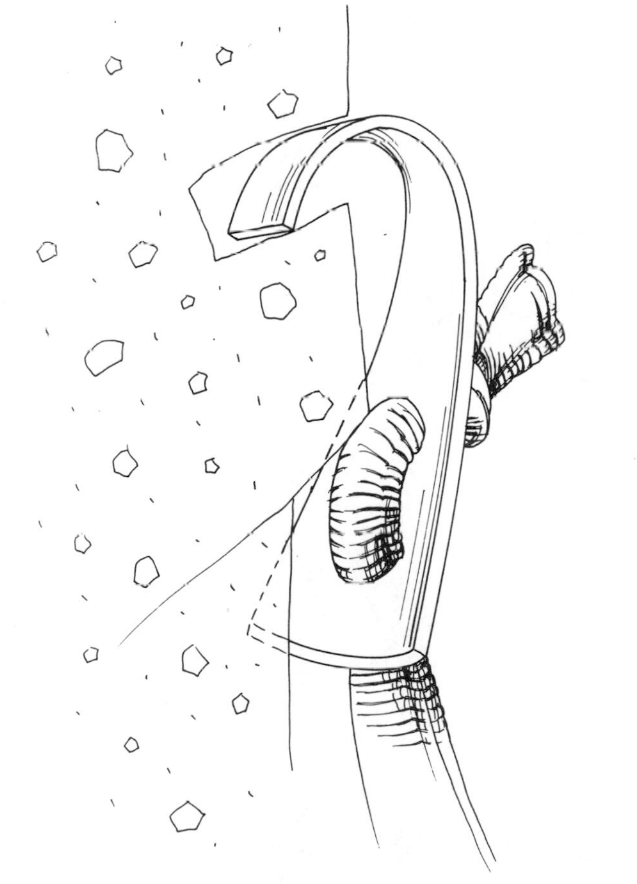

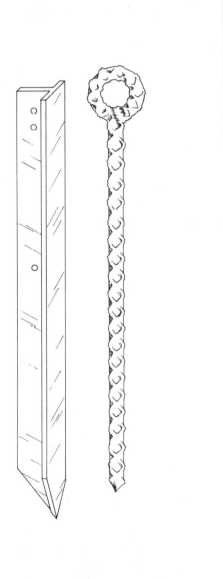

Fig. 8-3. Drilling angled holes for sky hooks allows short sections of blank wall to be climbed quickly.

Fig. 8-4. No. 5 steel reinforcing rod and aluminum "T" stock make good mud pitons.

The belayer should use a mechanical, friction belay device that could be attached to the belayer's harness. This will allow the forces generated in a fall to filter through the belayer before loading the belay anchor. See Chapter 9 for more on belaying.

Selection of the most useful gear is critical because too much gear can be frustrating, confusing, tiring and actually can contribute to a lead fall. However, having the right gear when needed can often mean the difference between completing the pitch or having to stop and return for the proper equipment. Knowing conditions and what gear to use is, again, one of those things that training and experience teach.

Ropes

The climbing team should use a dynamic rope, designed for the purpose of stretching when the forces of a fall are applied. These ropes are usually not desirable for single-rope techniques (climbing and rappelling in pits) in a vertical cave, due to their elasticity and low abrasion-resistance. The low-stretch, hard-wearing ropes made specially for vertical caving should be used when doing pit work. Static cave ropes should not be used for belaying the lead climber. The static cave rope does not provide enough "give" in the event of a leader fall.

Most underground climbers use a rope 7/16 inch in diameter and 165 feet (50 meters) in length, as is the normal practice with mountaineers. Due to the possibility of the leader dislodging debris, which could cut a single strand of

Fig. 8-5. A belayer must be able to provide the maximum amount of load absorption while maintaining his own safety.

rope, some climbers are using the European double-rope technique. This method uses two 3/8 inch diameter ropes to belay the leader, which lessens the odds of the rope being cut from rockfall or sharp limestone edges. This method has further advantages in that the team of two on the wall will have two ropes to work with in the event of self rescue. If they aren't carrying a static cave rope to fix their progress, they also have the ability to rappel 300+ feet instead of 150+ feet with a single rope. Another advantage of double ropes is the flexibility the leader has in route selection. She doesn't have to be as concerned about keeping the route straight to lessen rope drag. The leader can alternately clip each rope into protection, thereby lessening friction through protection points (Fig. 8-6). The double rope can also be clipped through protection points as if it were a single rope.

Ropes should be **thoroughly** washed, rinsed and inspected after each underground climbing trip. It is good to wash ropes even during the stay underground if a stream is available, because cave mud and grit are especially hard on dynamic climbing ropes.

The leader usually trails a haul line off the back of her harness to bring up extra equipment or a static rope to "fix" as progress is gained. The haul line is typically 1/4 inch in diameter to save on weight. More bolts, which can get heavy, can be sent up when the leader runs out (Fig. 8-7).

A static rope and any extra equipment is usually brought up on the haul line once the leader has

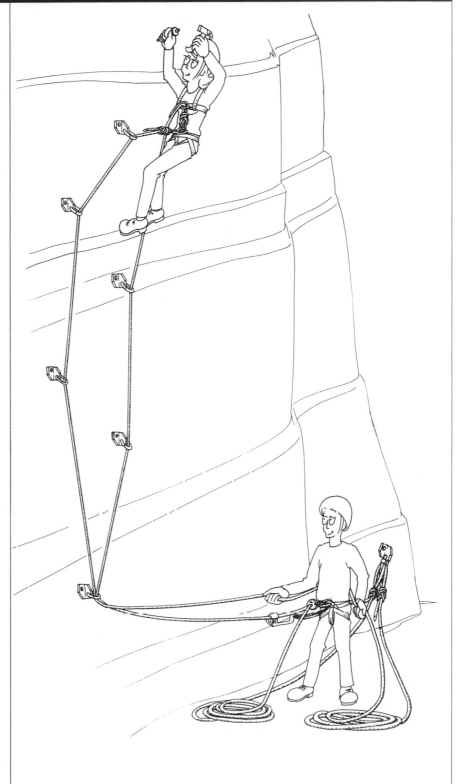

Fig. 8-6. Double rope can be used to lesssen friction through the series of protection points. Etriers not shown.

established the next belay. The second person or belayer then ascends the 7/16 inch static rope and cleans the pitch just led. If the rope traverses or zigzags, the second person may have to ascend the lead rope to be able to reach each piece of protection. It is a good idea for the leader to belay the second with the static rope in case the lead rope cuts on a sharp edge while the second is loading it. If the leader trails the static rope, it is possible to clip it in to selected pieces of protection to allow the second person to reach them for cleaning on a traversing route.

Special Techniques

In certain situations climbers may choose to aid climb with their prusik gear on over a rock-climbing harness. Or they may simply outfit themselves as they would for aboveground climbing. The choice depends on how much ascending and rappelling they plan to do. If they can get by with normal rock-climbing harnesses without adding their prusik rig, they will be less encumbered for difficult climbing situations. Each climber should definitely be using a recognized rock-climbing harness design and not just a diaper seat or minimally stitched together prusik rig (for static loading), which might rip apart in a fall.

Cheater Stick
An old telescoping car antenna, coat hanger or shock-corded tent pole can be used as a "cheater stick" to reach higher while lead-

Fig. 8-7. Haul lines can cut down on the amount of gear that the lead climber must carry.

Fig. 8-8. A cheater stick can allow a climber to reach formerly inaccessible placements.

ing to hang an etrier on a horn or place a chock (Fig. 8-8).

Scaling Poles

Extension ladders make for easy climbing, but in most situations it is impossible to transport anything that long or bulky to a climbing site. A scaling pole is an attractive alternative (Fig. 8-9). Typically, a scaling pole is an assembly of short pipe sections that allow a rope to be hung from the top. This in turn provides a route for a climber to carefully prusik up. This assembly may also aid the climber in reaching a promising ledge. It is also possible to climb from ledge to ledge in a tall, narrow dome.

The assembled pole, when leaned against a wall and loaded with a climber wants to curve outward like an archery bow. To overcome this hazard, the pole can be tensioned with lightweight cables and turnbuckles to add structural rigidity.

Helium Balloons

Helium balloons have been successfully used to float a haul cord high into a dome. The doubled cord along with the balloons was guided from the sides with light cord. The haul cord was positioned over a large projectile that had been carefully scrutinized from below with high-powered beacons. A regular-size climbing rope was pulled up and over the projectile and secured at the floor. This was then prusiked.

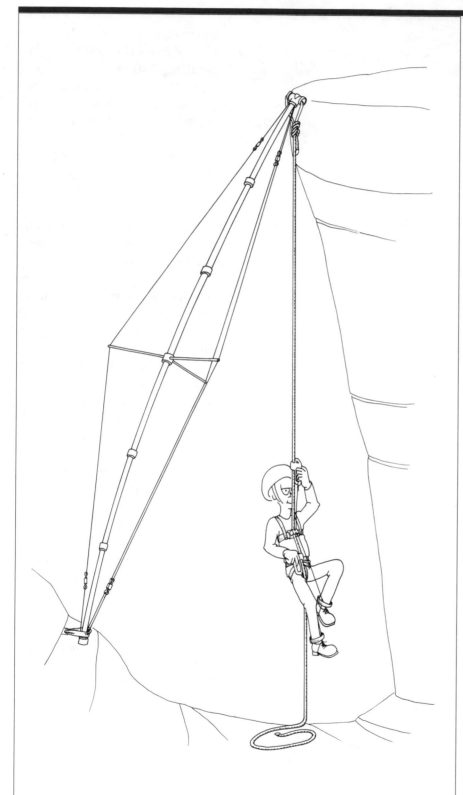

Fig. 8-9. Scaling poles require turnbuckle-tensioned cable to insure their rigidity.

Clothing on a Climb

Clothing is very important on a climb because it must serve a variety of functions for the climber. Without the proper clothing the climber and belayer can become chilled overheated, restricted and, certainly, demoralized.

The team should aim to select a clothing system that is very versatile. The cave may be dry and warm and the route may be free of mud and loose rock. These are approaching ideal conditions. More typically the cave conditions are cool, humid, muddy, with perhaps a slight breeze. Therefore the following considerations apply for the worst case scenario (barring heavy water or freezing conditions):

- Consider clothing that has an abrasion resistant outer layer (e.g. 60/40 cloth, 8 ounce pack cloth or cordura.

- Consider clothing that is fast-drying and wind and water-resistant.

- Freedom of movement is important.

- The belayer may get cold, waiting motionless for up to several hours at a time. Provide a hat or balaclava, food or one extra article for warmth.

- If wet mud or water is a problem, consider a vapor barrier system (VBL), such as a plastic trash bag over an insulating layer, such as polypropylene long underwear or a "pile suit."

- A wet suit may be necessary if under a heavy drip.

Foot gear ranges from jungle boots to heavyweight hiking boots. Usually whatever the climber uses for caving works well. A stiff sole is good when standing in aid slings for long periods of time. A boot that fits well and purchases well is good when free-climbing moves must be done. Smooth-soled, rock-climbing shoes should only be worn on a clean dry wall.

Helmet and Light

A good-quality rock-climbing helmet that offers maximum protection from falling objects and that will remain on the head in a tumbling fall is an essential piece of equipment. A more complete discussion on quality climbing helmets can be found in Chapter 10.

Primary and secondary light sources mounted on the helmet are obviously important. Individual preferences vary between all electric or a combination of electric and carbide. Carbide lamps can clog with mud or be extinguished by water, but they don't break like an electric light when accidentally hit with a hammer. The battery pack, as well as the light unit, needs to be securely fastened in the event the leader (or second) takes a wild fall. An auxiliary high-powered sealed beam is sometimes taken to aid with route-finding.

Route Selection

When the goal can be seen, the straightest line between two points is usually the best route, but not always. In the event of a waterfall or unstable rock zone, the route may come in from the side. In a traverse around a pit rim, the route would normally follow a horizontal path.

If the destination is unknown and cannot be spotted with powerful lights, then some detective work may help. A seam, fracture, or groove in the wall may speed up the climbing time. A drip, debris, shadow or stalagmite might indicate a clue as to possible upper level passage. For the most part, if the lead can not be seen and major water is not present, then it is anybody's guess as to what is up there. Two fairly long dome climbs have been done in the southeastern United States (Snowball Dome, 240 feet, and Topless Dome, 396 feet) in which no leads were found at the top.

If the route encounters problems such as mud, water or loose rock, it may be possible to avoid the problem areas by diverting the direction of the climb. Apparently the mud was so-o-o-o bad in Topless Dome that it was difficult to find the holes in the carabiners. Sometimes a change in direction will not avoid the problem, as in the case of sticky mud, a shale band or other rotten, unboltable rock that encircles a pit.

Mud and Rotten Rock

Cave walls commonly involve difficult climbing surfaces. Thick, deep, hard mud walls can be climbed using long 2- to 3-foot mud pitons. Often the walls are of rotten flaky rock or covered with thick liquid mud or guano.

Rotten Rock

Often drastic measures are necessary to overcome rotten rock, such as shale layers or fracture zones. It may be helpful to take an axe, shovel or spade and chop the rotten rock out. Large footholds, handholds, or mantles can be formed, affording the climber stable security.

Liquid Mud

Oozing, gloppy mud can be a real challenge. It is essential that the climber find solid rock in which to place his hardware. Liquid mud or guano should be first scraped off. After a vague outline of the wall can be determined, a chisel is an excellent tool to find solid rock. Define a 3 inch by 3 inch area and begin chiseling. The final surface needs to be flat, fracture-free and solid. After solid rock has been found, only then should hole-drilling begin.

Falling mud from cleaning or chipping activities can become a problem. The mud falls and seems to clog everything. The bolt kit bag can often become filled with mud. It is helpful to place anchors, cones, hangers and bolts in ziplock plastic bags. Muddy hardware can be very dangerous, for the mud can prevent the hardware from seating properly. The ropes, slings and etriers can also accumulate a lot of mud, to the point of clogging ascender teeth. A stiff bristle brush, water or a carbide tip cleaner all may be helpful tools when cleaning climbing hardware. In the final analysis, a method to clean climbing teeth and keep the hardware clean must be arranged.

MOVEMENT

It is difficult to discuss movement because each person often desires the freedom to make it up the wall his own way. There are basic moves to any aid climb that occasionally apply underground. If pitons, chocks or other quick-placement items are to be used as standard protection, then the typical aid-climbing sequence can be used.

Typical Aid Climbing

Movement on an aid climb is a sequential process:

1. Reaching as high as possible, securely place the desired piece of protection, whether it be a   piton, chock, cam or Friend.
2. Place a carabiner in the piece of protection.
3. Attach two etriers with two additional carabiners to the first carabiner.
4. An adjustable tether attached to the climber should be attached to the top carabiner if the angle is near vertical or overhanging. A daisy chain with a Fifi, or a short chain of carabiners can be used for this purpose.
5. The seat harness should have a 7/16 inch rope attached to it that also runs through the first   carabiner and then down to the belayer (Fig. 8-10).
6. The climber should work himself up the etriers while the belayer provides the necessary tension.
7. At the height of the climber's

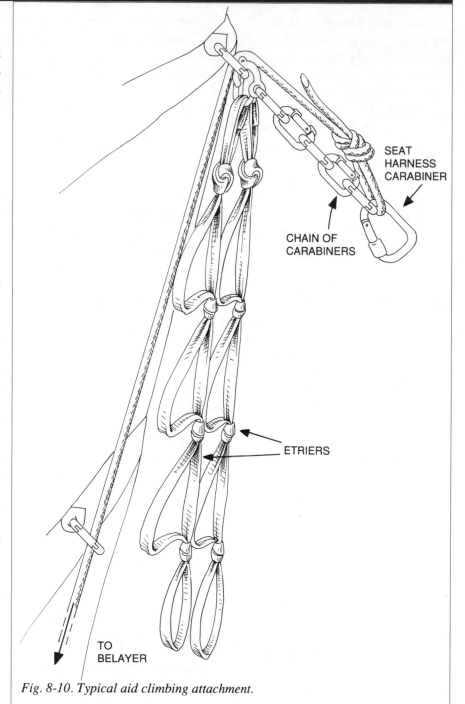

Fig. 8-10. Typical aid climbing attachment.

progress, he should analyze his next protection point, select the proper piece of protection, stand up, reach and place the piece of   hardware (Fig. 8-11). Obviously, maximum gain between aid points is an important goal.

8. Place a carabiner in the hardware as before.
9. Transfer one etrier to the new piece of hardware.
10. Test pull the etrier. Attempt to apply full weight while re-

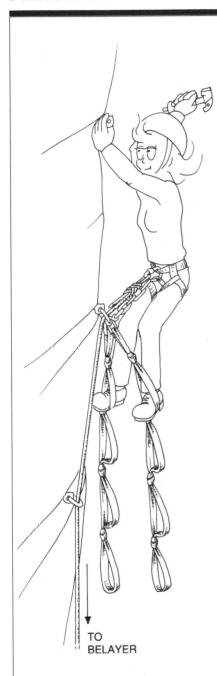

TO
BELAYER

Fig. 8-11. Movement from one piece of protection to another.

maining securely attached to the lower piece of aid.

11. If the placement appears sound, call for slack and move the 7/16 inch belay rope up into the top aid-protection carabiner. Do not remove the rope from lower aid carabiner.

12. Transfer the climber's weight from the lower etrier to the upper etrier.

13. Disconnect the seat harness tether.

14. Unclip the lower etrier and clip it into the upper piton carabiner.

15 The climber should move up the two etriers attaching the seat harness tether at first opportunity, all the while receiving tension from the belayer below.

16. Continue the sequence as long as necessary or possible. This procedure for vertical climbs can also be followed for horizontal traverses. Practice and experience can result in a graceful and efficient ascent.

CAUTION: Never allow yourself to hang from only one point of protection. With each new point of protection be sure it is backed up with a second piece of tested aid. Usually, this will be the last and probably closest lower piece of protection.

Bolt Climbing

Bolts are not considered quick-placement items and force modifications to the typical aid climbing sequence. It is extremely difficult to stand in floppy etriers for an extended period of time and place a bolt. The climber often finds it necessary to sit in his harness while placing the next bolt rather than enjoying the reach of a standing stretch. His sitting reach may only allow a 12- to 18-inch gain. It is better to reach fourteen inches comfortably and take take 10 minutes to place a bolt than to uncomfortably stretch 20 inches and take 30 minutes to place a bolt. There are several modifications to the rigging that can assist the climber.

Undercut Climbs.
Undercut climbs may require back support. The seat harness tether can easily become the main point of suspension and the belay line can be wrapped around the climber's upper torso and back through a carabiner attached to the piton carabiner (Fig. 8-12). The climber still remains attached to the primary point of protection by two independent means.

Alternatives

A climber can move up a wall without the assistance of a belayer by self-belaying. There are several methods that work. One involves the attachment of the belay rope to a lower protection point. The rope is placed through the carabiners attached to highest piece of protection. The climber can Texas-prusik up the rope using a very short seat-sling attachment (Fig. 8-13). When in position to place the next bolt, attach the seat harness tether to the upper point of protection. Note, with this method etriers are not needed. When moving between points, the seat prusik and the adjustable seat tether become the two points of weight transfer. While hanging from the seat tether the rope can be stretched upward to the next point of protection. The climber can easily reattach a seat Jumar onto the newly positioned line, ascend upward and release the tether when appropriate.

Fig. 8-12. The belay rope can be used to gain upper body support.

over 500+ feet of Fantastic Pit! This resulted in the discovery of the Attic with much more additional passage for Ellison's and a new rig point at 586 feet.

In what is probably the longest underground technical route in the world, Don Davison and Cheryl Jones worked on Topless Dome (a 555 foot long route which was 396 feet high) in Tumbling Rock Blowing Cave in Alabama over the course of a couple of years.

Many bolt climbs have gone undocumented, yet stratospheric passage is eyed and attained regularly. Many dome and wall climbs are not long and dramatic, rather involving one or two pieces of protection that allow a team to attain a high, previously unattainable goal.

Another method involves the careful attachment of the rope between the top and second point of protection (Fig. 8-14). This provides for a natural tight step (not a floppy etrier) whereby the climber can attain three or more feet between points of protection.

Leaving the Wall

Occasionally it is necessary to leave the wall and return to the floor. The rope should be securely tied to the second bolt and backed up to the top bolt (Fig. 8-15). The climber can do this while attached to either bolt with his seat tether. After the rope is secured, the climber should downclimb past the second hanger, change over to

rappel and descend to the floor. If bolts are to be left for a long time, it would be helpful to seal the holes with gasket sealer as mentioned in Chapter 4 to prevent water deterioration.

DOME ASSAULTS

One of the most exposed underground climbs to ever be done was when Don Davison climbed Seige Wall in Ellison's Cave, Georgia. He saw what he thought to be a ledge approximately 76 feet above the 510 foot balcony rig point. After running the route to one dead end, he backed up and angled it up the wall so that he ended up spending many hours bolting out

Conclusion

Climbing domes and underground walls is probably the most advanced form of rock climbing. The risks are high, the equipment very specialized, the strategies must be well thought through and the planning complete. More people risk the altitudes of Mount Everest than risk the lofty domes that exist deep underground. Domes remain one of the unconquered frontiers.

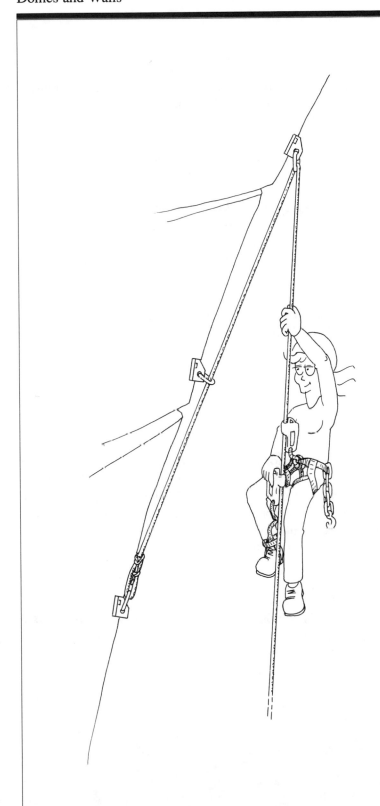

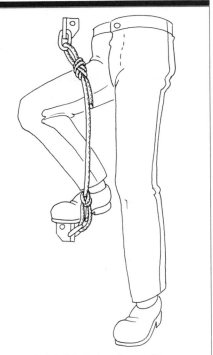

Fig. 8-14. Wedging foot between rope and wall gives secure footing.

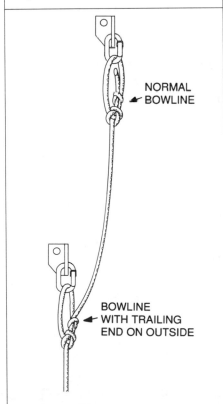

NORMAL ◄ BOWLINE

BOWLINE ◄ WITH TRAILING END ON OUTSIDE

Fig. 8-15. Never hang from just one lonely bolt. A back up makes good sense.

Fig. 8-13. Self belaying. A short seat attachment is essential when using this method.

REFERENCES

Dailey, Clark. "Camping Techniques of the Underground Climber." *NSS News*. Vol. 40, No. 10, 1982, p. 253.

Fischesser, Mike. "LRUES-System in Mammoth Cave." *NSS News*. Vol. 43, No. 8, 1985, pp. 266-270.

Fischesser, Mike. "Ascent of Snowball Dome." *Nylon Highway 18*. Vertical Section of the NSS, (1984), pp. 17-21.

Fischesser, Mike. "Some Thoughts on Brain Buckets." *NSS News*. Vol. 41, No. 7, 1983, pp. 203-204.

Isenhart, Kyle. "Bolts." *Nylon Highway 5*. Vertical Section of the NSS, (1976), pp. 13-15.

Jeffreys, Bob. "Rock Engineering on the Monster Wall." *NSS News*. Vol. 38, No. 11, 1980, pp. 307-308.

Jeffreys, Bob. "Topless Dome Revisited." *NSS News*. Vol. 40, No. 10, 1982, p. 252.

Jeffreys, Bob. "Skyhooking." *Nylon Highway 14*, Vertical Section of the NSS, (1981), p. 15.

Judson, David, Ed. *Caving Practice and Equipment*. London: David and Charles Ltd., 1984, p. 116.

Robbins, Royal. *Advanced Rockcraft*. La Siesta Press, Glendale, CA. 1985.

Profile of the Author

Mike Fischesser (NSS 18140). Fischesser's interest in ropework began with his active involvement with Scouting in western North Carolina in the early 1960s and on through the 1970s. His concerns for promoting safety and quality instruction prompted a 14 year appointment (seven years as program director) to North Carolina's Outward Bound School.

He has been the chairperson of the Safety and Techniques Committee of the NSS since 1983 and is responsible for the research and publication of a monthly article for the NSS's monthly publication. He has continued his Outward Bound career in Connecticut as the Director of its National Training Institute. In his position, he regularly participates and reviews programs at the various Outward Bound Schools. He focuses his efforts on rope courses, outdoor safety management, rock climbing, cave exploring and the related rescue associated with each category.

Fischesser has been on paddling, caving and climbing expeditions from Chile to the Artic. He is the designer and manufacturer of the Butt Strap Harness.

9 Belaying

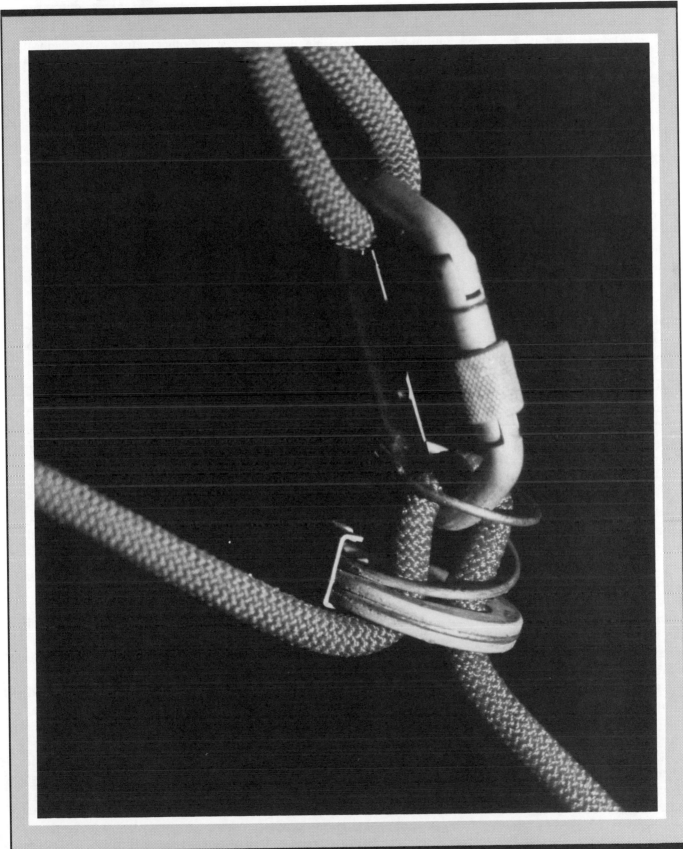

9 Belaying

In North America the term belaying implies an extended safety activity. Anytime a belay is being performed, some back-up or redundant safety activity is supposedly taking place. In Europe a belay refers to an anchor point, and belaying as North Americans have come to know it is referred to as lifelining.

In practice, ropework cannot be made perfectly safe, and a belay, although providing additional security, is no substitute for experience and careful execution of proven vertical techniques. Even with a belay, the risk of serious injury or death remains.

Belaying is controversial, complex and sometimes confusing. There are many forms of descending belays, including: top belays, bottom belays and spelean shunts. Then there are ascending belays, such as: top belays, self-lining and the use of a third ascender. Beyond this, there are a variety of rock-climbing belays. Rock-climbing belays are an essential skill for all those who ever ascend a wall or into a dome.

There is a school of cavers and climbers that feel "no belay" is the best belay. Their contention is that the bulky belay harnesses, the tugging belay rope, and hair-trigger mechanisms that sometimes activate belays, cause hassles and complicate a climber's or rappeller's enjoyment to the point of the caver's or climber's failure. They believe the best belay is the precise execution of a classic controlled rappel or the precise balance of a well rehearsed prusik. They believe the best belay is achieved by knowing exactly what to do, when, and, with deliberate precision, doing it. This approach to safety is, no doubt, for the purist, and for the most part will work for the experienced, careful rappeller and climber; however, many people need the assurance of a belay. In reality, a belay provides mental assurance first and may avert a tragic mishap second.

When Should You Use a Belay?

When to use a belay is often dependent upon the terrain. Exposure, steepness of the climb, and group/individual experience are all contributing factors, **but it is mandatory to belay any person who requests it.** It is a common error to assume everyone in a party is of the same ability. Even the best climbers have their days of uncertainty and may request a belay for a climb that would seem easy to some. Anytime any member of a party requests a belay, it should be given or arranged for without hesitation and without verbal abuse.

DESCENDING BELAYS

Among the many belays, several have specific application while descending. A descending belay adds a safety factor independent of the built-in safety of the rappelling device.

Self-Belays
Self-belays during a rappel are often referred to as spelean shunts or rappel safeties. These devices have been controversial for years, as some people swear by them, while others refuse to use them. It seems experienced rappellers have achieved the greatest success with these devices. This is usually the group of people that needs them the least. Their use can become complicated after engagement. To disengage a locked rappel safety, it is sometimes necessary to remove your weight via a foot loop. These devices and their use are discussed in detail in Chapter 5.

Top Belays
Top belays, as discussed in Chapter 5, have application during training sessions, short drops, and ladder climbs. This type of belay has drawbacks that should discourage its regular use, except when ladder climbing. It is the only belay that utilizes a second rope, which provides a redundant safety feature for the primary rope. A better option, if primary rope failure is a concern, would be to use two ropes and rappel on them both. Top belays are inappropriate and should be avoided as a general consistent practice, due to problems encountered by a moving rope causing rockfall at the edge and the possibility of the belay rope spinning around the rappel line, which could halt progress.

Bottom Belays
Bottom belays are commonly used and practiced in North America. During a rappel a person on the bottom can effect or control a rappel by pulling down on the bottom of the rappel rope, thus binding-up or increasing the friction in most standard rappel devices. If a rappeller were to become injured dur-

ing a rappel and unable to control her descent, a bottom belayer could perform this activity (Fig. 9-1). Bottom belays have their limitations. On long drops of over 400 feet, it is almost impossible to arrest an out-of-control rappel. Even climbing the rope hand-over-hand and applying full body weight may not slow a runaway rappel due to rope stretch and the pendulum effect. The belay will merely swing and move the rapidly descending rappeller about. This is especially true if the rappeller is using a rappel rack. Another drawback is the significant risk to the belayer. To effect a belay requires that the belayer stand in the rockfall zone. Every precaution should be taken, such as wearing a quality helmet, standing to one side of the rope or standing under a protective ledge. Looking up at the rappeller can also be risky, as a rock, if dislodged, could hit the belayer on his upturned, unprotected face. The most experienced group member should be the person monitoring the belay, unless the belayer is in training and being coached.

Fig. 9-1. A bottom belay can safely control descents if the belayer uses a mechanical friction rappel device and the drop is not too long.

ASCENDING BELAYS WHILE PRUSIKING

While prusiking, several safety measures can be initiated to increase the margin of security.

Top Belays

Top belays can be cautiously used on short drops, ladder climbs and during training exercises. As discussed in Chapter 5 and mentioned earlier in this chapter, this procedure often provides more problems than it solves. Fortunately, if the belay rope and the climbing rope twist together rendering the belay useless, a prusiker can still continue to climb up through the twisted ropes, usually without problem. However, it is best to attempt to untwist the ropes before continuing upward. This problem can be compounded by using laid rope.

Third Ascender

One of the safest methods of belaying during an ascent is to incorporate a third ascender into a climbing system. The theory suggests that as one ascender is moved up the rope, two ascenders (a nice margin of safety) remain locked on the rope. If one of the remaining locked ascenders fails during upward movement of the first ascender, the third ascender will keep the climber from falling.

Several Gibbs ascending systems already incorporate three ascenders. Other systems can occasionally adopt a third trailing ascender. Most trailing ascenders should be spring-loaded such as Gibbs, Petzl Croll, Petzl Jammer, CMI Shorti and others. Here are some suggested ways of attaching a third ascender to a normally two-ascender system:

Texas System. By floating a third ascender just above the foot ascender and attaching it to a second seat harness (Fig. 9-2) or a waist belt, three independent ascenders can be incorporated. Failure of any ascender or harness will still maintain the climber upright and holding on by two ascenders.

Mitchell System. A Gibbs ascender can be floated just above the ascender box with the attachment sling running between the box and the climber's chest, eventually attaching to the climber's seat sling (Fig. 9-3). Even though this may be the best place to attach a third ascender, it is less than desirable. The Gibbs placement will demand at least some loss per stroke and cause additional stress on the upper ascender arm. The Mitchell system may be one system that is not adapted to a third-ascender belay. However, Bill Cuddington advocates the use of this belay system and has found it to be an effective climbing option. If all the right tethers are in place and the rig is carefully fabricated, this system holds enough redundancy that it really doesn't call for a third ascender.

Inchworm System. By attaching a short trailing cam to the rope above the chest ascender and tethering it to the seat harness, a third ascender can be added to the inchworm system (Fig. 9-4).

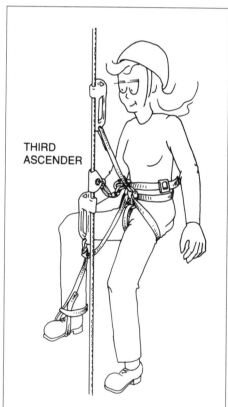

Fig. 9-2. Texas prusik system incorporating a third point of contact, a Gibbs attached to the waist belt.

THIRD ASCENDER

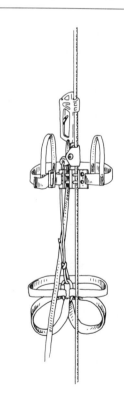

Fig. 9-3. Mitchell system's third point of contact inhibits full efficiency of the system.

Gibbs Ropewalker. If a chest roller is used, rather than a shoulder Gibbs, a Gibbs can be attached to the chest harness and ridden above the chest harness. Some Gossett boxes have been modified with a tooth cam that results in the rope locking in the box if descent or downclimbing were ever attempted (Fig. 9-5).

SELF-LINING

Self-lining is a belay method that is often used during rock climbs of low difficulty, during tricky downclimbs and often during lad-der climbs (see Chapter 6). Using a spring-loaded ascender attached with a short tether to one's seat harness, up and down maneuvering can take place with assurance (Fig. 9-6). Self-lining almost always uses some form of attached ascender. A somewhat more difficult version of a self-line climb involves the pushing of a safety Jumar up the rope by the climber while rock climbing. This is more difficult because it tends to be awkward, throwing the climber off balance, and forcing her to do something that is not part of what she came to do—climb.

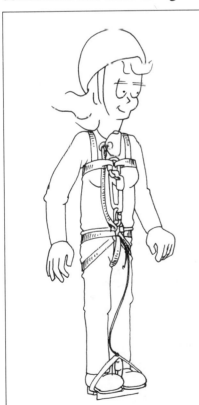

Fig. 9-4. Inchworm floats a Gibbs above the chest harness, with a sling attached to the seat harness.

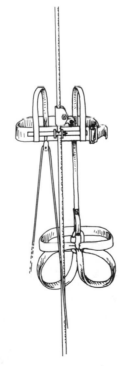

Fig. 9-5. Ropewalkers without shoulder cams need a third point above the chest roller, either a Gibbs or a Prusik knot.

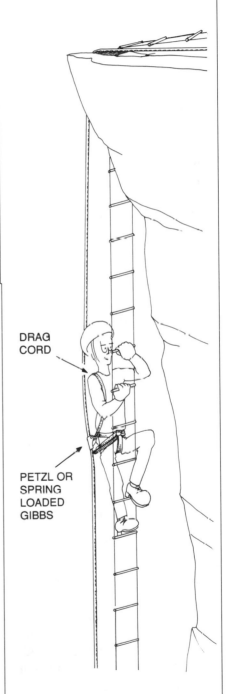

DRAG CORD

PETZL OR SPRING LOADED GIBBS

Fig. 9-6. Self-lining is a solo belay technique.

ROCK-CLIMBING BELAYS

Climbing belays, like the previously discussed belays, reduce the danger of injury and provide psychological reassurance. The fact remains that belayed falls will generate the highest forces experienced by rope, belay mechanisms, belayers and climbers. Equipment used by cavers and climbers is built to sustain these high forces. Regardless, the topic of belays remains quite controversial. Dynamic belays versus static belays along with mechanical belays versus body belays are two very much disputed topics.

Dynamic Belays

Early climbers using non-stretch manila rope adopted a dynamic or running belay procedure in which during a fall, the belayer would allow the rope to slide through his gloves and around his padded hips, creating a soft landing. Dynamic nylon ropes have eliminated the need for this procedure. In fact, the force of a fall, by its very nature, will cause the rope to dynamically slide through the belayer's hands in most situations. On longer falls, without choice, a dynamic belay will result, if only because of the stretch in the rope. Alpinists agree that the longer someone falls, the more opportunity exists for that person to hit something. Acceptable practice dictates that the climber be stopped quickly. Anchor strength influences this decision and will be discussed shortly.

Static Belays

Low-stretch, static kernmantle ropes make static belays practical. Many times rope bounce as achieved with dynamic rope belays is not helpful. Ladder ascents require a snug belay that is best achieved with a low-stretch rope. A climber can recover much quicker if his top-rope belay is a static rope. Slipping off the wall and dropping 10 feet can easily put a climber out of reach of his climbing line. Top belays, bottom belays and self-lining are all accomplished best with a static low-stretch rope. A good rule of thumb states that if a climber remains below her point of protection, static low-stretch rope should be used. If a climber ascends past or beyond her point of protection a stretchy, dynamic rope should be used.

Static belays definitely have their drawbacks. They can be harsh and put a maximum strain on the climber, anchor(s), belayer and rope. Static belays can be performed with dynamic rope, but the results will be dynamic in nature as the climber peels off the wall and bounces at the end of her dynamic rope. Regardless of the choice of rope, dynamic or static, the ultimate success of the belay depends heavily on many other critical factors, such as the anchor, the belay stance, the belay mechanism and the protection between the climber and the belayer.

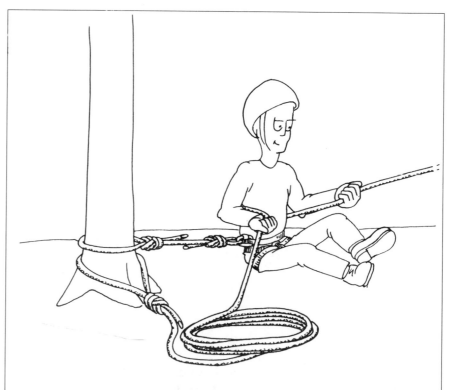

Fig. 9-7. The distance from the anchor to the belayer must be kept short, with no slack.

Belay Anchors

If a person jumps from a four-story building into your arms, you may experience a force equal to a falling climber. Obviously, if both individuals are to survive such an ordeal, some prior planning is required. The belay anchor must be bombproof and able to hold the strength of the rope. Typical wall bolts and pitons pull out at about 2000 pounds. If one great anchor, such as a large tree or seven-ton boulder, cannot be found, consider a multiple anchor and equalize the tension. The belayer needs to position himself in line with the anchor and the climber's possible fall trajectory or the direction of the first piece of protection.

There should be a minimal distance between belayer and anchor point with absolutely no slack (Fig. 9-7). If anchor direction is properly aligned and a fall should occur, the short connection will resist lifting, pushing, pulling and dumping the belayer. There should never be a chance for the belay rope to ride up on the mid-section. This could cause rope burns, organ damage and, possibly, spine damage.

Aiming the Belay

It should not be possible for a sudden force to rotate the belayer. Simply clipping the belayer's belt into a short anchor tether may be disastrous. If a fall were to occur that generated 500 to 1000 pounds of force, the belayer could find himself disadvantageously repositioned and possibly injured. If the belayer is not aimed, attached or gloved properly, or not adequately trained and practiced, he will become an insignificant influence in the outcome of the falling climber.

The belayer must be positioned in the direction of the anticipated fall or the point of the climber's first point of protection. If the protection should fail, where will the falling climber end up? Will the resultant forces and direction of pull be manageable? These and other "what if?" questions must be answered when positioning and aiming a belay.

Belay Stance

The position a belayer chooses to belay from is an important consideration. It is possible that the belayer may sit or stand for hours, and a position of comfort should be chosen.

Sitting Hip Belays
The sitting hip belay traditionally has the belayer sitting, legs spread apart for balance and feet braced against rocks. The stance features a low center of gravity and allows for a great deal of control (Fig. 9-8). It is considered among cavers and climbers to be the most often used belay stance.

Standing Hip Belays
Standing belays appear at first to be very unstable.

Fig. 9-8. A sitting hip belay properly aimed in the direction of the climber's anticipated fall.

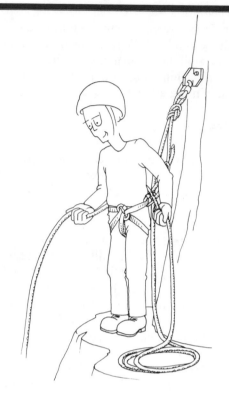

Fig. 9-9. Standing hip belay with anchor high above the waist.

However, if the anchor is placed above the waist, the ledge is small and the dynamics appear to be right, this stance may be the best option (Fig. 9-9).

Modified Hip Belays

Variation on standing or sitting hip belays allow a number of creative alternatives. Any hip belay that is terrain-dependent and deviates from the first two traditional belays is referred to as a modified hip belay (Fig. 9-10).

Climber Attachment

The method of attaching the rope to the climber is very controversial. Most sources just avoid the subject altogether. For years a waist loop or bowline on a coil were considered popular options. The problem with simple waist loops is that the fall invariably damages midsection organs, bruises ribs, causes severe rope burns, restricts breathing, restricts the circulatory system and can cause death in 15 minutes. Being jerked from a chest harness can also complicate recovery. A restriction around the chest when the wind has been knocked out of you greatly retards recovery. Falling onto a loop attachment requires the

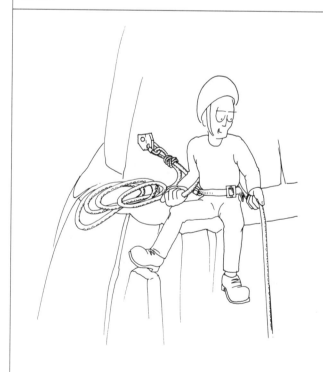

Fig. 9-10. Modified hip belays are situation dependent.

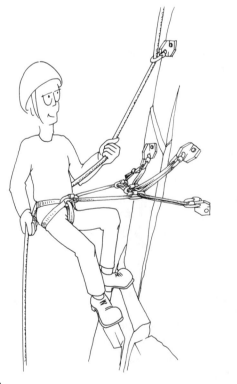

Fig. 9-10b.

quick action of transferring to a baboon hang (if the climber is conscious). See Chapter 11.

Low-attachment seat harnesses, such as those recommended for SRT, can result in an unsupported back at the moment of impact. Spinal damage is likely. Those using a low-attachment seat harness need only to place a short tether between the seat harness and chest harness and attach the belay rope to the chest harness (Fig. 9-11). Including an adjustable buckle in the tether allows for convenient adaptations to any situation. It is important to lock off the tab end of the buckle strap so that in the event of a fall, slippage will not occur. Carabiners of adequate strength must obviously be used on the chest harness. Simply running the belay rope through a chest carabiner and attaching it to a seat harness is an unacceptable alternative (Fig. 9-12). When a fall is stopped by a belay, the body gets pulled together and compressed beyond comfortable and normal limits. Any chest harness that may take a leader fall should be carefully restitched and strengthened overall.

Commercially made and purchased climbing harnesses that provide for mid-section attachment, for the most part, are the best option for a climbing harness and a climber's attachment. See Chapter 5.

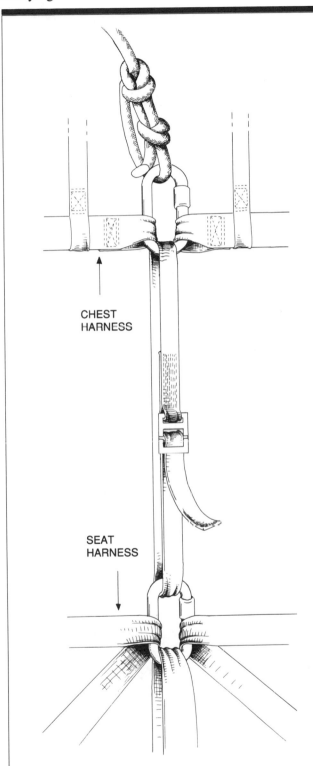

CHEST
HARNESS

SEAT
HARNESS

Fig. 9-11. Heavy-duty buckled tether connecting chest harness with low attachment seat harness. Strength of all components must withstand same load that rope may experience during shock loading.

Fig 9-12. If the rope is attached to seat harness, but is only passed through (not attached to) chest harness, a fall can severely injure spine, ribs and organs.

The Belay

Body belaying is often called soft belaying because the falling impact is traditionally very tolerable to the climber, assuming that the climber did not hit anything before the fall was finally arrested.

Navigating up or across the wall is difficult enough without the climber having to fight the belayer. The belayer needs to be highly alert and responsive to every command and signal given by the climber. See Chapter 10 for climbing signals. As the climber moves across the rock the belayer needs to coordinate his movements with the climber's.

Belayer

The belayer should verify that his staging area is ready for a belay:

- Belayer properly attached to a secure anchor?
- Belay pointed in the proper direction?
- Rope loosely laid out so as not to kink?
- Is the edge padded with a rope pad where the fall may occur? This is not always possible.
- Belayer wearing heavy leather gloves?
- Safety Jumar attached to a bombproof anchor? If a fall occurs, the belayer need only clip the safety Jumar onto the rope, enabling the belayer the freedom to do what he decides is necessary.
- Proper stance for the situation?

Regardless of right- or left-handedness, the hand closest to

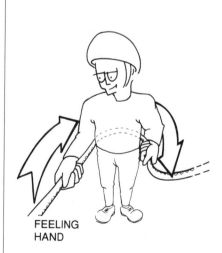

Fig. 9-13a. Snug up rope with both hands, leaving feeling hand extended.

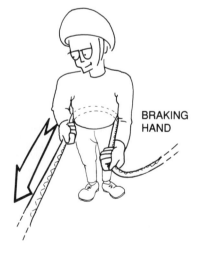

Fig. 13b. Tightly maintain a firm hold with braking hand while feeling hand is again extended.

Fig. 9-13c Grasp both ropes with feeling hand.

the climber is called the feeling hand, while the other hand is the brake hand.

UNDER NO CIRCUM-STANCES MAY THE BRAKING HAND BE RE-MOVED FROM THE CLIMBING ROPE UNTIL THE CLIMBER SAYS "OFF BELAY."

As the climber moves, the belayer's two hands work together providing tension or slack as requested by the climber. Moving the rope responsively and maintaining the snug security without upsetting the climber is one goal of the belayer. This movement is not totally natural and should be carefully analyzed and practiced (Fig. 9-13). If a fall should occur, the brake hand should pull the rope across the midsection while the rest of the body braces itself for impact.

Fig. 9-13d. Quickly slide brake hand back close to body always keeping it ready.

Fig. 9-13e. Repeat procedure.

Fig. 9-13f. If a fall should occur, wrap rope across midsection with brake hand and brace.

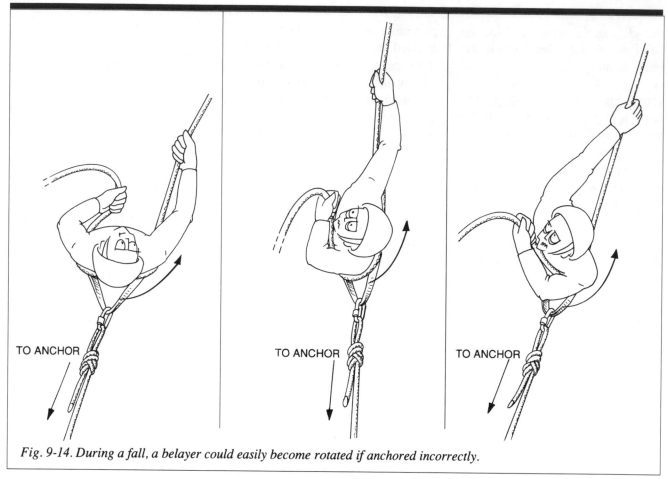

Fig. 9-14. During a fall, a belayer could easily become rotated if anchored incorrectly.

The Fall

The impact of a falling climber and the forces involved are traditionally grossly underestimated. Imagine attempting to catch a couple of falling truck tires or a car engine. The generated kinetic energy must be totally absorbed by the belayer. Often the belayer will feel as if he is not slowing down the falling victim. This may be true, but chances are the victim is not accelerating. A body belay invariably produces rope burns, smoking gloves, lint where denim used to be, and muscle strain. It is suggested by climbing veterans to practice belaying with falling weights. During the strain, the belayer could easily become rotated (Fig. 9-14). This must be avoided at all costs as once this occurs, the climber will surely continue the fall. A simple leg clip (Fig. 9-15) or the securing of the anchor tether to the belayer's brake hand leg (Fig. 9-16) can help keep the rope and belayer oriented during a soft belay.

Rope Burns

Rope burns can ruin a belayer's day, not to mention a falling climber's.

- A burned belayer becomes a victim and a less-than-helpful member of the group.
- A burned belayer may be unable to successfully complete the belay, dropping the falling climber.

The belayer will probably endure pain and skin loss to help a falling friend. The problem is far more severe than most realize. Rope burns are a common by-product of most soft body belays. The obvious solution is to use mechanical protection.

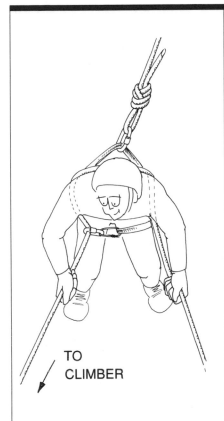

Fig. 9-15. A leg loop with a carabiner on the brake-hand leg can assist in preventing rotation.

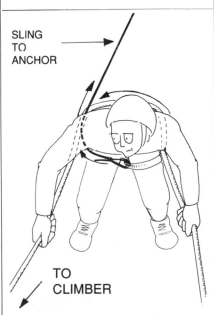

Fig. 9-16. Attaching the anchor tether to the brake-hand leg can also assist in preventing rotation.

Protection

There are a variety of stopgap measures that a belayer can take advantage of to assist and ensure a successful belay. Placing secure protection between the belayer and the climber is one of the best ways to thwart the high-impact forces on a belayer. As a rule, each carabiner that the rope takes a sharp turn through will reduce the impact force by 50 percent. The critical problem with protection, especially in caves and limestone, is that some of the aid that is placed to help the climber's upward movement is usually not strong enough to sustain the weight of a climber. Climbers boast of placing one or two flimsy bathooks between each piece of solid protection to speed up the climb. The ultimate in rock climbing in recent years has focused on unprotected, unroped free solo climbing. This, by its very nature, should be discouraged. Many excellent rock climbing books discuss this subject in great detail. It is suggested that one receive competent training prior to attempting underground rock climbing.

A belayer's best line of defense against loss of control, falling climbers and painful burns is the various mechanical belay aids that give the necessary margin of strength and assurance.

Figure 8

This device can obviously serve multiple functions. As a belay aid, it allows the climber the necessary freedom, adjusts readily and for the most part has a wide range of acceptable working limits. In ac-

tual use the figure 8 could be attached to an anchor and be controlled from the side by the belayer (Fig. 9-17). On the other hand, many climbers insist that the only way to get the proper pull-back braking angle on the belay device during an actual fall is to have the belay device attached to the belayer's seat harness. Attaching the device to the belayer's harness can assist in dissipating the fall energy before taxing the anchor. As a belay device, however, it should be restricted to top-roped climbs when using the larger eye. The smaller eye can occasionally second for a Sticht belay plate as discussed further in this chapter.

Sticht Plate

This device has proven superior to body belays (Fig. 9-18). Its attachment is simple. The climber's belay rope threads through the Sticht plate around a stout, anchored, locking carabiner, back through the same Sticht plate hole, ending in the firm grip of the belayer. A small keeper cord should be attached to the hole in the plate and looped inside the stout carabiner. During rope movement, this will prevent the plate from sliding out of reach.

With minimal effort, the rope will run free, unless the plate is jammed against the locking carabiner. A falling climber automatically causes the plate to snug up against the carabiner. One commercially available Sticht plate incorporates a spring that maintains the proper distance between the plate and the carabiner, which allows for the rope to pay out freely. To initiate a belay requires deter-

Fig. 9-17. *Figure 8s provide adequate protection against disastrous falls and belayer burns. Always wear gloves. The Figure 8 used in the rappel mode is ok for single climber top roping only.*

mined effort to snug the spring-loaded plate tight against the carabiner. Holding the rope with the brake hand at tight right angles (Fig. 9-19) will quickly arrest the fall. On longer leader falls, the Sticht plate falls short of effectiveness, even though it still maintains superior holding power compared to a body belay. Attaching the mechanical aid to the belayer will restrict his movements and, in the event of a fall, the belayer will find tying off somewhat troublesome.

The small eye of

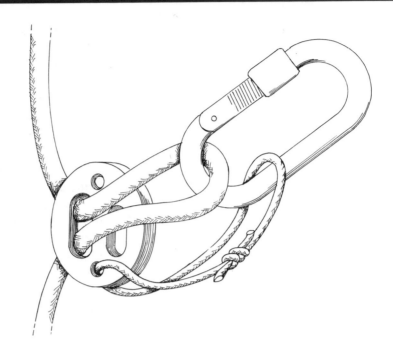

Fig. 9-18. A Sticht plate. A very popular belay device.

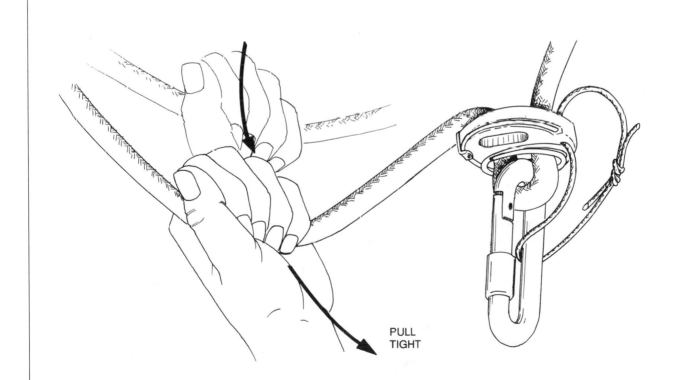

PULL
TIGHT

Fig. 9-19. During a fall the plate jams up against the carabiner. The belayer pulls the rope at right angles to the device to achieve the best results.

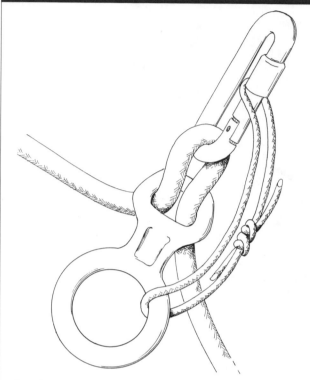

Fig. 9-20. Some Figure 8s have tailored their eye to second as Stitch plates.

The mechanical belays seem superior to all body belays during major long fall events. Some literature condemns these aids as gadget-dependency. It appears to be progress and the logical choice. That choice should be a joint decision between the belayer and the climber. What kind of protection does the climber feel secure with? Does the belayer prefer rope burns to gadgets? These questions, plus the consequences of the fall should weigh heavily in the decision.

After the Fall

The aftermath of any fall must be considered before the event takes place. Often the fallen climber will

some figure 8s can be used for a Sticht belay of sorts. If provided with a small cord for security, the figure 8 allows the climber to carry one less piece of hardware (Fig. 9-20).

Münter Hitch

Sometimes called the Italian friction hitch, this simple running knot has been condemned by some and sworn by by others. Claims that nylon rubbing on nylon will glaze or burn the rope are unjustified in that the areas of contact are constantly changing. Glazing primarily occurs when the rubbing is always in the same spot.

The knot is two-directional (Fig. 9-21), simple to tie (Fig. 9-22), easy to use and possesses the strongest holding and arresting force of the systems discussed so far. It is important to have a carabiner large enough to allow the knot to flip through. The knot automatically locks up during a fall with tension on the brake hand.

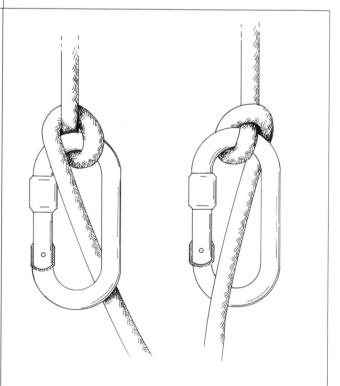

Fig. 9-21. A Münter hitch is multi-directional. Pull on either end and it forms the same friction knot.

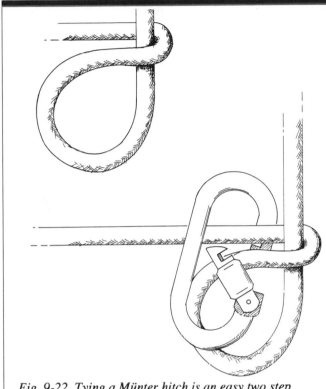

Fig. 9-22. Tying a Münter hitch is an easy two step process.

need only to be lowered to a ledge so he can regain composure. Any activity, other than lowering, requires the belayer to tie off or secure the fallen climber. Earlier, it was suggested that a safety Jumar be attached to the anchor. To secure the climber, simply clip in the Jumar onto the belay rope. There are few other one-handed activities that will accomplish this task as easily. Friends could help if they happen to be available. If the fallen climber is injured, and needs to be raised, a haul system may need to be quickly assembled in the staging area.

If the belayer chooses a body belay as the primary belay, he will undoubtedly experience difficulty securing his hanging partner, since both hands are busy preserving the life of his friend. Body belays are quick and convenient and for the most part are used out of habit. Belay devices are also quick and convenient and appear to be the superior choice. Mechanical belay aids provide the necessary edge to ensure that the falling climber is stopped quickly without injury to the belayer. Body belays cannot perform with the same efficiency.

REFERENCES

Conover, Keith. "Belaying." *NSS Caver Information Series*, 1971, Eight pages.

Ferber, Peggy, Ed. *Mountaineering, The Freedom Of The Hills*, The Mountaineers, Seattle, 3rd Edition, 1974, pp. 125-141.

Fischesser, Mike. "The Basics of Belaying Underground," *NSS News*, Vol. 43, No. 6, 1985, pp. 217-219.

Hudson, Steve. *Manual of U.S. Cave Rescue Techniques*, Second Edition, National Cave Rescue Commission of the NSS, 1986, Chapter 8.

Leeper, Ed. "Belaying: Forces and Stopping Distances." *Summit*, Jan. 1980, pp. 6-12.

Leeper, Ed. "Belaying: The Occupational Hazards," *Summit*, Jun. 1980, pp. 20-27.

Martin, Tom. *Rappelling*, Search, Mt. Sterling, KY, pp. 10-1 to 10-6.

Robbins, Royal. "Climbing Rope Myths," *Summit*, Mar. 1979, pp. 12-25.

Setnicka, Tim J. *Wilderness Search and Rescue*, Appalachian Mountain Club: Boston, MA, 1980, pp. 279-293.

Storey, J. Welborn. *American Caving Illustrated*, Atlanta, GA, 1965, pp. 128-137.

Williams, Toni. *Manual of U.S. Cave Rescue Techniques*, First Edition, National Cave Rescue Commission of the NSS. Huntsville, AL, 1981, pp. 55-56.

10 Vertical Potpourri

PHOTO BY BETH ELLIOTT

10 Vertical Potpourri

here are several related topics that need to be addressed regardless of whether a climber is going up or down in a cave, on a cliff, on a bridge or under a helicopter. These not only include philosophies, but techniques that are vital in all vertical work.

LEADERSHIP

The leadership of any vertical group is a controversial subject. Too often the delicate balance between meeting the objective and caring for the welfare of the group is not maintained. Many leaders do not realize that a leadership problem even exists. Some leaders will take too much responsibility. Rather than sharing a problem among party members, the leader stabs at a decision that is based on his experiences alone. The leader often emerges as the overwhelming problem. It has been well documented that many of the major vertical assaults were less than successful due to ineffective leadership. Many times, long ropes would sit idle for several hours during prime climbing/rappelling time because of leadership problems.

The "peerless leader" concept has proven to be less than effective. One dictator calling the shots causes bad feelings, one-sided decisions, and poor utilization of resources (mental and material). No one person is better than the combined efforts of an entire group. Each person should have the opportunity to give input to major decisions. The fact that the rope happens to belong to someone should not give that person the right to make all the decisions for a group.

A very effective leadership mode may be to form a consulting subgroup of two, three or four people and mutually agree on rope care, rig point(s), rappelling and prusik sequence, contingency plans, communication issues, derigging procedures, evacuation procedures, etc. This is not to say that someone shouldn't have the final say; rather the final say should be based upon experience provided by a consultation team. Members of this team should be allowed to express freely their opinions without feeling threatened. Everyone should be willing to abide by any decision made.

An effective leader plans, allows and encourages timely feedback. At the end of each day or at strategic times during a trip, the leader should ask questions of the group or of the consultation team such as:

- "Do you have any concerns or problems so far?"
- "Have you been able to 'live with' all the decisions made?"
- "Is the trip as you expected?"
- "What would you do differently?"
- "What could we do as a team to improve our experience (either for tomorrow or on the next trip)?"

This procedure will ensure open lines of communication, trip enjoyment, mutual understanding and enhance the learning process.

There are numerous leadership styles that have proven effective. Most of these can be graphed between the two extremes: goal-oriented leadership and people-oriented leadership. Many vertical people feel that because they own the rope and the four-wheel-drive vehicle that they fall somewhere on this graph line. When you read the final chapters in leadership books, they seem to all focus on the balance between a goal-oriented leader and one who uses the resources (party members around him) to accomplish that goal. A true leader leads for the success of the team, not the success of the leader. Having the party members succeed is a special part of leadership that is not easily attained.

THE COMPLETE CLIMBER

Each climber on any expedition, trip or drop should be completely outfitted with all the necessary gear. This means each person should be a self-contained unit with all the resources to climb, descend, stay warm, see in the dark, keep dry and protect himself. Borrowing equipment, sharing gloves or raising and lowering gear for the next person indicates that some of the members came unprepared. The exceptions to this lie under the subtitles of "Training" and "Emergencies."

A smart climber carries her survival pack with her. Too many times individuals find themselves separated from food, light and warmth only because a decision was made to pull all the gear up at once when the rope was pulled up during derigging. If an emergency were to occur (for instance, an injured climber on the rope), the appropriate gear necessary to handle the problem would not only be out of reach, but blocked by the injured climber.

Take It With You

Before attaching oneself to a rope and making the move either up or down, ASK!!!, "Do I have everything I need?" and, if appropriate, "Did I leave anything behind?" A very unpopular trip partner is one who is forgetful and constantly asks someone to grab his forgotten pack or delays the group because he needs to refit someone else's gear to his body. The worst case of this is someone who empties his ACE Hardware sack of newly purchased prusik cords and begins to cut them up and fit them accordingly at the bottom of the rope.

HELMET

The helmet is one of the most important pieces of equipment any climber will wear. Over the years, experience has shown us that looking for the cheap bargain is not the way to find a helmet.

The helmet should at least pass the industrial Z-89, test which states that a helmet should be able to sustain the impact of an eight-pound ball dropping five feet. The test also includes a penetration resistance test. A one-pound pointed plumb bob falling 10 feet should not penetrate the shell. The UIAA has more stringent tests for helmets. The helmet must sustain an eleven-pound ball dropped 6.5 feet. The helmet should not be penetrated if a 3.3 pound plumb bob is dropped five feet. The UIAA tests have specific

temperature ranges that the tests are carried out within. A UIAA helmet is considered a better helmet than one that only passes the Z-89 tests. In addition the helmet should be able to withstand glancing blows from the side in the event of a tumbling fall. The suspension should be able to absorb these shocks and yet keep the helmet on the climber's head. During inspection of a helmet, look for rivets in the suspension that may cause skull penetration if an unlikely blow were to occur. The chin strap should be attached to the helmet at 4 points and should be made of a non-elastic material (Fig. 10-1). It should be equipped with a quick-release mechanism. Among some of the proven quick release attachments are Velcro, Fastex buckles and properly cinched double-ring buckles (Fig. 10-2). Chart 10-A compares the features of some of the more popular helmets worn for vertical work.

Over the years Mountain

Fig. 10-1A four point attached chin strap is a key feature of a good fitting helmet.

Safety Research, along with the NSS, has laid down the criteria for helmet purchase. They are compiled and reviewed here:

- The helmet should have a rigid shell and pass the Z-89 (UIAA test would be better) impact test.
- The helmet should be able to pass the Z-89 (UIAA test would be better) penetration test.
- The helmet should have a suspension system that will absorb side blows and pad the skull.
- The helmet should remain on the head during a tumbling fall.
- The helmet should fit. It should not wobble on the head either front to rear or side to side.
- The chin strap should have a quick-release mechanism.
- The helmet should be well ventilated, lightweight, and allow effective hearing.
- The helmet should be of reasonable cost. What's your head worth?

If a heavy lamp, such as a carbide lamp, is to be placed on the front of a helmet with a bracket, it may be necessary to counterbalance the helmet in the back with a weight. A 10 oz. weight will counterbalance the average weight of a carbide lamp. A nape strap, a plastic helmet support that extends below the rim of the rear of the helmet and hugs the lower part of the skull, can assist holding the helmet in place if a heavy lamp is placed on the front.

	IMPACT ABSORPTION TOP	IMPACT ABSORPTION SIDE	HELMET RETENTION	MULTIPLE IMPACT RETENTION	COMFORT	VENTILATION	AVAILABILITY
CONSTRUCTION HARD HAT	Fair	Poor	Poor	Poor	Very Good	N	Excellent
MSA COMFO-CAP	Poor	Poor	Fair	Poor	Excellent	N	Very Good
MSR HELMET	Excellent	Excellent	Excellent	Very Good	Good	Y	Poor
SPELEOSHOPPE DELUXE	Good	Poor	Very Good	Good	Fair	N	Good
JOE BROWN	Excellent	Excellent	Excellent	Excellent	Fair	N	Excellent
ULTIMATE	Excellent	Excellent	Excellent	Excellent	Fair	N	Excellent
PETZL ECRIN	Excellent	Excellent	Excellent	Excellent	Excellent	Y	Excellent
PETZL DEVOLUY	Very Good	Good	Excellent	Excellent	Very Good	Y	Very Good
EDELRID ULTRA-LIGHT	Excellent	Excellent	Excellent	Excellent	Excellent	Y	Good

Legend:
- ▲ EXCELLENT
- △ VERY GOOD
- ◇ GOOD
- ▽ FAIR
- ▼ POOR
- Y YES
- N NO

Chart 10-1. Helmets

HELMETS

The ideal helmet protects the head and neck under all conditions. Besides absorbing impact from above and from the side, the helmet must remain on the climber's head. A four-point non-elastic chin strap assembly is the most desirable. Retention in multiple impacts is a must. A good helmet is comfortable and sufficiently ventilated to prevent heat buildup. The helmet should be lightweight so that the neck does not have to support an excessive weight load. When the helmet is used as a light holder, the lamp attachment should not extend inside the shell where it could cause possible injury in a fall.

COMPARISON CHART DISCLAIMER

Any rating or comparison is at best an educated opinion. Differing levels of familiarity with an item or differing applications can result in an entirely different rating score. The criteria used and the items rated are intended simply to show general opinions about these items. There will always exist isolated exceptions, and it is the authors' intent to avoid such "believe-it-or-not" discussion.

GEAR

There are three categories of equipment that should go with a caver or climber on any trip or expedition:

1. Gear that is always carried.
2. Survival gear that is also carried to the cave or drop (staging area).
3. Emergency gear that stays in the car until needed.

Gear That Goes With You

The gear that each person carries depends entirely on the assault/ trip/or drop. The transporting of emergency, rescue and "What if" gear can complicate a group's

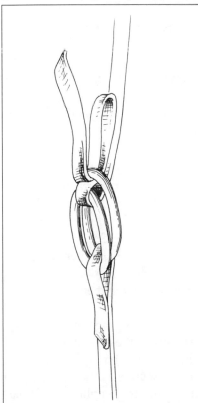

Fig. 10-2. A properly fastened double ring buckle can provide a quick release.

progress to the point of defeat or rescue.

Personal Gear

A caver/climber should travel light. The question, "What exactly will I need?" must be answered and may need a considerable amount of research. This may include contacting previous explorers, local individuals' data and records, trip reports and maps. Experience plays an important role. Ask any experienced backpacker how to prepare for a trip. It becomes apparent after 10 trips or so that the 10 extra carabiners and two pulleys never get used during routine exploration. It may be safe to surmise that all the extra baggage is just that. When the trip is over and you discover upon emptying your pack that everything was used and the trip was a success, then so was the packing for that trip.

Group Gear

Extra gear is trip-dependent. If an emergency were to happen, it would be helpful to have the basic necessary gear for a self, or partner rescue. Mike Fischesser, Chairman of the Safety and Techniques Committee of the NSS, feels that a group should carry: a minimum of three small rescue pulleys, two whistles, and a short rope (3/8 inch by 50 feet). Each individual should carry two prusiks (not incorporated in an ascending system), two spare carabiners and a knife or utility scissors. There will always be exceptions and extremes, but Mike's list seems to be a good place to start. Beyond that, travel light.

Rigging Gear

Ropes, pads, locking carabiners, pigtails, etriers, etc., are included in this category. The trip coordinator should be responsible for laying out and determining all the necessary rigging equipment required. All gear should be marked with the owner's name, initials or special code. This is especially important during a rescue operation. Often hundreds of items of gear may be necessary to facilitate a rescue. After it's over the nightmare of equipment return becomes reality.

Gear that should be included in the caver's/climber's pack may vary on the length and purpose of the trip. One should develop a checklist system to ensure that everything necessary is included. Here is a sample list of many common items found on a well prepared caver/climber. Realize that each trip dictates the necessary items that a team member will need to succeed.

CAVER/CLIMBER GEAR

- Helmet with appropriate chin strap
- Food   • Water
- Harness complete with harness carabiner
- Extra locking carabiner
- Carabiner to clip or attach gear with
- Rappelling device w/extra locking biner
- Gloves for rappelling
- Complete climbing system
- Chicken loops   • Safety Jumar
- Appropriate boots and socks
- Compass and maps
- Signalling device i.e. whistle or mirror
- Watch or time piece
- Appropriate clothing
- Large garbage bag stuffed in the top of helmet (warm and dry emergency)
- Primary light source w/spare batteries, bulbs, fuel and/or spares kit
- 2 additional sources of light, if caving. Butane lighter or flame source (heat, signalling, equipment repair e.g. nylon sealing)
- First aid kit (trip size and length will determine size). See first aid manuals.

SOME SPECIAL MISSIONS GEAR MAY INCLUDE

- Etriers, chocks, bolts, and/or scaling poles
- Tyrolean equipment   • Ladders
- Dye and traps   • Radios
- Survey equipment   • Sampling kit
- Life jacket(s)/Inner tubes • Wet suit(s)
- Rubber boats w/life jackets
- Cave-diving equipment
- Crampons, ice axe and ice screws
- Camera equipment

SURVIVAL GEAR

Survival gear is equipment that should be transported to the staging area. It traditionally falls under two categories:

1. The gear necessary to get the people from their vehicles to the cave or drop, as well as that gear neces-sary to keep the group warm, dry and fed until the time of the assault.

2. That equipment that has a better than fifty-fifty chance of being used during the trip.

The First Category May Include:

- Warm clothes (seasonal) • Rain gear
- Food and water   • Cooking stove
- Tarp/tent/shelter/ground cloth
- Sleeping gear   • Machete
- Maps, navigation equipment (i.e. compass)
- Binoculars/telescope

The Second Category May Include:
(Will vary depending on the goal of the mission)

- Pulleys   • Extra rope
- Digging tools   • Ax or saw
- Bolt kits   • Explosives
- Extra webbing   • Slings
- Duct tape
- Rescue call-out phone numbers

EMERGENCY GEAR

Emergency gear should remain in the vehicle and not be dragged to the staging area:

- Extra carabiners   • Large first aid kits
- Extra rope   • Extra webbing
- Litter and exposure bag • Tools
- Winches   • Come-along
- Hydraulic jacks   • Sewing awl
- Tow chain   • Jumper cables
- Snow/mud chains
- Emergency evacuation equipment

Adjustments to each category may be necessary, depending on the proximity of the assault area and its distance from the vehicle(s). The most important concept to pull from this section is the necessity to carry what is needed and not to complicate an expedition with fondue pots, troglodite repellent and a pool table. It is easy to "What if?" an expedition until the group is toting an entire sporting goods store.

GEAR TRANSFER: UP AND DOWN A DROP

The best way to transfer personal gear is for each person to carry his own. Personal gear should be a burden to no one but the person who brought it. Personal gear should always be within reach of the person who may need it. It should be attached somewhere below the climber's center of gravity, which is almost always below the seat-harness attachment point.

Lighter loads can be carried in small backpacks, side packs, hip belts and shoulder strap packs. If attached as a backpack, the additional weight above the climber's center of gravity can pull the climber upside down, causing severe complications (Fig. 10-3).

Proven attachment points are:

- To the seat-harness carabiner or eye of the rack (Fig. 10-4).
- There are several places on a seat harness that will accommodate a light pack. (Fig. 10-5).
- To one ankle ascender (Fig. 10-6). Ankle hauling does not work well on very heavy loads.

The important point here is that the attachment should aid the climber in remaining upright. There are other alternatives to carrying the gear.

Dropping Equipment
This practice should be highly discouraged on several counts:

- It is possible to hit someone, causing injury or death.
- Straps and slings tend to catch air currents and float. It is often unpredictable where they may land.
- Metal equipment could be permanently damaged if it hits a rock.
- Gear that lands in the dirt tends to collect that dirt and mud, causing weaknesses.
- If the equipment snags on the way down, it is often unretrievable.

On the positive side, tossing gear down a drop is quick and easy, but above 10 or 15 feet the risks outweigh the benefits. Gear that is too heavy or bulky to carry or throw must be raised or lowered on a rope.

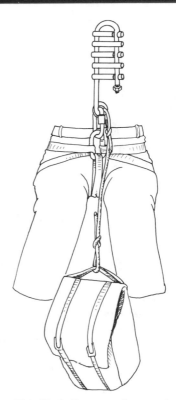

Fig. 10-4. Gear can be attached to a seat harness carabiner or to the eye of a rappel rack.

Fig. 10-3. A back pack can unbalance a climber. This is probably the worst place to carry a heavy pack.

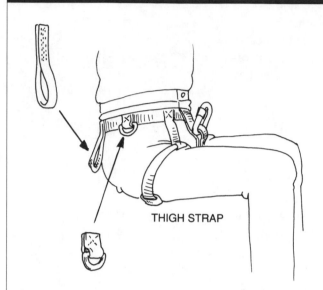

THIGH STRAP

Fig. 10-5. Lighter loads can be attached to seat harness loops or to a thigh strap.

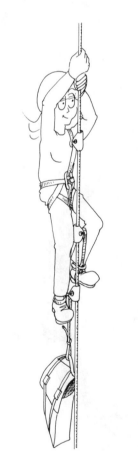

Fig. 10-6. Light to medium loads can be attached to an ankle ascender.

attractive alternative.

Zipline

A zipline is any angled rope that stretches from the top of a drop to the bottom and is used to slide equipment either up or down. The greater the angle away from the perpendicular, the safer and more controlled the transfer will be.

Transporting Gear Down

Large amounts of gear

Lowering Heavy Gear

The easiest way to lower gear is to rappel the gear down the drop (Fig. 10-7). Many alternative forms of this procedure will also prove successful. Two points are often suggested:

1. Be sure there is no opportunity for a pack or bag to snag on a rock protrusion. Straps, buckles, and catch points should be taped tightly to the side of the bag or removed if possible.
2. The person controlling the descent should be wearing gloves. If the drop is not free and there exists the chance that the gear may get snagged during lowering, a zipline is an

should be handled with a rappel rack as shown in Fig. 10-7 and a tether line. Small amounts of gear can often be slid down the line or "zipped". These dangling missiles have a tendency to act like the tip of a bullwhip when they hit the bottom of the rope. It is best to have the most experienced member of a team at the bottom to safely arrest the sliding gear. To guard against possible

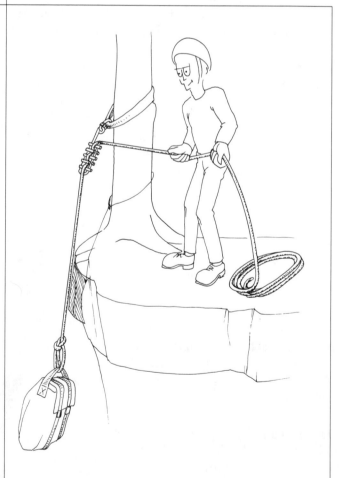

Fig. 10-7. A heavy pack can be rappelled down the drop with a rappelling device,

injury, three precautions should be taken:

1. Clear the area of all extra or unnecessary personnel.
2. Drape a line over the zipline and have two people hold it taut; one on each side.
3. Extend the angle as far as possible away from the perpendicular (Fig. 10-8).

Another method of slowing down sliding gear on a zipline is to oscillate the end of the rope in an effort to make waves up the rope. This will increase the friction at the attachment point (Fig. 10-9).

The most critical part of the sliding equipment, its safety and the participants' safety is the last minute relaxation of the tension from below by the person holding the line. Precision timing is necessary so that no equipment hits the ground or people. This procedure can be considered safe at vertical distances less than 50 feet. Over 50 feet the risk to equipment and personnel greatly increases.

Raising Heavy Gear

When it becomes necessary to haul up heavy loads of gear, a careful needs analysis should be done.

- How much gear needs to be lifted?
- How far does it need to be lifted?
- How much help is available?
- How much specialized equipment is on hand?

Raising heavy gear often necessitates a complicated raising system, as discussed later in this chapter. Pulleys incorporated into the raising system make the work much easier. Become acquainted

Fig. 10-8. Sliding gear down a zip line should be done with caution.

with quality rescue pulleys, and, as a team member, carry one (Fig. 10-10). Also take the time to become thoroughly familiar with a ratchet cam or progress capturing device and learn how to use it (Fig. 10-11). During a rescue, this device is often relied upon to support the victim's weight. Its rigging is often critical.

Transporting Gear Up a ZipLine

The use of a zipline to transport gear up allows for the easy clearance of trees, jagged rocks and nasty foliage (Fig. 10-12). Two methods are popular:

- The zipline.
- The clothes line zipline.

The zipline is a fixed line from top to bottom. A carabiner with gear is clipped to the line and pulled up the zipline with a tether line. It may be somewhat difficult to get the tether line back down for a second haul attempt, depending on the terrain and foliage. A second tether line extending the other way can easily solve this potential problem.

The clothesline zipline clips two ropes together or incorporates a butterfly in the center of a single line so a carabiner with gear can be clipped into the butterfly loop (Fig. 10-13). A person from above pulls while a person from below releases the rope while maintaining the proper angle and tension. This method is more

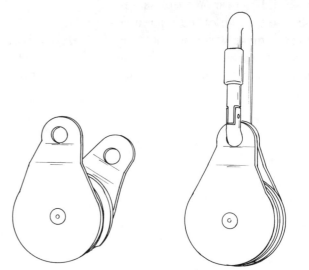

Fig. 10-10. Quality rescue pulleys will make the raising tasks much easier.

Fig. 10-9. Oscillating the line will increase the friction in the sliding carabiner and slow the gear down.

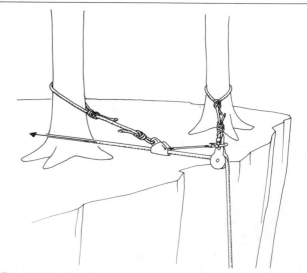

Fig. 10-11. A rachet cam or progress capturing device should be positioned near the edge.

taxing on all the individuals, but maintains the ease of multiple equipment transfers. In reality, if a clothesline transfer can be accomplished with minimal effort, most likely the packs are light enough to have been carried by the party members. Free-fall situations provide a new set of parameters and challenges when lowering or hauling gear.

Straight Pull

To accomplish straight pulling up a vertical drop, use the old formula that calls for a person for every 50 pounds of weight being lifted and a person for every 50 feet of vertical distance (Fig. 10-14). (Note: The earliest recalled use of this formula and probably the first descent into the 156 foot entrance pit of Hellhole Cave, WV, was in the early 1920s. Local farmers and townspeople would have a picnic in the field near the deep cave. For fun, they would lower and raise each other in and out of this deep cave.)

$$\frac{\text{Weight in pounds} + \text{Drop length in feet}}{50} = \begin{array}{l}\text{People} \\ \text{needed} \\ \text{for the} \\ \text{straight pull}\end{array}$$

Fig. 10-13. A clothesline zip may require added effort to successfully transport gear.

Fig. 10-12. The simple zipline.

Fig. 10-14. A straight pull of a 200 lb load up a 150 foot drop would require seven people.

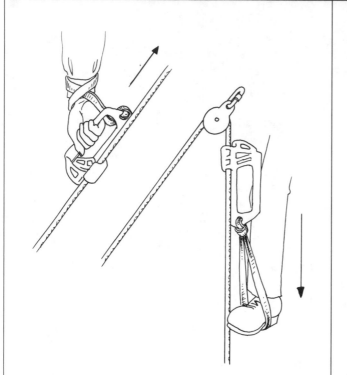

Fig. 10-15. An ascender can help as a hauler's aid.

Fig. 10-16. A 2-to-1 mechanical advantage may require a rope twice as long as the drop.

Members of the pulling team will find it helpful to use a Jumar or similar ascender to assist in grasping the rope (Fig. 10-15). Progress should be captured with a ratchet cam or Jumar as the mainline is hauled up.

Two-to-One Mechanical Advantage

A simple two-to-one advantage can be obtained by attaching a pulley to the gear and extending the rope from the top of the drop, down through the pulley and back up to the haulers. Realize that each pulley in a pulling system absorbs about 10 percent of the efficiency due to friction loss in the pulley. If the pulley is old or has lost its bearings, the lost efficiency could be considerably more. For example, a two-to-one system with one pulley lifting a 200 pound load will require about 120 pounds of force to raise the load. Using a carabiner in the place of a pulley can cause 50 percent efficiency loss.

To achieve one continuous pull to the top of the drop will require a rope that is double the length of the drop (Fig. 10-16). This is often impractical on long drops. A shorter piece of rope can achieve the same results if a mini version of the system is arranged at the top of the drop (Fig. 10-17). Pulling equipment up a long drop requires the hauling team to work in cycles. The purchase line is hauled, the ratchet cam is set, and the mechanical-advantage system is stretched back out and reattached to the rope, starting the cycle over again.

Typically, the hauling team members attach their ascenders to the rope and on the command of "Haul" pull together until the purchase advantage is exhausted, at which time someone shouts, "Set". The ratchet cam is secured, at which time the command, "Slack" is given by most likely the person setting the ratchet cam. The haulers release the tension, reset the hauling system and start the cycle over again on command of the ratchet cam tender.

Z Rig

A "Z" Rig, named for its shape, is a quick, simple hauling system that provides the pullers with a three-to-one mechanical advantage (Fig. 10-18). Two pulleys are necessary, as well as the use of one additional ascender as a ratchet cam. Friction loss in the pulleys (calculated at 10 percent) will amount to 14 percent of the load added to the purchase line. A 200-pound load will require at least 94 pounds of force to effect progress. If a pulley were used at the edge, an additional 20 pounds of friction loss can be added to the 94 pounds. The Z Rig is one of the most commonly used raising systems. This is not to say that this is the best. Many experienced climbers take the same hardware required to set up a Z Rig and fabricate a four-to-one system.

Piggyback Systems

A piggyback system (sometimes called "a pig") can achieve a four-to-one mechanical advantage. It is a combination of two two-to-one mechanical advantaged systems tied together (Fig. 10-19). Piggyback systems could be compounded to achieve much higher mechanical advantages. There is a point of diminishing return as the friction loss in the pulleys becomes too much to overcome. A disadvantage with any mechanical advantaged system is that the greater the advantage, the longer it takes to achieve progress. A 100 foot drop on a four-to-one piggyback system would require 400 feet of pulling. This takes a lot of time and, of course, energy.

Power Winches and Hand-Crank Winches

Power winches (e.g. winches attached to cars trucks or other motorized devices) are alternatives to the hoisting of heavy gear up a drop: however, power lifting is dangerous. A machine is often lacking in necessary sensitivity and will continue to pull even if the gear becomes wedged or snagged, causing the rope to break or the gear to tear free. Power winches should be used under ideal conditions and only by experts. Overloading the rope becomes extremely easy with a power winch and many knowledgeable climbers refuse to climb on a rope that had been subjected to power-winch use.

Blue Water advertises a hand-powered winch that provides a ten-to-one and thirty five-to-one true mechanical advantage. The precision engineering of this British-made winch puts the price at over $900.00. Hand-powered winches provide the necessary mechanical advantage, coupled with the necessary control.

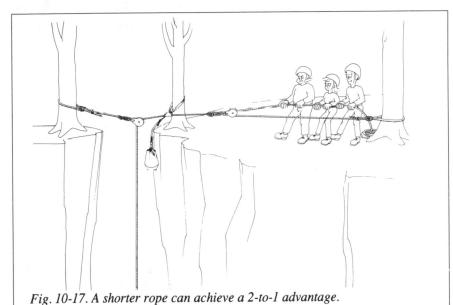

Fig. 10-17. A shorter rope can achieve a 2-to-1 advantage.

Fig. 10-18. A Z Rig can provide a 3-to-1 mechanical advantage.

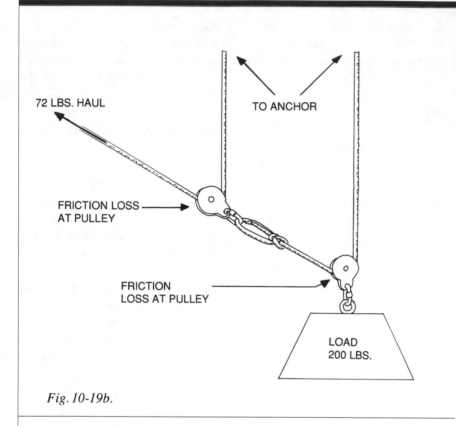

72 LBS. HAUL

TO ANCHOR

FRICTION LOSS AT PULLEY

FRICTION LOSS AT PULLEY

LOAD 200 LBS.

Fig. 10-19b.

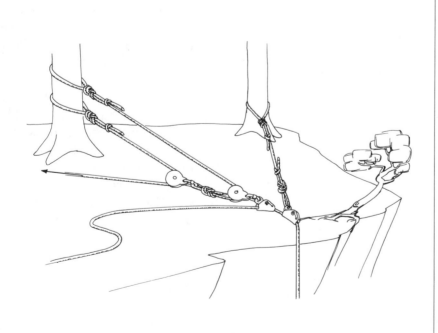

Fig. 10-19a. A piggyback system can provide a 4-to-1 mechanical advantage using the same hardware as the 3-to-1 Z Rig.

TYROLEAN TRAVERSES

Horizontal spaces may be crossed via a tyrolean traverse (Fig. 10-20). Tyroleans have gained increasing popularity for their usefulness in river rescue, mountain rescue, cave rescue, gear transporting, and as a sporting activity. These traverses are quite controversial because of the excessive stress that a rope experiences. There have been extensive computer studies to determine the actual stresses and tensions, but unfortunately, no conclusion as to the best procedure has been reached. This has developed into a complex and technical activity. It will be helpful when the entire topic is clarified and a general consensus obtained.

Rope

A static kernmantle rope is best. Steel cables and non-stretch materials should not be used as they will invariably break. It is important never to exceed 15 percent of the breaking strength of the rope. Field use requires some generalities due to so many uncontrolled variables. When the rope is rigged with a 15° angle of declination or sag from horizontal unloaded (Fig. 10-21), a 7/16 inch kernmantle rope will safely support 500 pounds. Use a field clinometer to measure the sag. A 1/2 inch rope with the same sag will safely support 650 lbs. while a 5/8 inch rope rigged with the same 15° sag will safely support 1000 lbs. A change in the sag will drastically effect these numbers. Some experienced tyroleaneers recommend a safe sag of 10 percent per person of the horizontal distance. For example, if the canyon to be traversed (by only one person at a time), is 350 feet across, the rope should sag, **unloaded,** at least 35 feet in the middle if one person intends to cross. If two people intend to cross together, a 70 foot sag would be necessary. It becomes difficult to measure this distance, especially while the rope is unloaded.

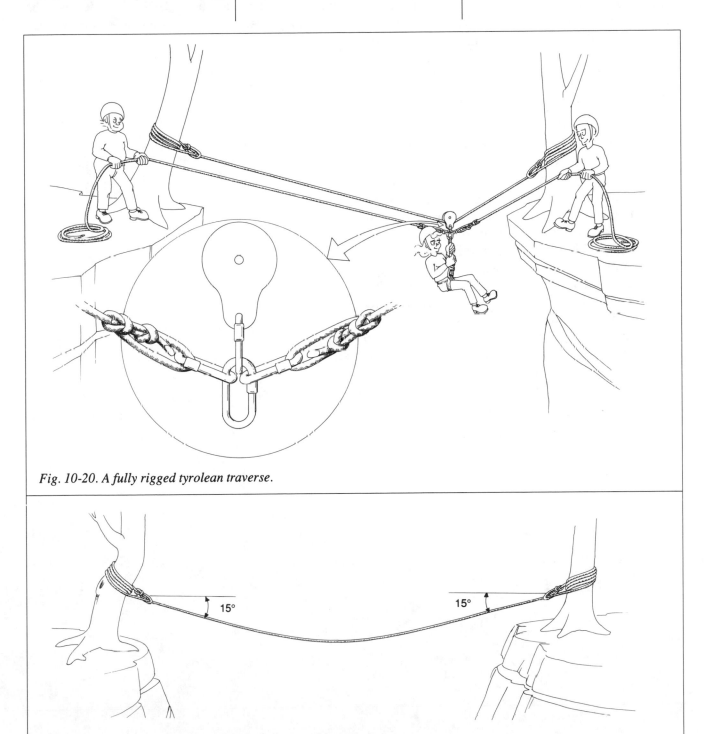

Fig. 10-20. A fully rigged tyrolean traverse.

Fig. 10-21. A 15° sag will place 200% of the load on each anchor point.

Rigging the Rope

There are not many easy ways to rig a tyrolean. Each canyon, each room, each expanse will have its own unique problems to solve. Some of the options available to a tyrolean rigging team include:

- Transport the entire rope to one side of the canyon, lower one end of the rope and walk/climb up the second side with the free end.
- Begin by lowering one end of the rope down one side, and, with a haul cord from the other side, hoist the free end of the rope into position.
- Drop two haul cords, one from each side and pull the rope into place.
- Use a line cannon and shoot a line across the space. The rope then can be pulled across.

Tie-Off

Because of the high tensions involved in tyroleans, the tie-off on either side should incorporate a tensionless knot if at all possible. Kyle Isenhart (caver and owner of Rescue Systems, Inc.), after extensive tyrolean research, suggests that the rope be fed through large pulleys and cinched up with a windlass type of winch (Fig. 10-22). With a winch a torque wrench can be used to precisely determine the rope tension. Caution must be used when a mechanical attachment (such as a Gibbs ascender) is to be used to secure the rope

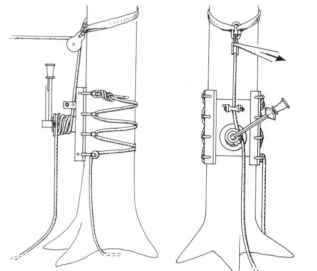

Fig. 10-22. Cinching up a tyrolean with a winch and a torque wrench.

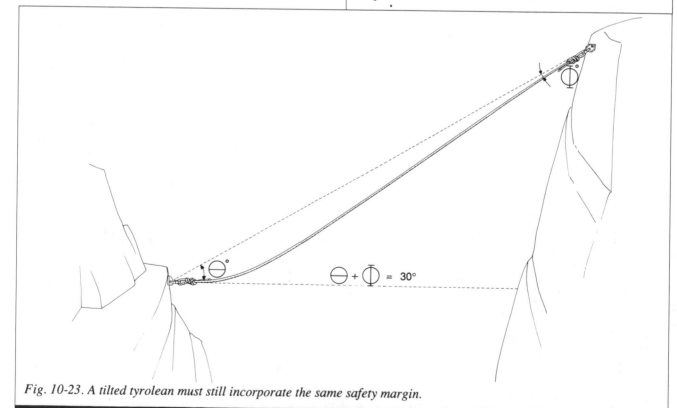

$$\ominus + \textcircled{} = 30°$$

Fig. 10-23. A tilted tyrolean must still incorporate the same safety margin.

or tighten it. During failure tests, the Gibbs ascender destroyed the rope by pinching it apart before the device failed.

Tilted Tyroleans offer a special challenge. They are not the horizontal trolley ride and they are not a free-fall drop climb. The calculation of the sag goes back to our 15° rule. Adding the degrees of declination on both sides of a horizontal tyrolean a total of 30° is achieved. On a tilted tyrolean, place an imaginary line between the two points of the tyrolean and measure declination below that imaginary line. The tyrolean may be so tilted that only 2° occurs at the top. That dictates that 28° of sag must occur at the bottom (Fig. 10-23).

Maneuvering Across

Experienced tyroleaneers use tether (tag) lines attached to the load from both sides of the canyon. These allow a way to maneuver people and gear back and forth, and they provide that mar-gin of safety in the event the main rope should break. Crossing usually involves the riding of a pulley half way across as the tyrolean slopes down and then struggling back up the other side with the use of ascenders, arm strength and assistance from members on the other side. Another very successful traversing method includes a shoulder Gibbs rig with a small pulley connection from the seat harness to the main rope (Fig. 10-24). This system makes the second half of the trip across very easy. Isenhart uses hand winches to crank the participants back and forth. Using only arm strength is the hardest and should be discouraged, along with the bicycle and unicycle.

Derigging

To derig a tyrolean, simply reverse the process used to rig. Lower the rope with haul cords or pull it across to one side with haul cords. It is unwise to drop the rope as damage may occur.

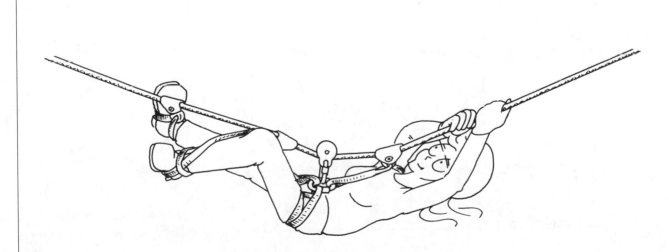

Fig. 10-24. Without a tether line, using a shoulder Gibbs rig makes traversing a tyrolean easy.

MAINTENANCE OF GEAR

All equipment should be carefully inspected after every use to determine whether it should be maintained or replaced. Nylon articles such as rope, nylon straps, harnesses, slings, belts, etriers and shock cords should be looked over and, if excessive wear is observed, should be discarded. Stitch patterns on harnesses need to be checked for integrity. Restitch the harness in the field if the situation calls for it. Evaluate harnesses for possible glazing that may have occurred during rappelling. Packs should be free of tears or holes to prevent gear loss. Metal equipment should be cleaned, especially teeth, hinges, and wheels. A climber should be prepared to clean the teeth of ascenders even during a muddy climb. A tooth brush and some water may be the answer to a slipping ascender.

Obviously, the use that equipment experiences will determine the extent of maintenance necessary. Polypropylene prusik cords could need replacing after only 500 feet of prusiking and yet may last through two or three thousand feet of the same. A climber who perhaps caves and climbs 30 to 50 times a year may need to replace all his slings annually. After every muddy cave trip or dirty experience, soil should be scrubbed off the webbing as soon as possible, preferably the same day. Prusik cords should not be allowed to stiffen up, but rather should remain supple. Prusik cords and webbing should be able to be pinched tightly between a thumb and forefinger (Fig. 10-25). If this suppleness is lost, chances are high that the space between all the yarns are filled with dirt. Under tension, this dirt will cut and tear the nylon fibers apart. If a puff appears, chances are that the rope or strap has already experienced internal cutting. Vertical gear should always look and operate like new. Old rope is a topic of

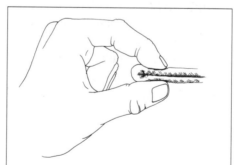

Fig. 10-25. Being able to pinch a prusik cord is one indication that the fibres are not filled with dirt.

increasing concern. Never risk your life on any questionable equipment.

Stitching Awl Use

The careful use of an awl during vertical gear construction or repair can become the key ingredient to a safe climbing system. The thread should be approximately 50 pound test and be of waxed nylon. Become well acquainted with the sewing awl (Fig. 10-26). The number of stitches and the stitching pattern will determine the holding power of the finished seam. A minimum safety margin would be to put in enough threads to hold 15 times the climber's weight. If a climber weighs 200 lbs. and the thread tests at 50 lbs. a minimum of 60 stitches should pass through the webbing or strap. Another goal would be to put enough stitches in the webbing to equal the testing strength of the webbing. A 6000-pound test two-inch strap would require 120 stitches.

Stitch Patterns

Analyze the weave pattern of the webbing or strap being stitched and the warp (vertical threads) and

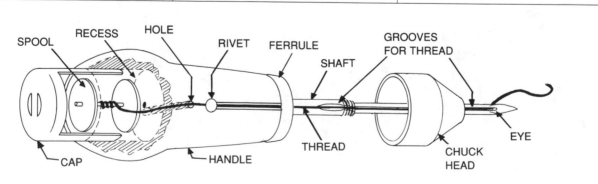

Fig. 10-26. Become well aquainted with a stitching awl.

woof (horizontal threads) will be evident (Fig. 10-27). It is best to form stitches that cross both the warp and the woof but trend in the general direction that the webbing or seam will experience stress (Fig. 10-28). This approach has proven the strongest of all stitch patterns. There are many standard stitch patterns that have evolved over the years (Fig. 10-29). It is interesting to note that the most popular pattern, a box with an X in the middle is the weakest of all the options. Carefully fit all the components to the system and pin, staple, tape, or place small basting stitches in the webbing so that it remains in place during sewing. One creative awl user recommends placing the webbing in a vise to hold it tightly together during sewing. With a pencil, chalk or other marking device draw the stitch pattern on the webbing. Load the sewing awl with thread and sew.

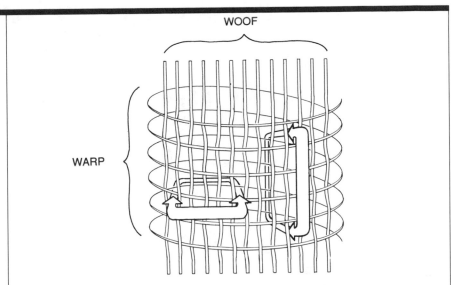

Fig. 10-27. Stitches should cross both the warp and woof.

Fig. 10-28. The strongest stitch pattern.

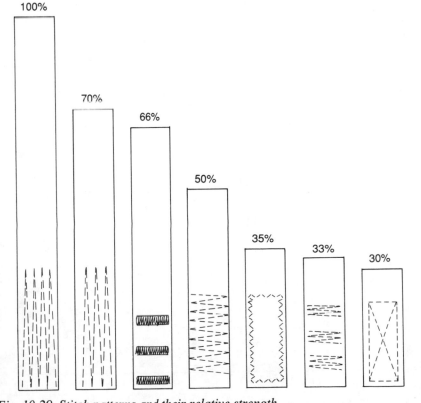

Fig. 10-29. Stitch patterns and their relative strength.

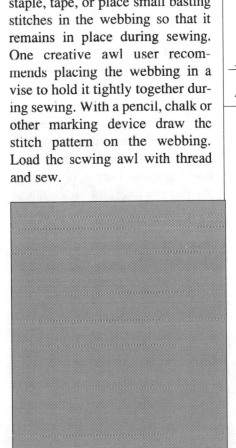

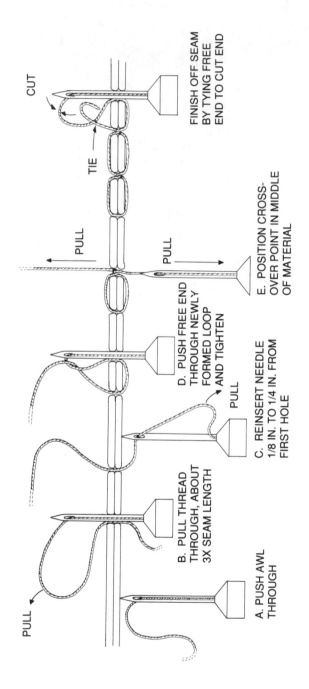

CUT

FINISH OFF SEAM
BY TYING FREE
END TO CUT END

TIE

PULL

PULL

E. POSITION CROSS-
OVER POINT IN MIDDLE
OF MATERIAL

PULL

D. PUSH FREE END
THROUGH NEWLY
FORMED LOOP
AND TIGHTEN

PULL

C. REINSERT NEEDLE
1/8 IN. TO 1/4 IN. FROM
FIRST HOLE

B. PULL THREAD
THROUGH, ABOUT
3X SEAM LENGTH

PULL

A. PUSH AWL
THROUGH

Fig. 10-30. Sewing awl techniques.

Sewing

Re-verify alignment and push the awl through the material to be sewn together at a corner of the drawn stitch pattern (Fig. 10-30a). Pull about 3 times the seam length of thread through the hole (Fig. 10-30b). Pull the needle back out and advance along the pencil line about 1/8 inch to 1/4 inch and reinsert the needle (Fig. 10-30c). Push the free end through the loop formed by the new needle loop (Fig. 10-30d). Continue in this manner positioning the cross thread point in the middle of the material during each stitch (Fig. 10-30e). After each stitch, draw up the tension and attempt to bury the thread deep into the webbing. This will ward off the possibility of snagging. At first, it may be wise to practice on something that one's life will not depend on. After stitching the entire stitch pattern, finish the sewing line off by pushing the awl through the material one last time and cut the thread at the awl. Tie the two ends together and melt the ends of the threads to prevent unravelling (Fig. 10-30f).

Securing Along the Way

Often it is difficult to secure each stitch as precisely as a sewing machine. It is possible to tie square knots every so often so that if a thread gets snagged, the effects will be minimal throughout the seam (Fig. 10-31a). It is also possible to twist the threads together and pull the twisted bundle into the material (Fig. 10-31b). If there is any uncertainty about the quality of the finished seam(s), take the harness down to the nearest cobbler or harness shop and have him reinforce the seams.

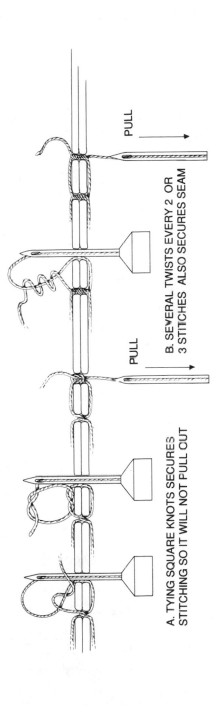

PULL

B. SEVERAL TWISTS EVERY 2 OR
3 STITCHES ALSO SECURES SEAM

PULL

A. TYING SQUARE KNOTS SECURES
STITCHING SO IT WILL NOT PULL OUT

Fig. 10-31. Sewing securing methods.

Sewing Machines

Due to the thickness of webbing and the size of the thread required, most normal household sewing machines will not work for sewing climbing gear. Industrial, shoe shop, or upholstery sewing machines will usually do quite well. When using a machine, it is important to make **absolutely** sure that both bobbins are loaded with nylon thread (Fig. 10-32). For machine sewing use 50 lb. tensile, size No. 6 thread. Use sufficient overlap and passes (a pass is one stitching line from one end of the overlap to the other) (Fig. 10-33). The overlap should be three times the width of the webbing being sewn. The number of passes should be nine per inch of width of webbing. If 1 inch webbing is being sewn there should be three inches of overlap and at least nine passes.

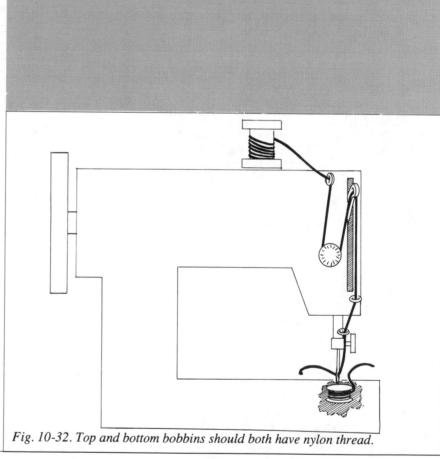

Fig. 10-32. Top and bottom bobbins should both have nylon thread.

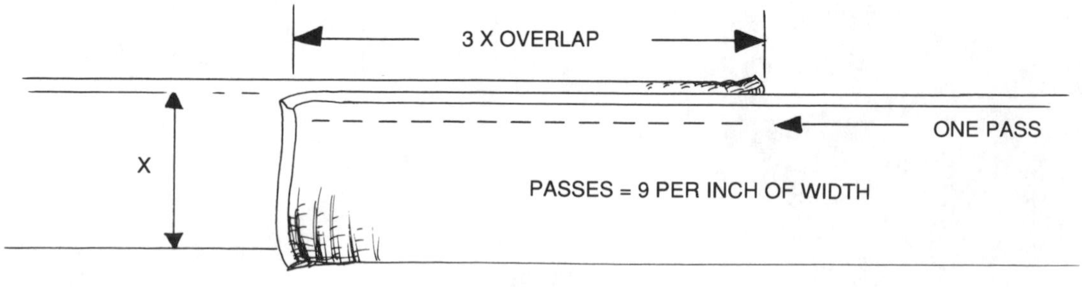

3 X OVERLAP

X

ONE PASS

PASSES = 9 PER INCH OF WIDTH

Fig. 10-33. Proper overlap of a seam should be three times the width.

ETIQUETTE

There is a pattern of protocol and unspoken pleasantries that has evolved over the years among vertical people (Fig. 10-34). Courtesy and etiquette play important roles in the relationship between climbers, cavers and property owners. By no means consider this list all-inclusive.

General Etiquette

1. Always tell a reliable person where you are going and when you expect to return. Include a plus factor and call if plans change.

2. Car keys should be stashed near the vehicle and group members should be informed of the hiding place. This allows for vehicle access, as people may return at different times.

3. Share vehicle expenses.

4. Always obtain the appropriate permission to be on private property or in government controlled areas. Thank the same individual upon departure.

5. At a drop, never touch, adjust, retie or fool with another person's rigging, unless a life-threatening situation is about to, or is, taking place as a result of a dangerously rigged drop.

6. Never walk up to a rigged drop and toss rocks over the edge to see how deep it is. Be careful not to accidentally dislodge anything into the drop.

7. Ask permission from the leader of another party and the rope owner before using someone else's rope or gear.

8. Ask permission from the leader of another party before rigging a rope beside another party's rope. Your rope could easily interfere with theirs.

9. Never throw a rope down a drop, rather lower it and only after one is sure there are no climbers below either rock-climbing or prusiking.

10. Climb with a system that can maintain the pace of the other party members. A two-knot Texas climbing rig is inappropriate on a long drop trip unless everyone chooses to use knots.

11. Finish a climb as quickly as possible. In a cave, those waiting below may be threatened by hypothermia.

12. Use appropriate signals at all times. Frustration is no excuse for silence or non-communication.

13. Always answer signals if physically able.

14. Be prepared. Practice putting gloves on while you're moving. A gulp of water can be on the go. Clothing adjustments should be made as the group moves or when the entire group decides to stop and rest. Many explorations are on timetables and multiple stops by individuals that hold up an entire party can often jeopardize the party's chances for success, as well as lead to hypothermic conditions in some situations.

15. Don't take anything that is not yours.

16. Leave nothing but footprints and leave them in the right places.

17. Maps, surveys or test results should be shared with owners, from whom original permission was obtained.

18. There exists an obligation to protect onlookers and stop them from attempting vertical work on your rope. If they are curious, they should be provided with information on how to find out more. Conversations with bystanders should be non-condescending. After all, everyone was a rookie once.

19. Report accidents or incidents so that others may learn from prior mistakes or trouble-some-causing circumstances.

20. Share the responsibility for carrying ropes, and other heavy gear during a trip.

21. Help to pull up the rope during derigging and share the coiling or stuffing responsibilities. Help carry all the gear back to the vehicles.

22. Stay together on the trail to and from the drop. No one likes to be left behind to worry about the route. Multi-drop situations often dictate the opposite.

23. The group has an ethical responsibility to preserve the natural environment. Will the group size be detrimental? Will someone be able to tell that a group climbed or camped if he were to come along the next day?

24. A group should respect another group's exploration efforts. Scientific experiments, dye traps and exploration digs that are obviously currently in progress should not be tampered with.

25. An experienced climber has a responsibility to teach proper, safe techniques to novices and share his knowledge and experience with climbers of all levels of experience.

26. Consider rescue feasibility. If efforts to explore take a group beyond the edge of where safe, experienced explorers go, then the consequences should be clearly discussed. Endangering others needlessly is a bad decision.

27. There exists an ethical controversy as to whether it is okay to make a drop or cave easier. Should standing ropes be left in a cave? Are explosives okay? Is it okay to dig or divert waterfalls? The authors of *On Rope* choose not to make ethical judgments on these issues, but their importance and ramifications dictate that they appear on this list.

28. There exists an ethical responsibility to tactfully tell someone if she is doing something unsafe. The difficult question that must be answered before someone comes off as "Super Vertical Know-it-all" is "Is it fact, or only my opinion?"

Caving Etiquette

1. First in should be first out. However, experience of the group members may dictate differently. If novices are along, the experienced member should be at the bottom during rappels and he should also be the first to climb.

2. Do not shine your light in someone's eyes.

3. When it is your turn to climb, be fully prepared and ready to go. When the rope is clear, attach your ascenders to the rope and immediately begin climbing.

4. Give novices the chance to lead and experience the cave or rockface whenever possible. Dis-

covering the beauties of nature loses its impact and thrill when the view always includes someone's backside.

5. Carbide cavers should be constantly aware of their flame and avoid close contact with others, especially other's hair.

6. Share your photos. Copies are often appreciated.

7. Carbide cavers should either recharge at the same time or each individual should be prepared to recharge as he walks or maneuvers down the passage. Electric cavers can give light to carbide cavers while they refuel.

8. Electric cavers should be careful to keep batteries and ropes physically separate.

9. Carbide cavers should be careful to keep their flame away from ropes or rigging.

COMMUNICATIONS

Communication is critical to the success of any mission. To ensure continuous communication, several modes of communication must be available. All members of the party must be able to understand and use all modes. Communications really fall into two categories:

1. Signals, the most commonly used method.

2. Telecommunications, high-tech, which is more commonly used on major assaults and rescue work.

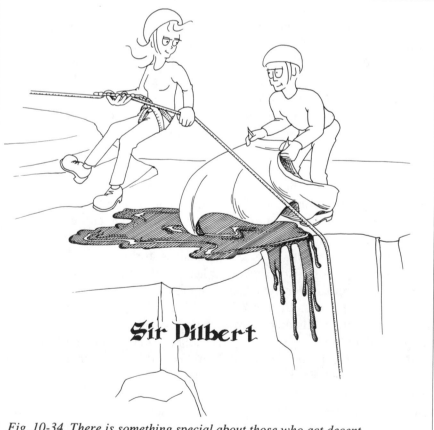

Fig. 10-34. There is something special about those who act decent.

SIGNALS

Signals convey precise, quick messages that answer the need for communication and ensure progress toward an objective. All members of a party must be familiar with verbal and whistle signals. Because there is no universal standard at this time, codes **MUST** be reviewed by everyone prior to any vertical activity. The following signals are recommended signals for common ropework communications.

WHISTLE OR SHOUT SIGNALS

Verbal   **Whistle**

STOP   Tweet (Quit whatever you are doing. Stop feeding out line. Stop hauling up line. Stop rappelling. Stop ascending. Wait for further communications, etc.).

UP   Tweet-Tweet (Pull up the line. Tension. I'm climbing up. I'm on rope, etc.).

DOWN   Tweet-Tweet-Tweet (Lower the line (when hauling). On rappel. On rope. I'm coming down, etc.).

LINE   Tweet-Tweet-Tweet-Tweet   (Off
FREE   rope. Come on down. Come on up, etc.).

HELP!!   Long Blast (In difficult situations a long blast is always discernable while separated tweets can involve echoes and confusion resulting in miscommunication).

VERBAL SIGNALS

"ON ROPE"   Spoken by the climber when he is attached to the rope, slack has been removed and the climber is ready to climb. This signal may also be used to indicate that a rappeller is attached to the rope, tension has been applied between the rappeller and the anchor and the rappeller is ready to enter "neitherspace" or the transitional time before full weight is hanging on the rope.

"OFF ROPE"   Climber/rappeller has completed either the rappel or the climb, is in a safe area where rockfall danger has been minimized, and another climber or rappeller can place her weight on the rope and begin rappelling or climbing. The first climber/rappeller may or may not have removed her gear from the rope.

"OK"   Acknowledgement that a signal was received and understood.

"ON BELAY"   Acknowledgement to rappellers "on rope," which indicates that a bottom belay is ready to be applied.

"ROCK"   This warning should be given whenever ANY object is accidentally dropped or dislodged. The size of the falling object should be distinguishable by the volume and urgency of the voice.

OTHER VERBAL SIGNALS

Other verbal signals that exist under the general heading of belay commands fall under SRT Signals. Climbers above and below ground use the following interplay which assists in everyone understanding what is happening.

BASIC DYNAMIC BELAY COMMANDS

Climber   "On belay" (I am tied securely into the rope).
Belayer   "Belay on" (I am in belay position).

Climber	"Ready to climb" (I am preparing to move).		**Climber**	"Tension" (I want you pull the rope tight).
Belayer	"Climb" (I am expecting you to move and will begin hauling up or letting out slack).		**Belayer**	(Pulls the rope tight, preparing for a possible fall).
Climber	"Climbing" (I am climbing)		**Climber**	"Falling" (Obvious).
			Belayer	"Fall" (Catches fall in the prescribed manner, saving life of fellow climber).
Climber	"Up rope" (I want you to pull up the rope and remove any slack).			
Belayer	(Would adjust the rope accordingly).		**Climber**	"Off Belay" (I am detached from the rope and have moved to a safe place, out of the rockfall zone, and/or away from the lip, etc.).
Climber	"Slack" (I want you to pay out the rope, thus releasing the tension. Often necessary to afford the climber freedom to make a move).			
			Belayer	"Belay Off"(Okay! I can relax and the rope is free for the next person).
Belayer	(Would afford the necessary slack).			

TELECOMMUNICATIONS

Telecommunications involves the use of radios or telephones and can be divided into two basic categories; wired and wireless communications.

Wired Communications

Cave rescue and expedition cave exploration may require wired communication. Solid rock and irregular passageways make line-of-sight radio communication a hopeless fiasco. Radio waves will not penetrate rock. There are several particulars with regard to field phone set-up and use. The owner of a set of field phones must know how to properly assemble and hook up the equipment. She should be able to instruct others in the proper use of the equipment. All party members must take full responsibility to protect the wires that are strung along the passageways.

Field Phone Use

The use of the communications equipment is formal in nature and follows a standard format. A pad and pencil should be with each phone to allow complex messages to be written down rather than chance someone's memory.

Speaking Techniques:

- Keep the mouthpiece one-half inch to one inch from the mouth and talk directly into it.
- Talk in a loud, clear voice, as if talking to someone across a room. Do not whisper, do not shout. The phone station should be positioned away from waterfalls and streams to avoid noise.
- Talk slightly slower than normal. Break words into syllables. Say individual words distinctly.
- Spell out unusual words and those likely to be misunderstood.

Line Discipline: A few simple common sense rules can ease communication frustration.

- Keep unnecessary chatter off the circuit. If there is something to say, say it briefly and then clear the line.
- Do not key the handset unless talking. Background noise picked up by a keyed handset can drown a weak signal.
- Do not leave the station unmanned. If it is necessary to leave for a minute or so, inform the other party.

Message Format: Every transmission should include basic compenents:

1. State the name of the station BEING CALLED.
2. Give the name of the station CALLING.
3. Wait for a response from the station being called.
4. State the message clearly and briefly.

5. Wait for the receiving station to acknowledge the message by stating the station name followed by "Roger." If the message is not understood completely, the station should request the sender to "Say again."

6. To sign off, "Station Clear."

WIRELESS COMMUNICATION

Two-Way Radios

Wireless communications are used in open spaces to avoid the weight and hassle of wired phones. The use of radios requires the same discipline as field phones.

While CB radio equipment may be the cheapest, it does not perform well over great distances or in other than line-of-sight situations. CBs are susceptible to interference from other radio users. Frequently, in populated areas this interference can render the radio useless.

FM radios provide range, power and compactness. They are priced accordingly. Due to battery drain, their use must be strictly controlled. When radio use is extended into several days or weeks, a time schedule should be established. (for instance every two hours for five minutes). If the other party fails to respond during this period, do not extend the radio-window. Wait for the next window. Battery life is shortened in cold or wet weather. Spare batteries should be kept warm. Lithium batteries, though expensive, are the best alternative in cold climates.

Climber's Radio

Although the best use of radios during any assault occurs during rigging and derigging, it may be helpful for the first rappeller to carry a radio so they are able to report any problems that others should be aware of. Subsequent climbers or rappellers may also find it useful. Even though the person on rope cares little about top or bottom activities (she has enough problems of her own), a radio conversation may be helpful in passing the time. It would be unreasonable and discourteous for base stations, either top or bottom, to demand communication and continuous up-to-the-minute reports from a climber making her way up a long drop. Any climber using a radio should make sure that the radio is securely fastened to her gear.

REFERENCES

Fischesser, Mike. "Some Thoughts on Brain Buckets." *NSS News* Vol. 41, No. 7, 1983, pp. 203-204.

Fischesser, Mike. "More On Caving Helmets." *NSS News* Vol. 43, No. 7, 1985, pp. 240-241.

Folsom, Franklin. *Exploring American Caves*. New York: The MacMillan Co., 1962 (etiquette in the underworld) pp. 238-246.

Isenhart, Kyle. "Rigging the Tyrolean Traverse." *Nylon Highway 12*, Vertical Section of the NSS, (1980), pp. 10-20.

Isenhart, Kyle. "The Seneca Rocks Tyrolean Traverse." *Nylon Highway 20*, Vertical Section of the NSS, (1985), pp. 22-24.

Magnussen, Cal. "How Strong Is A Stitched Splice In Nylon Webbing?" *Nylon Highway 3*, Vertical Section of the NSS, (1974), pp. 11-14.

Montgomery, Neil R. *Single Rope Techniques*, Sydney, Australia: Sydney Speleological Society, 1977, pp. 103-104.

Penberthy, Larry. "MSR Climbing Helmets." *Mountain Safety Research*, Issue 8, March 1974. p. 22.

Smith, Bruce. "When to Retire a Prusik Cord." *Nylon Highway 3*, Vertical Section of the NSS. (1974), p. 17.

Smith, Bruce. "Lifting With Pulleys," *Nylon Highway 5*, Vertical Section of the NSS, (1976), pp. 2-6.

Tomer, Darrel. "Using a Stitching Awl." *Nylon Highway 17*, Vertical Section of the NSS, (1983), pp. 2-6.

Williams, Toni, ed. *Manual of U.S. Cave Rescue Techniques*, 1981 ed. Huntsville, AL.: NSS, 1981.

11 Teaching and Practicing Ropework

11 Teaching and Practicing Ropework

It is not possible to master the physical skills of ropework by simply reading a book. A book can organize the material, but it is necessary to practice the skills. The two steps in acquiring any skill are first learning and then practicing that which has been learned.

Learning requires an attitude that makes us open to information and ideas regardless of our level of skill. Learning should be an evolutionary process. While the end may seem near, it should never be reached. Ropework is serious business. Failure to grasp the subject matter could result in the death of a student, trainer or both. It is not like failing Music Appreciation 101. A little bit of Music Appreciation might be useful, but a little vertical skill can be very dangerous. Disaster is often closely associated with the semi-trained, word-of-mouth-trained, or the I-think-it-works-this-way-trained person.

There is more to learning a skill than just knowing the steps to perform it. A novice rappeller can complete the sequence and arrive safely at the bottom, but until he understands rappel theory, he is not trained. A trainer should be able to answer the question, "Why?" for every statement he or she makes. As the reader moves through this text, he or she should be able to answer "Why?" for every statement before it is passed on to another learner. It is not just knowing HOW to do something, but also understanding WHY something is done that brings the student out of dangerous ignorance (Fig. 11-1). If something is about to go wrong, he can sense this and devise a solution to the problem.

Basic Training

The initial training session is important to the novice. The instruction should take place in a controlled environment such as a small cliff, gymnasium or tree. A beginning class on items of safety and procedures should precede the actual training session.

It is important to allow plenty of time for careful instruction and to prevent confusion. Class size should be kept small (10 to 12 students maximum, although one-to-one training is considered best) and sufficient gear should be available to lend to all students (helmet, seat harness, carabiners, gloves and Prusik knots).

A copy of the course outline and other diagrams of knots, gear, etc. should be available for free distribution. The goal of basic instruction is to cover only the simple, necessary skills and give an overview of ropework. Learning should take place through instruction and direct experiment.

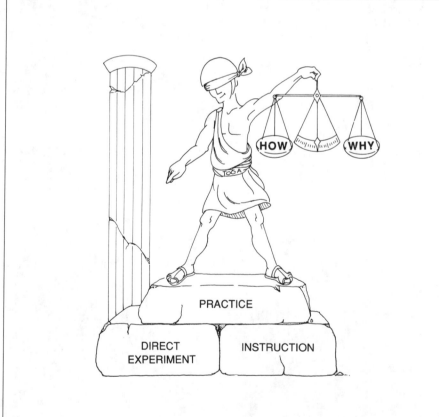

Fig. 11-1. It takes both the HOW and the WHY, as well as PRACTICE to learn.

BASIC ROPEWORK COURSE OUTLINE

1. Introduction.
   A. Instructors and their background.
   B. Safety parameters of the course.
   C. Information sheets:
      1. Safety rules.
      2. Course outline.
      3. Loaner gear.

2. Rope.
   A. Fiber types.
   B. Construction.
   C. Strength, abrasion resistance, and load absorption.
   D. Rope care.
   E. Webbing.

3. Knots.
   A. Terms and Considerations.
   B. End-line knot.
   C. Mid-line knot.
   D. Prusik knot.

4. Rappelling.
   A. Theory: Friction controls energy.
   B. The harness.
   C. The rappel device.

   D. Style: Checklist.
      1. Loose clothing.
      2. Helmet.
      3. Signals.
      4. The edge.
      5. Rate of descent.
      6. Bottom belay.
      7. Landing.

6. Prusiking.
   A. Theory: Upward movement using devices.
   B. Sit-stand classic 3-knot prusik method.
   C. Sling length and attachments.
   D. Moving a Prusik knot.
   E. Chicken loops.
   F. Getting started.
   G. Climbing rhythm using correct muscles.
   H. The lip.
   I. Getting off rope.

6. Review.
   A. Return of loaner equipment.
   B. Quick review of the outline.
   C. Questions.
   D. Emphasis on how little has been taught at this point.
   E. Practice and recommend further reading.
   F. Intermediate training session.
   G. Course—instructor critique.

INTERMEDIATE TRAINING

After a basic class and a fair amount of novice practice, the ropework student should then be formally instructed in intermediate skills. This gives a chance for review of the basic skills and learning of new skills. By this time the students should possess their own gear. This session will develop skills using each student's own equipment. A course outline and information sheets should be available.

INTERMEDIATE COURSE OUTLINE

1. Introduction.
    A. Instructors.
    B. Course content.
    C. Information sheets.
        1. Safety rules.
        2. Course outline.
        3. Further information source sheet.

2.. Quick review of basics.
    A. Rope.
    B. Knots.
    C. Rappelling.
    D. Prusiking.

3. Rigging.
    A. One strong anchor.
        1. Back-up anchors.
        2. Self-equalizing anchors.
    B. Natural anchors.
    C. Artificial anchors
    D. Rope pads.
    E. Hazard avoidance.
    F. Knot in rope end.
    G. Gear transfer.

4. Belaying.
    A. Self.
    B. Top.
    C. Bottom.

5. Advanced rope travel.
    A. Changeover from rappel to prusik.
    B. Changeover from prusik to rappel.

6. Self-Rescue.
    A. Lost gear.
    B. One ascender fails.
    C. Hair caught in rappel device.
    D. Recovery from a heel hang.
        1. Baboon hang.

7. Partner Rescue.
    A. Haul systems.
    B. Rescue using the same rope.

8. When and how to get outside help.

ADVANCED ROPE TRAVEL

Changeover is a necessary skill with which all climbers or rappellers should be familiar. It can and should be practiced in a non-threatening situation such as on a short cliff or tree.

To Changeover from Rappel to Prusik

1. Lock off the rappel device. The rappel device should have a connecting locking carabiner between it and the rappeller's seat harness.
2. Attach the upper ascender or safety Jumar to the seat harness with an extra carabiner. Attach the safety Jumar to the rope above the rappel device (Fig. 11-2).
3. Attach any and all lower ascenders to the rope well below the rappel device as the second and possibly the third attachment point (Fig. 11-3).
4. Unlock the rappel device and slip down the rope until full weight is on the upper ascender. Then remove the rappel device from the rope (Fig. 11-4).
5. Bring the lower ascenders into play and begin climbing.

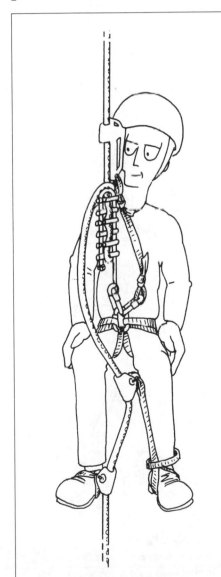

Fig. 11-2. Attach a safety Jumar above the rappel device.

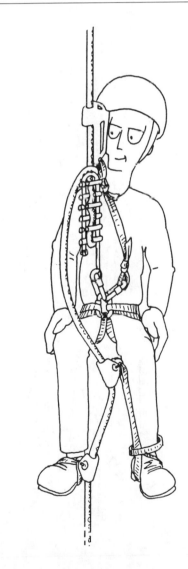

Fig. 11-3. Attach all other foot and knee ascenders to the rope.

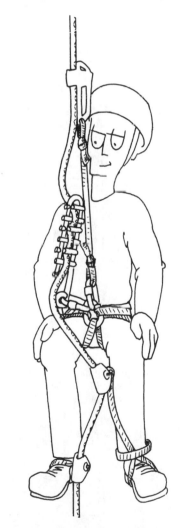

Fig. 11-4. First shift weight to seat harness, then remove rappel device from rope and harness. Don't open the seat harness carabiner.

To Changeover from Prusik to Rappel

1. Attach an ascender or safety Jumar to the rope and sit down, placing all weight on the seat harness.
2. Attach a rappel device to the rope under the safety Jumar (Fig. 11-5).
3. Attach the rappel device to the seat harness with an extra locking carabiner. **Do not open a loaded seat sling carabiner.**
4. Lock off the rappel device.
5. Stand up on the lower ascender(s).
6. Release all upper ascenders, rollers, safety Jumars, and shoulder cams (Fig. 11-6).
7. Sit in the rappel device, which is locked off, and remove all lower ascenders.
8. Unlock the rappel device and begin rappelling.

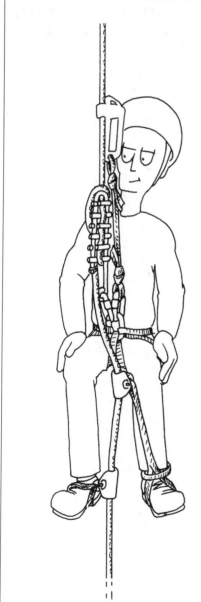

Fig. 11-5. Attach a rappel device below the safety Jumar.

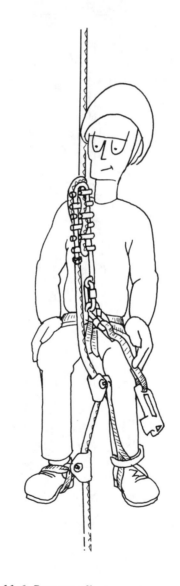

Fig. 11-6. Remove all upper rope attachments from the rope first.

Fig. 11-7. Passing a knot requires you to changeover to prusik and downclimb past the knot. Always maintain at least two points of contact with the rope.

Access to a safety Jumar makes both of these maneuvers easier. Due to particular features of each prusik system, subtle differences will occur that will require practice with each person's personal gear in a controlled situation prior to actual need. See Chapter 6 for a further discussion on changing over.

To rappel past a knot in the main rope requires the ability to change over. The climber rappels down near the knot, changes over to prusik, downclimbs past the knot, keeping at least two points of contact while moving the ascenders past the knot, changes back over to rappel and continues downward (Fig. 11-7). Again, the safety Jumar will greatly ease this operation.

To ascend past a knot requires only that two points of contact be maintained at all times. Because Prusik knots are slow and inconvenient to place on or remove from a rope, a safety Jumar or a fourth knot is necessary to prevent a heel-hang upset.

Self-Rescue

What if an upper strap were to break, or an upper attachment were to fail, inverting the climber? If the climber's chicken loops remain functional he will find himself in an uncomfortable, yet salvageable position known as a heel hang. If the chicken loops fail, or if they were forgotten, the climber needs to prepare for "battle" with the bottom. Sometimes the distances involved in an inversion can be great. The head may travel as much as 12 feet be-

Fig. 11-8. In case of a heel hang, first tighten up all of the body muscles to gain approximately 10 to 12 inches.

fore stopping. A good helmet is essential because of the possible impact with the wall or floor.

Recovering From a Heel Hang

Realize that to right oneself takes a lot of effort, and each movement should be carefully planned and deliberately executed. Rarely will a climber have the strength to make this effort twice. Practicing is a must. Keep in mind that if the climber is muddy, wet, injured, tired, or, possibly, hanging in a waterfall, she will have a whole

new set of problems to overcome that weren't a part of the practice session. It is important to be successful on the first attempt:

1. If wearing a backpack or toting a heavy rope, remove it and reattach it to the rope with an ascender or anything easily available. Unneeded equipment can be dropped. Remember, there may be only three minutes or so before exhaustion and blackout occur.

2. Bend both knees, bend at the waist and pull the body up

about 10 to 12 inches (Fig. 11-8).

3. Take the lower or free leg and hook it over the top of the opposite foot (Fig. 11-9).

4. At this point all the balance points, counterbalance forces and pivot points are in place to right the climber. A simple forward rocking motion, assisted by the pull of the arms will raise the climber, who will find herself sitting on her foot (Fig. 11-10). Hanging by a foot Gibbs requires substantial effort to accomplish the same move.

5. Clip into the rope with a safety Jumar.

Prevention

The best remedy for a heel hang is prevention. Prevention can be easily arranged with a short tether from one's seat harness to one of the foot ascenders.

The **Texas System** requires a small tether between the lower ascender and the seat harness (Fig. 11-11).

The **Gibbs Ropewalker Systems** require a small tether from the knee cam ascender to the seat harness (Fig. 11-12).

A **Mitchell System** requires a tether from the short foot ascender to the seat harness (Fig. 11-13).

The **Inchworm** requires a tether from the Mar-bar to the seat harness (Fig. 11-14).

The **Pygmy Prusik System** requires a tether from the lower ascender to the seat harness (Fig. 11-15). Regardless of the system being used, in case of catastrophic failure of any part, a climber should never be allowed to become separated from the rope and fall and never be allowed to fall upside down.

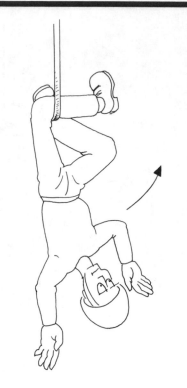

Fig. 11-9. Hook the lower or free leg over the opposite foot.

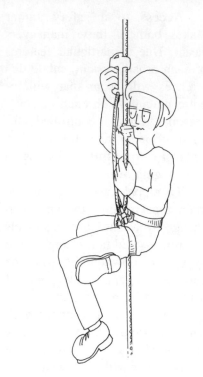

Fig. 11-10. A simple rocking motion will right the climber.

Fig. 11-11. The Texas system requires a tether between the lower ascender and the seat harness.

Fig. 11-12. *Gibbs ropewalker systems may need a small tether between knee ascender and seat harness.*

Fig. 11-13. *The Mitchell system requires a short tether from the lower Jumar to the seat harness.*

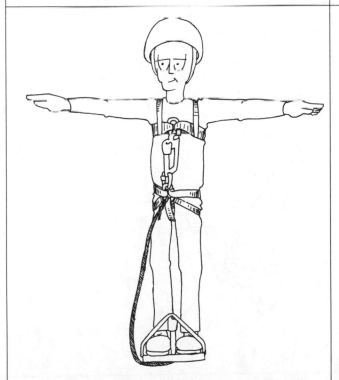

Fig. 11-14. *For the Inchworm, attach a tether from the bottom of the Mar-Bar to the seat harness.*

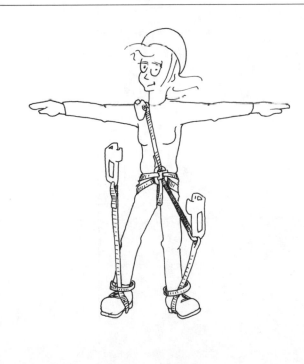

Fig. 11-15. *The Pygmy prusik system needs a tether from the lower ascender to the seat harness.*

The Baboon Hang

If a climber should take a fall and end up suspended by a waist loop, she can act fast and relieve the abdominal pressure by maneuvering into a baboon hang. Simply slip an endless loop over the thighs like a girdle, and rock back into the upright position (Fig. 11-16).

Fig. 11-16a. Hanging upside down, hook one foot around the rope.

Fig. 11-16b. Slide a sling over the non-hooked foot.

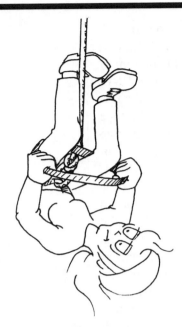

Fig. 11-16c. Hook the rope with the opposite foot and slide the sling over the other leg. No need to twist the sling.

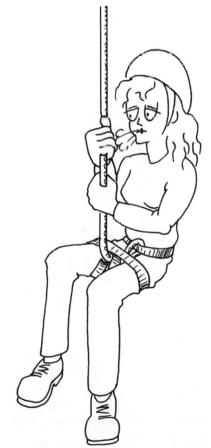

Fig. 11-16d. Rock forward and sit up.

Problem Solving

Intermediate ropework skills involve training in problem solving. If hair or a shirt gets caught in a rappel device, there is a correct way to get unstuck. The procedure as outlined in Chapter 5 requires an ascender, not a knife. During intermediate training, the procedure should be practiced close to the ground. Let the rappel device eat a shirt tail and use the ascender to cure the jam.

What if, on a two ascender system, one ascender fails or is lost? Haul out a spare and rig a compromise system. The most common compromise system is based on the Texas sit-stand system. The **bad case** involves no spare ascender. Rig the remaining ascender to the seat harness and have it serve as the upper Texas ascender. Pull up the main rope and tie a figure eight loop. Place a foot or both feet in this loop and stand up while advancing the top ascender. Sit down and retie another foot knot. This is slow and tedious, but it works. To make the system safe, a tether clipped into the figure eight knot and extending to the seat harness could add security (Fig. 11-17). Many climbers use webbing or chained 3/16 inch rope for a belt, which could be substituted as an ascender in a matter of minutes. Like all skills, practice ahead of time in a controlled situation.

A **worst case** would involve being at the bottom of a cave with no ascenders. Perhaps a flooded cave has swept away all existing gear. One could sit and wait for help, risking possible hy-

pothermia and starvation, or risk an attempt to get out. If there is some excess rope at the bottom of the main rope, simply cut 10-12 feet off and fashion a seat sling. If a knife is unavailable, cut the rope by bashing it apart between two rocks. Cut two more sections of rope and fabricate prusik slings. However to grip the main rope securely the prusik cords should be smaller in diameter. Strip the sheath from the core and use the sheath for prusik cords. If excess rope is in short supply, braid the core strands to form the second prusik cord. The core strands could also be used to form chicken loops. The braided sheath usually works best when used in an ascender knot configuration (Fig. 11-18). Again, the best system in this case may be to sit back and wait.

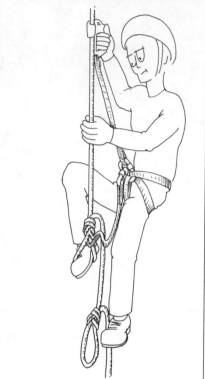

Fig. 11-17. Climbing with one ascender lost needs innovation.

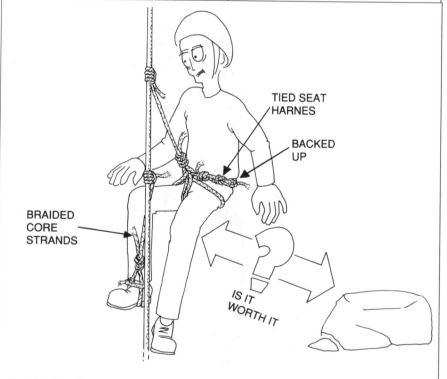

TIED SEAT HARNES

BACKED UP

BRAIDED CORE STRANDS

IS IT WORTH IT ?

Fig. 11-18. The worst case may result in the use of pieces of the main rope to formulate a climbing system.

Practice both: sit in a chair and see how safe it is, then climb using a field-generated rig. A climber should enter into such a climbing contract with his eyes wide open.

Partner Rescue

Self-reliance in vertical work is necessary, but accidents can and do happen, requiring assistance from others in the party. The skills necessary to rescue a partner from mid-rope are complex. Training and practice are essential in this intermediate skill. The primary thing to remember is that if the problem that caused the rescue cannot be safely solved mid-rope, the victim must be brought down or up to solid ground quickly.

If enough rope or an extra rope is available a lowering system can be quickly arranged (Fig. 11-19). One person can effect this solution. However, if tension must be relieved, a haul system must be arranged to raise the victim. Additional gear and rope are necessary. See Chapter 10.

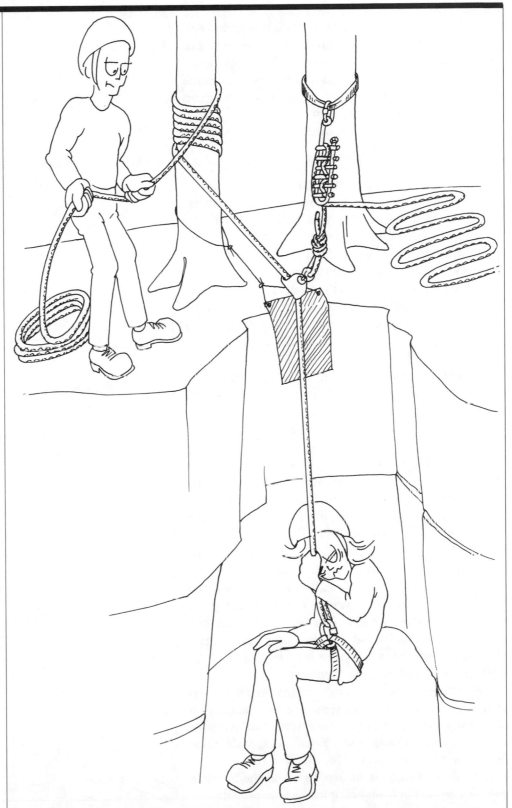

Fig. 11-19. In partner rescue, rappel the victim to a secure place where first aid can be administered.

Often the quickest and best solution is to descend or ascend to the victim, administer essential first aid, replace any faulty gear or provide necessary assistance. It may be necessary to attach a harness to the clinging victim. Using a sling and a quick-attachment procedure can avert an accident:

1. Drape the endless loop over the shoulders of the victim (Fig. 11-20a).
2. Reach from the back around the sides through the legs and grab the dangling harness (Fig. 11-20b).
3. Pull it up through the front of the crotch. Grab the sling from both sides and pull it around the victim's sides and waist (Fig. 11-20c).
4. Allow the sling to fall from the victim's shoulders. Pull the front crotch loops through the back sling and back again to the front (Fig. 11-20d).
5. Attach a carabiner through the front loops and the victim is ready for attachment to any other rescue tether (Fig. 11-20e).

NOTE: The rescuer's arms are around the victim during the entire process. If by chance the person starts to fall, the rescuer can easily grab him, preventing disaster. The entire process takes only seconds.

To continue with the assistance, the rescuer should attach a strong tether from his harness to the victim's harness, get positioned above the victim and remove all the victim's rope attachments. The victim is now being totally supported by the rescuer (Fig. 11-21). If the rescuer has tremendous strength he can climb up the rope with the load. A much quicker approach would be to change over to rappel and descend to the floor. If possible, changeover should take place before the extra weight is suspended from the rescuer's harness. David Judson aptly says, "Prior training is essential; willingness is no indication of the skill, strength and stamina necessary."

Further study and information on Rope Rescue Procedures can be obtained by consulting some of the excellent rescue texts available such as Caving Practice and Equipment, Wilderness Search and Rescue and the NCRC Manual.

Once the victim is on solid ground the problem can be assessed and several questions answered:

• Can the victim recover and exit with minimal help?

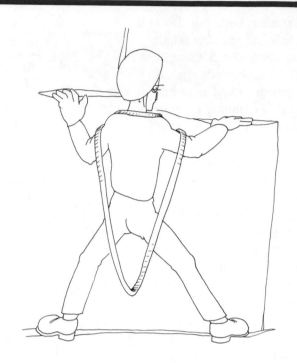

Fig. 11-20a. When attaching a clinging victim to a new harness , the quick-attachment procedure can be most helpful. Drape the sling over the victim's shoulders.

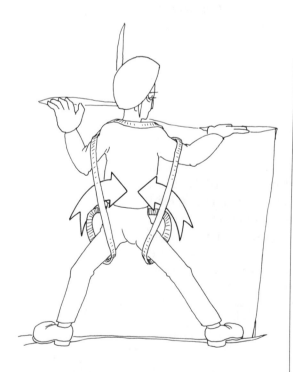

Fig. 11-20b. Grab the sling by reaching around the sides and through the victims crotch.

Fig. 11-20c. Pull the sling through the crotch and around both sides.

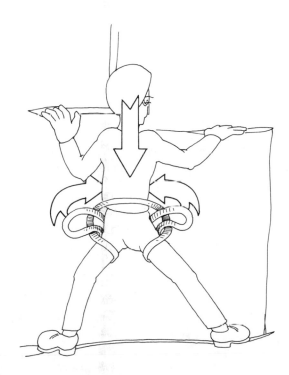

Fig. 11-20d. Let sling fall from victim's shoulders.

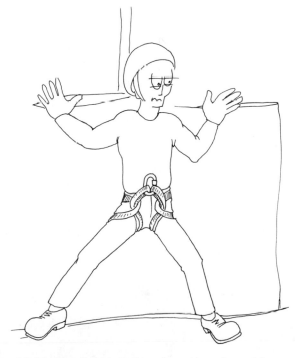

Fig. 11-20e Hook the two front loops together with a carabiner and attach to a secure line.

- Can the group effect a rescue on its own?
- Should experienced help be sent for?
- Should the group present start the rescue and send for outside back-up help or relief?

If the group is faced with a serious injury requiring specialized first aid, evacuation equipment, or if there is any doubt about the ability of the group to effect a safe rescue, the problem is best left to an experienced rescue team. Before making a decision, be absolutely confident of the outcome. A mistake may kill the person being rescued or violate the first rule of rescue: "Don't get dead."

Basic rescue skills and ways of contacting rescue authorities should be thoroughly covered during intermediate training sessions.

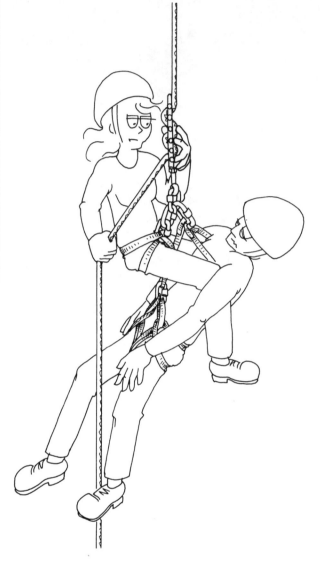

Fig. 11-21. In partner rescue, the victim can be attached to rescuer's seat harness and both rappel down together.

Practicing

Learning is a continuing process. Practice and actual use bring about a honing of skills, an opportunity for problemsolving and the development of a routine. Along with skills, strength and endurance are also enhanced.

Actual use can teach a lot, but to experiment with new procedures and techniques a controlled environment is useful. By enlisting a friend to carefully lower the rope as it moves through a pulley, the practice climber can climb a great distance and never get 10 feet from the ground (Fig. 11-22). For adjusting gear, the pulley practice system is useful in that the assistant can lower the climber at any time to make adjustments, then he can climb again.

Difficult maneuvers can be learned while using this system. So if the procedure is done incorrectly, the assistant can lower the climber, sort out the mistake and the climber can try again. Pulley climbing also allows for strength and endurance building at home.

For a rope-climbing treadmill, an endless rope loop can be rigged to allow solo practice. The system speed is controlled by the climber. First, an endless rope loop must be made. Static kernmantle rope does not splice well, so a **weak** splice is all that is possible. However, on the pulley rig the climber is not at any serious risk if the splice fails. To splice the rope (Fig. 11-23), take the two fresh cut ends, push the sheath back 6 inches or so and cut the core strands out. Pull the sheath back and on one end melt the sheath into a solid button. Lightly fuse the fiber ends on the other sheath end to prevent unravelling. Push the melted button up into the other sheath until the core is met. Pull the overlaying sheath tight and whip tightly with nylon thread to hold the joint solidly. This is **NOT** a strong splice and should only be used for the treadmill loop splice where the consequences are minimal if it breaks.

The rope loop is then rigged across a pulley and rappel device (Fig. 11-24). A weighted bucket hung on the bottom is lifted by elastic to the climber, reducing tension in the rappel device, allowing the rope to slide. If the climber stops or slows, the

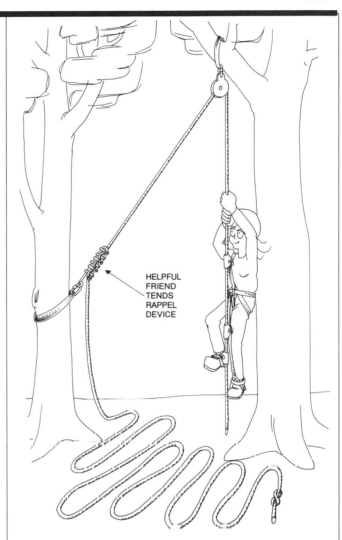

HELPFUL
FRIEND
TENDS
RAPPEL
DEVICE

Fig. 11-22. Use a practice pulley to ensure that a system works properly.

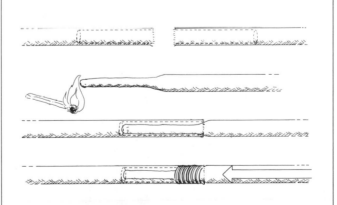

Fig. 11-23. Making a WEAK kernmantle rope splice for home or treadmill use.

bucket weight settles and the rappel device tension slows the rope. With fine-tuning, the system is remarkably smooth and allows the climber to practice any distance and at any rate.

Teaching

There are two ways to learn: through direct experiment or through instruction. The problem with North American rope techniques, in general, is that people have experimented too long and passed on their ancestral vertical rope techniques to all those that they come in contact with. Even the best and most experienced climbers learned from the experimenters and hearsay. Proper instruction provides us with an opportunity to learn the proven methods and avoid the unsafe practices. There is always a place for experimentation, but it should be used to advance our technology, not relearn it.

Teaching is passing on expertise and knowledge, but most importantly, it involves the transfer of skills. Without this critical element the students do not learn and the teacher does not teach. College degrees in education are granted to those who possess the basics of knowing how to teach. Having knowledge of a subject does not qualify one to teach, but it is a good start.

The person attempting to teach vertical work should not just "wing it", but rather should prepare a lesson plan. This should include visual aids, props, learning aids and printed information sheets. Above all, the lesson plan should be written, whether on 3 by 5 cards or a legal pad. Never rely on one's memory to get through a training ses-sion. The teacher has a grave responsibility if he chooses to teach this subject.

Safety and conservation should be stressed. Many resources, such as caves, are non-renewable. Along with protecting the environment, the instructor has a duty to protect the unknowing students as they learn. The instructor should be proficient in rescue and first aid skills. The instructor should have the ability to understand the fears and limitations of those with less experience than himself. The students can be provided with a twin rope rigging as shown in Fig. 11-25. This allows one instructor to be alongside the student while another instructor can lower the student safely to the ground if any problem develops.

The student should be made aware that the basic skills learned are not the end. Intermediate skills and experience are necessary to become competent and knowledgeable. It is important to not only know the how, but also the why.

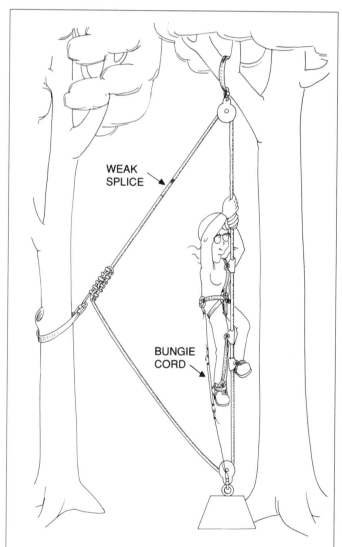

WEAK SPLICE

BUNGIE CORD

Fig. 11-24. A home treadmill can provide climbing practice and endurance training.

Continuing Education

Whether novice or expert, learning is a continuous process. Experimentation and research lead to innovations and new skills to learn. Discovery of new information can lead to safer techniques for all. Teaching defines the basics for the learner and refreshes the expert as he instructs. Answers to questions should include the why of the answer as well as the answer. Accident reports are vitally important, for these become an analysis of what went wrong without having to repeat the incident. Instruction rather than direct experiment is the obvious benefit.

Learning continues with our participation in vertical work. The more we learn the more we enjoy the experience.

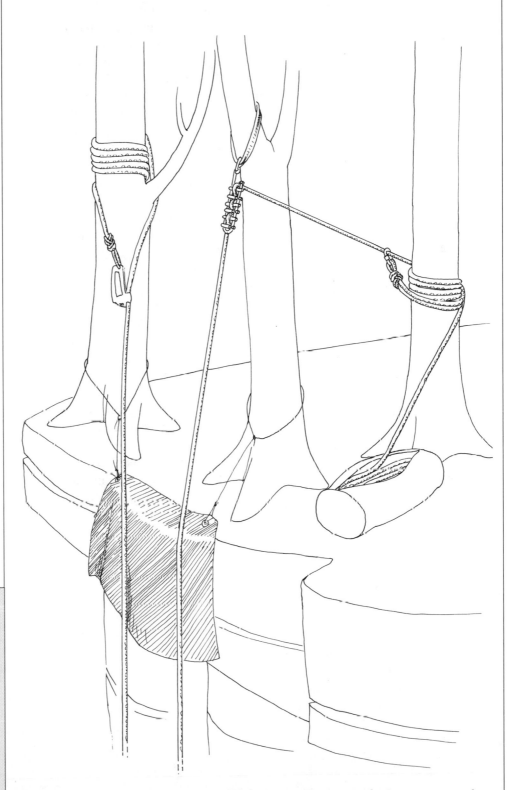

Fig. 11-25. A training situation almost always has two ropes, one for instructor, one for learner. Learner's rope is attached to a rappel device in case lowering is needed.

VERTICAL CLIMBING CONTEST

The vertical climbing races have fostered many developments in equipment and style. These ideas and devices have practical application in the real world of climbing because that which is fast is efficient and easier to use during actual climbing situations.

North Americans will make a contest out of anything. In 1966 at a regional cavers meeting, the "Prusik Contest" saw its beginnings. It then went national at the 1967 NSS Convention in Alabama. The contest, now a two-day event, takes place at each annual convention of the NSS, with certificates and prizes awarded for outstanding performances.

The climbing setup is the same as a pulley practice rig. The rope is fed through a rappel device such as a spool or rack, then down through a pulley to the climber. Below the climber are safety padding mats. The event is usually held in a gymnasium or theater and the padding is to prevent injury in case of equipment failure. To provide tension below the climber "puller(s)" keep the rope tight. Three official timers use stopwatches to record the time.

Distances for the contest, now international, are measured in meters. The two distances are 30 meters and 120 meters. Set up like a track meet, there are men's and women's divisions with age categories 0-12, 13-16, 17-19, 20-29, 30-39, 40-49, 50-59, 60-69, 70-up. These divisions are divided between the two ascending styles. The first category, Mechanical,

includes anything metal or hard touching the rope such as Jumars or Gibbs. Motorized ascenders do not qualify. The other major category, "Classic Three-Knot," in an effort to maintain a long-standing tradition, limits innovation and insists on three soft knots moved in the historical fashion. To race using knots requires near-flawless technique and lots of stamina.

Each climber is allowed three attempts in each style and distance category. To race, the climber ascends off the floor to a single red mark on the rope (fig. #11-a). She then stops her top attachment point just below that mark. The timers ready their watches and as the climber, when ready, moves across the mark, the watches are activated, the spooler allows the rope to slide as needed and the pullers maintain the proper lower tension. Time splits and distances are called out at the marks as requested by the climber. Time stops when the top attachment point (ascender, roller, etc.), crosses the finish mark.

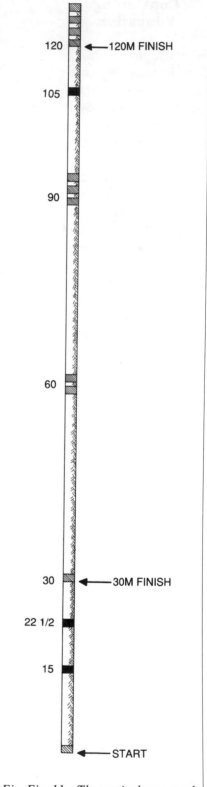

Fig. Fig. 11a. The vertical race track. Mark points are red, splits are black.

PRUSIK CONTEST RECORD TIMES				
		MEN		**WOMEN**
Mechanical 30M	25.7	Rossano Boscarino '87	43.4	Martha Clark '85
Mechanical 120M	4:10.7	Rossano Boscarino '87	5:40.1	Louise Hose '87
Classic 3-Knot 30M	1:37.1	Jeff Forbes '81	2:05.0	Martha Clark '84
Classic 3-Knot 120M	9:39.2	Trick Howard '85	12:29.3	Martha Clark '84

REFERENCES

Ferber, Peggy, ed. *Mountaineering. Freedom of the Hills*, Seattle: The Mountaineers, 1974, pp. 138-139.

Fischesser, Mike. "Teaching Single Rope Techniques Safely." *Nylon Highway 15*, Vertical Section of the NSS, (1982), pp. 9-11.

Judson, David. *Caving Practice and Equipment*, London, Newton Abbot, 1984, pp. 90-99.

McClurg, David. *Adventure of Caving*. Carlsbad, NM: D & J Press, 1986, pp. 297-302.

Meredith, Mike. *Vertical Caving*, Kendal England: Westmoreland Gazette, Kendal England, pp. 56-59.

Seaman, Ed. "Teaching New People Vertical Techniques." *Nylon Highway 15*, Vertical Section of the NSS, (1982), pp. 7-9.

Smith, Bruce. "The Heel Hang." *Nylon Highway 23*, Vertical Section of the NSS, (1986).

Weinel, J.E. "Continuous Loop Slings." *pamphlet*, Valencia, PA, J.E. Weinel, Inc. 1986.

12 Further Information

12 Further Information

There are several sources of information on ropework that are important to climbers. As techniques are evolving, so should climbers who practice SRT keep currently informed.

Many practices that were popular only 10 years ago are now condemned as dangerous and unacceptable procedures. Looking into the future, it would be presumptuous to think that every-thing between the *On Rope* covers will remain the state-of-the-art. These information sources are some of the best in the world:

National Speleological Society (NSS) Cave Avenue Huntsville, Alabama 35810. 205-852-1300
   Membership services of the NSS:

- *NSS News*—Professional monthly publication that includes advertisements.
- *NSS Bulletin*--Scientific research published semi-annually as a separate publication.
- *Membership Manual*—Annual issue with member services and membership list.
- Bookstore—Retail books in print for sale.
- Library—Vast resource of archives, books and periodicals, some lending available.
- Convention—Annual week-long event crammed with information and fun. The vertical contests take place at the NSS Convention.
- *American Caving Accidents (ACA)*—Published annually since 1967.

- *Speleo Digest*—A collection of all the best published cave articles that appear in the various publications in North America. Published annually.
- Vertical Section—Publishes twice a year the *Nylon Highway*. Group also sponsors annual Vertical Technique Workshops and the Vertical Climbing Contests.
- National Cave Rescue Commission (NCRC)—Publishes a how-to manual and sponsors an annual week long training symposium and numerous weekend seminars. The NCRC coordinates the cave rescue network nationwide.
- Grottos (Local chapters or clubs)—The NSS organization includes local groups as a part of its overall structure. Most grottos publish local cave information monthly.
- Safety and Techniques Committee (STC)—Published monthly as part of the NSS News. Performs evaluations, testing, and an annual workshop at the Convention.

- Cave Rescue Section: National Cave Rescue Network: 804-323-2300 for West Virginia, Virginia, Maryland, Pennsylvania, New Jersey, North Carolina, Tennessee and Kentucky. 800-851-3051 elsewhere in the USA.

National Association for Search and Rescue (NASAR) P. O. Box 50178 Washington, D. C. 20004. 703-352-1349
   Member services of the NASAR:

- *Response*—Magazine published bi-monthly which includes advertising.
- Membership list—Annually published.
- Bookstore—Discount sales of search and rescue titles.
- Convention—Annually featuring workshops, presentations, discussions and displays.
- North American Technical Rescue Symposium—Annual forum on technical rescue topics.
- Training classes—Three classes offered, Managing The Search Function, Managing Emergency Operations, Basic SAR Skills.
- Data Collection—Compile data on all SAR missions.
- Government Liaison—National voice to all agencies concerned with SAR.

National Fire Protection Association (NFPA) Batterymarch Park Quincy, MA. 02269

- Establishes standards for safety in the fields of fire service, life safety rope, harnesses, hardware, definitions, testing methods and the proper conditions for equipment use.

International Society of Fire Service Instructors (ISFSI) 20 Main Street Ashland, MA. 01721. 617-881-5800

Membership services of the ISFSI:

- Publication—Professional 20-page; distributed monthly.
- Resource Catalog—Listings of audio-visual materials, texts and manuals for the fire service is available.
- Annual Conference—International annual meeting organized for fire department instructors.
- Standards—Establishes professional standards for terms and methods used by emergency companies.

British Cave Research Association (BCRA) c/o David Stoddard 23 Claremont Ave. Bishopston, Bristol England   BS7 8JD
Membership services of the BCRA:

- *Caves and Caving*—Professional quarterly publication that includes advertising.
- *Cave Science*—Published three times a year. Contains scientific cave research papers.
- National Caving Conference—Annual convention.
- Meetings—General information sharing get-togethers throughout the year.
- Library.
- Foreign contacts—keep current through worldwide contacts.
- Insurance—Public liability is provided to BCRA members free.

American Window Cleaners Newsletter   P.O. Box 5653 Berkeley, CA 94705. 415-547-8651

MANUFACTURERS, SUPPLIERS AND RESOURCES

Listed here are some of the manufacturers and suppliers of equipment and supplies that are generally used during ropework. Most manufacturers will supply to individuals as well as retailers.

B&B Enterprises, P.O. Box 411P, Lewisburg, WV 24901, 304-772-5049. Retailer of rescue and climbing equipment.

Backwoods Equipment, 5011 S. 79th E. Ave., Tulsa, OK 74145, 918-664-7850. Retailer.
Base Camp, 1730 Chestnut St., Philadelphia, PA 19103, 215-563-9626. Retailer.

Base Camp Supply, 3730 South Pine Street, Tacoma, WA 98409, 206-472-4402. Retailer.

Bat Sew Products, 2842 NE 14th Dr. Gainesville, FL 32609, 904-376-6051. Custom sewn harnesses and related gear.
Blue Water LTD, P.O. Box 1465, 131 Lovvorn Rd. Carrollton, GA 30117, 404-832-9694. Ropemaker, rope/rescue/equipment distributor.

Bob & Bob, P.O. Box 441R, Lewisburg, WV 24901, 304-772-5049. Retail supplier of rope, and caving supplies.

Boulder Mountaineer, The, 1335 Broadway, Boulder, CO 80302. 303-442-8355.
Butt Strap Harness Makers, c/o Mike Fischesser, 121 N. Sterling St., Morganton, NC 28655.

Buzzard Mountain Shop, 250 Moraine Ave., Estes Park, CO 80517, 303-586-4638.

California Mountain Co., P.O. Box 6602, Santa Barbara, CA 93160, 1-800-235-5741, CA 805-867-5654. Technical rescue equipment.
Canoeist Headquarters, 4825 Hixson Pike, Chattanooga, TN 37443, 615-877-6256. Retailer for the hiker, climber, and paddler.

Caves Unlimited, 4956 Asbury Circle, Dubuque, IA 52001, 319-582-7756. Retail supplier.

Climb High, P.O. Box 9210, South Burlington, VT 05401. Retail supplier hardware.
Colorado Mountain Industries (CMI), P.O. Box 535, Franklin, WV 26807, 304-358-7041. Manufacturer of chocks, ascenders, hardware.

Columbian Rope Company, P.O. Box 270, Guntown MS 38849, 601-348-2241. Rope manufacturer.

C.S.A. Outdoors, Rt. 2 Box 68-A Leetown Curve, Grundy, VA 24614, 703-935-4808. Retailer.

Diamond Brand Camping Center, Highway 25, Naples, NC 28760. 704-684-6262. Retailer.

Dive Rescue, Inc./International, 2619 Canton Court, Fort Collins, CO 80525, 1-800-248-3483, CO 303-482-0887. Rope and rescue equipment.

Exkursion, 4123 William Penn Hwy., Monroeville, Pa 15146, 412-372-7030. Retailer.

Fire Brand, Inc., 3025 S. Military Highway, Chesapeake, VA 23323, 804-487-4646. Retailer of rope/rescue equippment/fire department supplies.

Forrest Safety Products, 4550 Jackson St., Denver, CO 80216. Manufacturer of harnesses and rescue equipment. 1-800-223-2102.

The Gendarme, Box 53, Seneca Rocks, WV 26884, 304-567-2600. Retailer.

Gibbs Products Co., 202 Hanpton Avenue, Salt Lake City, UT 84111. Gibbs ascenders.

Great Pacific Ironworks, P.O. Box 150, Ventura, CA 93001. Manufacturer of Chouinard products.

High Country Sports, 500 Idaho St., Boise, ID 83702, 208-344-3821. Retailer.

Holubar Mountaineering, 2490 S. Colorado Blvd. Denver, CO 80222, 303-758-6366. Retailer.

Inner Mountain Outfitters, c/o Alex Sproul, 102 Travis Circle, Seaford, VA 23696, 804-898-2809. Retail rope and rescue equipment.

International Mountain Equipment Inc., P.O. Box 494, Main Street, North Conway, NH 03860, 603-356-6316. Mountaineering clothing and climber's hardware.

Inward Bound, 378 Webster Street, Manchester, NH 03104. Cave diving retail supplier.

JRAT Designs, 1833 Pearl Street, Boulder, CO 80302, 303-444-2779. Retailer.

Juniper Junction, Smith Rock State Park, 9297 N.E. Crooked River Drive, Terrebonne, OR 97760. Retailer.

K.H.S. Sales, 7247 Oak Ridge Hwy, P. O. Box 7101, Knoxville, TN 37931, 615-691-7660, Hm. 615-690-6706. Rappelling and vertical rescue equipment retailer.

Lane Equipment Sales, P.O. Box 71857, Chattanooga, TN 37407, 615-867-2846. Retailer of caving/rescue equipment.

L & S Sporting Goods, P.O. Box 176, Philippi, WV 26416, 304-457-2567. Retailer.

Lirakis Safety Harness, Inc., 30 Greenough Place, Newport, RI 02840 401-846-5356. Harnessess and accessories.

Lost Creek Packs, 1600 West Bloomfield Rd., Bloomington, IN 47401, 812-336-4941.

Mammoth Sporting Goods, Sierra Center Mall, Mammoth Lakes, CA 93546, 619-934-3239.

Mar-Mex International Ltd., P.O. Box 723126, Atlanta, GA 30339, 404-394-4413. Manufacturer of Escapeline.

Midwest Mountaineering, 309 Cedar Ave So. Minneapolis, MN 55454. 612-339-3433. Retailer.

Mountain Affair, 226 Ocean Ave., Laguna Beach, CA 92651, 714-494-3844. Retailer.

Mountain Gear, 12 West Sprague, Spokane, WA 99204, 509-838-8040. Retailer.

Mountain Safety Research, (MSR), 1100 East Pike Street, Seattle, WA 98108. Research and climbing equipment.

Mountain Shop, The 126 West Laurel, Ft. Collins, CO 80524, 303-493-5720. Retailer.

Mountain Sports, 821 Pearl Street, Boulder, CO 80302, 303-443-6770. Retailer.

Mountain Ventures, 3040 North Decatur Rd. Scottdale, GA 30079, 404-378-5789 Retail outfitters.

Mountaineering South, 791 Merrimon Ave. Asheville, NC 28804, 704-254-6419. Retailer.

Northern Lights Trading Co., 1627 W. Main, Bozeman, MT 59715, 406-586-2225. Retailer.

Outward Bound USA, 384 Field Point Rd., Greenwich, CT 06830, 203-661-0797. Adventure education.

Para-Gear Equipment Co., 3839 W. Oakton Street, Skokie, IL 60076, 312-679-5905. Hardware, buckles, webbing, thread supplier.

Petzl, F., Cidex 105 A/Z.I. Crolles, 38190 Brignoud, France, phone 76-08-10-53. Ascenders and other climbing equipment.

Pigeon Mountain Industries, (PMI), P.O. Box 803, Lafayette, GA 30728, 404-764-1437 1-800-282-ROPE. Ropemaker, rope/rescue equipment distributor. U.S. Petzl distributor.

Recreational Equipment Inc., 1525 Eleventh Ave, Seattle, WA 98122. Retail supplier.

Rescue Systems, Inc., Rt. 2, Box RSI Little Hocking, OH 45742, 614-989-2860. Blue Water equipment retail supplier, features rescue equipment.

Roco Rescue, Inc., 1945 Candlewood Avenue, Baton Rouge, LA. 70816, 1-800-647-ROCO, LA: 504-647-1420. Rope/rescue equipment supplier.

SMC (Seattle Manufacturing Corp.), 12880 Northrup Way, Bellevue, WA 98005, 206-883-0334. Manufacturer of hardware, carabiners, pulleys and racks.

Smith Safety Products, Dan Smith, Box 36, Petaluma, CA 94953, 707-763-5946.

Speleobooks, c/o Emily Davis Mobley, Box 10 Schoharie, NY 12157, 518-295-7978. Literature retail supplier.

Speleoshoppe, P.O. Box 297, Fairdale, KY 40118, 1-800-626-5877 or 502-367-6292. Retail supplier of rope and caving equipment.

Sunrise Mountaineering, 2636 Vista Pacific Dr., Oceanside, CA 92056, 619-724-0533. Retailer.

Walter Marti Apparatebau, CH-3713 Reichenbach, Switzerland. Jumar ascenders.

Weinel, J. E., Inc., P.O. Box 213, Valencia, PA 16059, 1-800-346-ROPE, PA 412-898-2335. Retail distributor of rescue equipment, climbing and caving supplies.

Wellington Puritan, P.O. Box 521, Madison, GA 30650, 1-800-221-5054 or 404-342-1916. Rope manufacturer.

Complete Information
For a complete look and analysis of all the pros and cons, research data and scope of that which is available, the authors recommend the reading of the references listed at the conclusion of each chapter throughout the book, as well as subscribing to the regular publications produced by the various vertically oriented organizations.

13 History

Before modern vertical techniques evolved, drops and pits were either avoided, or done with ladders or with hauling systems. In the early 1800s, several deep pits were descended using these lowering and raising techniques.

In mountaineering the problem of crevasse rescue was similar to vertical cave exploring. Dr. Karl Prusik in 1931 described in an Austrian mountaineering journal a new knot and a method of ascending a rope with this knot (Fig. 13-1). Dr. Prusik, who died in 1961 at the age of 65, was twice president of his Austrian mountaineering club and pioneered 70 new mountain routes and ascents.

Early Approaches

An article in the Washington Star in 1938 described what is best termed an assault on Schoolhouse Cave, WV. This article attracted the rock climbing section of the Potomac Appalachian Trail Club. This group investigated the cave as though it were a mountain underground. Their method of entry was to body rappel down and use rope ladders to ascend. This group, which included several early cavers, brought mountaineering skills into early cave explorations. This same group of explorers, along with others, determined that an organization could further their cause.

Bill Stephenson, an early caver, was the catalyst that formed the Speleological Society of the District of Columbia on May 6, 1939. On December 1, 1940, a group of cavers ratified the constitution of the National Speleological Society and on January 1, 1941 the NSS became an officially recognized organization. On Oct. 17-19, 1941, the first "convention" of the young society was held in Aurora, West Virginia with vertical demonstrations and a trip to Schoolhouse Cave as a part of the program. This society, through its publications and conventions, allows for the transfer of information throughout the country and the gathering of inventive minds to discuss vertical caving.

The Modern Era

In the summer of 1952, a young Virginia caver, Bill Cuddington, was unable to round up enough cavers in his area to use the existing hauling system techniques. He had done many drops on cable ladders and knew how to body rappel, but with this small caving group enough ladders were often unavailable. Having heard of Prusik knots, he looked them up in a 1942 mountaineering book. As a result of his research, the summer of '52 found Cuddington in Haynes Saltpeter Cave, W.V. where he both rappelled and prusiked a 40-foot pit for the first time in a cave. In 1953, at a Virginia Region Meeting, Cuddington, and Richard Sanders walked up to Sites Cave (180 foot entrance pit) and Cuddington rappelled and prusiked the drop. In a local club newsletter, the D.C. Speleograph, Marguerite Klein, in writing about the trip, coined the nickname "Vertical

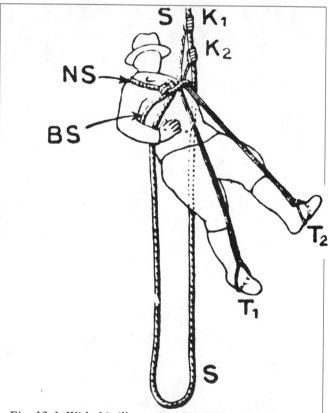

Fig. 13-1. With this illustration, Dr. Prusik showed how to climb using his new knot.

Bill" and the legend was born.

Though the rappel and Prusik knot had been discussed in Europe in the '30s, it never received a lot of attention and it's use died out. After Cuddington brought the system to the caving world, it became apparent that others had also experimented with Prusik knots. Charles Fort (Kentucky) and Bob Handley (West Virginia) were two individuals who had tried the prusik technology even earlier than Cuddington. However, Cuddington became the ambassador of vertical caving, instructing all who would inquire. As the news spread, excitement in the North American caving world ran very high. People began dropping pits and prusiking out with great regularity.

Again, out of the mountaineering circles in Switzerland, a game warden named Jusy and an engineer named Marti built 10 trial pairs of Jumar ascenders in May 1958. They were first described in the September 30, 1958 issue of *Mountaineering*, the official Journal of the British Mountaineering Council. Jumars were first imported into the U.S. in 1962 and introduced to cavers at the 1963 NSS Convention. There were changes in the frame shape in 1972 and 1979. The original Jumars were painted gray. In 1973, they were plastic coated, and, with a frame change in 1979, their color changed to yellow. In 1981 a control number was introduced, that is, a Jumar bearing #3 was manufactured in 1983.

Developmental Years

By the mid '60s, vertical caving had become extremely popular. This was assisted by the publication of a book, *American Caving Illustrated*, by **J. Welborn Storey** in June of 1965. Almost 100 pages of this 300-page book were devoted to vertical techniques. Henshaw and Morehouse described the "Iowa Cam" at the 1965 NSS Convention and the story was carried in the November 1965 *NSS News*. The "Iowa Cam" formed the basis for the production of the Gibbs cams, which were first constructed in 1968. They were introduced at the 1969 NSS Convention. The '68 models had wire retainer pins and sand-cast molded cams. In 1970 the

LOOKING BACK

After looking up Prusik knots in the mountaineering book, the young Bill Cuddington began to practice. At night he rappelled and prusiked out of the second story window of his bedroom. His folks at one time thought he was a burglar! With this practice, he learned several important things. The step method shown in his reference book was wrong. The sit/stand method was much more efficient. He also discovered that the sling rope needs to be smaller in diameter than the main rope.

When Cuddington used the rappel/prusik system the first time in Haynes Saltpeter Cave, W. Va., Tom Barr, Larry and Betty Sabatinas were along to witness his climbing procedure. Cuddington talked Larry Sabatinas into trying the system. Cuddington's enthusiasm was not shared by Sabatinas who declared prusiking "a last-ditch system."

Because many felt this way, Bill often had trouble finding others to go with him. Another breakthrough came when Cuddington soloed Hess' Hollow Pit in Pig Hole Cave, VA. After ascending 20 feet of the 80-foot climb, he discovered that his Prusik knots began to slide because the lower part of the rope was covered with mud and guano. Slowly he made his unplanned descent to the bottom. At first, he thought he was trapped, but remembered experimenting with tying the Prusik knots with extra wraps during his practice sessions. The additional wraps overcame the slick rope and he successfully finished the climb.

In the early years, Cuddington was criticized by many cavers because his technology was new and different. They felt he was an "insurance risk." As a result of this, Cuddington did not really "talk up" his system or write about it. He only taught the technique to those who came to him and asked. But the ability to explore pits with his climbing techniques set the caving world on fire. "Vertical Bill" and his quiet ways are to caving as Bell's work is to telephones or Edison's work to the electric light. Development continues with Bill and Miriam Cuddington quietly leading the way. One fact will always remain: the birthplace of rappel/prusik systems was North America.

quick-release pin became an option, and in 1977 the spring-loaded model was introduced.

The development of mountaineering equipment assisted with the evolution of caving techniques. Aluminum carabiners, brake bars, figure 8 descenders and the development of kernmantle dynamic ropes are only a few examples.

The vertical rope climbing contest originated at the 1966 Southeastern Regional Association (SERA) of the NSS and became a national event in 1967 at the Huntsville, Alabama NSS Convention. The contest became an official and popular international event at The Eighth International Congress of Speleology in Kentucky in 1981.

Development of rappel devices also continued and John Cole of Huntsville, Alabama, introduced the rappel rack in 1966. At the same time, Dick Mitchell introduced the Mitchell System, "The Fastest Method With Jumars."

Appearing on the scene in 1969, Blue Water II became the first rope "made for caving by cavers." Richard Newell of Carrollton, Georgia, founded Blue Water Ltd., and one of the first products besides rope was a Mitchell system ascender box. This dual chest-pulley box was first introduced at the 1969 NSS Convention in Lovell, Wyoming, by Keith Wilson. Blue Water products became the first commercially available cave gear on a large scale.

Providing an encyclopedia of information on prusik devices and methods, Bob Thrun introduced his book *Prusiking* in 1971. Across the United States there are several hotspots of vertical activity and development. Most notable are the TAG cavers of the Southeast, The AMCS (Association for Mexican Cave Studies) and Texas cavers of the Southwest. Included in this group of pacesetters are some of the Virginia/West Virginia cavers. This group is able to practice their skills locally but often travels long distances to enjoy the deeper pits and longer drops of the South and West. In 1972 at the NSS Convention in White Salmon, Wash., the NSS Vertical Section, a group of cavers interested in vertical rope work, was chartered, bringing together on a national level all of the vertically oriented groups and people from across the country.

In 1977, Pigeon Mountain Industries, Inc., a company dedicated to quality products, was formed. This company began manufacturing kernmantle rope and offering various rope- related equipment.

Neil Montgomery's book, *Single Rope Techniques*, published in Australia, in 1977, introduced the term SRT to North America.

Recent Trends

Cavers and climbers have joined forces on many fronts, sharing and refining equipment and techniques. Since the mid '70s, efforts have focused on deeper and higher drops and higher and longer tyroleans. Many of these techniques are now being adopted by the fire, rescue and EMS groups across North America. For over 10 years, no major revolutionary breakthrough has developed with regard to equipment or techniques. However, a great deal of refinement has taken place in the sophistication of roller systems, double-bungie systems, chest plates, sewing methods, harness comfort, and space-age alloys that have enhanced the fabrication of vertical gear. Many people speculate that the vertical world is on the threshold of a great revolution. What often boggles reason is that the extensive history of vertical ropework happened as a result of personal desires to achieve, whether those achievements have been physical, technical, ethical, artistic or theoretical. Money, and marketability have had little to do with this great history, yet our vertical past will undoubtedly repeat itself many times over.

REFERENCES

Arnold, Jay, Ed. "American Caving Ropes Special Issue." *NSS News*, Vol. 41, No. 9. 1983.

Barr, Thomas C. Jr. *Caves of Tennessee*. Nashville: Tenn. Div. of Geology, 1961, fig. 5 page 21, Bill Cuddington on his first vertical cave trip where prusiks were used.

Boyd, Dick and **Carl Foster**. "New Jumar System." *Wisconsin Speleologist*, Vol. 5, No. 2, 1966, pp. 49-55.

Cole, John, "A New Rappel Device." *NSS News*, Vol. 24, No. 6, 196, pp. 154-5.

Gibbs, Charles and **Warwick Doll**. "Vertical Caving and the New Cam Ascender." *NSS News*, Vol. 27, No. 2, 1969, pp. 28-31.

Gibbs, Peter. "A Short History of Gibbs Products, Inc." *Nylon Highway 15*, Vertical Section of the NSS, 1982, pp 5-7.

Henderson, Kenneth, *Handbook of American Mountaineering*. Boston: Houghton-Mifflin Co. 1942.

Henshaw, Robert E. and **David F. Morehouse**. "The Climbing Cam: A New Ascender." *NSS News*, Vol. 23, No. 11. 1965, pp. 158-160.

"Jumar Climbing Clamp." *Mountaineering*. Official Journal of British Mountaineering Council, Vol. III, No. 4, Sept. 1958.

Mathews, L.D., Ed. "Vertical Caving Issue." *NSS News*, Vol. 27, No. 2. 1969.

Moore, George W. Ed. "Jubilee Issue." *NSS Bulletin*, Vol. 28, No. 1. 1966, pp. 38-53.

Prusik, Karl, "A New Knot and Its Application." *Osterreichische Alpenzeitung*, Dec. 1931, pp. 343-352.

Smith, Marion O., Ed. "Descents Issue." *Journal of Spelean History*, Vol. 18, Nos. 3 & 4, 1984.

Storey, J. Welborn. *American Caving Illustrated*. Atlanta, GA: Dogwood City Grotto, 1965, pp. 96-190.

Thrun, Robert. *Prusiking*, Huntsville, AL, NSS, 1971.

Whittemore, R.E., Ed. "A History of the Virginia Region." *The Region Record*, Vol. 3, No. 4, 1979.

14 Glossary

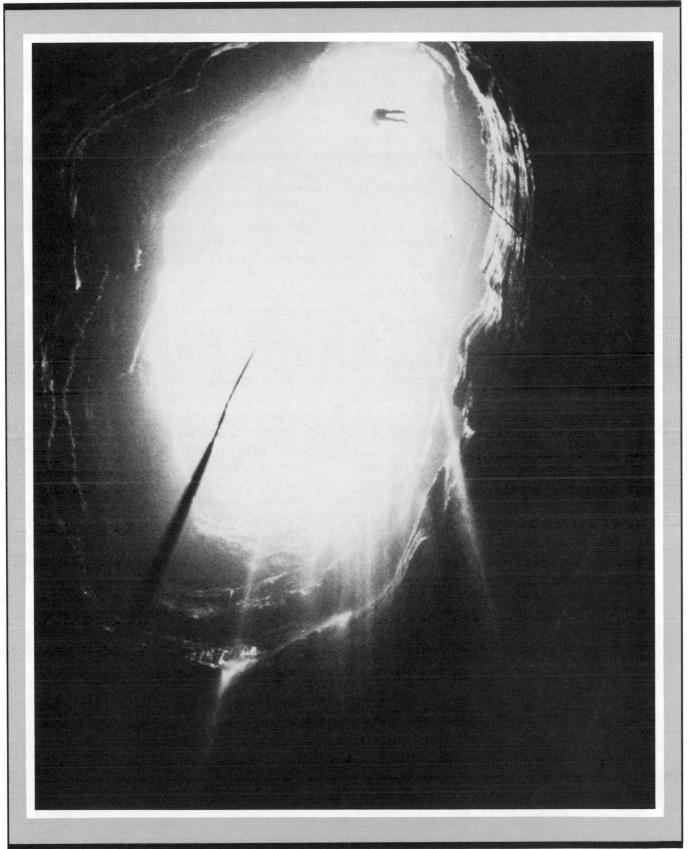

14 Glossary

A

abrasion resistance The ability to retard or withstand wearing away by friction. This is a very important design quality of caving rope as one of the greatest single dangers in SRT is that of abrading the rope against sharp edges while rappelling and prusiking. Also a factor in determining a rope's useful life.

abseiling A German-Swiss term for rappelling; widely used in Europe.

abyss A dark canyon, space, or drop.

adventure Occurs when the best laid plans go awry. (see diplomacy)

aid Climbing in which devices such as pitons and bolts are used for body support and upward progress.

aiders See etriers.

air rappel Slang for fall.

air voyager A sling that has been stitched with bar-tacks. Used as a form of shock absorber in the event of a fall. The air voyager can be placed anywhere between the anchor and the climber. Each set of bar-tacks explodes at approximately 600 pounds.

ambient abrasion The wearing away of the outer sheath of a rope due to occasional rock rubbing, dragging and other activities.

AMCS Association for Mexican Cave Studies.

American Descender A rappelling device available from American Rescue Systems designed for lowering heavy loads. It looks like a double sided whale-tail with two swing gates. There are a variety of rigging combinations to achieve the best results. Source: Tom Martin's book *Rappelling Edition II*.

anchor 1. (Br. **belay**) A secure point, such as breakdown, rock projections, cave features, trees, expansion bolts and other hardware, to which a ladder, rope or belayer can be safely attached. 2. An encasement. After drilling a hole in rock, this part is inserted into the hole, then expanded to secure it. The bolt or hanger is then attached.

Anderson, Russ 1. A designer and manufacturer of figure 8 rappel devices and other rescue hardware. 2. A brand name.

angle pitons A piton used in cracks 1/2 inch and wider. A cross section resembles the letter "U".

arm rappel See hasty.

arrest a fall Stop a fall. Commonly in belaying.

ascender A climbing device.

ascender box In some climbing systems, a metal housing with rollers or pulleys, usually worn high on the chest, to keep the upper body parallel to the rope.

ascender knot An excellent climbing knot that slides easily, yet locks tightly. Isolated testimonies warn against downward pressure on the top of the knot when loaded as it may release.

ascendeur French for ascender.

ascending The process of moving upward, usually using a rope or ladder.

Assaultline A supple, dark-colored kernmantle rope manufactured by Blue Water Ltd. Inc. for military and S.W.A.T. purposes.

A.T.E.P. All Terrain Edge Protector. An edge roller manufactured by Rescue Systems, Inc, that looks like a large bicycle chain.

Australian rappel A rappel down a cliff face whereby the rappeller faces down or out while the rappel device is attached to the seat harness in the back. This is primarily a S.W.A.T. or military maneuver and considered dangerous. It should be done only in rare emergencies.

aven (Am. **dome**) A vertical extension up from a cave passage or chamber, not open to the surface, though many sometimes lead to an upper passage.

awl A single-stitch sewing device used for hand sewing canvas, leather, straps, harnesses, etc.

B

bachmann knot A semi-mechanical climbing knot that uses a rope sling and an oval carabiner.

back-up Any redundancy for safety.

bankl plate A very small rappel device made by Edelrid of Europe. It also has belaying applications.

bar-tack A stitch pattern in which tight clusters of stitches are sewn at right angles to the direction of the webbing.

bashies Soft malleable blobs of copper or aluminum fixed on loops of aircraft cable. When hammered into seams and grooves they sometimes hold body weight. Used only for aid climbing and should be considered a last resort before drilling a hole for a bolt.

Batbrake A very small belaying/rappelling device manufactured by Edelrid. It is made of aluminum and often needs a steel carabiner to back it up. Source:Tom Martin's *Rappelling Edition II*.

bathook A small steel hook that fits in shallow-drilled holes. Used to save time while rock climbing on long, blank walls since the hole only needs to be 1/2 inch deep. Should be used in very hard rock.

BCRA British Cave Research Association.

belay 1. (Br. **lifelining**) A method of protecting a climber in case of a fall. A safety rope tied to a climber is payed out or taken in by a second person (the belayer) as the climber moves. By controlling this rope, the belayer can stop the climber from falling. 2. (Br.) A natural or manmade attachment point for a ladder or rope.

bend A knot term. Any knot that fastens two ropes together at their ends.

bight A U-shaped bend in the rope.

biner (Proper spelling 'biner) See carabiner.

bivouac A planned or unplanned camp using minimal or no gear. Used for the purpose of resting, eating and/or sleeping.

blade A thin piton.

blind pit A pit with no horizontal passage.

block See ascender box.

block down (tree surgeon's term) Act of lowering sections of trunk to the ground.

Blueline Static kernmantle rope manufactured by Blue Water Ltd. Inc.

Blue Water Brand name of the first ropes specifically designed for vertical caving. These first nylon ropes were of kernmantle construction and featured low stretch, high strength and high abrasion resistance. Blue Water Ltd. is located in Carrollton, GA.

Blue Water Gold Static kernmantle rope manufactured by Blue Water Ltd. Inc.

bo Shout used in signaling while ridgewalking, looking for caves, in thick woods, or on mountainsides. This shout has been proven to carry farther than other yells.

bob 1. Slang for descending and ascending one or more pits, usually open air, quickly, without spending time exploring the bottom. Also yo-yo. 2. Descending and ascending the same pit repeatedly.

bobbin (Fr. **bobine**) 1. French descending device. It is the leading rappel device in Europe and consists of two fixed pulley sheaves inside an aluminum frame. 2. Thread holders on sewing machines.

body rappel Any rappel that is primarily controlled by the friction generated between the rappel rope and the body. These rappels often demand heavy leather padding. Arm rappels are not included in this category.

body thrust (tree surgeon's term) A method of climbing a tree using a doubled rope. One end is tied to the saddle of the climber, the rope travels up and over a tree crotch and back into the hands of the climber. A special tree climber's knot captures progress after each body thrust.

Bogibbs European Gibbs cam version that incorporates a side slot in the shell for engaging the rope.

bollard A hanger that is used with a self-drilling anchor for a looped rope. Comes in 8 and 10 mm sizes.

bolt 1. The part of an artificial anchor that the hanger hangs on. The bolt often screws into an anchor. 2. A generic term for artificial, drilled anchors.

bombproof Slang for something that is designed rigidly and able to withstand large amounts of punishment, abuse or shock loading.

bong A folded steel piton used for hammering into a wide crack in the rock to form an anchor.

booger Slang for a wear spot on a rope due to ambient or external abrasion. Characterized by a soft fuzzy area larger than the diameter of the rope due to the wearing of outer sheath fibers. Also known as a caterpillar.

bop See bob.

bottom belay A safety maneuver whereby a person at the bottom of a rope pulls down on the rope while someone is descending. The added friction in the rappel device due to this downward pulling will bind up the system and arrest the rappel. A bottom belay can also control a descent.

bounce 1. See bob. 2. The action or movement generated by a climber who climbs rope in a jerky manner. Due to the slight stretch in a static rope. Bouncing can lead to rope abrasion.

bowline A knot commonly used to make a non-slipping loop in the end of a rope. One of the basic knots any person doing single rope techniques should know.

box See ascender box.

braid on braid A solid braided core rope covered with a braided sheath.

braided sheath The protective outer covering or mantle on kernmantle ropes. It is constructed by weaving yarn together uniformly, much like braiding hair. It constitutes about 30% of the total strength of kernmantle rope.

brake bar A short metal bar with a hole at one end where it is threaded onto a rack or carabiner. On the other end is a slot which fits snugly against the other arm of the rappel device. These bars provide the primary source of friction for both the carabiner (or brake-bar rig) and the rappel rack. Some variations are constructed differently.

brake hand Hand used to control the rope feeding into a descending device. Braking, for the most part, is provided by friction generated between the rope and body. Often referred to as the control hand.

brake plate A rappel device that is a metal rectangle with a number of deep grooves around the edges allowing for a number of friction-related combinations.

break The action necessary to loosen a tightened knot.

breakdown Rock slabs, blocks or chips on the floor of a cave that have fallen from the walls or the ceiling, usually in considerable accumulations.

breakover See lip.

bridle A harness, made primarily of straps, used to attach objects to a suspension system. Commonly a bridle is used when attaching to a litter.

bucket Rock climber's term for a great handhold with a shape similar to the rim of a bucket.

bullrope (tree surgeon's term) Large-diameter low-

ering line; half inch or greater.

bungie cord An elastic cord made of multiple rubber band-like strands, tightly wrapped with a fabric sheath. Often used to provide continuous tension on an ascender during climbing or when used as a ratchet cam.

burn the rope Slang for climbing or rappelling the rope rapidly.

Butt Strap Harness A three-cam ropewalker system utilizing a unique strap under the buttocks for additional comfort and safety. Produced by Butt Strap Harness Makers.

cable ladder A flexible ladder made of strong aircraft cable and aluminum alloy rungs.

cam 1. The working or moving part on most mechanical ascenders. It pinches the rope against the shell or body of the ascender when a directional load is applied. 2. A generic term for an ascender using a cam device such as a Gibbs ascender.

carabiner Also biner, krab, karabiner or snaplink. An oval or offset oval shaped, aluminum alloy or steel link with a spring-loaded gate in one side. Used as a universal connector in climbing and rappelling.

carabiner brake bars See tandem bars.

carbide lamp A miner's lamp used by cavers. Acetylene gas produced by dropping water onto calcium carbide is ignited and burns in a jet, positioned in a reflector.

caterpillar See booger.

caver Also a spelunker. Someone who explores caves in a safe manner while showing respect for the cave, other cavers and the land above the cave. Cavers call other cavers cavers. Non-cavers call cavers spelunkers. Scientist cavers call themselves speleologists.

chain structure (re: webbing) Weak webbing construction that may unravel under certain conditions.

changeover Going from rappel to prusik or from prusik to rappel while on rope. This may be necessary if the rope is too short, when attempting to pass anchors, obstacles or attempting to change ropes.

cheater stick Used to extend a climber's reach when placing slings or protection during a climb.

cheeks The sides of a pulley that encase the sheave.

chest block See ascender box.

chest box See ascender box.

chicken head Description of the shape of a handhold, place to rig or a place for a good pull-down.

chicken loops Sewn, tied or buckled bands of webbing or rope that fit onto the ankle. Their function is to keep ascender stirrups from slipping off the climber's foot. They should be strong enough to hold a climber's weight in the event of a heel hang.

chimney 1. A narrow canyon or fissure in a cave passage. 2. A technique used to freeclimb up through a narrow passage.

chocks Also nuts, wedges or crackers. Small aluminum alloy blocks, primarily used by rock climbers, that wedge into various sized cracks. Usually they can only permit tension from one direction. Developed by and for rock climbers, they are increasingly being used in SRT. Chocks are a part of the clean-climbing evolution of the early '70s.

chockstone Stone or boulder wedged between two walls or in a crack. Can sometimes be used as an acceptable rope anchor.

Chouinard steels Small stainless steel wedges used by rock climbers for micro-cracks.

clean a pitch Remove all pieces of hardware and protection that may have been used to climb a wall.

climb 1. To ascend a rope. 2. To ascend the face of a rock using rock climbing skills.

climber's knot (tree surgeon's term) A variation on a Prusik knot or taut line hitch.

climbing 1. To go up under one's own power. 2. To ascend a rock face. 3. To climb a rope with prusik equipment.

climbing line (tree surgeon's term) A 120 foot piece of woven or twisted static rope. The knot can be used to both prusik and rappel.

Clog A British company that makes climbing hardware. The term often refers only to their manufactured ascender.

CMI Colorado Mountain Industries. A manufacturer of ascenders and other climbing-related equipment, located in Franklin, WV.

Coe A rappelling device manufactured by Pentiction Engineering. It looks like a tandem brake bar configuration, however all the oval carabiners are solid ovals of stainless steel. Source: Tom Martin's book *Rappelling Edition II*.

Cole rack The rappel rack as designed by John Cole.

compact (re. knots) Knots small in size, that are used when rope has to travel through a pulley or be climbed or rappelled over such as butterfly, figure 8 bend, water knot, or grapevine knot.

contraction bolt A bolt that applies pressure to the sides of the predrilled hole. These require very hard rock for an effective placement. The primary supplier of such bolts is Rawl. Product name is Rawl Drive.

control line Secondary ropes that control the movements of personnel and equipment on the main line of a tyrolean traverse. Also called tether lines.

copperheads Developed by Bill Forrest for rock climbers. They are cylindrical copper swages on a wire.

core The inner part of a kernmantle rope. It consists of bundles of continuous, parallel fibers that contribute about 70% of the strength and mass of rope, and determines its breaking strength and stretch.

cow's-tail Safety attachments used in the frog system. Used when passing anchors or knots in the middle of a drop, or for protection on a roped traverse. Usually consists of one short (18 inch) and one long (28 inch) 8-10 mm rope. North Americans generally use a safety Jumar for a similar purpose.

crack-n-up Chouinard anchor-shaped aid.

cradling hand The hand that varies the friction in a rack by moving the bars up or down, or removing them as needed for control of the rappel. Also referred to as the balance hand.

crater in Slang for falling to the surface below.

crossover 1. To go past a knot, anchor or other obstacle on rope while ascending or descending. 2. A cave trip where two separate groups enter from two separate entrances and pass each other under-

320

ground. A vertical trip crossover implies that each group prusiked up using the other group's rappel rope(s).

D

daisy chain A runner that has numerous loops through its entire length, either sewn (bar-tacked) or tied, in which carabiners and climbing hardware, can be clipped. It can be used as an adjustable seat harness tether for use in aid climbing.

death rig Climbing system or rope anchoring rig that is blatantly unsafe.

delta maillon rapide link A triangular-shaped maillon rapide link that lends itself to multi-directional pulling. Often used with seat and chest harnesses.

deprusik See downclimb.

derig 1. To pull up the rope and remove all rope anchoring devices and pads after completing a drop. 2. To remove one's climbing or rappelling gear from a rope.

descender A rappelling device.

descendeur French for descender.

Descent-Master A cast aluminum rappel device made by Atlas Safety Equipment Co. which features an internal shunt. The device tends be complicated to use, requires time to engage on a rope and only semi-variable when it comes to friction control. Source: Tom Martin's *Rappelling Edition II*, 1987.

deviation A method of redirecting the rope to avoid abrasion. Another anchor is used to pull the rope away from a rub point by means of a sling and a carabiner clipped around the rope.

diaper sling A common, easily tied harness for rappelling and ascending, usually made of 1 inch or 2 inch webbing. A separate, redundant waist loop can add the necessary safety in case the webbing should break or cut.

diplomacy Necessary when there is too much adventure. (see adventure)

directional Route changing pulley. See deviation.

D.M.M. Denny Morehouse Mann. Manufacturer of carabiners, figure 8s and other vertical gear. Key

person in the development of the Clog.

doline A sinkhole in limestone.

Dolt hook A climbing hook, manufactured by Bill Dolt who was an early manufacturer of vertical gear.

dome (Br. **aven**) A roughly circular natural cave shaft above a room or passage, created by solution. Does not reach the surface, however, may connect to upper passage.

domepit A solution area of a cave that includes a dome and a pit in the same vertical area. A dome-pit has a passage intersecting this vertical shaft somewhere in the middle or at the top as well as the bottom.

donut Slang for a figure 8 descender.

double bungie system A ropewalker system where both the knee and foot ascender are floated using two shock or bungie cords, or one bungie cord looped through a pulley at the chest box or roller.

downclimbing 1. Descending a rope using an ascending system. Also deprusik. 2. Reversing moves while free climbing or scrambling.

dress (said of a knot) To orient the rope parts of the knot, so that they are properly aligned, straightened or bundled and thus look like the drawings of knots in books.

dressler A descender similar to a bobbin.

D-ring A carabiner that is usually larger than a standard oval and looks like the letter "D".

drop A steeply descending slope, pitch or pit. To descend, it is usually necessary to rig a rope; otherwise it is known as a climb.

dulfersitz See hot seat rappel or body rappel.

dyeing Coloring. See solution dyeing or surface dyeing.

dynamic belay A belay using a dynamic rope. If the climber were to fall, the stretchy rope would cushion the impact much like a rubber band's ability to absorb shock. Many years ago dynamic belays called for letting the rope run or slide through the hands of the belayer. This is no longer an acceptable practice.

dynamic ropes Ropes that stretch 10% or more of their length with a load of approximately 180 lbs. Generally used for rock climbing, where much greater stretch or shock absorbing ability is needed to protect a falling climber.

E

ears The protrusions on some models of figure 8 descenders.

edge rollers Stationary pulley-type device used at the edges of long drops or buildings to lessen or soften the angle of the lip and avoid rope abrasion.

elephant tracks Slang for a blatantly obvious and well worn path through a cave or through the woods to a cave or drop.

elevation 1. A view from the side or profile, i.e. in a cave on a survey. 2. Height in feet or meters above sea level or a determined point.

EMS Emergency Medical Services.

Escapeline A rappelling device that squeezes the rope to achieve friction. Manufactured by Mar-Mex International Ltd., Atlanta, GA.

Estralon Brand name of rope used by tree surgeons.

etrier Also aider. A webbing ladder or aid sling developed by rock climbers, now used by cavers primarily in negotiating hard lips. Made by tying loops in a step fashion with flat webbing.

European style Rigging methods using bolts to reanchor rope whenever it touches rock.

expansion bolt A type of anchor for ropes. It is placed into a hole drilled into rock and it expands as it is driven or twisted in. Hardware for rope connection is attached to it.

expedition A trip requiring special resources, planning and equipment.

exposure 1. A subjective measure of the insecurity induced by a void beneath. 2. Cooling of the body resulting from an inability of one's metabolism to generate heat as rapidly as the environment is removing it. Hypothermia.

extra passenger (tree surgeon's term) Object caught in a line. Often given as verbal command for the ground crew to clear the line.

eye 1. Hole in a brake bar. 2. The hole in a rack frame. 3. The hole in a sewing needle. 4. The hole in just about anything can be referred to as the eye.

eye-hole A natural hole in the rock. Jughandle.

EZ-Bend A soft, supple static kernmantle rope produced by Pigeon Mountain Industries, Lafayette, GA. See Flex.

F

face climbing Rock climbing using hand and footholds on an open-air rock face.

fall factor The length of the fall divided by the length of the rope in actual use.

fall line Vertical path followed by a hanging rope.

Famau A small cast aluminum rappelling device that is rigged similar to a figure 8. Source: Tom Martin's book *Rappelling Edition II*.

feed or **feeding** 1. The act of pushing a rope through a rappel device. 2. To pay out rope over the edge.

fiffi hook A piece of hardware used when performing single-line pull-down rappels. Also used in bolt and wall climbs.

figure 8 Rappelling device that looks like an eight.

figure eight A very useful knot that looks like an eight.

figure nine A knot that incorporates one more turn than a figure 8 around the standing part of the rope before pushing the end back through the loop. This knot is much easier to untie than a figure 8.

finishing a knot Involves dressing (orientation of parts) and setting (tightening of all parts).

Fire Cross A rappel/belay device available from J.E. Weinel, Inc. The device can be rigged several ways including a rigging similar to that of a Sticht Plate. Source: Tom Martin's book *Rappelling Edition II*.

fixed friction A term describing a rappelling device with no friction adjustment at all.

flaky Describes rock that is unstable to bolt into due to fragile, peeling, layered platelike characteristics.

flatrock Slang for kill or attempt to kill with large rock dropped from the top of a drop.

Flex An old product name of Pigeon Mountain Industries (PMI) version of more flexible kernmantle caving rope. It is constructed using a looser braid than their first introduced sport rope

(Max-Wear). Thus, this rope is somewhat easier to tie knots with, particularly after much use. See EZ-Bend.

floating cam systems Climbing systems that use ascenders (usually Gibbs) which are attached to foot stirrups, but are not attached to a knee even though the ascender is usually positioned in the proximity of the knee. The cam is held in place and advanced with elastic cord, which can be fastened in a variety of ways.

footlock (tree surgeon's term) also **footlocking.** Climbing a rope hand-over-hand but using a special leg wrap and instep grab to pinch the rope which enables the climber to stand in place.

footlocker One who climbs a rope using a footlock.

free climbing Term used by rock climbers to signify climbing without artificial aids such as slings, chocks, pitons or other hardware. However, rock climbers are normally belayed on all but the easiest climbs, whether free or aided.

free drop Occurs when rope does not touch a wall or obstacle when hanging down a drop. Drops are often described by the measurement free from the lip, e.g. 587 foot free drop.

freefall A drop that can be rigged without the rope touching a wall.

free hanging (Brit.) See free drop.

French descending hook Pierre Allain made this cast aluminum descending device which has proven to be tricky and possibly a dangerous device to rappel with.

friction climbing Climbing in which the feet and hands are "smeared" onto the rock using sloping holds.

friction hitch See Münter hitch.

Friends Spring-loaded expanding cams designed as a piece of protection, that rock climbers have popularized. This bombproof anchor, invented by Ray Jordine in the late '70s, enabled easier ascents of many routes that were all but unclimbable before.

friends The people that are nice to have around.

Frog A belay device available from Edelrid, European company, that incorporates a version of a Muenter hitch to engage the friction. Looks similar to a small horseshoe with attachment holes·at the ends of each leg for carabiner attachment.

Source: Tom Martin's *Rappelling Edition II.*

frog system A sit-stand ascending system widely used in Europe. Equipment consists of a seat harness, chest harness, two ascenders, foot slings and two cow's-tails. This system is characterized by its excellent performance in crossing reanchors, knots and performing other on-rope maneuvers common in European SRT.

G

gardening (Brit.) Clearing debris, loose rock and old beer cans from a vertical route, where they present a hazard to climbers.

gear Equipment. Often in the form of packs or transportable stuff.

generic rope Ropes manufactured by those not directly related to the evolution and development of rope technology.

Gibbs A cam-loading ascender made by Gibbs Products. Used in many ropewalker systems due to its free-running characteristics. Consists of a cast aluminum alloy cam, U-shaped aluminum alloy plate rope housing and a steel quick-release pin.

glaze or **glazing** Overheating of an area on a rope or webbing to the point of melting the nylon sheath fibers momentarily and cooling in a hard crystalline coating. Heat generated during rappels and the other dynamics of SRT can cause this condition.

Gossett block A chest box named after Jim Gossett.

gouffre A French term for pit cave.

grapevine knot Usually used in forming loops in rope for slings. Also a good knot for tying two ropes together when more length is needed. Also known as a double fisherman's knot.

grotto 1. A small side chamber of a cave usually decorated with formations. 2. A local chapter or caving club affiliated with the National Speleological Society.

gut knot See water knot.

hairy Slang for an especially frightening, difficult, exposed or dangerous climb, maneuver, lip, descent or ascent.

Hall Sidewinder A rappelling device made by Li-rakis. It is made of stainless steel and comes in two sizes. Source: Tom Martin's book *Rappelling Edition II.*

handline A rope rigged down a moderately steep slope. Ascending and descending equipment are rarely needed on such a slope.

hanger Part of an anchor bolt assembly to which rope or a carabiner is attached.

hardcore Slang for anyone (usually caver or climber) willing to risk life and limb while participating in their sport or hobby. Also used as an adjective to describe a particularly difficult climb, crawl, trip, etc.

hard nailing The process of getting hardware to adhere to a climbing wall.

hardware Cave gear that consists of metal, i.e. carabiners, ascenders, buckles, Jumars, etc.

harness Strapping or equipment used to connect rappel devices, tethers or ascending equipment to the body.

harpoon An Australian rappelling device made of aluminum alloy. It is a variation of the figure 8.

hasty A form of a body rappel, sometimes called a double arm rappel, whereby the rope passes across the back, under the armpits, wraps around both forearms and ends in the palms of the hands. Handy on short sloping rappels where a handline may be rigged. Proper heavy clothing to protect one's arms and gloves to protect the hands from burns are essential.

haul bag Large packs used for carrying ropes, anchoring equipment and possibly camping gear through a cave. Designed not to snag when being dragged through cave passages or hauled up drops. Haul bags are modern versions of the early metal Gurnee cans.

H.B.s After Hugh Banner. Small brass or stainless steel wedges for mirco-cracks.

headache Tree surgeon's term for "Rock".

Heddon A climbing knot first made popular by Chuck Heddon.

helical knot See ascender knot.

helmet Hard-shell head protection, retained with a chin strap to protect the head from falling objects and the impact of falls.

hexentric Eccentric hex nut that fits into a crack four different ways.

Hiebler A German mechanical climbing device that has proven inefficient and occasionally dangerous when used.

high angle Refers to drops approaching the vertical plane of 90°.

high line A rope stretched sideways between two points used to support and transport people and equipment laterally. Has naval origins whereby gear and personnel were transferred between ships at sea.

hip belay A soft belay whereby the belayer uses his hip(s) as the primary load absorption point.

Hobbs Hook A complicated aluminum rappelling device made by Bry-Dan Corp. Source: Tom Martin's book *Rappelling Edition II.*

hoehle German for cave.

hold Small ledge, knob or crevice that can provide assistance in climbing, chimneying or scrambling. Could be a foothold or handhold.

hollow brake bars A steel alloy brake bar that is hollow, allowing for twice the surface area for heat dissipation.

horn Term for a handhold or rig point that protrudes from the surface of the rock face.

horror hole Slang for cave or pit presenting combinations of many difficulties and obstacles.

hot seat rappel A type of body rappel. Descent without use of a harness using the body to provide friction.

H.R.T. Hostage Rescue Team.

hypothermia A physical condition caused by the extremes of the elements. Significant lowering of the body's core temperature due to exposure to wet and cold.

inchworm system Ascending system that later was the basis for the development of the frog system. Major difference is that the Jumar attached to a foot bar, called a Mar-bar, was replaced with an upper double slinged ascender that attaches to the climber's feet.

internal abrasion Rubbing of dirt and grit particles trapped between the fibers inside a rope. Use of a rope filled with these particles may cut the rope from the inside out.

inverting a knot Some knots, when loosened or tensioned incorrectly, can unfold, forming different loop patterns, often changing the original knot entirely.

Iowa cams Early rope cam predecessor to Gibbs designed by Morehouse and Henshaw in 1965.

ISFSI International Society of Fire Service Instructors.

J & K

jam 1. A technique used in free climbing to enable one to make progress or rest by lodging a fist, foot, body or fingers into a constriction in a crack. 2. European usage as a verb. To climb a rope using climbing equipment such as Petzls or Jumars.

jam crack A crack running vertically, which can be climbed by wedging part of the body into the fissure. These cracks may range in size from fingertips to body-swallowing.

jammer Any handled European ascender. Specifically a brand name of handled ascender made by Petzl.

jug Slang for Jumar.

jughandle Small tunnels or arches in the rock. Strong jughandles can make very good anchors because they are usually very secure.

Jumars A spring-loaded cam ascender made by Walter Marti Apparatebau of Switzerland. Used in ropewalker climbing systems as well as sit-stand systems due to its versatility and ease of clipping on and off rope. Consists of cast aluminum alloy frame and a replaceable spring-loaded cast alloy steel cam.

Jumar safety See safety Jumar.

karabiner See carabiner.

kern See core.

kernmantle Rope construction consisting of a core or kern of more or less parallel bunches of fibers.

These are contained in a tightly woven protective sheath.

kit-bag European pack used for holding vertical gear.

krab See carabiner.

L

laid rope A type of rope construction, usually made of three main twisted strands of continuous filament nylon. Now mainly used by commercial users such as powerpole linemen and tree surgeons. However, Goldline, made by the Columbian Rope Co., Auburn, NY, is still widely used by climbers and cavers.

Latok Tuber A rappelling device used in conjunction with a steel carabiner. It is made by Lowe Alpine Systems and seconds for a belay device. Source: Tom Martin's *Rappelling Edition II*.

layback Crack climbing, using counterpressure between feet and hands. A strenuous technique useful for cracks that have one side offset from the other.

lead climbing In rock climbing, the first climber up a face sets a route and establishes protection for himself using aids. He is often belayed with a climbing rope that is threaded through the various pieces of protection below him.

leader fall An accidental fall taken by the lead climber. Leader falls are potentially the worst type of controlled fall because the protection is almost always below the climber, which can generate high forces on the system.

Leeper Manufacturer of "Z-shaped" pitons, nuts and hangers. After Ed Leeper.

leg wrap 1. An emergency maneuver in which an out-of-control rappeller rotates his leg rapidly about the rope generating the necessary friction to slow his descent to a point of control. 2. A method of securing one's descent on a rappel by wrapping the rope back and forth between the thighs in a figure-eight pattern.

Lewis Autolock A rappelling device made by Lewis which features an autostop function. Source: Tom Martin's book *Rappelling Edition II*.

lifeline 1. Term used by rescue and professional

groups, referring to a horizontal line between two fixed points similar to a tyrolean. It should be capable of supporting 5400 pounds in the center. 2. (Brit.) A safety rope used in vertical work or in other dangerous situations. 3. (OSHA) A safety line that backs up platforms, ladders, etc. Must be attached with a separate harness or belt.

lifelining British term for belaying.

life-safety harness Standard term used by fire and rescue people for a harness that supports people.

life-safety rope See lifeline.

lightening holes Holes drilled, punched or cast in metal equipment that allow the piece of equipment to weigh less.

line See rope.

lip The edge of a drop or cliff, especially where rope falls from the edge to hang free.

Lizard 1. A company in Britain owned and operated by David Elliot which supplies cave exploring equipment. 2. A common name for a bolt hanger similar to the Troll Bollard.

load absorption A rope's capacity to withstand a shock load. Depends on the amount of stretch built into it.

locking carabiner A carabiner equipped with a locking sleeve.

locking off To wrap a rappel device with the rappel rope in such a way that descent is positively stopped.

Logan hooks Small hook-shaped pieces of aid that hook in convenient horizontal cracks. Often called sky hooks.

logistics The details of transport, camping and supply of an expedition or trip. The act of getting all the right equipment in the right place, with the right people, at the right time.

long dong Largest of Chouinards lost arrow pitons, now used as a nut tool.

long drop Any vertical expanse over 500 feet containing a predominant percentage of freefall.

long rack Rappel racks longer than the standard 14 inch six-bar racks. These racks are preferred on drops longer than 1000 feet, where control by bar sliding alone is desired.

longhorn A rappelling device formerly made by Mountain Safety Research. Works similar to a figure 8.

lost arrow A forged, hard alloy piton capable of being driven and removed repeatedly. Developed by John Salathe.

lowering line (tree surgeon's term) A large static kernmantle rope used to lower large sections of trees.

MAD Motorized Ascending Device. Developed by Nevin Davis in the late '60s.

Magnus hitch Original name for the Prusik knot.

maillon rapide link Solid metal links closed by a screw sleeve rather than a hinged gate, and thus capable of load applied in any direction. Used whenever strong, secure fastening is required that need not be opened and closed quickly.

mainline The principal load-carrying rope.

man-made fibers Also synthetic fibers. Usually petroleum-derived fibers, which all modern climbing rope is constructed of due to the desirable properties of continuous fiber, weather and water resistance and superior strength.

mantle 1. Outer braided protective sheath on kernmantle ropes. 2. Technique used in free climbing to gain a shelf or ledge.

Mao method A climbing method preferred by the Italians which utilizes an upper ascender with a pulley. A short rope passes through the pulley and connects the seat harness with the climber's boot(s). Another ascender is attached the climber's harness to capture progress. Good system for the tired climber. Source, Mike Meredith's book *Vertical Caving* 1986.

Mar-bar The foot ascender of the inchworm climbing system. Consists of a Jumar to which a horizontal step plate is attached. A piece of webbing is stretched across the top of the ascender and back down to the ends of the step plate, which holds the climber's boots in place.

Max-Wear A stiff, very abrasion-resistant static kernmantle rope produced by Pigeon Mountain Industries, Lafayette, GA.

maypole British term for scaling pole.

mechanical advantage (MA) The ratio of the load, to the pull required to lift the load.

memory A term describing rope and its return back to its original length after being stretched.

Metoulius Manufacturer of sliders and T.C.U.

Miller Descent Device A rappel device similar to a Sky Genie. The internal spine has spiral rope guides unlike the Sky Genie. Source: Tom Martin's book *Rappelling Edition II*.

Mitchell system Climbing system developed by Dick Mitchell, which utilizes a chest harness and two Jumar-type ascenders attached to the feet with stirrups.

monofilament One extended solid piece of nylon. Like fishing line.

moulin A domepit-like structure of glaciers.

move During rock climbing, an individual movement or step progressing to the next position.

multi-directional anchor An anchor that can be loaded from several directions.

multi-drop See multiple drop.

multi-filament Rope bundles composed of tiny hair-like fibers.

multiple-drop Term describing a cave containing a series of pits or pitches.

Münter hitch A sliding knot used for belaying.

Munter An aluminum rappelling device manufactured by Eiselin-sport. It is made to enable several rigging options such as a Sticht Plate rigging or a figure 8 rigging. Source: Tom Martin's book *Rappelling Edition II*.

NASAR National Association for Search and Rescue.

natural anchor A solid object occurring naturally such as a boulder or tree. The anchor should be at least as strong as the rope being tied to the anchor.

natural fibers Organic in nature. Ropes made of natural fibers usually employ a twisted construction e.g. hemp, manila and sisal.

NCRC National Cave Rescue Commission of the NSS.

neitherspace That uncertain or precarious feeling a rappeller experiences when transferring his or her weight from solid ground to the rope. Also, that unstable time when a climber is taking the slack

out of the rope and is transferring weight from the floor to the rope. It is often an unbalanced or unstable situation physiologically as the mind attempts to shift from the familiar stable support state to the less familiar, less stable supported state. An invented word by the book's authors.

NFPA National Fire Protection Association.

Niteline A static kernmantle rope manufactured by Blue Water Ltd. Inc.

novice A person who does not know enough hows and whys to be independent with ropework skills.

NSS National Speleological Society.

Nylon Highway A newsletter/magazine published by the Vertical Section of the NSS, which specializes in ropework articles.

off belay 1. A signal or shout indicating that the climb is over and the belayer is no longer in position. 2. Name of a popular climbing magazine, now no longer being published.

off rope Signal or shout up or down a rope indicating the rope is free and safe for the next person to approach and use.

offset carabiner A distorted D-shaped carabiner where one end is larger than the other.

offset drop A drop where the rope needs one or more additional anchors in order to hang free or pads to prevent abrasion.

on rope 1. The title of this book. 2. Signal or shout up or down a rope indicating that the rope is being loaded by a person either climbing or rappelling.

open-air pit (Br. **pothole**) (Fr. **gouffre**) (Sp. **sotano**) A shaft whose entrance is open or exposed to the surface. Generally larger than ten feet in diameter.

OSHA Government agency. Occupational Safety and Health Administration.

pad See rope pad.

pad rope A second rope whereby several pads can be attached at various points.

parapet The 90° edge of a pit, cliff or drop. Below,

the edge is characterized by a sheer vertical wall.

partner rescue Technique for getting a partner out of trouble while on rope.

pear carabiner A carabiner shaped narrower at one end than the other. The sides are not parallel.

Pecker Crackers Early British nuts.

peg See piton.

perlon European trade name for type 6 nylon.

Personnel Lowering Device A military descending device that is used to rappel on webbing. Source: Tom Martin's book *Rappelling Edition II*.

pic The short exposed distance of a sheath bundle between two other crossing sheath bundles.

pig See piggyback.

piggyback A haul system traditionally using a 2 to 1 system to pull another 2 to 1 system resulting in a 4 to 1 system.

pigtail A short rope with a knot in its end, which extends below the lip on an overhang. Rigged beside the main rope, it is used to aid in crossing difficult lips.

pins See pitons.

pit (Br. **pot**) A hole or shaft of some depth that may require the use of vertical techniques to descend or ascend.

pitch 1. An uninterrupted drop. Of European origin, one long drop could be rigged with several ropes, each one anchored in the European style. Each section drop then becomes a pitch. 2. Also a term used by rock climbers to describe a segment of a climbing route.

pitch head The top of a pitch, including the rigging, anchors and staging area.

pitons (Br. **pegs**) Flat spike-like anchors used in rock climbing. Pitons are driven or tightly wedged in existing rock cracks.

PMI Pigeon Mountain Industries. Brand name for a rope manufactured by Pigeon Mountain Industries Inc. of Lafayette, GA.

pompier hook An oversized pear-shaped carabiner used for rappelling, and a universal attachment device.

potpourri A miscellaneous collection of related topics.

pro Short for protection. Common term among rock climbers.

Pro-Pak A descending device made by Rappel Rescue Systems, Inc. and designed to be used with Kevlar webbing. Source: Tom Martin's book *Rappelling Edition II*.

protection A point of security such as a chock, nut, piton, bolt or other rock attachment device, whereby climbers can attach themselves.

Prusik knot An ascending knot popularized by Dr. Karl Prusik. It is the basic knot used for climbing a fixed rope. Ashley lists it as a variation of the magnus hitch.

prusiking A method of climbing up a fixed rope by means of rope-gripping devices such as knots or mechanical ascenders.

puff Exposed core of kernmantle rope poking through the sheath.

puit, puits (Fr.) Vertical shafts or pits.

pull-down The act of pulling the rope down and taking it with you after rappelling a drop. A pull-down trip often means that no one will retrace their steps. There is a note of finality with a pull-down.

push Slang for exerting oneself continuously, vigorously or obtrusively to gain an end or completion.

quick lag Rock climber's term for runner.

quick link See maillon rapide link.

Quickies Opposing wedges used by rock climbers similar to sliders.

R

rack See rappel rack.

rapide link See maillon rapide link.

rappel 1. (verb) To descend by sliding down a rope in a controlled manner. 2. (noun) The event or act of rappelling. NOTE. The word in French, means "to recall". Hence, its original meaning: a method of descending a retrievable rope, doubled through the anchor point.

rappel device An device used to rappel with.

rappel rack A multiple brake bar descending device which features variable friction control. Considered by some as the ultimate descending device.

Rappelevator A rappelling device made of a circular ring of steel and used similar to a carabiner wrap rappel. Source: Tom Martin's book *Rappel-*

ling Edition II.

rappelling (Verb) To slide down a rope in a controlled fashion as to prevent injury.

ratchet cam A safety cam used in rigging to capture progress during hauling or maintain control during lowering.

RBS knot A semi-mechanical climbing knot using a rope sling and an oval carabiner.

reanchor (Br. **rebelay**) An intermediate anchor, used primarily by Europeans, at each point where rope touches rock, or just below the rub point, so that rope again hangs free.

redundant system A system with extra or additional parts of a life-supporting system (i.e. harness, anchor, ascender) installed to take over if a primary part fails. Also a backup.

reef knot A square knot.

Reepschnur system A method for arranging a pull-down rappel with a single rope and a light cord.

REI Recreational Equipment Inc. A well known company that supplies quality equipment to cavers and climbers. Located in Seattle, WA.

relief straps Foot stirrups attached to a seat harness. When stood in, blood circulation is allowed to return to areas previously cut off. Worn during situations which may require a lot of seat harness time.

rescue pulley A substantial quality pulley that tests at least 6000 lbs.

rig 1. (noun) A climbing system. 2. (verb) To tie-off the main rope. 3. (verb) To get on rope.

rigger Someone who arranges the tying-off of the main rope or any other rope system that the team finds necessary, i.e. a tyrolean, hauling system or lowering system.

rigging A completed mainline tie-off.

Rigging Buddy (tree surgeon's device) A friction device comprised of two metal rings and 2" strapping that enables the treeman to create a false crotch or point of friction to lower heavy objects such as limbs.

Robot A small light weight rappelling device made by Bonaiti. Source: Tom Martin's book *Rappelling Edition II.*

rock 1. Trade name of Wild Country for stoppers that incorporate a subtle curve that acts as a cam in small parallel cracks. 2. Standard shout or signal signifying a falling object. The volume and urgency of the shout should be directly proportional to the size of the rock. 3. Stone.

rockfall zone Possible landing area of any item dropped from any point within that drop.

roller 1. Component part of a chest box. 2. Used as a noun in place of a Simmon's roller or other chest roller. 3. Fixed wedge with a sliding stainless steel roller. Useful in parallel cracks.

Roloff Ascender A homemade rope-climbing device resembling a Jumar. Manufactured by members of a California Grotto, they have been nicknamed the Mother Lode Grotto ascenders. They are no longer available.

rope 1. Flexible cordage. Commonly made of synthetic materials such as nylon. 2. A command given before tossing a rope down a drop.

rope bag A canvas duffel or nylon bag used to store a rope, to keep it clean during transport.

rope down The act of descending a drop using rope, e.g. "I intend to rope down this drop after I've secured my seat harness."

rope pad A protective piece of canvas or carpet placed to prevent abrasion.

ropewalker Someone who climbs a rope with a system that is very much like climbing stairs.

ropework American term for single rope techniques (SRT).

R.P.'s After Richard Paullick. Small brass or stainless steel wedges or small nuts used in micro cracks.

Ruapehu A versatile aluminum alloy fixed-friction rappelling device.

runaway rappel Out-of-control descent.

runner 1. Any attachment configuration using nylon strap or webbing with a sewn or tied loop in each end. Used often as a tether. In climbing they are used to extend slings on chocks with wire cables. Also known as "quick lags." 2. Endless loops or slings.

RURP Realized Ultimate Reality Piton. Postage-stamp size piton used for tiny, incipient cracks. Very scary to use.

S

saddle (tree surgeon's term) Seat harness.

Safetyblue Tree surgeon's rope made by Plymouth.

safety-cord See cow's-tail.

safety Jumar A one-handed quickly attachable mechanical ascending device attached to a seat harness. This device could be a Jumar, Petzl, Clog, CMI, or any easy-to-use mechanical ascender. Used to lock a climber on the rope to rest, change over, negotiate a lip, cross a knot, for rescue and for many other purposes.

safety strap A strap used by tree surgeons to hold the climber to the tree when spiking up a tree.

salle (Fr.) Room.

SAR Search And Rescue.

scaling pole (Br. **maypole**) Sectional metal pole used with a ladder or rope to gain access to an upper cave passage.

scoot or **scooter** A person who leaves a drop area immediately after finishing the drop without assisting to derig or carry gear back to vehicles.

screamer Slang 1. A long fall. Someone who takes a 200 foot screamer falls 200 feet, traditionally screaming all the way. 2. A term used for a particularly long, scary and/or dangerous lead fall.

scree The rock that forms a talus slope.

SEA Self-equalizing anchors. An anchor that provides several places to tie in a rope so that the weight of the rope can be dispersed equally between all the anchor points.

seat sling An endless loop that can be worn as a diaper seat harness.

seilbremse A 3 oz. rappelling aid used with carabiners to assemble a rappelling system.

self-belay A method whereby a rappeller can, independent of a rappel device, stop a rappel.

self-locking carabiner A carabiner with a spring-loaded locking collar.

self-rescue Techniques for getting oneself out of trouble on rope.

semi-variable friction device A device that provides limited friction adjustment, usually in stepped amounts.

set a knot Tightening all parts of the knot so that the rope parts touch, grab and cause friction upon the other parts of the knot rendering it operational.

Loosely tied knots can easily deform under strain and change in character.

sewing awl See awl.

shakehole (Brit.) See doline.

shear strength Resistance to being broken by forces acting at 90° to the major axis.

sheath See mantle.

sheave The grooved wheel or pulley of a pulley block.

shock-loading Causing a sudden force or impact on a rope or anchor.

shunt A safety device used during rappelling that is supposed to stop a rappeller's descent in the event he rappels out of control or wishes to halt downward progress.

signals Words or sounds that have been agreed upon to convey a particular message.

Simmons Roller A single chest roller invented and manufactured by Ron Simmons. The single roller is inserted and removed from the shell by a quick-release pin.

sit harness See seat harness.

sit-stand Prusik style involving repeated application of a sit-stand motion.

Sky Genie A rappel device that requires the use of special rope.

sky hook A small steel hook used on tiny rugosities and ledges for aid climbing. Very scary to use. See Logan hook.

slack Signal or shout signifying that more loose rope is needed by the person attached to the rope.

slider Camming device utilizing opposing wedges for protection in thin parallel cracks.

sling An endless loop made of rope or webbing, used primarily for forming knot climbing systems or for wrapping around a stationary point when rigging.

slippery hitch A method of arranging a pull-down rappel using one rope. This method is highly discouraged and very dangerous.

smart loop An easily attached chicken loop developed by Jim Moore and advertised by Gayle Smart at the 1986 NSS Convention.

snake A rappel device that looks like a couch spring. Tom Martin features this device in his book *Rappelling*.

snap link See carabiner.

software ropes, slings and harnesses.

solution dyeing Adding color to nylon resin, which can result in a weaker finished product.

sotano (Sp.) A pit.

spaghetti A pile of tangled up rope.

Spectra A Blue Water, Ltd., Inc. prototype cord.

spelean shunt See shunt.

spelunker See caver.

spider A harness used with stretchers. See bridle.

spike (verb) To climb up a tree or pole using spikes.

spikes Climbing spurs used by tree surgeons and pole lineman.

spine A term often referring to the long straight axis of a carabiner.

Spit Brand name for a Europeon self-drilling anchor.

spiral structure Webbing weave that is very strong.

split-nail A Rawl product (Rawl drive) in which the shaft of the bolt is split. When the anchor is driven into a pre-drilled hole, the spoons lock the bolt tightly in the hole. This anchor should only be used on very hard rock. Also called contraction bolts.

Spong knot A climbing knot considered by many climbers to be an unacceptable alternative to the Prusik knot.

spool An early rappelling device that incorporated a drum on which the rope was wrapped providing the necessary friction.

sporting Challenging, requiring skill.

SRT (Am. **ropework**) Single-rope techniques or static-rope techniques. Methods of descending and ascending a single fixed rope. Recognized as the best general method for pit-cave exploration.

SSP 1. Smith Safety Products. 2. Brand name of static kernmantle rope manufactured for Smith Safety Products.

standard oval A carabiner featuring parallel sides and a round top and bottom. Probably the earliest as well as the simplest design.

standing part of the rope Includes all the rope that is not fastened at the rigging point.

static belay A belay that uses a low-stretch rope. The climber does not fall away from the point where he slipped, but rather remains in the same approximate location so reattachment can take place. A top belay is considered static belay.

static rope Ropes that stretch between 2% and 4% under a load of approximately 180 lbs. Also called no-stretch or low-stretch rope. Most ropes used in vertical caving have this property.

STC Safety and Techniques Committee of the NSS.

stemple (Brit.) A beam or expanding bar wedged across a narrow place for support or safety.

Sticht plate A mechanical belaying device.

stirrup Any loop made of webbing, strap, rope or metal that is stood in.

Stop A bobbin type rappelling device made by Petzl that incorporates a parking brake.

Stoppers Trade name for a Chouinard wedge shaped nut. They range in size from 1/16 inch to 4 inches.

strung-out Climber's term referring to the distance between pieces of protection. Aid points with large distances between are referred to as being strung-out.

stuttering The uneven jerky movement of a climbing knot sliding up a rope, or the jerky movement of rope in a dynamic situation.

style An accumulation of techniques. Performing in a characteristic manner.

summit rope On long drops, an additional rope used at the top for multiple jobs, typically about 10-20% of the length of the main rope.

Superline Plus An orange static kernmantle rope produced by Blue Water, Ltd. Inc.

surface abrasion See ambient abrasion.

surface dyeing Adding color to the yarns after the nylon fibers have been formed. This method of dyeing does not weaken the yarns.

S.W.A.T. Special Weapons And Tactics.

Swiss seat Generic term for a tied seat harness or diaper seat. A sewn harness is not a Swiss seat.

switch The act of changing hands while Mitchell prusiking, i.e. upper right hand drops to pull up the lower lefthand ascender while the lower left hand operates the upper righthand ascender. This has often been called the "Cuddington Switch" and is used when shoulders become fatigued when climbing.

Symplex Slot harness A one-size-fits-all seat harness, designed by John Markwell and made by Rescue Systems Inc.

system 1. Short for climbing system, which includes an entire climbing rig. 2. The general category of climbing rig, i.e. Mitchell system, ropewalker system, 3-knot system.

T

tackle (Brit.) equipment, gear, collectively.

TAG 1. Tennessee, Alabama, Georgia. At the approximate junction of these three states lies an abundance of caves. 2. An association of young cavers in the late '60's from the TAG states.

tag line A rope used to pull people and equipment across a tyrolean. See tetherline.

talus slope A sloping mass of rocks, dirt and debris at the base of a drop.

tandem Two climbers ascending a rope together, one just above the other, separated only by a few feet.

tandem bars also **tandem brake bars** A method of rappelling using two carabiners with brake bars attached connected with a chain link or another carabiner. The rope is wrapped back and forth through the configuration providing six points of friction. This rappelling method is considered unsafe because the primary pressure of the system is sideways against the carabiner gates, the weakest part of the carabiner.

tape 1. Webbing, flat or tubular. 2. A measuring tape.

TCU Three-cam unit used by climbers. Developed by Steve Byrne and made by Metoulius.

technique The manner in which something is done.

Telpher See tyrolean.

tensile strength Breaking strength with the major axis.

tension traverse Any movement across an area whereby a snubbed-up belay has been provided for protection.

tether 1. See tetherline. 2. (Brit.) A length of wire rope with eyes at each end for rigging wire ladders. Also called a wire belay.

tetherline 1. An auxiliary line used with tyroleans and highlines that assist in pulling people and gear back and forth. 2. Any connection between two things that is intended to prevent separation.

Texas prusik system A climbing system that incorporates two points of ascender contact, one attached to a seat harness, the other attached to either one or both feet.

thimbles Grooved sleeves that allow for ropes and

cables to curve gently through an eye.

Thor tree Metal cylinder plate acting as a "tree" in a tensionless rigging.

thumb the cam A method of releasing the cam of a handled ascender with one's thumb. This technique aids in downclimbing a rope or starting from the bottom without tension on the rope from below.

thumb the knot Part of the Prusik knot loosening process in which the thumb of the break hand pulls on the bar of the knot.

tie-off An anchor.

top-roped A belay or climbing safety system where a rope attached to a rock climber is strung through a carabiner at the top of the drop and into the hands of the belayer. If the belayer is positioned at the top of the drop it may not be necessary to use a carabiner.

traveling distance The length of the short leg of a rappel rack expressed in inches. The greater this distance, the more friction flexibility the rack provides.

traverse line A horizontal rigged rope or cable, onto which climbers can tether as a self-belay and maneuver across the rock face.

tri-cam A camming device used by rock climbers. Is used in severely flaring or shallow cracks while being lighter and more compact than Friends.

Triton A rappelling device made by Forrest Mountaineering. This cast aluminum device can be used with either single or double rope and is rigged similar to the fashion of a Sticht plate. Source: **Tom Martin's** book *Rappelling Edition II.*

Troll European equipment and harness manufacturer.

Troll bollard A hanger for a bolt anchor.

trou (Fr.) Hole as in Trou de toro (bull-hole), or trou de vent (wind hole).

tuber Belay device imported by Latok. Used primarily by rock climbers. Works well with 9 mm rope.

tubular webbing Nylon strapping that appears flat, yet when pinched from the sides reveals its hollow weave. Commonly available in one-, two- and three-inch widths.

tyrolean A rope stretched sideways and attached at two points whereby people or gear traverse back

and forth. This includes horizontal and tilted traverses.
tyroleaneers People who traverse across tyroleans.

U & V

UIAA Union of International Alpine Association. Organization that sets standards for climbing and mountaineering.
variable friction A term used to describe a rappel device with a gradual friction adjustment, such as a rack.
Vertical Bill Refers to Bill Cuddington, who has often been named as the father of North American single-rope techniques.

W

Warden Ascender A mechanical cam ascender developed by Tom Warden, which is considered an early predecessor to cam ascenders.
water knot 1. Originally any knot used by fishermen or anglers. The fisherman's, grapevine and barrel knot were once all known as water knots. 2. Present day, it refers to the original ring bend.
webbing Nylon strapping. Commercially available in flat or tubular construction.

whaletail A machined fixed bar position rappel device. This device became popular in the early '70s. Commercially made by Spelean in Australia.
wrap Commonly used when discussing knot tying. The turns made around something with rope.

X, Y & Z

yo-yo 1. To go down a pit or drop and come right back up. Sometimes more than once. 2. A person who does #1.
z rig A type of 3 to 1 mechanical advantage hauling system. It gets its name from the "Z" shape the rope makes as it is threaded through the rigging.
zip down the rope Rappel very fast.
zipline A fixed line from a high place to a low place. Used as a high line to transfer gear either up or down.
zipper A rack rigged backwards.

Index

Index

abrasion 25-26
    ambient 74
    direct 74
    protection 76-77
abrasion resistance 14
Accidents in N. American Caving 55
acid 25
aid climbing 230
aiders 222
ambient abrasion 25-26, 74
anchors 54-93, 241
    two 58, 60, 61
artificial anchors 64
ascender box 163, 165, 178
ascender knot 152
ascenders 146-7
ascending
    getting started 175
    Gibbs rig 176
    long drops 212-4
    Mitchell system 176
    power 187
    preparing 174
    sit-stand systems 175
Ashley, Clifford 36, 50

baboon hang 290
back-up 58, 60
barrel knot 48, 51
bars, brake 112, 120, 204
belay
    aids 247
    aiming 241
    anchors 241
    attachment 242
    burns 246
    event 244
    falling 246
belays
    ascending 238
    body 246
    bottom 127, 236-7
    descending 236
    dynamic 240
    no belay 236
    top 135-7, 150, 236, 238
    rock climbing 240

    self 128, 231, 236
    self-lining 150, 239
    static 240
    third ascender 238
    when to use 236
belay stance
    modified hip 242
    sitting hip 241
    standing hip 241
belayer 223, 244
belaying 22, 236-251
bight 36
binoculars 202
block and tackle hauling 148
blood knot 44
Blue Water 16, 265
Blue Water II 16, 305
Blue Water III 16
bobbin 109, 116-7
body rappel 98
bollard 72
bolt hangers 72-74
bolts 65, 66, 222, 231
    criteria 67
    drilling 66, 67-70
    types 66, 67, 90-93
    self drilling 67-70
    sleeve type 90-91
Boscarino, Rossano 171, 301
bottom belay 127
bottomless pit 84
bowline knots 37-42
    bowline 37, 51
    mountaineering 38
    double-knotted 38
    high-strength 38
    French 38-39
    double-turn 38
    round-turn 38
    on-a-bight 41, 51
    triple 42
    three loop 42
brake bar 112, 120, 204
buildings 216
bungie cord 166-7
Butt Strap Harness 172-3
butterfly knot 43, 51

"Off Rope."